How Can We Solve Our Social Problems?

Third Edition

To Alex and his generation—let us work to make a more humane and just world.

How Can We Solve Our Social Problems?

Third Edition

James A. Crone

Los Angeles | London | New Delhi
Singapore | Washington DC

Los Angeles | London | New Delhi
Singapore | Washington DC

FOR INFORMATION:

SAGE Publications, Inc.
2455 Teller Road
Thousand Oaks, California 91320
E-mail: order@sagepub.com

SAGE Publications Ltd.
1 Oliver's Yard
55 City Road
London EC1Y 1SP
United Kingdom

SAGE Publications India Pvt. Ltd.
B 1/I 1 Mohan Cooperative Industrial Area
Mathura Road, New Delhi 110 044
India

SAGE Publications Asia-Pacific Pte. Ltd.
3 Church Street
#10-04 Samsung Hub
Singapore 049483

Printed in the United States of America

Library of Congress Cataloging-in-Publication Data

Crone, James A.
How can we solve our social problems?/James A. Crone.—Third Edition.

pages cm
Revised edition of the author's How can we solve our social problems?, 2011.
Includes bibliographical references and index.

ISBN 978-1-5063-0483-0 (pbk.: alk. paper)

1. Social problems. 2. Sociology. 3. Social problems—United States. 4. United States—Social conditions—21st century. I. Title.

HN18.3.C76 2016
306.0973—dc23   2015027937

This book is printed on acid-free paper.

Acquisitions Editor: Jeff Lasser
Editorial Assistant: Alexandra Croell
Production Editor: Bennie Clark Allen
Copy Editor: Michelle Ponce
Typesetter: C&M Digitals (P) Ltd.
Proofreader: Rae-Ann Goodwin
Indexer: Wendy Allex
Cover Designer: Glenn Vogel
Marketing Manager: Johanna Swenson

15 16 17 18 19 10 9 8 7 6 5 4 3 2 1

Detailed Contents

Preface to the Third Edition

How can we solve our social problems? For example, how can we solve the problem of poverty or the world's population problem? We have certainly made progress in dealing with a number of social problems. We have college student loans for poor people to allow them to get ahead in life. We have passed civil rights laws so that all Americans can vote and go into public places, such as restrooms, restaurants, hotels, and parks. We have health care for older people (Medicare) and for poor people (Medicaid), and with the Affordable Care Act, we are starting to offer more affordable health insurance for millions of Americans whose companies and businesses do not offer health care.

How can we solve more social problems for our fellow Americans and fellow humans of the world? For example, can we someday provide health care for all Americans, can we get more Americans out of poverty by providing jobs that pay above poverty-level wages rather than pay below poverty-level wages, can we stop the warming of our planet by decreasing the production of carbon dioxide and other pollutants by using more wind, water, and solar energy to create a cleaner, healthier, and more survivable environment, and can we slow the growth of the world's population so that current and future humans can share more of the resources we have and hence have a higher standard of living instead of existing in dire poverty for generation after generation? I believe that we can tackle these above problems and, in the coming pages, I discuss specific steps we can take to decrease or solve our social problems.

I outline a number of realistic steps we can take to solve or at least decrease the severity of a number of social problems. Notice that I say "can" rather than "should." I present what we *can* do, but you will need to decide what we *should* do. As a sociologist, I cannot answer the "should" question for you because a science (natural or social) can deal only with the "is" part of phenomena, that is, description, causes, consequences, and prediction.

Consequently, as you make your way through the book and read and think about how we *can* solve each social problem, I also want you to think about what we *should* do.

As you read the chapters, I remind you from time to time how challenging it will be to solve our social problems. In Chapter 2, for example, I discuss a number of barriers we face when we try to solve our social problems. By discussing these barriers and making them conscious in your mind, I do not intend to make you feel that the situation is hopeless. What I do intend is to urge you to develop a realistic outlook. Neither a pessimistic outlook nor a naive outlook will help us solve our social problems. To address these problems, we need to have a realistic outlook where our feet are firmly planted on the ground and where we are open to new ideas and possibilities that will give us hope that we can indeed solve our social problems.

Acknowledgments

I thank all of the reviewers who made many constructive suggestions to improve this book: Chris Adamski-Mietus (Western Illinois University); Elsa Valdez (CSU, San Bernadino); and Laci A. Fiala (Walsh University). I greatly appreciate their time, effort, and insight. At SAGE Publications, I thank the acquisitions editor, Jeff Lasser, and his editorial assistant, Alexandra Croell, for their patience and continual support of me and my work. I am grateful to production editor Bennie Clark Allen for making the production process go smoothly and to copy editor Michelle Ponce, who did a superb job in making this book flow much more smoothly. Finally, I thank the hundreds of students I have taught in social problems courses over the years who have asked important and challenging questions and created enlightening discussions that, collectively, were the stimulus for my writing this book.

About the Author

James A. Crone earned his PhD in sociology at the University of Kansas. For 33 years, he taught seven sociology courses in the Department of Sociology and Anthropology at Hanover College. Over the years, he served as chair of the department and as chair of a number of faculty committees. He won the Arthur and Ilene Baynham Award for Outstanding Teaching. He has published articles on the sociology of sport and teaching sociology and edited the book *15 Disturbing Things We Need to Know*. He has served the larger community by being president of the Hanover Town Council, president of the local chapter of Habitat for Humanity, and member of the Jefferson County Council. He ran for the U.S. Congress in 2012 and is currently chair of the Jefferson County Democratic Party. In his leisure time, he likes to work out and play basketball, especially with people considerably younger than he is. His son, Alex, is a mechanical engineering student at the University of Southern California.

1

Preparing to Solve
Our Social Problems

Have you ever been concerned about a social problem? I imagine that you have. You may have been concerned about poverty, racial prejudice and discrimination, or the inequality between men and women. Well, you are not alone. Many other Americans and people in other countries are also concerned about these and other social problems. One way to address these problems is to read about and study social problems and think about how we might address these problems realistically. This book is a good place to start.

Before we begin to study specific social problems and consider how we can solve them, we need to learn a few things that will provide a foundation on which to build a more comprehensive understanding of social problems. With a fuller understanding, we will be better prepared to think about how we can solve these social problems. So, let us first build this foundation of understanding in Chapters 1 and 2, and then we will be ready to address our social problems.

What Is a Social Problem?

Before we turn to the main emphasis of this book, namely how we can solve our social problems, we need to define what a *social problem* is. One thing it is not is a personal problem that others do not experience. As C. Wright Mills, a respected American sociologist, pointed out, a personal problem can also be a social problem if a number of people experience the same personal problem when certain social conditions are causing these people to experience the same personal problems. For example, many families experience poverty personally, but all of them are a part of a larger social pattern of unemployment, a social factor not caused by these families (Mills, 1959). Consequently, a key element in deciding whether something is a social problem is to discover how people's personal problems, for example, experiencing unemployment, poverty, prejudice, and discrimination, are related to the social conditions of a society.

Many social problems, such as poverty, racial/ethnic discrimination, and gender inequality, occur at the societal level. Also, local communities can define certain social conditions such as high rates of unemployment, juvenile delinquency, gangs, illegal drug use, and family break-up as social problems (Fuller & Myers, 1941). In addition to recognizing local and societal social problems, we are becoming more aware of global social problems, such as the world's population problem where many people throughout the world do not have their simplest needs met, for example, enough water to drink and enough fertile land to grow a minimum of food, just to survive each day. A social problem can therefore be at the local, societal, or global level.

Part of defining a social condition as a social problem is that we subjectively say to ourselves that something is wrong and that we believe it should be changed. For example, we say that we believe poverty is wrong and that we as a community, society, or world should do something about this. In addition to our personal concerns, Fuller and Myers (1941) asserted that social problems need to have objective elements to them (p. 320). That is, we need to show that there is empirical evidence of a social problem. For example, when we collect data to show that poor people have lower incomes, lower quality of housing, and overall lower quality of life than people who are not poor, we demonstrate that a social problem also has an objective element to it. We therefore need to have both subjective and objective elements in a definition of a social problem.[1]

Taking all of these things into consideration, we include the following elements as part of a definition of a social problem. First, certain social conditions cause personal problems. Second, social problems can be local, societal, or global. Third, social problems consist of both subjective perceptions and objective evidence. Hence, we use the following definition:

A social problem exists when people subjectively perceive and have empirical evidence to show that social conditions combine at a local, societal, or global level to cause personal problems.[2]

History of Studying Social Problems

People have thought about social problems for a long time. In fact, the field of sociology—the scientific study of society and social interaction—developed during the early 1800s. Early social thinkers (they were not called *sociologists* back then) during the late 1700s and early 1800s were concerned about all of the social changes that were occurring and wondered whether societies were falling apart. At that time, more and more people were moving from rural areas to cities to get new kinds of jobs called *factory jobs*. Slums and crowded housing began to emerge. Some people lost their jobs and experienced extreme poverty. The people who had no jobs and therefore no income would at times steal or rob, thereby making crime a social problem. As a result of these social changes, social problems of unemployment, poverty, slums, crowded housing, and crime grew and became a typical part of the urban scene.

So much social change was occurring that some people such as Auguste Comte, a social thinker in France during the early 1800s, became conscious of and concerned about these social changes and resulting social problems.[3] He believed that society was falling apart due to too much disorder and therefore believed that something needed to be done to bring some semblance of order and harmony to people's lives. Comte concluded that a new discipline was needed to study society—how it works, why it works that way, and where it is headed. He was concerned about what could be done about all of the social problems people were facing. He created the new discipline of sociology to study society scientifically in order to see what could be done to make a more stable and orderly society, under these newly emerging social conditions of urbanization and industrialization and resulting unemployment, poverty, and crime. Hence, the new discipline of sociology was born.

Later during the 1800s and early 1900s, other social thinkers began to study the society in general and social problems in particular. Emile Durkheim, a French sociologist, had concerns similar to those of Comte.[4] With the fall of monarchies and the apparent decline in the influence of religion, Durkheim, like Comte, wondered how modern society could keep any sense of order. German social thinkers, such as Karl Marx during the mid-1800s and Max Weber during the early 1900s, also became interested in how society worked and the social problems people faced.

Marx was greatly troubled by the increasing poverty and inequality he saw around him.[5] He was concerned that people had factory jobs that were alienating because the jobs were so boring, people were paid so poorly that they could hardly survive, and yet they worked 12 hours per day, 6 days per week. Moreover, they did not have much choice in life. They either took alienating factory jobs or had no jobs and hence no means to sustain themselves. They were stuck in a social system that was brutal and inhumane, and they did not know what to do about their situation. As Marx pointed out, previous generations created the very conditions that factory workers lived in—unemployment, poverty, alienating jobs, and the lack of much choice in life. He further asserted that because our ancestors created these social conditions, we could—and should—change these social conditions. Marx helped us realize that we humans created our existing social conditions; therefore, we can change our social conditions. That is, we did not need to accept the existing social conditions as the only way to live.

Marx developed solutions to these problems that he thought would create a more humane society. He focused on what he thought was the main cause of many modern social problems: capitalism. He noted that although capitalism produced material benefits for many people and much profit for some people, at the same time it created alienating jobs, unemployment, poverty, and much inequality. He concluded that since we humans created our own social conditions and that we could change these social conditions, we therefore had the power and the responsibility to create a more humane and just society and world.

Another giant in the field of sociology was Max Weber.[6] He was concerned about the modern social problem of all the bureaucracies and institutions we live in and how these bureaucracies and institutions have considerable power over us. If we want to work within these bureaucracies and institutions (and therefore survive in the society we are living in), we must go by their norms, values, beliefs, and regulations—even if we do not agree with these things. He predicted that individuals would feel helpless in the face of such large and powerful institutions. Consequently, Weber wondered how we would be able to solve the problem of our powerlessness in the face of these modern bureaucracies and institutions.

As you can see, from its beginning, the new discipline of sociology focused on the study of social problems and how these problems could be solved. Contemporary sociologists have the same focus. We too are curious about how society works, why it works the way it does, and what may happen in the future. We too are interested in how social conditions create social problems. And we too are interested in how we can change our social conditions to solve our social problems.

Teaching About Social Problems in Today's World

In sociology today, there are courses and textbooks devoted solely to the study of social problems. In these courses and the textbooks that are used for these courses, there is usually a focus on 10 to 15 social problems that are of current concern. Some of these problems are a concern and have been so for many years. For example, in our country we have been especially troubled about poverty, crime, and racial prejudice and discrimination. Other social problems have become of increasing concern to us since the 1950s, including the growth in the world's population and the burden it plays on our limited resources, the deterioration of our global environment, and the inequality between women and men in our country and throughout the world.

In our social problems courses, we focus on certain aspects of a social problem. For example, we describe a social problem, such as how many people are affected and where the problem is most prevalent (in cities, in the lower social classes, among women, and so forth). We search for the causes of the problem, usually finding that there are a number of causes for each social problem, and that some causes have greater impacts than others. We point out the intended consequences that are readily apparent and dig deeper to discover the unintended consequences that are not so apparent. We also make predictions as to what will most likely occur given certain social conditions. Finally, we discuss possible solutions, which is what this book addresses specifically.

How Can Sociologists Address Social Problems and Yet Remain Objective?

The study of social problems presents a dilemma for sociologists. The dilemma does not occur at the point of choosing a topic of research, of gathering facts in the research process, or of choosing certain methods of gathering data such as the survey, participant observation (when a sociologist lives with a certain group for a period of time to learn about the group), or the interview. Sociologists, in general, agree that these kinds of activities are what sociologists need to do. These activities are an integral part of our being sociologists. The dilemma also does not occur at the point of discovering the causes or uncovering the unintended consequences related to each social problem. Sociologists, in general, seek to pinpoint causes and find unintended consequences.

The dilemma, however, occurs at the point of dealing with the solution part of social problems. That is, what should we say about the solving of social problems? Should we say what we personally think should be done? Should a group of sociologists come together to decide what should be done? Should we remain objective and not take a personal stance on what should be done and yet, in some way, contribute to what we know about the solving of social problems?

Many sociologists contend that our role is to state only what is—that is, to study only what occurs, focusing on description, causes, consequences, and prediction but not saying what should occur.[7] They begin to feel uncomfortable when it comes to the solving of social problems because they worry that they or other sociologists may go beyond their role in being objective. They fear that if the general public no longer sees sociology as objective, sociology will lose its credibility.

The result would be that sociologists would be seen as just another interest group with its own vested interests, with sociologists looking out for what benefits them instead of being a group that the public and government can trust to report valid data and provide objective knowledge about a subject so that others can make more informed judgments as to what should be done. Consequently, a number of sociologists conclude that, rather than risk losing our credibility as an objective source of data, knowledge, and understanding, maybe it is better to stay away from recommending solutions. Instead, we need to leave this area to the policymakers of the society, such as members of Congress or state legislatures, and focus solely on descriptions, causes, consequences, and predictions.

There is another group of sociologists who see their role not only as stating what *is* but also stating what *should be*. Their belief is similar to that of Marx ([1845]1972), who said, "The philosophers have only interpreted the world, in various ways; the point, however, is to change it" (p. 107). That is, these sociologists ask, "What is the point of doing all of this studying of society, collecting mountains of data, and discovering causes and consequences if we do not take the next step to change the society for the better?" They argue that if we study the problem more than anyone else in society and understand it best, especially its causes and consequences, why not take the next step and say what should be done about it? After all, they say, sociologists are the most expert on the study of social problems.

It seems to be a great waste of our knowledge and understanding of social problems if we cannot, in some way, venture into the realm of solving social problems. The key question then becomes the following: How can we study the solving of social problems and yet maintain our objectivity and credibility? Is there, in other words, a common ground to stand on for all sociologists?

Yes, there is a common ground on which we all sociologists can stand. On this common ground, there are at least five areas within which we can achieve the goal of contributing to the solving of social problems and yet remain objective and maintain our credibility.

One way sociologists can help to solve social problems is to look at what sociologists know about social patterns in social problems and how knowing about these social patterns can help us to solve our social problems. We have a good idea of a number of social patterns that typically occur within various kinds of social problems.

A second way in which sociologists can contribute to the solving of social problems and yet remain objective is to study the aspects of a social problem that prevent it from being solved. That is, sociologists can help us to become more aware of the barriers that prevent a social problem from being solved. Once we know these barriers, we can focus on how we can work around these barriers.

A third way sociologists can remain objective and yet contribute to solving our social problems is to study empirical examples of how social problems have been solved in the past in this or in other countries and reflect on how these solutions could be applied to solving our current social problems. That is, what can we learn from the social problems that we have already solved that can be applied to the solving of our current and future social problems?

Fourth, all sociologists stand on a common ground when they make predictions about potential new social problems on the horizon and about where existing social problems are likely to go in the future, given current social policies and attempts to solve these social problems. By predicting new and emerging social problems and predicting where current social problems are likely to go in the near future, sociologists can provide information that can be of considerable use to policymakers.

A fifth common ground for all sociologists is the ability to suggest various solutions and what their consequences might be for individuals, groups, communities, societies, and global social systems. Note that sociologists are not recommending a preferred solution. Instead, we are pointing out what we think are the possible solutions, thereby helping policymakers to know more clearly what options they have and what combinations of options they have in order to address a specific social problem. Contributing such knowledge could provide a great service to policymakers, because this knowledge will give our policymakers (for example, the President, members of Congress, and state legislators) a fuller picture of what actions they can take to solve or at least reduce a social problem.

What Social Problem Should We Solve First?

Given our limited resources, we cannot solve all of our social problems at one time. Consequently, it would help to have criteria to decide what social problem we should tackle first, then second, and so on.[8] This leads to the question: What are the most important criteria in deciding which social problem to address first? The following criteria can help us to get started. One criterion is the degree to which a social problem seriously endangers the lives of people; for example, one social problem causes little more than an inconvenience to people, whereas another social problem endangers their lives. A second criterion is the number of people being hurt by the social problem; for example, one social problem hurts hundreds of people, whereas another social problem hurts millions or billions of people. Using these two criteria, we can create the two-by-two table shown as Figure 1.1 as a visual means of deciding what social problem we should address first.

Figure 1.1   Two-by-Two Table for Addressing Social Problems

	Not Endanger Lives	Endanger Lives
Affect Some	Least serious	
Affect Many		Most serious

Applying these two criteria, we can conclude that a social problem that endangers the lives of people and affects many people (lower right cell) could be the one we address first, whereas a social problem that does not endanger people's lives and affects relatively few people (upper left cell) could be the social problem we address last. As to the other two cells, I am not sure what would need to be chosen next. Maybe additional criteria will help us to answer this question. The point, however, is that given the limited resources we can apply to the solving of social problems, it is fruitful for us to use criteria to help us gain clarity as to what social problem we may want to tackle first and then second and so on.

How Might Sociological Theory Help Us to Solve Social Problems?

If we can understand the nature of a social problem better by applying socio-logical theory to it, we are in a better position to solve that problem. Let us first define what *theory* is before we begin using it. In sociology, theory has usually meant one of two things: either it is a collection of interrelated con-cepts and ideas, or it is a set of interrelated propositions that are applied to social phenomena to help us understand social phenomena.[9] The "interrelated propositions" kind of theory needs a little bit of explanation, so we discuss this type of theory first before discussing a number of theories that consist of a collection of interrelated concepts and ideas.

With respect to a theory that is a set of interrelated propositions, you may ask, "What is a proposition?" A *proposition* tells us how one variable causes another variable to change. For example, say that you are interested in what causes poverty. You create a hypothesis, which is a predicted causal relationship between two variables, in which you hypothesize that as the rate of unemployment (one variable) goes up, the rate of poverty (the second variable) goes up. Because unemployment is doing the "causing," we call this variable the *independent* variable. Poverty is the *dependent* variable, because it is being influenced by unemployment.

We test our hypothesis to see what is really occurring. We collect data in some way, such as through participant observation, the interview, or the survey, to see whether or not our hypothesis is supported by the data. If we test our hypothesis a number of times and find that, indeed, as the rate of unemployment goes up, the rate of poverty goes up, we begin to conclude that our hypothesis is probably true. As a note of caution, however, we know that we might never be 100% sure, because there could be another independent variable that is causing the rate of poverty to go up. However, we can do what is called *controlling for other possible independent variables;* that is, if we have a random sample of data that does not allow for other variables to vary, such as a sample made up of all females (no males so that the variable of sex cannot vary), all African American women (no White, Hispanic, Native American, or any other kind of racial/ethnic group so that the variable of race/ethnicity cannot vary), all high school-educated women (no middle school- or college-educated women), only women with two children under 5 years of age (no women with no children, with one child, or with three or more children), all women who are 30 years of age (no women who are any other age), and so on, we now know that these variables cannot vary in our study.

We test our two variables. As these women in our sample increase in unemployment, do more and more of them also fall into poverty? If the data show that there is still a relationship (or correlation) between the rate of unemployment and the rate of poverty, we are closer to being confident in saying that unemployment is probably a cause of poverty. Once various sociologists find the same data in different studies, we begin to be cautiously confident that the independent variable in our hypothesis is a cause of the dependent variable in our hypothesis.

Once our hypothesis is firmly established, we can begin to say that it may be a *theoretical proposition,* that is, a hypothesis that not only is found to be true but also is more abstract; that is, it can apply to various social conditions in this society and other societies, and it can apply over time or to various times in history. In other words, the more a proposition applies to more diverse social conditions and the more it applies throughout more of history, the more abstract the proposition is. Ideally, we in sociology—as well as researchers in other social sciences—would like our theoretical propositions to be more abstract so that they apply to more social conditions over more time. In reality, some theoretical propositions are very abstract (apply to billions of people over thousands of years), and some are more concrete (apply to thousands or millions of people in the last 100 years).

Let us go one step further and connect one theoretical proposition with another theoretical proposition, that is, where one of the variables is present in both propositions. When we begin to do this, we begin to call this *theory*. For example, let us relate the proposition—the higher the rate of unemployment, the higher the rate of poverty—to another proposition, where either the rate of unemployment variable or the rate of poverty variable is one of the variables in the second proposition.

Let us say that the United States is losing factories to other countries and that nothing else is taking the factories' place in the United States. Companies are moving their factories to Mexico, South Korea, Thailand, and China to get the benefit of paying lower wages and not having to provide workers with health and retirement benefits, thereby making more profit for the companies and making more money for the investors who own stock in those companies. This process has been occurring since the 1960s and is known as *deindustrialization*.

We can now make a second proposition that connects to our original proposition: The greater the rate of deindustrialization, the greater the rate of unemployment. Notice that we connected this second proposition with the original proposition by using one of the variables that occurs in both propositions, that is, the rate of unemployment. Here are the two propositions so that you can see how they are connected:

Proposition 1: The greater the rate of deindustrialization, the greater the rate of unemployment.

Proposition 2: The greater the rate of unemployment, the greater the rate of poverty.

Notice that the rate of unemployment is the dependent variable in the first proposition but the independent variable in the second proposition, thus connecting the two propositions and therefore beginning to create a theory. Now we can create more propositions that help us to further develop this theory, say of poverty. We could, for example, state the following proposition: The greater the rate of poverty, the greater the rate of homelessness. Notice that the rate of poverty becomes the independent variable, which we predict causes the rate of homelessness to increase.

Now that you know what a theory of interrelated propositions is, I share with you what I call a *theory of conflict and social change* as a way to help us better understand and solve our social problems.

A Theory of Conflict and Social Change: A Way to Better Understand and Therefore Solve Our Social Problems

In this theory, I have created a number of interrelated propositions that will help us to understand how social problems can be solved or at least lessened. I have not included here every variable that influences a social problem, but I have included a number of variables that I believe play a key role in what happens to social problems.

Before we talk about specific variables, I mention again that we, as humans, have socially constructed our reality.[10] That is, whether you realize it or not, humans have created all kinds of social phenomena, such as slave systems; various kinds of prejudice and discrimination; democracies and dictatorships; economic systems such as capitalism and socialism; and norms, values, and beliefs that are important in one culture or at one point in history and are not important or even present in another culture or at another time in history. We humans have created all of these things and yet, as Marx ([1844]1964) pointed out, these human creations can come to control us—many times for hundreds or thousands of years. Over the years, we come to forget that someone back in history socially constructed these social phenomena and typically created ideologies, laws, and customs to legitimize or to justify these social creations. Over time, we come to accept society the way it is and live a certain socially constructed way of life for generations. It is as though we say to ourselves, "This is the way it is and has been, and this is the way it will always be."

Then something happens in society (I elaborate soon) to cause people to realize that what seemed to be beyond us as humans was actually constructed by us and therefore could be changed. Once this realization occurs, there is also the possibility that people can seek social change. The opposite is also true. If people never realize that social phenomena are socially constructed by people who have lived before us, they are much less likely to seek social change.

Given these initial ideas on the human constructedness of our social world, we can now proceed to create a theory of conflict and social change that consists of a number of interrelated propositions where each proposition consists of one variable influencing another variable. Taken together, these propositions create a theory that will help us not only understand the nature of social problems but also solve these problems.

One key variable that seems to be related to many social problems is the amount of inequality in a community, society, or global social system. By *inequality*, I mean that some people, groups, organizations, and societies have more money (income and/or wealth), power, and prestige than do others.[11] There are many causes of inequality in contemporary society, but I assume that the following social factors explain much of the inequality that we have had, and currently have, in our society: various kinds of prejudice and discrimination, a capitalistic economy, and unequal exchange relationships that are supported by the accepted norms, vested interests, ideologies, laws, and customs of a particular society.

As you may already know, those who experience prejudice and discrimination will have fewer chances and opportunities than others who do not experience prejudice and discrimination, hence creating more inequality. In capitalism, some people are owners and make a profit while many other people are workers and earn a wage. Typically, owners make a lot more money in making profit than workers do in earning wages, thereby creating inequality. In every society, there are exchanges of goods and services. Sometimes those exchanges are unequal; the norms that are created say, "This is the way it should be; when we exchange something for something, you get this and I get that." This kind of norm is called a *norm of reciprocity,* in which people accept the prevailing exchange relationships as legitimate (Gouldner, 1960). Once people accumulate more money, power, and prestige, they develop *vested interests* in keeping or increasing these resources. Given these vested interests, they will socially construct ideologies, laws, customs, and informal norms to justify and maintain the resources that they have accumulated. If these ideologies, laws, customs, and informal norms are accepted as legitimate by the rest of the people, those who have the extra resources will be more likely to retain and increase their unequal resources. All of these socially constructed social factors together create a certain amount of inequality in a given society. Consequently, here are the first theoretical propositions dealing with what contributes to inequality in a society:

1. As more prejudice and discrimination develops, more inequality will occur.

2. As capitalism develops (some people will make profit while many others will earn wages), more inequality will occur.

3. As unequal exchanges are created, more inequality will occur.

4. As norms of reciprocity that justify unequal exchanges are created, more inequality will occur.

5. As people who accumulate more money, power, and/or prestige develop vested interests to maintain or increase their money, power, and/or prestige, more inequality will occur.

6. As people who accumulate more money, power, and/or prestige create ideologies, laws, customs, and norms to maintain or increase their money, power, and/or prestige, more inequality will occur.

Another key variable is the amount of opportunity people have. Some people have many opportunities, whereas others have few opportunities. For example, we know that poor people, African Americans, and women have not started at the same "starting line" of equal opportunity as have others such as middle-class Americans, White Americans, and male Americans. Consequently, here is the next theoretical proposition:

7. The more inequality there is in a social system such as a group, organization, community, society, or global social system, the less opportunity people will have who are at the bottom of the system of inequality.

As people have less opportunity, they will be less likely to be upwardly mobile. This situation is especially important in a class-type society versus a caste-type society. People in a class society are socialized to "get ahead," whereas people in a caste society, such as India in the 1800s, are socialized to "stay in their place." In a class-type society such as the United States, people who have less opportunity to get ahead will be less upwardly mobile than people who have more opportunity. In other words, given the structural situation of less opportunity, we should predict that people with less opportunity will experience less upward mobility. Consequently, we add another proposition:

8. The less opportunity people have, the less upwardly mobile they will be compared with people who have more opportunity.

Assuming that no other variable influences people at the bottom of a system of inequality, people are likely to accept the prevailing system of inequality as legitimate and will therefore live within this system and do nothing to attempt to change it. However, if these people are able to and begin to communicate with each other about their respective conditions and if a charismatic leader communicates dissatisfaction regarding the current system of inequality, these people can begin to develop an awareness of their unequal situation. These additional variables of the ability to communicate and the presence of a charismatic leader suggest two more propositions:

9. The more people at the bottom of the system of inequality can and do communicate with each other about their situation, the more aware they will become of their unequal conditions.

10. The more a charismatic leader communicates the unequal conditions that people experience at the bottom of a system of inequality, the more aware they will become of their unequal conditions.

As people communicate with others who are at the bottom of a system of inequality and as a charismatic leader is successful at communicating about their unequal conditions, the situation is ripe for these people to begin to develop a feeling of unfairness. Hence, the need for the next proposition:

11. The more aware people become of their unequal conditions, the more likely they will develop a feeling of unfairness.

As people continue to talk about their unequal conditions and develop a feeling that their situation is unfair, they are more likely to do something that those in power and those who want to maintain the status quo of existing inequality do not want them to do. That is, they are more likely to question the legitimacy of the existing social construction of inequality. In other words, they are more likely to question the legitimacy of the existing ideologies, laws, customs, and informal norms that justify inequality and to question the legitimacy of why some people have so much money, power, and/or prestige and the rest of the people have so little money, power, and/or prestige. They are more likely to say to themselves, "Why do we need to live like this? Why should we have so little while they have so much?" This kind of thinking can lead people to question the very foundation of a society.[12] These thoughts suggest another proposition:

12. The more that people develop a feeling of unfairness about an existing system of inequality, the more likely they will begin to question the legitimacy of that system of inequality.

Given these conditions, we may begin to see the formation of a group or organization that begins to organize itself around solving a social problem. For example, in 1955, Martin Luther King Jr., a soon-to-become charismatic leader, and members of the African American community of Montgomery, Alabama, began to focus their efforts on forming an organization to boycott the segregated bus system. Hence, we need another proposition at this point:

13. The more that people question the legitimacy of a system of inequality (such as racial, gender, religious, wealth, or power inequalities), the more likely they will form a group or an organization to take action to address that social problem of inequality.

Once people have formed a group or an organization, they are more likely to take some kind of action to change the current social situation of inequality (again, such as racial, gender, homosexual, religious, wealth, or power inequality), which will mean that they will have some kind of conflict with people, groups, and organizations who do not want to change the existing status quo, that is, the existing social system of some form of inequality. The conflict can be peaceful or violent. Both types of conflict, peaceful and violent, can be used by people who want change and the people who do not want change. Or one group can use one type of conflict, and the other group can use the other type of conflict. For example, people seeking social change and the solution to their problem can use peaceful means of conflict, such as writing letters to legislators; attending town meetings to express their grievances; walking in protest marches; and boycotting stores, buses, and restaurants. They can also use more violent methods, such as rioting. Those who want to keep the status quo can urge the seekers of change to "go by the law" and "stay in your place" and use laws to enforce the status quo, that is, the existing social conditions of inequality. If need be, they can use governmental force in the form of the police or the military or use informal methods of threat, torture, and murder, such as those of the Ku Klux Klan, an organization of Whites started in the late 1860s who were prejudiced against and discriminated against African Americans.

With conflict (peaceful or violent) comes the possibility that something can change in the social system and possibly solve or ameliorate a social problem. Once conflict has occurred, we can notice various kinds of social change. We can see social change in ideologies: for example, from a racial segregation ideology to a racial integration ideology. We can see laws change: for example, the Civil Rights Act of 1964 through which public places such as drinking fountains, rest rooms, motels, restaurants, and stores were open to African Americans and the Title IX Act through which females were given equal opportunity in schools that receive funds from the federal government. We can see change in informal norms: for example, people of different races, genders, sexual orientations, or religions are expected to be friendlier toward each other and more respectful of each other. We can see, at times, where people of different religions actually give each other dignity and respect and even care for each other instead of what has happened so much throughout human history where people of one religion hate people of another religion. We can see a change in the redistribution of money, power, or prestige or a combination of these three dimensions of inequality in the form of new social services offered: for example, the creation of Social Security, Medicare, and public schools that are open to all people. We can see more opportunities made available to people so that they can be more upwardly mobile: for example, programs such as Head Start and grants and loans for poorer people to go to college or trade school. Hence, the need for two final propositions:

14. The more a group or an organization carries out conflict (peaceful or violent) with the intent of solving a social problem, the more likely one or more kinds of social change will occur and result in a new social construction of reality.

15. To the degree that social change occurs (for example, changes in laws, informal norms, ideologies, values, and beliefs) with the intent of solving a social problem, the more likely a social problem will be solved.

Causal Model: A Picture of Our Theory

Now let us create a picture of our theory to visualize how the propositions are tied together. When we create a picture of a theory, this is called a *causal model* (Turner, 1991, pp. 15–28). That is, we show how the preceding propositions are related by connecting them with arrows indicating the direction of causality (Figure 1.2).

As you can see when you analyze Figure 1.2, the variables at the left of the causal model influence the variables to the right. As you can also see, there will be some kind of conflict that can result in some type of social change. Part of this social change can involve the solving or reduction of a social problem. Given that our theory of conflict and social change is valid,[13] we should be better able to analyze numerous social problems and arrive at ways to solve these problems because we will be more conscious of the key variables that are a part of social problems. The more conscious we are of these key variables, the more we can change these variables to solve social problems.

Figure 1.2 Causal Model: Theory of Conflict and Social Change

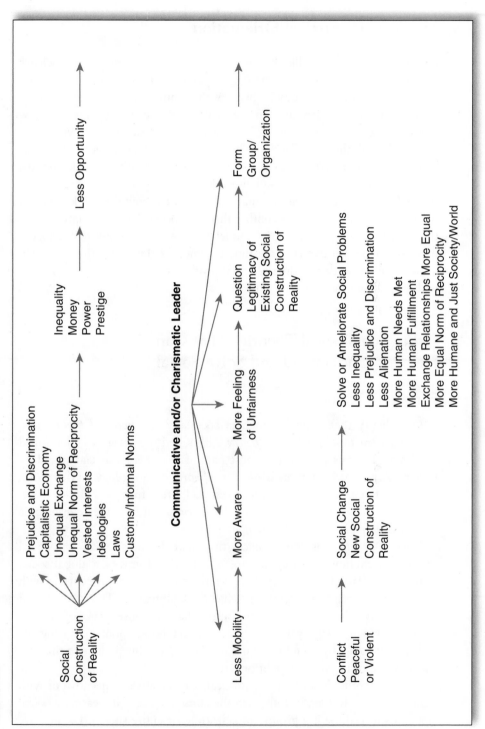

Social
Construction
of Reality

Prejudice and Discrimination
Capitalistic Economy
Unequal Exchange
Unequal Norm of Reciprocity ⟶ Inequality
Vested Interests   Money
Ideologies   Power
Laws   Prestige
Customs/Informal Norms

Less Opportunity ⟶

Communicative and/or Charismatic Leader

Less Mobility ⟶ More Aware ⟶ More Feeling
                             of Unfairness

Question
Legitimacy of
Existing Social
Construction of
Reality

Form
Group/
Organization

Conflict   ⟶ Social Change
Peaceful   New Social
or Violent   Construction of
                   Reality

Solve or Ameliorate Social Problems
Less Inequality
Less Prejudice and Discrimination
Less Alienation
More Human Needs Met
More Human Fulfillment
Exchange Relationships More Equal
More Equal Norm of Reciprocity
More Humane and Just Society/World

My Own Theoretical Orientation

Professors in sociology, like professors in other social and natural science disciplines, tend to favor one theoretical perspective over others when analyzing certain social phenomena because they think that a particular theory provides a fuller explanation. In the analysis of social problems and how these problems can be solved, I favor a conflict theoretical perspective because I think the reason why we have a social problem typically has a lot to do with the interrelations of money, power, inequality, vested interests, ideologies, and legitimation—all of which are integral parts of a conflict theoretical approach. So, as you make your way through this book, you will notice that I continually use conflict theory, especially as formulated in the theory, propositions, and causal model that we just discussed. I also use other sociological theories, from time to time, if I think that they will help us increase our understanding of social problems. With this in mind, I share with you these other sociological theories.

Other Sociological Theories That Can Help Us Understand and Solve Social Problems

Functional Theory

One theory that is well known in sociology is *functional theory,* also known as *structural–functional theory.* Although it was originally developed by Talcott Parsons (1951), I use just part of this theory, as elaborated by Robert Merton (1967) in his work, *On Theoretical Sociology.* In this work, Merton defined the concepts of manifest and latent functions and dysfunctions. Here I define these concepts and elaborate on how they can help us understand and solve social problems.

I define *function* as consequences that increase the survival of a social system, for example, a group, an organization, a society, or a global social system. For example, let us say that Company A gets a major contract with Company B to produce a certain product for Company B. This is functional for Company A because getting the contract has the consequence of increasing the company's survival. Notice that I am talking about increasing the survival of Company A and that I did not make the value judgment that this was positive or negative or right or wrong.

In other words, function does not deal with positive or negative or with right or wrong. Rather, it deals with the consequence of increasing a social system's survival, be it a group, organization, or entire society. Let me give an example in American history to show the distinction. We can hypothesize that the laws in the southern states during the 1700s and early 1800s had the consequence of increasing the survival of the slave system. These laws were therefore functional for the survival of the slave system. However, whether the slave system was positive or negative, or whether it was right or wrong, is another question. So, we might personally believe that the slave system was a terribly wrong system. However, as a sociologist, we want to discover how something, whether we like it or not, is functional for a certain social system, that is, how something increases the survival of that social system. Consequently, being a sociologist helps us look at a social situation objectively in order to see why it is surviving, regardless of whether we personally like it or not.

Another concept, *dysfunction,* deals with consequences that decrease the survival of a social system. For example, prejudice and discrimination against a group of people will have the consequence of decreasing the survival of that group. Given prejudice and discrimination against that group, they will have fewer choices of jobs, fewer chances to get more education so as to get better-paying jobs, and fewer chances to join voluntary organizations—such as churches, country clubs, and other organizations—that provide the opportunity to get to know networks of people who have connections that help people to get jobs, give advice on how to get ahead, and give financial support so that they can get ahead. In other words, prejudice and discrimination will have consequences for decreasing the survival of a certain group of people by decreasing their chances at gaining more money, power, and prestige. Again, even though we may not personally like prejudice and discrimination, we, as sociologists, can remain objective and discover how prejudice and discrimination is dysfunctional for a certain group of people.

A function can be either *manifest* (that is, intended) or *latent* (that is, unintended). For example, when there is intended prejudice and discrimination against Group A by Group B, the members of Group B will increase their survival because the intended prejudice and discrimination will typically have the consequence of giving them more choices, chances, and connections. Hence, a manifest function states that there are intended consequences that increase the survival of a certain social system. Again, notice that I am not saying that this is positive or negative or that it is right or wrong; rather, I am saying that something has the consequence of intentionally increasing the survival of some social system.

A manifest dysfunction, in contrast, states that there are consequences that are intended to decrease the survival of a social system. For example, using the preceding example, whereas Group B's intended prejudice and discrimination have consequences of increasing its members' survival, it has consequences of decreasing the survival of Group A members who are being prejudiced and discriminated against. Thus, what is functional for one social system (group, organization, society) can be dysfunctional for another social system (group, organization, society).

Finally, something can be a latent function or a latent dysfunction for a certain social system. That is, a function or a dysfunction can have an unintended consequence for a certain social system. For example, many African Americans migrated from the southern states to northern cities during the 20th century in search of better-paying jobs and more freedom. That is what they intended to do. However, what they did not intend to do, but what ultimately happened, was that as Blacks congregated in certain inner-city neighborhoods in northern cities because of intended racial segregation by Whites, they became a political power by voting in Black mayors, Black city council members, and Black members of Congress. Increasing their political power was not what Blacks originally intended when they moved north. They moved north because they intended to get better-paying jobs and experience more freedom. However, their migration north also turned out to be a latent function for them, that is, an unintended consequence that increased their survival in that they began to have more political power in local, state, and national governments.

So, you can see how using the concepts of function, dysfunction, manifest and latent function, and manifest and latent dysfunction can help us understand many social problems and therefore help us solve our social problems.

Symbolic Interaction Theory

Another well-known theory in sociology is *symbolic interaction theory*. Whereas functional theory deals with the functions and dysfunctions of social systems, symbolic interaction theory focuses on the micro level of society, on interactions between and among small numbers of people. We use ideas such as Cooley's (1902) concept of the "looking glass self" (looking glass was the term used for mirror at that time), in which he pointed out that we will many times look to others and observe how they see us and judge us as a way to decide how we see and judge ourselves. For example, how have African Americans, women, and poor people at various times in American history been seen and judged? And how did they come to see and judge themselves?

These looking glass selves can help us understand social problems in that the perception of the self, as taught to us by those around us, can be a barrier to our being able to get ahead. That is, not only do objective conditions of prejudice, discrimination, and poverty affect people's chances of getting ahead in life, but also the kinds of selves people are socialized to have can act to hold them back. Hence, we need to apply theoretical ideas from symbolic interaction theory to help us gain a greater understanding of our social problems and what steps we can take to solve these problems.

Anomie Theory

Another well-known sociological theory that will help us understand social problems such as crime and deviance is *anomie theory* by Robert Merton (1938). In his article titled "Social Structure and Anomie," Merton noted that most people are what he called *conformists,* meaning that they have the legal opportunities available to them, without breaking the laws of society, to gain the goals of society such as money, power, and prestige. However, there are others in society who, because of their social conditions, face blocked opportunities as they attempt to attain the goals of society. Due to these blocked opportunities, they are more likely to use illegal means to attain the goals of society. Merton called these people *innovators.* That is, people become innovators because the social conditions in which they live make it much more difficult for them to use legal means to achieve the goals of society. Merton's theory will help us understand the deviance that occurs in a society because of the blocked opportunities that the existing social structure creates for certain groups of people, for example, poor people, people who receive poor education, and people who have been prejudiced against and discriminated against. Using his theory will help us reflect on how, at times, we need to change the social structure in order to give legal opportunities to people, as a way to solve or reduce social problems such as juvenile delinquency, adult crime, and escape into such behaviors as alcoholism and drug abuse. As we give legal opportunities to people who do not currently have these opportunities, we will unlock another door that will help us solve a number of our social problems.

Reference Group Theory

Another theory that will help us understand our social problems and how to solve them is *reference group theory* (Merton, 1968a, 1968b). This theory asserts that we all refer to various groups in our lives to decide how to think, feel, and act. We use a number of different groups as reference groups such as our family, our friends, a team, a fraternity or sorority, a church, a college or university, the place where we work, or some other social organization. While we are members of some of these groups, we may not be members of others—yet we can still refer to them to decide how to act, think, and feel. These groups, whether or not we are members of them, can be positive or negative in our eyes. Regardless, we still refer to them. We may refer to our family and how we were socialized to decide how to act in a certain way. For example, let us say that you were taught by one of your reference groups, such as your family, to be considerate of all people, regardless of their race, gender, ethnicity, religion, or sexual orientation, and you act in that way. Another individual, however, may have been taught by their family to be prejudiced and to discriminate against a certain group of people, and—not surprisingly—he or she thinks, feels, and acts differently from how you do. So, two families act as reference groups on two different individuals with the result that these two individuals act, think, and feel differently about the same group of people. Interestingly, when these two individuals become roommates in college, are in the military together, or work next to each other in the same work place, there is the chance for disagreement and conflict, due to how their reference groups socialized them.

Reference group theory does not say that you act exactly the way you were taught by the reference groups you have, but it does say that you will refer to these groups in *deciding* how you are going to act, think, and feel. Remember that outside social factors in our lives do not totally determine how we think, act, and feel, but they do tend to have a substantial influence on us even though we are not always aware of such influence. This is what Emile Durkheim ([1895]1938) meant when he said that society is external to us and yet coercive on us. That is, society's laws, values, beliefs, and customs are outside of our minds when we are born, but through the process of socialization, these social phenomena are put into our minds and influence us more than we realize. Most of the time, we go through our daily lives and do not realize how much we are influenced by what we have been taught by our reference groups. This is especially true if we stay with the same people we grew up with, but if, as we go throughout our lives, we encounter new groups of people, we will become more conscious of how we were socialized by our reference groups versus how others were socialized by their reference groups.

Differential Association Theory

Another sociological theory that can help us gain greater clarity, especially with respect to social problems such as crime, drugs, and the problems of families, is Sutherland's (1940) *differential association theory*. Sutherland, in focusing on crime, hypothesized that criminality "is learned in direct or indirect association with those who already practice the behavior" (p. 10) and that "those who learn this criminal behavior are segregated from frequent and intimate contacts with law-abiding behavior" (pp. 10–11). Knowledge of this theory will help us, for example, understand why people depart from the norms of the society and commit crimes and other acts of deviance, for example, a member of the Ku Klux Klan may be more willing to discriminate against African Americans, Catholics, Jews, and homosexuals because he or she learns this behavior while associating with others who have learned this same behavior. We can apply this theory to various social problems to help us better understand how the associations people have can cause them to be prejudiced against and discriminate against certain groups of people. Likewise, a change in their associations, for example, moving to a new area of the country, going to college, or going into the military will change their original associations and can possibly lead to new ways of thinking and acting, such as not being prejudiced and not discriminating.

Original associations can be very powerful on an individual, especially if everyone else in that social situation is also acting and believing the same way. However, new associations can also act as a powerful influence on the individual, which can lead to life-changing values, beliefs, actions, and a new and different world view. Hence, whether we realize it or not, the associations we have, from the beginning of our lives and throughout our lives, can have a huge effect upon us.

Exchange Theory

Finally, one more sociological theory that I apply is Peter Blau's *exchange theory* (1964).[14] Blau asserted that we not only exchange material goods but also exchange nonmaterial things such as love, time, attention, support, and sympathy. Many of our interactions with other people, groups, and organizations are interactions that include some kind of exchange—even though much of the time we do not realize that many interactions also involve exchanges. In addition to going to a car dealer and exchanging money for a new car or going to a grocery store and exchanging money for food, we give our time to someone or some group and typically receive something in return, such as approval, honor, respect, prestige, acceptance, love, or attention.

A parent gives us love, and we give back love, time, and/or trust to that parent. We give a girlfriend or boyfriend time, attention, and love and hope that he or she gives us these things in return. In fact, relationships tend to continue as long as there is mutual giving and receiving. However, the relationship is in jeopardy if, for example, you give love, time, and attention to your boyfriend or girlfriend, but he or she no longer gives these things to you. When someone gives something to someone else (for example, love, time, attention) and expects something similar in return but does not receive anything in return, this is called *breaking the norm of reciprocity* (Gouldner, 1960). Whether we realize it or not, when we create new relationships, we also create new exchanges, for example, parent–child, boyfriend–girlfriend, husband–wife, teacher–student, coach–player, or employer–employee relationships. In other words, we create norms in relationships where if we give something, we expect something in return. The exchange might not necessarily be equivalent, but there is an expectation of receiving something in return. For example, if you are a college student and say hello to someone you know as you walk across campus, you probably expect a hello in return. If that person looks the other way and ignores you, you will probably become immediately conscious that there was a breaking of a norm of reciprocity between you and the other person. That is, when someone says hello to another person, there is the expectation that the other person will say hello back. Hence, even in the simple saying of hello, there is the creation of the norm of reciprocity.

Bob likes Sue. Sue likes Bob. They want to give each other time, attention, sympathy, and love. Bob, however, is also a football player and spends 2 to 3 hours each day practicing or playing in a game. He is also expected to spend time with his fraternity brothers. He has little time left to be with Sue. Sue, on the other hand, has lots of time to be with Bob. She is not in a sorority or on a team. She wants to spend more time with Bob. Bob cannot spend as much time with Sue as she wants. He cannot be with her on Friday nights, on Saturday afternoons, or at other times. Sue pays a lot of attention to Bob (calling him and asking him, "When can we be together again?"), but Bob can spend only a certain amount of time with Sue. Sue's feelings are hurt because she tries to give so much time and attention to Bob, but he does not reciprocate with the same amount of time and attention. In sociological terms of exchange theory, Sue feels that the norm of reciprocity is broken, and this can place the relationship in jeopardy.

Although this example is a romantic example, exchange theory and the norm of reciprocity can also be applied to social problems. Millions of people in our country work 40 hours per week but get paid wages considerably below the poverty line. These people may conclude that this relationship is an unfair exchange and may go on strike, demonstrate, march, or take some other social action because they believe that the norm of reciprocity has been broken. Hence, the breaking of the norm of reciprocity can lead to conflict and possibly some kind of social change. So, exchange, the norm of reciprocity, and the breaking of the norm of reciprocity all can be integral parts of social problems. Thus, the creation of new exchanges and new norms of reciprocity can lead to the solving of social problems, for example, between Blacks and Whites, males and females, employers and employees, and the poor and nonpoor. Consequently, you can see how exchange theory can be an integral part of the theory of conflict and social change where the discovery and the analysis of the ideas of exchange and the norm of reciprocity can help us understand the nature of existing social problems and what we can do to address these social problems.

Concluding Thoughts on Theory and Social Problems

Note that as we work our way through this book, we continually use the theory of conflict and social change as a main means of understanding and solving our social problems. But we also apply the other theories just outlined to give us additional insight into a particular social problem. As you make your way through this book, you will see how beneficial it is to apply sociological theories to social problems in order to better understand them and solve them.

Addressing Social Problems Within Capitalism

I want to make a comment on the context within which we address our social problems. I suggest actions to solve or reduce our social problems within the context of a U.S. and worldwide capitalistic economy. The reason I say this is that I think that we Americans, as well as many people throughout the world, will live our lives, at least for the immediate future, within a capitalistic economy. How long will this be? I do not know, and I imagine that no one else does either.[15] Capitalism during the past 300 to 400 years has continued to evolve, adapt, and adjust to the times. Will it continue to do so? I do not know. However, given capitalism's ability to adjust so far, its current pervasive influence in the world, and the legitimacy it carries among many powerful people, I predict that a capitalistic economy will continue to survive in the United States and throughout the world for some time to come. So, with this in mind, my book is about what we can realistically do to solve or at least reduce our social problems within the context of a U.S. and worldwide capitalistic economy.

The Next Chapter

Before we discuss our first social problem, we focus in the next chapter on three things: (1) the barriers to solving our social problems, (2) the possibilities for solving our social problems, and (3) how sociology can help us solve our social problems. So, read and reflect on Chapter 2 to prepare yourself to tackle the specific social problems we address in later chapters.

Questions for Discussion

1. Should we, in sociology, go beyond our role of being objective and say what we think should happen?

2. How much should sociologists be a part of changing society?

3. What might be other criteria, besides the number of people affected and the problem's potential to endanger lives, which we could use to decide which social problem we should tackle first?

4. Can we do without bureaucracies such as the government and large corporations?

5. If we need to have bureaucracies, are there some ways that we, as individuals, cannot be so powerless against them and be able to feel that they are not so impersonal to our human needs?

6. Why do people, at times, accept their unequal situations as long as they do?

7. What are some ways that we can become more aware of social problems in our current society and world?

8. What is the relationship between capitalism and a certain social problem?

9. Do you think that we will ever go beyond capitalism and create some new type of economic system or not?

10. What are some things we can do in society and the world that can help us to have peaceful conflict versus violent conflict?

2

Barriers, Possibilities, and How Sociology Can Help

T here are a number of barriers that either prevent us from solving our social problems or slow us down in making progress toward solving our social problems. At the same time, however, there are also possibilities for solving our social problems. In this chapter, I discuss both barriers and possibilities so that you can become more aware of a number of the key factors that influence the solving of social problems. Our discussion of these barriers and possibilities does not exhaust all of the factors that influence the solving of social problems. However, the barriers and possibilities we discuss are the key factors in addressing our social problems. Finally, I share with you how the discipline of sociology can help us solve our social problems.

Barriers to Solving Our Social Problems

In the forthcoming pages, I discuss a number of barriers that prevent or at least considerably slow down the solving of our social problems. These barriers, as you will soon see, are formidable and hence difficult to overcome. I discuss these barriers not to make you pessimistic about the solving of social problems but to show you the daunting challenges we face when we attempt to address our social problems. Discussing each of these barriers, however sobering this discussion may be, will help you become aware of and understand these barriers and, in doing so, help all of us take steps toward solving our social problems.

Power

One of the largest barriers to the solving of our social problems is the existing power structure, power elite, and powerful corporations that together will not want the solving of social problems if this means that people in positions of power and powerful organizations—especially large multinational corporations—will lose their power. Put simply, once people and organizations have power, they do not want to give up this power and all of the material and nonmaterial amenities that go along with it.

Throughout history and in today's world, people who have power do not want to give it up. They do all kinds of things to hold on to power, such as constructing ideologies (for example, religious, economic, and political) to justify their staying in power, giving a portion of their money and resources in the form of wages and social services as a way to stay in power, creating laws to legitimize the existing social conditions and hence the existing conditions of inequality, and using force (if needed) in the form of the police and military to maintain the status quo.

People and organizations that have power many times get their power from the money they have. So, whoever makes a lot of money, especially in the capitalistic societies of today's world, can and often will wield much more power than the rest of us. Of all the barriers that we discuss, this barrier of power and who has it will continually play a major role in how we deal with our social problems. In other words, to understand why we do not readily solve or diminish the severity of our social problems, we need to discover and continually be aware of who has power and how they use their power.

What I am saying is not new. Various people throughout history have been aware of the relationship between power and what occurs in society. For example, during the mid-1800s, Marx and Engels ([1848]1978) wrote in *The Communist Manifesto,* "The ruling ideas of each age have ever been the ideas of its ruling class" (p. 40). Whatever the type of society, whether ruled by kings or dictators or owners of capital in a modern capitalistic society, those who have the power will tend to protect their own vested interests, which are usually to remain in power and to retain a disproportionate share of the material comforts of life. Hence, they will not want to solve social problems if solving those problems means that they will lose their power and/or lose their material way of life. At times, the powerful can even support the alleviation of deplorable conditions of the masses so long as they do not lose their power and privileges (Lenski, 1984).

During the middle of the 20th century, Mills (1956) hypothesized that there was a power elite in American society that made a disproportionate number of the decisions in our society. Mills hypothesized that people in the top positions in the corporate world, the military world, and the political world are the "movers and shakers" of our society. In the early 21st century, Kerbo (2006) asserted that sociologists need to speak of a new social class, namely the corporate class. He noted that the very largest corporations in our country have huge amounts of power, such as the ability to lay off workers in one community, move a plant or factory out of the country, decide how taxpayers' money is spent, and influence the making of laws in communities, states, and nations. To show the potential power that the largest 100 American corporations can yield, he noted that there "are about 200,000 industrial corporations operating in our country today, but almost 75 percent of all the industrial corporate assets are in the hands of 100 (0.0005 percent) of these corporations" (p. 179). In other words, there is a huge concentration of capital in relatively few hands in the United States. Moreover, Kerbo reports that of the top five stock-voting positions in the largest 122 corporations in the United States ($5 \times 122 = 610$ positions in all), "just 21 investors accounted for more than half of all these top five stock-voting positions" (p. 184). So, a few people and a few corporations wield vast amounts of power as a result of their control over huge amounts of corporate assets. Today, in the 21st century, this is where much power appears to be shifting—to the very largest multinational corporations and to those people who run these corporations.

The bottom line for the solving of our social problems is that the vested interests of these very powerful corporations who seek their own survival and profit do not coincide with the vested interests of others seeking to solve certain social problems. Hence, we now discuss vested interests as a powerful barrier to the solving of social problems.

Vested Interests

Another big barrier to solving social problems is the vested interests of the people in a society who have power. *Vested interests* are the concerns, perceived rights, or "stakes" that individuals or larger social systems want to protect and hold. Individuals, groups, organizations, communities, states in a country, and entire societies will support, defend, and preserve what is to their benefit and will struggle against what can hurt them such as a loss of income, wealth, power, prestige, and way of life. Individuals, groups, and larger social systems will, throughout human history, lie, cheat, and even resort to violence to protect their vested interests. In all probability, we humans underestimate how powerful an influence vested interests happen to be. For example, individuals or groups may be sympathetic to changes that could be made that could help others. But if these proposed changes go against their own vested interests (loss of money, power, prestige, and/or way of life), these individuals and groups may still be against any changes such as social policy that could solve social problems. Moreover, as Blumer (1971) suggested some years ago, "A social problem is always a focal point for the operation of divergent and conflicting interests" (p. 301).

Let us elaborate on the above thoughts by giving an example that occurred throughout the 20th century. What would you do if you were in this situation? It is just after World War II; Wil, who is White and has a family, has been back from the war for 2 years. While serving in Europe during the war, Wil met Al, an African American soldier. They found out that they both were from Atlanta, Georgia, and over time they became good friends during the years they were in the war.

Soon after the war, Wil and his family bought a house in a middle-class, all-White neighborhood in Atlanta. Al's family visited Will and his family and really liked the neighborhood. Al decided that he would try to buy a house that had a "For Sale" sign in the front yard just a few houses away from Wil's house. Al talked with the realtors (that is, people who sell houses for home owners). He was ready and financially able to buy the house.

However, the realtors felt social pressure not to sell to an African American family because it was thought that an African American family moving into an all-White neighborhood would bring down the value of all the houses in the neighborhood; there was a fear that other African American families would want to move into the neighborhood and that White families would, in turn, panic and sell their houses below market prices. Also, besides the fear of losing the value of their homes, a number of White families in the neighborhood were still prejudiced and did not want to live near African American families or want their children to go to the same school as African American children. Remember, this was in the late 1940s in the South, where public schools were segregated; segregation was the law at that time and went along with the strong, informal norms of that time.

From a friend perspective, Wil might have had no reservations about Al and his family moving into the neighborhood. However, from Wil's vested interest of wanting to keep up the value of his house, he may be ambivalent and somewhat fearful of Al moving into the neighborhood.

Stories like the one that I made up occurred numerous times in our country during the past 100 years. Even when people are personally sympathetic, their own vested interests may still outweigh their sympathies. This goes for getting a job, attending a school, belonging to a country club, or even being a member of a church. Sympathies and friendship can be strong, but vested interests can be even stronger. Hence, vested interests can serve as a strong barrier to the solving of our social problems. Therefore, if we want to understand the nature of social problems and why they are so hard to solve, we need to discover all of the vested interests involved that are related to a certain social problem. Once we know all of the vested interests involved, we can begin to see how we can address the various vested interests as a way to address a particular social problem.

Legitimation

A third very powerful barrier or impediment to the solving of social problems is legitimation. *Legitimation* occurs when people with power and money have the ability to socially construct beliefs, laws, informal norms, and traditions in such a way as to make it appear that it is just and right for them to be and stay in power. In other words, if the people in power can convince the rest of us that the current situation is the way it should be, it is highly likely that the existing situation will continue; hence there will be no social change and no progress toward the solving of social problems.

These first three barriers to the solving of social problems—power, vested interests, and legitimation—can serve to maintain the status quo, that is, the current social conditions, with all of its attendant social problems, for years—even hundreds of years; for example, slavery survived in the United States from the early 1600s to the 1860s—around 250 years. Although these three barriers are extremely powerful in maintaining existing social conditions and therefore inhibit the solving of social problems, there are other barriers that we now discuss so that you can be more fully aware of the challenges we face in solving our social problems.

Redefining the Social Problem

Another deterrent or barrier to solving our social problems has to do with how we define them. A group of people, such as a civil rights group or a group concerned about the environment, may define a social problem one way, whereas political authorities who deal with the social problem define it another way. A third group, the people who carry out a social policy to solve a social problem (usually people in government bureaucracies), may define it a third way. Given these different definitions, these three groups can disagree on what social policy is best to solve a certain social problem and hence slow down the solving of the problem.

Disagreeing With Social Policy

Even when various groups agree on the definition of a social problem, they can disagree on social policy. Different political philosophies, for example, will often result in different social policies. Let us use poverty as an example. *Conservatives* may suggest decreasing taxes on businesses so that these businesses will have more money to expand existing facilities, thereby creating more jobs. *Liberals* may suggest increasing social programs, such as job training and loans and grants to get more education, reasoning that if the poor get an opportunity to be trained or educated, they can fill new types of jobs that provide higher incomes and chances for upward mobility. *Radicals*, on the other hand, may assert that capitalism is the problem in that it does not provide enough jobs, does not provide enough jobs that pay above the poverty line, does not distribute services (such as education and health care) equitably to all people, and hence does not address the needs of many people. Thus, radicals' solution is to change to a more socialistic system where every citizen would be guaranteed a job at a decent income and where their essential needs (such as food, shelter, safety, freedom from discrimination, health care, and opportunity to get a decent education) would be satisfied. As you can see, even though everyone might agree that there is a social problem of poverty, they may disagree on the specific social policies to use to solve it.

The above discussion raises the question, "Why do people have different political views?" There are a number of reasons. One reason relates back to what Durkheim (1933) suggested is the nature of modern society. That is, people in modern society are allowed a greater variety of values and beliefs than did people in societies of the past. In societies of the past, there were typically kings, emperors, and dictators who expected and usually got obedience to certain norms, values, beliefs, and ideologies. If individuals did not conform to these social regulations, they could be threatened with the loss of their life or family members' lives or property; they could be imprisoned or tortured to get them to change; or, if a person still did not relent, the person could be killed through various violent and painful means such as beheading, crucifixion, burning alive, drowning, and suffocation. As such, for thousands of years, humans pretty much had to conform to the views of those in power, whether they be governmental or religious leaders.

However, only in the last few hundred years of human history, our human ancestors began to create constitutions, bills of rights, democratic assemblies, and new values and beliefs that suggest that people should have more freedom to have different beliefs and values. Although this relatively recent human trend has afforded people more freedom in what to believe and value, it has also presented the new challenge of how people of different beliefs and values can get along. For example, a conservative may value individualism and freedom to make as much money as possible, even though this may result in some people having millions of dollars while others are homeless and penniless. A liberal, on the other hand, may value having more equality in society, where money and access to resources are distributed more evenly at the expense of some losing some freedom to make as much money as is possible.[1] These different values and beliefs cause people to create different social policies, making it difficult for everyone to settle on an agreed-on social policy that will solve a social problem.

Desiring a Minimum of Government

Some people, called *libertarians,* hold a personal philosophy that there should be little or no government.[2] They believe that more government means less freedom for people. Even though they might agree that some social condition is a social problem, they do not want the government to help solve the problem because that would mean creating a larger government. Libertarians argue that other methods, such as more individual determination and responsibility, should be used to solve the social problem. Consequently, they will fight against nearly any expansion of government, even though the use of government could be a major means to solve a number of social problems.

Although conservatives are not as extreme in their desire to limit the government as are libertarians, conservatives also believe that a minimum of government is best. When libertarians and conservatives combine to form a coalition, they can be a powerful force that restricts the use of the government as a means to solve social problems. As you go through life, you will probably notice a trend in politics in which libertarians and conservatives will work to limit or decrease the programs and services of the government, while liberals will work to retain or increase programs and services of the government. This trend is the result of two different philosophies: libertarians and conservatives will emphasize less government and less government regulation, potentially at the expense of having more poverty and inequality; whereas, liberals will emphasize less poverty and inequality, potentially at the expense of having more government and more government regulation.

As a side note, if you are taking a course in social problems or a course related to social problems and are reading this book, you may, as you work your way through the course, want to think about your own political philosophy as it relates to what social policies you believe should be used to solve social problems. If you find inconsistencies between your beliefs and the social policies you think will solve social problems, you may want to rethink your political philosophy. So, ask yourself the question, "Where do my social policies fit—as a libertarian, a conservative, a liberal, or a radical?"

Given that libertarians want to have a minimum of government and not use government and its resources to solve social problems, you might wonder how they would go about solving social problems of poverty, crime, homelessness, and so on. Their answer is that each person should be responsible for himself or herself, and therefore each person should rely on himself or herself to solve his or her own individual problems. They assert that if we all are responsible for ourselves, we will solve our social problems.

The libertarians have been criticized for this stance because a number of problems in our society are caused not by individual inadequacies but rather by the social structure. Some individuals are indeed able to solve the difficult situations they are in by themselves, but by and large, if some aspect of the social structure causes a social problem, most people experiencing the social problem will not be able to get out of their situations merely by taking more personal responsibility. For example, no matter how much people take more responsibility for themselves and their situations, this will not change the lack of enough jobs or the lack of enough decent-paying jobs in a country. In other words, to solve social problems, something more needs to be done than merely expecting individuals to take on more personal responsibility. In other words, various aspects of the existing social structure, such as more jobs and more decent-paying jobs, must change if we want to solve our social problems.

You may ask what I mean when I say that the social structure causes a social problem. Maybe one way to show you this is to give the example of African Americans living in our country during the 1950s. There were laws and informal norms during the 1950s that did not allow African Americans to go to the same schools, eat in the same restaurants, stay in the same motels, swim in the same swimming pools, sit in the same movie theaters, live in the same neighborhoods, worship in the same churches, or join the same clubs as did Whites. These laws and informal norms also did not allow African Americans to vote or hold various political offices. All of these beliefs, laws, informal norms, and customs that prohibited African Americans from doing these things combined to form what sociologists call a *social structure*: that is, social patterns that occur over and over and that, in this case, caused African Americans to have less opportunity, less upward mobility, and hence less income, wealth, power, and prestige.

To the degree that the social structure of a society limits the opportunities of groups of people (for example, African Americans, Native Americans, Hispanic Americans, gays, women, and the disabled) and therefore limits their upward mobility, we can say that the social problems that develop from such a lack of opportunity, upward mobility, and hence lack of money, power, and prestige are caused largely by the social structure rather than by the actions of individuals. In such a situation, for the social problem to be solved, it is the social structure rather than the individuals that needs to change. For example, during the 1950s, individual African Americans could be honest, hardworking, and responsible, but because they did not have the opportunities that Whites had due to the existing social structure, their individual behavior typically had little or no effect on their life situations. The social structure, rather than their own individual efforts, largely determined what they could do. Hence, in order to solve their social problem of lack of opportunity and upward mobility, the larger social structure of laws, beliefs, values, norms, and ideologies needed to change.

Individual Change Versus Social Structure

An additional barrier or obstacle to the solving of social problems has to do with how much social policies emphasize changing only individuals. If the social policies applied are calling for individuals to change, the social problems will not be solved. Why? Because the real causes of the social problems are structural. One of the key things we need to do as we study social problems is to discover how the existing social structure causes social problems. If we are not aware of this connection, we are less likely to solve our social problems.

Values

The values that we embrace can be an impediment to solving our social problems. As hard as it may be to believe at first, our own values might not always be the same as other people's values. This greatly hinders the solving of certain social problems. Let us take the example of gender inequality. When asked, most people in our society would say that they believe in equal opportunity. Given the ideology taught to us and how we have been socialized, most Americans would say, "Yes, of course, I believe in equal opportunity."

However, a number of people in our society take the Bible and what it says as the literal truth. Certain passages suggest that women are supposed to be subordinate to men. For example, in the Book of Leviticus (27:3–4) in the Old Testament, the Bible implies that women should be paid 60% of what men are paid. In the Book of Ephesians (5:22–24) in the New Testament, the Bible says, "Wives, submit yourselves unto your own husbands." A third passage is in I Peter (3:1 and 7), in which wives are told to "be in subjection to your own husbands" and a wife is described as "the weaker vessel."

For a number of people in our society who take a literal interpretation of the Bible, the value of equal opportunity and the values of the Bible pose a dilemma such as the following:

> If I go by the society's value of equal opportunity, I will break biblical teaching by treating women equal to men. If I go by biblical teaching, I will break society's value of equal opportunity by treating women unequal to men. What should I do?

One of the consequences of these conflicts in values is that social problems are not solved. Instead of changing laws and informal norms and other aspects of the social structure in order to solve a social problem, individuals and groups argue over values. As a result, social change comes about more slowly, with the result that social problems are solved more slowly.

This situation becomes especially difficult when the values, along with beliefs, laws, and informal norms in question are seen as having been created by God. We can predict that whenever God and religion are connected to values, beliefs, laws, and informal norms—for example, in such areas as gender inequality, abortion, gay marriage, and teaching evolution[3]—there will be long and emotional debates that will result in taking more time to create a social policy to solve social problems.

Existing Social Policies Versus New Social Policies

An additional barrier or obstruction to the solving of a social problem is that other policies that dealt with this problem previously may conflict with new policies. Peyrot (1984) noted, for example, that we have responded to drug abuse via both a criminal justice policy and a medical treatment policy. These two models have not always meshed well to create a coordinated social policy toward drug abuse (p. 91). Is the person a criminal and should be sent to prison, or is the person ill and should be seen as a patient and therefore sent to a hospital or addiction center? In other words, separate and discordant policies can work to slow down the process of solving the overall problem.

Once a social policy is implemented, there is a time period when the new policy is observed or measured to see whether it works. In a number of situations in the past, social policy did not work in practice the way it was intended to work on paper. Unexpected things happened, there were not enough resources to solve the problem, and so on. When this happens, those who were skeptical of the policy now have new ammunition to fight it. The policy can be attacked, thereby decreasing enthusiasm for the policy and making more people question whether the policy will really solve the problem.

If the skeptics are powerful enough to make their doubts about a new policy known to the policymakers, resources can be cut back or the social policy itself can be dismantled. A result of this process is that we do not solve the social problem. This does not mean that the policy was the wrong policy, even though it may have had flaws. It does show the power of interest groups and how they can negate a social policy that could have solved, or at least ameliorated, a social problem.

Mass Media as a Business

The mass media can act as a barrier to the solving of a social problem. The mass media may be seen as seeking the truth. In many cases, this is true. However, we need to remember that the mass media, such as newspapers, radio stations, and television networks, are businesses that seek profit. Consequently, they may play up a social problem that will sell newspapers or increase listener or viewer ratings, and, in so doing, they may downplay another social problem. The result is that the less publicized social problem does not get the attention it needs to be addressed satisfactorily.

Lack of the Best Information

Even if social policymakers in state legislatures and Congress are genuine in their attempt to solve a social problem, they might not always have the best information on the topic with which to make the right decisions. For example, policymakers might not read a sociological study that has important information on a social problem. Sociologists, like other academicians, report their research in professional journals that, many times, are read mainly by other academicians. This situation can create a *closed loop* of information. Academicians will read each other's published research and understand the implications of the research, but policymakers might not always be aware of such research. Hence, the research that could be crucial to the solving of a social problem goes unread by the policymakers. For example, in reference to a piece of sociological research, Wilson (1993a) noted, "These important findings, buried in an academic journal, were apparently not discussed by the media and were probably ignored by policymakers" (p. 17). So long as the findings of sociological research and other social science research are not employed to address our social problems, as a society we are more likely not to have the most comprehensive and most up-to-date knowledge with which to create the best social policy possible in order to solve our social problems.

Recipients of Government Services

Another obstacle to the solving of a social problem is the fact that as recipients of government services receive the services that bring relief to their daily situations, they may consider the social problem as being solved because they are getting help. The social problem, in reality, has not been solved; rather, some of its effects have simply been alleviated. For example, people cannot find a job because of increasing unemployment due to a recent recession. They are given food stamps to alleviate their situation, but they are still without jobs, income, and housing and hence unable to live on their own. The result may be to "cool out" and "cool down" these recipients and other people who are advocating for them (Piven & Cloward, 1971). But the social problems of unemployment, poverty, and dependence still remain.

Nature of Congress

Finally, another barrier to the solving of social problems has to do with the nature of the U.S. Congress. Many times, Congress is more of a reactive institution than a proactive one. Typically, as a social problem occurs, Congress reacts to address the problem rather than acts to prevent the potential social problem from materializing in the first place. In other words, members of Congress do not plan ahead and are therefore not as visionary as they could be.[4] David S. Broder, a prominent newspaper editorialist, stated, "Our system of government is notoriously short-sighted; we do not act until a crisis is upon us" (Broder, 2002, p. A11).[5]

Why is this the case? A key reason is that members of Congress know that they can be voted out of office rather quickly (every 2 years for a member of the House of Representatives) if they wander too far from their constituents' views. Most members of Congress want to continue to be re-elected every 2 years. Hence, even though they may have some very creative ideas to help us solve our social problems, they first go by their personal vested interests of wanting to be re-elected and therefore "tone down" their ideas in order to fit with their constituents' prevailing view and end up being less bold, farsighted, and visionary and, thus, less likely to solve our social problems. In other words, their primary concern is to hold onto their jobs first and the power (money and prestige, too) that comes with their positions.[6] Schumpeter (1976) put the situation this way: "We must start from the competitive struggle for power and office and realize that the social function is fulfilled, as it were, incidentally—in the same sense as production is incidental to the making of profits" (p. 282).

As you can now see, there are many barriers to hinder, slow down, or even stop the solving of our social problems. You might be rather pessimistic at this point. However, "take heart" as the saying goes. There are also a number of possibilities that we need to consider to help us realize that not all is "doom and gloom." Let us look at these possibilities.

Possibilities for Solving Our Social Problems

Yes, as you may now agree, there are a number of formidable barriers to the solving of social problems. But there are, at the same time, many possibilities to our solving our social problems. In the coming paragraphs, there are numerous steps that we can take to solve or at least greatly reduce our social problems and hence give us hope that we can indeed do something about our social problems.

Change Our Social Construction of Reality

We created our social world, and we can change it. Our ancestors created beliefs, values, customs, laws, norms, political systems, economic systems, religious systems, and so on. Over hundreds or thousands of years, we, as humans, have many times forgotten that we created these social phenomena. Once we realize that we created social phenomena, we are more likely to realize that we can indeed make changes in our social phenomena. We do not have to put up with things of the past. For example, we have gotten rid of the slave system in the United States and have decreased racial prejudice and discrimination and have replaced these human creations with new human creations that provide more equal opportunity for African American people. So, the more we realize that we socially constructed this reality and that we can change it, the more likely that we are to take the next step of changing it. The more we realize this, the closer we will be to solving, or at least decreasing, our social problems.

Address Social Problems

We have made progress with a number of our social problems. We have recognized different kinds of prejudice and discrimination (for example, racial/ethnic, religious, gender, sexual orientation, disability, age) and have constructed new beliefs, laws, norms, and customs to decrease these various kinds of prejudice and discrimination. Our society is far from being perfect, but compare our society today with our society of 1950, for example, when African Americans were not allowed to go to many schools, live in many neighborhoods, or have many kinds of jobs; when women could not play sports and were not encouraged to go to college or to become doctors, lawyers, professors, ministers, or chief executive officers; when gays and lesbians were not even allowed even to express who they were and how they felt personally; and when disabled people could not make their way downtown, through a college campus, or to another floor in a building. All of these examples show that we have made substantial changes, just with regard to various kinds of humanly constructed prejudice and discrimination and that more of our fellow Americans are being taken into consideration and being given more equal opportunity and being treated with dignity and respect.

Raise Consciousness

More people in the United States and throughout the world are becoming conscious of what hurts them, what alienates them, and what holds them back. Computers, e-mail, the Internet, travel within a country and to other countries, study in other countries, the reading of books and newspapers, and the watching of television—all have at least one thing in common: namely, that they increase the consciousness of humans around the world, whether they intend to or not. News, knowledge, information, insight, new ways of thinking, and different ways of thinking are spread via computers, travel, the mass media, and so on. Whether we want consciousness about the world and the conditions of the world to spread or not is one thing. The fact is, regardless of whether we want such consciousness about world conditions to spread at what seems like a geometric rate, it is spreading quickly. Recall in our theory of conflict and social change and the accompanying causal model (Chapter 1) that a key factor in social change is the consciousness or awareness of existing social conditions and their inequalities. No doubt, as more people become conscious of these conditions, it is only a matter of time before they will form groups and organizations to address these concerns.

With regard to these first three possibilities: (1) we socially constructed this social world, (2) we can already see progress on a number of fronts, and (3) we are increasingly conscious of the social conditions and social problems within which we live, these three possibilities are powerful engines for social change and for the addressing of our social problems, at the local, state, national, and world levels. In addition to these three powerful influences, there are other possibilities that will help us solve our social problems.

Redefine Problems

One way we can solve social problems is to redefine them as no longer being a problem. At first thought, this may sound ludicrous, but this was done in 1933 when we repealed the Prohibition amendment, thereby making alcohol legal to drink again. At one time, we defined drinking alcohol as a social problem and made it illegal. At another time, we ceased to define it as a social problem and made it legal.

This act of redefining has also gone in the other direction, that is, the labeling as a social problem a situation that, at one time, was not seen as a social problem. Peyrot (1984), for example, noted that until 1875, "there were virtually no legal restrictions on the use of drugs such as opium, heroin, morphine, codeine, cocaine, and marijuana" (p. 86). He pointed out, however, that between 1875 and 1912, most cities and states began passing laws against these drugs out of "fear of minority-group drug users" (p. 86). Note that the act of redefining occurred over a period of time during which much discussion and debate occurred, leading to the eventual social construction of new ideologies toward these drugs. As we might expect, with the changing of laws and ideologies came the relabeling of people who used and sold drugs from a good label to a bad one. As you can see, this redefining process is political.

At first thought, we may think that redefining a social problem as no longer a social problem is the easiest way to solve a social problem. However, redefining a social problem is not that easy. A great deal of convincing needs to be done before any social problem gets redefined as no longer a social problem. For example, whether or not marijuana should be legalized has been discussed and debated since the 1960s. Although various states have begun to legalize marijuana to various degrees, other states are still struggling as to what to do. Likewise, we can say the same thing about homosexuality. Various states have created laws for and against the legalization of gay marriage. In all probability, the status of marijuana and homosexuality will continue to evolve.

Great amounts of time, energy, and money have been expended by the pro- and anti-marijuana and the pro- and anti-gay marriage groups. These two social problems suggest that any attempt to redefine a social problem typically requires the substantial use of valuable resources such as money, time, and people. As a result, redefining a social problem is not necessarily easy, quick, or inexpensive—but it has happened such as with regard to racial and gender inequalities and is now happening with regard to marijuana and gay marriage. Consequently, if we only take a short-term view of looking at a social problem, we may not recognize and appreciate the importance of redefining it. However, if we take a longer view of looking at a social problem, we can see how important it is that the redefining of social problems can be an integral part of solving them.

Make It a Concern of Powerful People

Another way a social problem can get attention and increase the possibility of getting solved is for it to become a great concern to powerful people whose vested interests are at stake. When their interests are threatened, people in power will not only have the motivation to solve a social problem but they will also have vast resources such as access to influential networks, access to much money, and access to people working for them who can work full time on the social problem. Thus, if powerful people have vested interests in solving a social problem, the chance of solving that problem becomes much greater.

Give It Attention

Sometimes, political authorities are in a social situation in which they are almost required to pay attention to a social problem. This situation is shown most clearly by the news media and their influence. For example, the media can give a social problem much visibility and attention and not let the controversy of a social problem fade before the reading and viewing public and political authorities. If the media champion a particular social problem and persist in covering it, that social problem is more likely to be addressed than are other social problems not discussed by the media. In a sense, if and when and for as long as the media trumpet a particular social problem, the powerful people of the society may have to address that social problem whether they want to or not. Consequently, the mass media, by paying attention to a social problem for an extended period of time, can be a key factor in solving a social problem.

Be Realistic

A fact we must accept in solving social problems is that many social problems will be solved by a matter of degree rather than in an all-or-nothing way. It would be nice if social problems got totally solved once they were addressed. That may happen at times, but the more realistic course of events is that, because the solving of a social problem can conflict with the power, vested interests, and values of various groups of people, we should expect various compromises to occur. The result of these compromises is that many social problems will be addressed to some greater or lesser degree, rather than solved completely.

Moreover, it takes time for the various elements of a society to change. For example, there are laws, informal norms, values, attitudes, beliefs, and ideologies that may need to change for the social problem to be more completely solved. Some of these parts of society may, and often times do, change at various rates. For example, the law may change, but the attitudes, beliefs, and ideologies will take longer to change. Societies are complex with all their various socially constructed parts. It therefore takes time for all of these parts of a society to realign themselves. Just with respect to racial equality, we are still "realigning ourselves."

Work Toward Shared Values

Although people's conflicting values can stop or slow down the solving of social problems, at times, commonly shared values can help to solve social problems. There are some values in our society, such as equal opportunity, fairness, freedom, justice, and democracy, that are widely accepted among the American people.[7] These shared values can be a starting point in how we solve our social problems.

The importance of shared values in solving social problems can be seen in the civil rights movement of the 1950s and 1960s. Martin Luther King Jr. applied the previously mentioned values to prompt Whites and political leaders to reformulate laws. Before the 1950s, although African Americans believed in these values, they did not get to experience them in their daily lives. For example, African Americans could not attend the same public schools that Whites attended, could not attend public universities such as the University of Alabama and the University of Mississippi, and could not join country clubs. In addition, they could not stay in the same motels or eat in the same restaurants as did Whites, shop in certain stores, work in certain jobs, vote, or hold public office. The values of equal opportunity, fairness, freedom, justice, and democracy rang hollow for them. King and other civil rights leaders used this gap between our shared values and the existing laws to justify changing the laws in the direction of these values.

When King began pointing out the discrepancy between our shared values and our laws, our society began to make changes to solve the social problem of racial prejudice and discrimination. Laws were enacted so that African Americans could attend public schools and universities, play sports at southern universities (Eitzen & Sage, 1997, p. 263),[8] live in dorms on campus rather than live off campus in private homes and need to commute to the university,[9] vote in elections, run for and hold public office, live in any neighborhood they could afford, and work at any job they were capable of doing. The changes in these laws allowed African Americans not only to believe in these values but also to experience these values.

Is everything perfect, and is there no more racial prejudice or discrimination? No. We still have work to do in our society and in our world. However, sharing values in common and working to see that our laws are consistent with our values is a step in the direction of solving the social problem of racial prejudice and discrimination. As you can see, values, especially values that are shared by most Americans, have the potential to play a key role in solving our social problems.[10]

Coordinate Social Policies

Another key area in helping us to solve our social problems is how social policy is carried out. If a new social policy is coordinated with other existing social policies, the social problem has a better chance of being solved.

Schoenfeld, Meier, and Griffin (1979) and Peyrot (1984) discussed the situation of new social policies coming into conflict with existing social policies, with the result that the social problem is less likely to be solved or is more likely to be solved at a slower rate.

Consequently, one crucial step in creating new social policy is to study how new and existing social policies can relate to and complement each other. If there are potential points of conflict between new and existing policies, how can we smooth over these rough spots before we carry out the new policy? If we do not answer this question first, we build into the new social policy a predisposition for failure or at least for a slower pace at solving the problem. So, to solve or at least reduce social problems, we need to think ahead and coordinate new social policies with existing social policies.

Collect Valid Data

We are more likely to solve our social problems when political authorities draw on valid data as they consider what social policies to create. This kind of data is collected by sociologists and other social scientists. For example, in sociology we use certain research methods (participant observation, experiment, survey, interview, and/or historical research) to collect the best possible data on a social problem. Once the data are collected, we analyze the data to see what conclusions we can draw. Once we know what the data are saying, we can share our findings with political officials. The political officials can then, in turn, use this objective and valid information to make better social policy. In other words, the use of excellent data will give our policymakers a better idea of how to solve our social problems.

Create More Incentives Than Disincentives

Another key factor in solving social problems is to have more incentives to solve the problem than disincentives. As we begin to see an increasing number of incentives if we solve a social problem, we are more likely to join in the support of creating a new social policy. The more these incentives are made known—such as through the mass media—there is an increasing probability that something will be done about the social problem. In other words, as people become aware of more incentives versus disincentives, they will be more likely to act to solve social problems.

Related to the idea of incentives and pointing them out to people as a means of solving a social problem is how these two actions relate to exchange theory (see Chapter 1).[11] As we discussed previously, social problems are not as likely to be solved when people believe that a proposed solution means that they have to give up resources (such as pay additional money in taxes) and yet receive nothing in return. However, if people are shown how they can benefit from giving up some of their resources to solve a social problem, they will be more willing to part with some of their resources in the form of taxes. For example, if they believe that paying more taxes will decrease crime and that this drop in crime will make the streets safer for them and their families, they may be more willing to pay more taxes. In other words, part of the process of solving social problems will be to help people realize "what's in it for me."

Perceive the Problem as Urgent

A social problem is more likely to be solved when political authorities and the general public begin to see the urgency in addressing the problem—that is, when there is a feeling that something must be done and must be done *now*. Such a state of urgency can act as a stimulus to address a social problem. We observed this phenomenon after the attacks on the World Trade Center in New York City and the Pentagon Building in Washington, DC, on September 11, 2001, when the U.S. government took a number of steps to beef up security at our airports, and in the recent recession, when the government (both Bush and Obama administrations) moved quickly to stimulate the faltering economy to avert a potential depression. In both cases, perceived urgency was the catalyst that jump-started concerted action.

Realize How Many People Are Affected

In some social problems, relatively few people are negatively affected. In other social problems, many people are negatively affected, and many others feel the negative effects indirectly. When many people are affected either directly or indirectly, we are more likely to address a social problem. Hence, the more people are affected by a problem, the more likely society will address that problem.

As you can see, there are a number of situations that can lead to conditions conducive to solving our social problems. So, even though there are a number of barriers to solving our social problems, we need to "take heart" when we realize that there are also a number of factors that create possibilities for solving our social problems.

How Can Sociology Help to Solve Social Problems?

There are a number of ways in which we, as sociologists, can contribute to solving our social problems. For example, we can help people become more aware of social problems, we can do research and report our research to the public, we can suggest to Congress and other political entities the various options that are available to address social problems, and we can analyze current social policy to see how well it is working. Let us now discuss the various steps that sociologists can take to solve our social problems.

Play a Consciousness-Raising Role

One way sociologists can help to solve social problems is to analyze social phenomena to identify new social problems that might be arising in the society and to inform the media and political authorities of our findings. In a sense, we can serve a consciousness-raising role by pointing out what we see as the social problems of our times (Wilson, 1993b). We can be guided by the criteria suggested in Chapter 1, that is, the number of people being affected and whether or not the social conditions endanger lives (refer back to Figure 1.1).

We can also carry out this consciousness-raising role when we teach and publish books and articles about social problems. Our teaching and publishing activities can serve to legitimize certain social conditions as social problems in the eyes of the public. We can also use the theory of conflict and social change and causal model discussed in Chapter 1 to help people become more conscious of the key variables that are a part of the process of a social problem.

Do Research

Sociologists can help to solve social problems through the research we do. For example, we can pinpoint causes, locate what stage the social problem is in, uncover the values and vested interests that are in conflict, and analyze to what degree current social policy has an effect on the solving of the social problem. Kingdon (1993) noted, "Social scientists can be very good at documenting the existence, frequency, incidence, and intensity of a condition" (p. 48). As a result, our analysis will provide a clearer understanding of the social problem for the general public and for political officials. For example, former Senator Bill Bradley of New Jersey told William Julius Wilson, a sociology professor, that Wilson's research in his book *The*

Truly Disadvantaged (1993b) "illuminated their [the senators'] understanding of the problems of ghetto poverty, raised their consciousness, and increased their awareness of the need for effective public policy to address these problems" (Wilson, 1993a, p. 9).

Use "If, Then" Statements

Sociologists can also help to solve social problems by making what Berger and Kellner (1981) called "if, then" statements (p. 76). Berger and Kellner asked the following: *If* certain social conditions exist, *then* what can be done? For example, *if* in capitalism there is unemployment and there are jobs that pay below the poverty line, *then* what can we do to solve poverty? In other words, sociologists can specify the given social conditions and proceed to create the various choices of social action that can be taken within those conditions. By creating "if, then" statements for social problems, sociologists can get a clearer idea of the possible social policies that can be attempted and the possible consequences for each social policy. Such knowledge will prove to be invaluable for those who create social policy.

Analyze Social Policy

Another way sociologists can contribute to the solving of social problems is to study the various social policies that address a particular social problem, see how these policies are related, and suggest how they can be further interrelated to do a better job of solving the social problem. Given that different social policies are created at different points in time, under different political administrations with different political philosophies, such an array of social policies addressing a specific social problem can contain duplication in some areas, big holes in other areas, and work at cross-purposes in still other areas. When sociologists discover these problem areas about the current social policies, they can analyze these areas and suggest how they could be addressed so that the existing social policy is more efficient and effective.

Sociologists can also study the potential impact of a new social policy that's been implemented to solve a social problem. We can see whether the policy is doing what it is supposed to be doing. We can assess how successful the new policy is at solving or decreasing the problem and what the unintended consequences (both beneficial and harmful) of this new policy are. With such data in hand, political authorities will be better able to decide how well a new social policy is doing and make adjustments to the social policy if necessary.

Determine Which Problem to Address First

Solving some social problems, it appears, is the key to solving or lessening the severity of other social problems. For example, it seems that reducing poverty will help to diminish other social problems such as crime, spouse and child abuse, divorce, drug abuse, and poor health. That is, poverty is a key independent variable that contributes to these other social problems. Although we do not claim that the solution to poverty is the panacea for all of these other social problems, we do predict that a decrease in poverty will also bring a decrease in the rates of these other social problems.

Because poverty exacerbates other social problems, one of society's primary concerns could be the focus on poverty. One of the key factors that could solve the problem of poverty is a sufficient number of decent-paying jobs, that is, jobs that pay above the poverty line. Consequently, social policies that increase the number of decent-paying jobs would be at the top of the list of the policies political officials might want to address first—at the local, state, and national levels.

Given how one major social problem can have a substantial influence on other social problems, it would therefore be very beneficial to study how social problems interrelate. Such analysis will provide us with a clearer idea of which social policy will give us "the biggest bang for the buck"—that is, how solving one key social problem could simultaneously go a long way to solving or reducing a number of other social problems. Once we understand how social problems affect other social problems, we can choose more accurately which social policies will decrease the most social problems possible, given the limited resources that local, state, and national governments can put toward the solving of their respective social problems. Sociologists can therefore play a key role in the larger process of solving social problems by discovering the interrelationships among social problems.

Study the Social Policies of Other Countries

Sociologists can also study the social policies of other countries to learn how other countries' policies might address our social problems. We can find out what specific policy was attempted, what resources were used, what the unintended consequences of the social policy were, and how the other country is similar to or different from the United States. For example, we would need to take into consideration the population of the other country and the degree of its people's heterogeneity in race, ethnicity, and religion. For example, let us say that we wanted to study the country of Sweden and how it has addressed the social problem of poverty. We would need to keep in mind that

Sweden is a much smaller country with a more homogeneous population than the United States. With these differences in mind, we could assess Swedish social policy to see how suitable it would be for the United States to apply Swedish social policy. In other words, sociologists could collect comparative information on the social policies of various countries as a means of having a larger pool of information to draw from in deciding which kind of social policy we need to try in the United States (Eitzen & Leedham, 1998, 2001).

Collect Data About the Victims of Social Problems

Sociologists can also collect data on the victims of a social problem. For example, we can find out the answers to the following questions. What are the victims experiencing day to day? How are they coping? What is happening to them that they believe the rest of society does not realize? What do they think needs to be done to solve this social problem? These are some of the questions that sociologists can answer by doing research on victims. What we find out from this research can guide political authorities in the development of social policy to address these social problems.

Develop a Sociological Perspective

Sociologists can help others to develop a sociological perspective with which to view social problems and their solutions. Policymakers are already using sociological theory, hypotheses, concepts, and research findings to analyze social problems. Weiss (1993) asserted,

> Evidence from social science research can reduce disagreements over matters of fact (e.g., whether fewer pregnant women are receiving prenatal care, whether vocational education improves employability and job performance). In doing so, it helps to raise the level of debate, freeing policy actors to talk about matters of value—which is their proper province. Analogously, the concepts and theories of sociology make a difference. They are helping to make public decision makers more sophisticated about social structure and group processes (less content with individual-level explanations for social phenomena), and they are gradually infusing political thinking with more complex and subtle notions of conflict, social disorganization, community norms, social movements, and other sociological constructs. (p. 29)

Weiss (1993) urged that sociologists undertake two actions as a means of solving social problems: (1) make a sustained effort to reach policymakers by giving them sociological findings and conversing with them and (2) share not only specific findings but also the larger sociological perspective with policymakers so that they can gain a much greater "understanding of the forces and currents that shape events" in our society (p. 37).

Remember That There Is No Crystal Ball

As you can see, sociologists can contribute in a number of ways to solve our social problems. Yet we do not have a crystal ball. That is, we cannot say for certain that if a certain social policy is attempted, it will solve the social problem. There are three reasons for this. First, social life is complex in that there are a number of independent variables (that is, causes) that influence every social problem. Second, we do not always know precisely to what degree each independent variable influences a social problem. Third, we do not always know all of the independent variables causing a social problem.

However, sociologists know many of the independent variables that influence social problems. Much research has been done to give us good ideas about these independent variables and their influences. We have already collected immense amounts of data and discovered many interrelationships. We are continually learning more and more about social phenomena in terms of how certain independent variables influence social phenomena. Consequently, we have a clearer and more comprehensive picture of what is occurring in social life than ever before in human history.

Because sociologists have gathered considerable data on social problems, because we have discovered many social patterns within social problems, and because we have isolated many independent variables that cause social problems, it is evident that sociology needs to play an important role in solving our social problems. Beginning with Chapter 3, I share with you how sociology and the sociological perspective can be used to solve our social problems.

Questions for Discussion

1. What might be some things we could do to overcome the problem of conflicting vested interests in a social problem?

2. How could Congress become a more visionary body and plan ahead instead of reacting to what goes wrong?

3. When should we consider a social problem to be solved?

4. There are different political orientations that want different social policies to solve a social problem. What are some steps we can take to resolve these differences?

5. How can we be more confident that the social policies we use will work?

6. What other values besides equal opportunity, fairness, freedom, justice, and democracy do you think we share in common in the United States that could serve as a starting point to solve our social problems?

7. Which political orientation do you think is the best for solving our social problems? Why?

8. Which political orientation do you think will be used the most during the next 10 to 20 years to address our social problems? What is your reasoning?

9. Should sociologists say what social policy should be applied or should they remain objective and leave that up to the politicians?

10. Given their knowledge about social problems, should more sociologists run for political office? Why or why not?

3

How Can We
Solve the Problem
of Increasing Inequality?

One of the biggest social problems in the United States, as well as around the world, is the problem of growing inequality. In this chapter, I define inequality, present statistics on it and how it is growing, note some of its key causes and consequences, and suggest what we can do about it. Do we want to continue to increase inequality? Do we want to maintain the current amount of inequality? Do we want to decrease inequality? As you read this chapter, keep these three questions in mind and consider what you believe we should do.

Definition and Statistics

Inequality in a society occurs when people have differing amounts of money, power, and/or prestige.[1] I define these terms here so that we will think the same things when these terms are used throughout this book. There are two kinds of money: income and wealth, hence, two kinds of money inequality. The kind of money that we call *income* is typically money that we get from a job. *Wealth*, the other kind of money, represents what we own. For example, if you own a home and own stock, you have a certain amount of wealth. Some people have a lot of wealth because they own a very expensive home (even in the millions of dollars), and some of these people also own more than one home. Also, some people have a lot of wealth in how much stock they own. Some people own millions or even billions of dollars worth of stock. They have seen their stock value rise sharply from 2008 when the economy was entering a recession and the Dow Jones average (a way to measure the overall value of stocks in our country) was at 6,000 to late 2014 when the stock market rose to 18,000, tripling its value in 6 years (Waggoner, 2014, p. 1B). In other words, people who own stock have tripled their wealth in the last 6 years! At the same time, many other people own no stock, especially poor and working class people. As a result, they were not able to take advantage of the growing stock market and could rely only on their income from their job.

Yet incomes have not risen nearly as much, especially since the 1970s when many companies began to move out of the United States (called deindustrialization) in order to pay lower wages and provide little or no benefits such as health care and retirement benefits. By moving to other countries and paying lower wages and providing few or no benefits, companies made more profit. As a result of this deindustrialization process, many jobs were lost, which caused American wages to stagnate in many industries as the same number of American workers competed for fewer jobs, hence allowing factories not to have to raise wages since there were so many people searching for jobs. For example, the mean annual income for the bottom 20% of the American people decreased 8.3% from 1980 to 2011 (Macionis, 2015, p. 264).

So, in order to understand inequality in our country, we must be aware of how income from jobs rises or does not rise and how wealth, especially in the form of stock ownership, rises or does not rise. These two factors will play a major role in how much inequality, especially money inequality, there is in a society.

I define the term *power* by using the definition of the great German sociologist of the early 20th century, Max Weber: "We understand by 'power' the chance of a man or a number of men to realize their own will in a social action even against the resistance of others who are participating in the action" (Weber, [1914]1968, p. 926). Simply put, power is the ability to make people do things, even against their will. If someone is holding a gun on you, he or she can take your money. If someone has the legal ability to make people do things against their will, I label this as *authority*. For example, a police officer has the authority to give you or me a speeding ticket when we go above the speed limit.

Finally, the third dimension of inequality is prestige. By *prestige,* which is sometimes referred to as *status,* I again use Weber's ([1914]1968) definition:

"We wish to designate as status situation every typical component of the life of men that is determined by a specific, positive or negative, social estimation of honor" (p. 932). In other words, when we give people high honor or high respect, we give them prestige. For example, we tend to give higher prestige to medical doctors and U.S. Supreme Court Justices and to give lower prestige to garbage collectors and custodians. As you may already know and have learned about life and about human beings, humans, throughout history, greatly seek out and wish to have glory or honor or what we call prestige. People will go to great extremes in their lives, even to the extent of losing their lives in order to gain prestige. Medals, ribbons, trophies, pictures on the wall of a school gymnasium or on the wall of a government building, or statues—all have been and are presently ways to get people to exert themselves greatly—and all of these ways are indicators of people desiring glory, honor, or prestige.

So, sometimes, people will go after prestige more than they will money or power while other people will be motivated to go only after money. Still, others are motivated to go after power. People will be motivated differently to gain these different dimensions of inequality. Also, some people will seek just one kind of inequality while others will seek two or all three of these dimensions of inequality. How people have been socialized coupled with the experiences that they had as they grew up will combine to influence which dimensions of inequality they seek. For example, someone may have parents who own a business and emphasize making money. At the dinner table and at other times of informal conversation, the parents socialize the child, knowingly or unknowingly, that it is good to make money. So, many conversations between the parent and the child center around the making of money. Given this kind of socialization over a period of years as the child is growing up, there is a higher probability that this child will want to make money. On the other hand, another child grows up in a family that emphasizes seeking social change to create a more just society. So, his or her socialization has nothing to do with making money. This child is being socialized to seek social change of some kind, for example, racial, gender, religious, or sexual orientation equality and is oblivious to the making of money. Still, another child is socialized soon after he or she is born to be an Olympic ice skater and some day to win the gold medal and gain great prestige. So, he or she spends his or her youth practicing to be the best ice skater in the world—pretty much to the exclusion of anything else. Whether right or wrong, good or bad, people will spend much of their lives seeking one, two, or all three of these dimensions of inequality.

In sociology, we gather data on how much money, power, and prestige people have. For example, with regard to money inequality, some people in our country earn incomes at the minimum wage level and earn only $7.25 per hour or $290 per week, for a total of $15,080 per year (assuming a worker works 40 hours per week for all 52 weeks of the year and never takes a vacation). Other people, such as teachers, carpenters, and plumbers, typically make yearly incomes in the range of $30,000 to $70,000. Medical doctors, dentists, lawyers, and some businesspersons tend to make from $200,000 up into the millions of dollars per year.

Not only is there substantial inequality in our country, but statistics suggest that it is growing. Let us look at money inequality—both wealth and income —and see how it has been on the rise. With regard to wealth inequality (again, wealth is what people own in the form of homes, stocks, bonds, land, and buildings), in 1962, 20% of the richest Americans owned 76% of the country's wealth (Brinkerhoff & White, 1985, p. 210). By 2011, 20% of the richest Americans owned 88.9% of the nation's wealth (Macionis, 2015, p. 253). So, we are getting closer and closer to 20% of Americans owning 90% of the wealth and 80% of Americans owning the remaining 10% of the wealth—hard to believe but that is nearly where we are in the early 21st century. In 1972, the richest 1% of Americans owned 21% of the wealth (Brinkerhoff & White, 1985, p. 210). In 2011, the richest 1% of Americans owned 35% of the wealth (Macionis, 2015, p. 253). Clearly, in terms of wealth, the rich are getting richer; so, we are becoming much more unequal with respect to wealth in our country.

Income inequality has also been increasing since 1970. For example, in 1970, the richest 20% of Americans made 43.3% of all the income. By 2011, they made 48.8% of all the income (Macionis, 2015, p. 253). At the same time, the poorest 20% of people earned 4.1% of all the income in 1970 (Eitzen, Zinn, & Smith, 2009, p. 37) but earned only 3.8% by 2011 (Macionis, 2015, p. 253). In a study of rising income from 1972 to 2000, while the income of Americans in the 90th percentile of income rose 34%, the income of Americans in the 99.99th percentile of income rose 497%— nearly 15 times faster (Krugman, 2006b, p. A7). Economist Paul Krugman reported that data for 2004 show that "a small fraction of the population got much, much richer" (Krugman, 2006a, p. A9). The tax cuts under former President George W. Bush meant that middle-class people received a 2.3% increase in their incomes after taxes, whereas upper class people (those earning more than $1 million per year) received a 7.3% increase in their incomes after taxes, thereby creating more income inequality. Consequently, in the last 40 years, the gap between the rich and those who are not rich has grown both with regard to wealth inequality and income inequality. The old saying, "The rich are getting richer, and the poor are getting poorer," appears to be true for the United States.

Moreover, people who have a lot of wealth and income will typically have more power, too, because they can use their wealth and income to protect their own vested interests and therefore get what they want, sometimes at the expense of other social classes. For example, they can run for political office and have more money than any other candidate and therefore be more likely to win. They can give large contributions to groups and organizations who believe as they do and therefore perpetuate their own values, beliefs, and ideologies. They can threaten to not give to charities unless these charities conform to their values, beliefs, and ideologies. Consequently, those who have more money and power will have more influence in a society. For example, they can decide whether factories in communities move or do not move out of these communities and can therefore have great influence in deciding the economies of communities, such as, the unemployment rate, the poverty rate, the homelessness rate, the crime rate, and the rate of spending for public schools. They will have more influence in proposing bills in city hall, in a state legislature, or in Congress, and they will have more money and influential networks to lobby for the bills they want passed in favor of their vested interests and potentially against the vested interests of other social classes. So, money inequality can lead to power inequality, and those who have both money and power will have a disproportionate influence on how society develops—its social policies, its laws, its ideologies, its tax structure, its job structure, its chances for upward mobility, its overall economy, and the overall inequality of a society.

Causes of Growing Inequality

Most people in our country earn income from their jobs, and that is their only way of making money. Some people, on the other hand, not only make money from their jobs but also make money from the wealth they own. What seems to be one cause of growing inequality in our country is that people with higher incomes tend to get bigger raises than do people with lower incomes. Also, people who own stock, buildings, and land can make additional money (dividends from stock and rent from buildings and land) from these investments. Moreover, millions of Americans who gain income solely from their jobs have minimum wage jobs and typically do not receive raises each year. For example, the federal minimum wage was raised to $7.25 in the summer of 2009—6 years ago. Yet, inflation tends to go up each year and eats away at those workers who make a minimum wage. As you may or may not know, the minimum wage is thousands of dollars below the poverty line for a family of four (the poverty line for a family of four in 2015 is $23,850 while the minimum wage makes only $15,080 if the worker works all year at 40 hours per week, resulting in the full-time worker making $8,770 less than the poverty line). So, a minimum wage job will not put families above, at, or even near the poverty line. As a result of all these factors, there is growing inequality between people who have high incomes and much wealth versus people who have moderate to low incomes and no wealth.

Another cause of growing inequality is the relationship between those who have much wealth and income and power and those who have no wealth, little income, and little or no power.[2] For example, when someone has a lot of money, he or she can give more contributions to elected officials in the hope of receiving favorable legislation in return. People with more money can afford to run for political office and spend more money than other candidates to win the office. People with higher incomes and wealth will also have jobs that allow them to interact with other people who have high incomes and wealth and also much power.[3] For example, a person who is a president or vice president of a large corporation, say one of the 100 largest corporations in our country (for example, Wal-Mart, Exxon, or General Electric), will not only know people in the top positions in the other large corporations but will also serve on the boards of these corporations.[4] Assuming that 35 people are on a corporate board, there are 35 x 100 of the largest corporations, or 3,500 people, who control 75% of all the industrial assets in the United States (Kerbo, 2009, p. 188). Moreover, because a number of these 3,500 people serve on one, two, or three other boards, there could actually be 2,000 or fewer people holding these 3,500 board positions who are the "movers and shakers" of much of our economy. Moreover, as the largest 100 corporations become even larger, they will also wield more power.

When these powerful corporate leaders speak, the rest of us listen and are influenced by what they decide to do. For example, if the board members of one of these corporations decide to cut thousands of jobs and close a number of plants, not only will workers in those plants lose their jobs, but the communities in which those plants are located will be hurt. Stores in those communities may close or suffer great financial losses; schools might not have enough money for enough teachers, up-to-date equipment, or renovation of buildings; and city governments may lose tax revenue that would have gone to pay the salaries of the police and fire department members and workers who maintain the streets and sewage and water systems.[5] So, a decision made by board members at corporate headquarters in a distant city can devastate workers and their communities (Mills, 1959b).

Another cause of growing inequality has to do with our capitalistic economy, in which some people are able to own factories and businesses where they can make a lot of money compared with people who are their employees. It is in the nature of capitalism that employees will earn wages (paid by the hour) or salaries (paid weekly, biweekly, or monthly) while owners will make profits. In other words, built within the nature of capitalism is the process of growing inequality—wages versus profits.

Also, the ideology in a capitalistic culture typically asserts that everyone is responsible for himself or herself and that there is much emphasis on the individual, with the individual getting ahead and surviving in a "dog-eat-dog" world. This ideology tends to justify or legitimize the idea of some people making a lot more money than others and therefore justifies substantial inequality and increasing amounts of it. This ideology is taught to us from the time we are born, so that it seems like human nature to us to be individualistic, look out for ourselves, live in a "dog-eat-dog" world, and accept this capitalistic culture as the only way to live. As a result, this ideology we are socialized to believe in promotes the acceptance and legitimacy of inequality—and a lot of it. For example, for many Americans, it is fine and acceptable that a number of Americans make minimum wages that are thousands of dollars below the poverty line while other Americans make millions of dollars per year. So, it is acceptable by many Americans that one American makes hundreds of times more than another American while this other American, though working full time, has a difficult time just surviving.

Another significant cause of growing inequality in a capitalistic society is the belief that the influence of government should be kept to a minimum, therefore, needing to collect fewer taxes, for example, providing mainly for the national defense. With less tax to pay, the wealthy can keep more of their wealth, which, in turn, increases the money inequality in society. Moreover, with less tax revenue going to the government, the government has less tax revenue to provide for various services for the middle, working, and poor classes, for example, less extensive health care for the retired middle class and working class via Medicare, less extensive health care for the poor and near-poor via Medicaid, not providing paid maternity leave for the birth of a baby like most other industrialized countries (Kerbo, 2009, p.294), not having a health care system that covers all of its citizens like all other industrialized countries (Kerbo, 2009, p. 41), not providing subsidized child care for both parents who work for poor and near-poor parents like other industrialized countries, providing less quality public education, and so on.

In other words, lower taxes means less money the government has to pay for the aforementioned services to middle class, working class, and poor people. As there are fewer services for the middle, working, and poorer social classes, there will be greater inequality. So, the ideology of limited government, which on the surface sounds okay and fairly benign, translates into lower tax revenue coming to the government, which, in turn, means that the government can provide fewer services to the middle, working, and poor classes. Providing fewer services to the middle, working, and poor classes means that these social classes are more unequal to the rich, which, in turn, means more inequality in the society.

As you can see, the belief in limited government can have dire consequences on middle, working, and lower class Americans. With limited government, two things occur: (1) the rich pay less in taxes and therefore keep more of their money and (2) with lower tax revenue coming in to the government, the government cannot offer as many services to the middle, working, and lower classes—these two things together cause more inequality in our society. Greater inequality may not be the intent by those who want limited government, but greater inequality is the unintended consequence.

Another cause of increasing inequality is the degree to which wealthier people can influence the government to decrease the progressive income tax. A *progressive income tax* is one in which people with higher incomes pay a higher proportion of their incomes in taxes than do people with lower incomes. If the tax system becomes less progressive, wealthier people pay less in tax, allowing them to keep more of their money and thereby increasing the overall inequality. Because wealthier people can typically use their money and political connections to influence public officials much more so than do people who are not wealthy, they can have more influence on how people are taxed. They do not have total influence, but they have more influence than the average citizen in our country.[6] Hence, it is in the vested interests of wealthier people to have less government that provides fewer services, so that fewer taxes will be needed, thereby allowing for and justifying a lower progressive income tax. Moreover, it is in the vested interests of wealthier people not to have the government provide for as many services since they are less likely to need or use these services, for example, welfare, food stamps, college student loans, subsidized child care, Medicaid, and so on. The bottom line is that with a lower progressive income tax, wealthier people keep more of their money, which results in greater inequality.

Other kinds of taxes can also cause more inequality in our society. For example, if there is less tax on people who inherit wealth, the people who inherit wealth will be able to keep more of their wealth, resulting in greater inequality. Former President George W. Bush sought to abolish the inheritance tax, which would work to the vested interests of wealthier people and would also increase inequality. Typically, political conservatives want to abolish or at least minimize the inheritance tax while political liberals want to keep and even increase the inheritance tax. This is a constant battle in Congress. Whatever happens will influence the amount of inequality in our country.

The same idea can be applied to the sales tax. A sales tax is a *regressive tax*, meaning that lower-income people pay a higher percentage of their incomes in taxes than do higher-income people. For example, a higher sales tax on products that everyone needs (for example, soap, shampoo, shaving cream) means that people with low to moderate incomes will pay a larger percentage of their incomes in sales tax for these products than will people with higher incomes. Hence, as the sales tax goes up, inequality also goes up.

Another cause of growing inequality is the degree to which people of low to moderate incomes working for industries and businesses cannot organize into unions to protect their financial interests. The less they are able to join unions to seek higher pay and more benefits such as health care and retirement plans, the more likely it is that those at the top of these corporations will be able to keep a larger proportion of the profits of the corporation for their stock holders and higher officials of the corporation. For example, German workers are the highest paid among the seven most highly industrialized nations, whereas American workers are the second to lowest paid (Kerbo, 2000, p. 28). A key factor in the difference of pay between German and American workers is the strength of unions in each country. Labor unions are strong in Germany, whereas they are relatively weak in the United States. In fact, in Germany, it is legally mandated that employees make up one half of the board of directors in a company (p. 510). This difference gives German workers much more power than American workers and, thus, enables them to seek and get higher wages and more benefits. Hence, this creates less inequality in Germany.

A key problem for workers in the United States that has hurt the amount of unionization and power of unions and hence the power of workers is the process of corporations moving their plants outside of the United States (known as *deindustrialization*) to other countries that allow for lower labor costs in the form of lower wages, no retirement benefits, and no health care benefits. Paying lower wages, providing no retirement benefits, and giving no health care benefits together save a great deal of money for these corporations and therefore allows them to make more profit. In fact, just the threat by a corporation of moving out of a community can make workers become less aggressive in seeking higher wages and more benefits. Corporations know this situation; workers know this situation. This situation began being the case for workers since deindustrialization began in the 1970s. As you can see, this deindustrialization process has had negative consequences for workers attempting to increase their wages and benefits, with the result that our country has become more unequal.

For much of our country's history, prejudice and discrimination against various minorities, such as African Americans, Native Americans, Latino

Americans, Chinese Americans, Japanese Americans, women, homosexuals, and the disabled, have hurt members of these groups immensely. They were hurt because when they were discriminated against; they were not given the same opportunities as were other Americans. As a consequence, they were forced to settle for lower income jobs or no jobs, fewer benefits such as health and retirement benefits, little or no power, and little or no prestige. Prejudice and discrimination have therefore caused much inequality throughout the history of our country.

Our country has been reducing these kinds of prejudice and discrimination during the past 100 years. So, over time, this particular cause of inequality has begun to recede as we, as a country and as individuals, have worked to eliminate the various kinds of prejudice and discrimination in our country and in ourselves. The current situation in our country is not perfect, but we are headed in the direction of decreasing various kinds of prejudice and discrimination. As this process continues, we should find that this factor will be one cause of growing inequality that will become less and less influential. With the election of Barack Obama as President of the United States (which meant that many White Americans voted for Mr. Obama), we have taken yet another important step to show that we are decreasing this major cause of inequality in our society.

Consequences of Growing Inequality

One consequence of growing inequality is that people in the higher social classes are more socially and physically distant from people in the lower social classes. That is, those in the higher social classes are more likely to live in different neighborhoods, go to different public schools or attend private schools, attend different places of worship, and so on, than do people with lower incomes. With rising inequality, the higher social classes, by being more socially and geographically distant, can be less understanding and consequently less sympathetic of the members of the lower social classes. This situation increases the possibility that certain ideologies, such as "The reason why the poor are poor is that they are lazy," will be constructed and will be used to justify or legitimize the existing inequality.

Another consequence of growing inequality is that the higher social classes will have more opportunities, and the lower classes will have fewer opportunities. For example, for the higher social classes, there will be more chances for travel throughout the world, for more years of education and for higher quality education, for more consumer goods, for more and better health care, and for better retirement lifestyles. Unless some outside source, such as the government, intervenes by providing lower classes with opportunities that the society, in its normal functioning within a capitalistic system, does not provide, the gap will continue to widen between the higher and lower social classes.

This process of a widening number of opportunities can lead to what sociologists call *feelings of relative deprivation,* when people in the lower classes compare their situations with the situations of people in the higher classes and feel deprived as well as resentful. This situation is especially likely to occur if the society socializes people that there is equal opportunity in life, but in reality there is not (refer to our theory of conflict and social change causal model in Chapter 1). If people feel relatively deprived and resentful, they may begin to question the legitimacy of the existing social conditions.[7] These circumstances can lead to riots and various outbursts of frustration from the lower classes and can, in turn, lead to less stability in society.

Options We Have With Inequality

In a society, we can increase inequality, keep the existing inequality, or decrease inequality. Let us discuss each of these options and consider the implications. As we discuss these three options, think about what you believe we should do in society.

Increase Inequality

The first option is to increase our inequality even more. If we wish to increase inequality, we can do this by taxing the poor, working, and middle classes more and taxing the rich less. For example, we can increase the federal income tax on the poor, working, and middle classes and decrease the federal income tax on the rich. We can also increase the sales tax, knowing that this will hurt people in the poor, working, and middle classes more than it will rich people because everyone needs to buy similar amounts of certain products like soap, toothpaste, toothbrushes, toilet paper, shaving cream, razors, and shampoo. Poor people pay the same prices for these products and pay the same sales tax as do rich people. Consequently, when we raise the sales tax in a state or city, poor people will be poorer relative to rich people, thereby creating greater inequality.

Another way to increase inequality is for wealthier people to pay little or no tax when they inherit wealth from their deceased parents. As of 2015, when the last parent dies, the children, usually adult children, can inherit up to $5.43 million without paying any taxes (personal communication from

B. Foley, tax accountant, January 26, 2015). Most Americans do not inherit anywhere close to $5.43 million. Typically, poor Americans inherit nothing, while working-class and middle-class Americans inherit somewhere less than $100,000 to $200,000. But adult offspring who come from wealthy families can inherit $1 million, $2 million, $3 million, $4 million, or even $5 million and not pay any taxes. As a result of paying no taxes on these millions of dollars, these Americans can become instantly wealthy, which results in growing inequality. A key point to remember is this: as there is less tax on inheritance, this will cause more inequality and, vice versa, as there is more tax on inheritance, this will cause less inequality. Hence, how Congress and individual states tax inheritance has a direct influence on how much inequality we have in our country. As you can see, the making of laws—in this case, the making of tax laws—has a direct bearing on how much inequality we have. So, depending on how we tax people, we can increase or decrease the inequality in our society.

Another way to increase inequality is to decrease or abolish taxes on dividends from stocks and to decrease or abolish the capital gains tax on stocks, thereby allowing those who own stock and are making money from stock to keep more of their money. Given that 10% of Americans have typically owned 80% or more of all the stock in the country since the 1980s (Kerbo, 2009, p. 35), people in this group can increase their wealth considerably, depending on how much their dividends and capital gains are taxed, with the result that inequality increases.

In addition to changing taxes that create more inequality, we can create more inequality by decreasing or abolishing social services that help the poor, working, and middle classes survive or live better lifestyles. For example, if state legislators, governors, members of Congress, and the President decrease social services such as Social Security, child care subsidies for mothers who are getting off welfare in order to work, college loans and grants, money for public schools, Section 8 subsidized housing, money for Head Start and Upward Bound programs, money for unemployment compensation, money for health care, and so on, the poor, working, and middle classes will be poorer, with the result that inequality will increase in our society.

So, increasing taxes on the poor, working, and middle classes, decreasing taxes on the rich, and decreasing social services for the poor, working, and middle classes are three ways to increase inequality in our society. Many Americans would find these actions to be extremely distasteful given that these methods will make it harder for the poor and working classes to get by each day.

When I have given an anonymous survey in my social problems classes and asked my students whether they think we should increase inequality, keep it the way it is now, or decrease inequality, no one has ever voted to increase inequality. This does not mean that there are not Americans who do not want more inequality, but it does suggest that when students discuss the consequences of increasing inequality, some students opt for keeping it the same, while most students vote to decrease it.[8]

Maintain the Current Amount of Inequality

The second option is to maintain the current inequality in our country with a certain combination of taxes and social services. Some of my students have voted for this option. Probably a number of people in our country, without any discussion about this issue, would vote for maintaining the current amount of inequality. However, from what I have observed in my social problems classes, if Americans discuss this issue and realize the negative consequences of rising inequality or maintaining the current amount of inequality in our country, I predict that if given the opportunity, the majority of Americans would, like the majority of my students, vote to decrease the amount of inequality in our country.

Decrease Inequality

The third option is to decrease inequality in our society. If we, as a society, choose to decrease inequality, we can do a number of things. We can decrease various kinds of taxes on the poor, working, and middle classes and, at the same time, increase taxes on rich people. For example, we can make the federal income tax more progressive, so that the poor, working, and middle classes pay a lower percentage of tax and the rich pay a higher percentage of tax on income. Besides taxing income, we could tax the wealth of the rich more, and this would decrease inequality.

Another kind of tax we could change is the Social Security tax. As of 2015, only the first $118,500 that Americans earn each year is taxed at 6.2% (personal communication from B. Foley, tax accountant, January 26, 2015). People no longer pay Social Security taxes on income they make above $118,500. So, a poor person making a minimum wage of $7.25 per hour, or $15,080 per year, will pay 6.2% of his or her income in Social Security tax. At the same time, someone who earns $300,000 per year (such as a medical doctor) will pay only 2.4% in Social Security tax (6.2% × $118,500 = $7,347 / $300,000 = 2.4%)—that is, less than one half of the rate of what a poor person pays. A rich businessperson, pro athlete, rock star, or movie star making $10 million per year will also pay only $7,347. So, the pro athlete or movie star or rich business person will pay less than one tenth of 1% of his or her income in Social Security tax. This is an example of what is known as a regressive tax, where poorer people pay higher tax rates, and richer people pay lower tax rates.

It is hard to believe that rich people pay a lower tax rate than poor, working, or middle-class people, but that is the way it is. Hence, if we want to decrease inequality, we can have rich people pay more in Social Security tax by not having a limit on how much Social Security tax they pay, while having poor, working, and middle-class people pay a lower tax rate.

By the way, having the rich pay more in Social Security tax would also help to provide enough Social Security income for our elderly in the future, thereby solving our Social Security problem due to more Americans retiring and therefore more Americans being eligible for Social Security. Consequently, by increasing the Social Security tax on the rich, we could solve two of our social problems: (1) decrease our inequality and (2) make the Social Security system solvent for our children and grandchildren.

Another way we can decrease inequality is to decrease the sales tax, making it not so hard on the poor to buy everyday products to survive day to day, and, at the same time, depend more on progressive taxes of various kinds, such as federal and state income taxes and federal Social Security taxes. That way, more of our taxes would be structured so that the ability to pay taxes will be tied to one's income and wealth—the more income and wealth, the more taxes people pay; the less income and wealth, the less taxes people pay.

Another way we can decrease inequality is to increase social services such as the following:

- Provide health care for all Americans
- Increase unemployment compensation
- Create more college grants and loans for people in the poor, working, and middle classes
- Create more child care subsidies for lower-income, single parents who are working at or near minimum wage jobs so that they can work and survive at these kinds of jobs
- Create more housing subsidies for poor and lower income families
- Expand Head Start and Upward Bound programs for poorer and lower income people
- Increase funding for public schools located in poor and lower income neighborhoods so that children from these neighborhoods get the same quality public education as do children in middle-class and upper-middle-class neighborhoods

In other words, three ways to decrease the inequality in our country are (1) tax the poor less, (2) tax the rich more, and (3) provide more social services for the poor, working, and middle classes. Figure 3.1 shows diagrammatically the three ways we could decrease inequality.

What Should We Do?

What should we do? This is a question that neither sociology nor any other social science (for example, economics, political science, history, social psychology, anthropology, communications) can answer, because science cannot tell us what we should do. Science, whether natural or social, can

Figure 3.1 Three Ways to Decrease Inequality

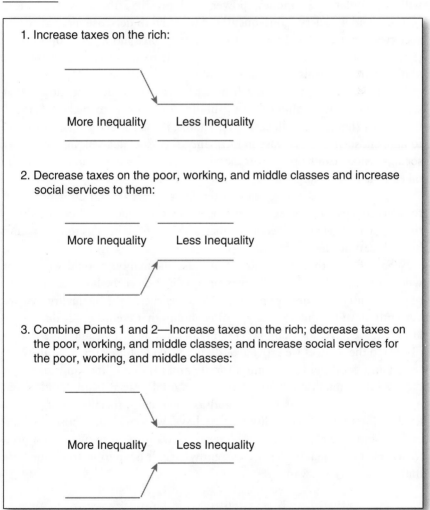

tell us many things. For example, it can give us the statistics on the unemployment rate, poverty rate, and homelessness rate. It can tell us what causes something to happen, such as what causes unemployment, poverty, and homelessness. It can tell us consequences, such as that more unemployment can lead to more poverty, homelessness, family stress, and crime and less tax revenues to pay for more police, courts, and prisons. It can also predict what may happen in the future. For example, given various kinds of prejudice and discrimination (for example, racial, gender, or sexual orientation), people being prejudiced against and discriminated against will have fewer opportunities than people who do not experience prejudice and discrimination. Having fewer opportunities will mean that these people will accumulate less money, power, and prestige, thus, creating more inequality in a society. Consequently, if we wish to decrease inequality in a society so that various groups of people will have more equal opportunities, then we will need to continue to work to decrease and eventually abolish various forms of prejudice and discrimination.

What science cannot do is tell us what we should do. The closest that science can come to answering a "should" question is to make "if, then" statements (Berger & Kellner, 1981). That is, if the society wants something to happen, such as a decrease in inequality, then sociology, along with other social sciences, can help us more clearly understand what actions need to be taken to achieve that goal.

In other words, sociology cannot tell us what we should do with regard to rising inequality. However, if the society wants to move in a certain direction, such as to decrease inequality, then sociology can help us to understand how we can do this.

What do you think? Should we increase inequality? Should we keep it where it is now? Should we decrease inequality? Over the hundreds of years of our country's history, we have socially constructed the inequality that we currently have (1) due to the type of economy that we have; (2) due to the laws that we have, for example, certain tax laws on income and inheritance; (3) due to the services we provide or do not provide, for example, health care for all and good public education for all; and (4) due to the kinds of prejudice and discrimination that we have, for example, racial, gender, and sexual orientation. Since we, as humans and as Americans, socially construct the kind and amount of inequality that we have, we can change both the kind and amount of inequality that we have if we want to do so. We do not need to accept the inequality that we currently have. It is up to us to decide how much inequality we want.

Questions for Discussion

1. Should we try to decrease inequality, or should we let it grow as it is currently doing?

2. Should we increase taxes on the wealthy as a way to decrease inequality?

3. Should we decrease taxes on the poor, working, and middle classes as a way to decrease inequality?

4. Should we provide more social services for the poor, working, and middle classes as a way to decrease inequality?

5. Where do you think inequality will go during the next 10 to 20 years—higher, lower, or stay where it is now? Why?

6. What are other ways we could decrease inequality?

7. How does having a capitalistic economy affect inequality?

8. Should the government be more involved in decreasing inequality?

9. How does the amount of inequality we have affect the other social problems we have?

10. What do you think most Americans think about inequality? Why?

4

How Can We Solve the Problem of Poverty?

In this chapter, our focus is on how we can get rid of poverty in the United States. By getting rid of poverty, we mean getting all poor Americans above what the federal government says is the poverty line. For example, the 2015 poverty line for a family of four is $23,850 in annual income (U.S. Department of Health and Human Services, 2015). So, the key question of this chapter is as follows: What can we do in our country to get all poor Americans out of poverty or, more specifically, above the poverty line? Let us first make some assumptions and then discuss what we can do.

Assumptions We Can Make About Solving Poverty

Before we begin to discuss what we can do to solve the problem of poverty in our country, we need to make a number of assumptions about our current situation in the United States in relation to what we can and cannot do to get all Americans out of poverty.

Our first assumption is that the economic system of capitalism will not provide enough good-paying jobs for all of the adult Americans in our country who are capable of working and want good-paying jobs. For example, as of December 2009, the unemployment rate in our country stood at 10% (Aversa, December 29, 2009, p. A1).

This means that nearly 1 out of 10 working-age Americans was out of work and searching for a job. If we rely on capitalism only to solve our poverty problem, we will not solve it because cycles of moderate to high unemployment occur regularly within a capitalist system. For example, in 2003, before the deep recession of 2008 to 2012, our country had 6.4% unemployment, which is still considered somewhat high ("Unemployment Hits 9-Year High," 2003). The unemployment rate has decreased to 5.5%, as of February, 2015 (Waggoner, March 7, 2015, p. 1B). Consequently, if we want to solve the problem of poverty, we will need to do more than rely on capitalism only.

Second, even when capitalism produces a cycle of many new jobs and the unemployment rate goes down to 3% overall, which is roughly as low as it typically goes, we cannot assume that the jobs created pay above the poverty line. For example, Sanders (2000) noted that "30 percent of American workers earn poverty or near-poverty wages" (p. 3). This raises the question of how to get people out of poverty in an economic system in which 30% of the jobs pay at or below the poverty line. Because capitalism produces such a high proportion of jobs below the poverty line, we will need to do something more than rely on capitalism only to reduce poverty.

Third, since our capitalistic economy does not produce enough jobs for Americans who want them (again, the current unemployment rate is 5.5%) and, furthermore, when our capitalistic economy does create jobs, it creates 30% of jobs that pay below the poverty line, then the government will need to be a part of solving poverty in at least three ways: (1) provide subsidies of food, housing, and income that bring the poor above the poverty line so that they can survive day to day; (2) provide services such as health care when the poor work for employers who do not provide health insurance or when the poor cannot find jobs and thus have no health insurance unless the government provides it; and (3) collect enough taxes from those of us who are not poor to fund public programs to help the poor to get out of their poverty.

Fourth, there are probably some lower income people who are poor because they are lazy. Our country will need to face the problem of how to deal with these people. Even though these people represent only a small number of the overall number of poor people, this problem needs to be addressed.

Fifth, because there are different groups that make up poor people (for example, people without jobs; people with jobs but the jobs pay thousands of dollars below the poverty line [the current minimum wage of $7.25 an hour will give a full-time worker an annual income of $15,080, but the current poverty level for a family of four is $23,850, which means that the worker, and his or her family, is $8,770 below the poverty line]; people who cannot work, such as children,[1] the elderly, and the disabled; people who do not want to work and do not work), we will not be able to solve poverty by creating just one solution, such as creating more jobs. Instead, we will need to create a number of solutions to get all people above the poverty line.

Sixth, to solve the problem of poverty in the United States, we will need to solve it within the context of a capitalistic economy. Some Americans may want us to go from capitalism to some form of socialist economy in which all adults are guaranteed jobs. As a result, there would be no unemployment. I do not think that this is a realistic option now or in the near future. The simple reason is that so many of us who are not poor have benefited from, and are still benefiting from, capitalism, with nice homes, good incomes, and many consumer goods and services. Too many of us currently benefit from the existing economy to realistically consider changing to socialism. Furthermore, from what we have heard and read about the standard of living in the Soviet Union during the Soviet-socialist era (1917 to 1990), and what we have read about the East European countries under the control of the Soviet Union and what has occurred so far in China and Cuba, we know that the people living in these countries have had standards of living considerably below those of us who live in capitalistic countries. They have also had less freedom. Consequently, given our hesitancy to change to a socialistic economy, we will need to consider, for the time being, solutions that we can carry out within a capitalistic economy.

Seventh, given that capitalism cannot solve poverty by itself due to (1) periods of moderate to high unemployment and (2) 30% of the jobs created paying at or below the poverty level, and given the need to add the help of the government, we, as taxpayers, will need to give some of our resources in the form of taxes to solve poverty. This is not a pleasant situation to face for those of us who are not poor, but I see no other realistic way given the preceding assumptions. As to who pays taxes and how much, this will need to be decided by the Congress, state legislatures, and county and city governments. It would seem, however, that the most humane, fairest, and least hurtful way of collecting the needed taxes to address poverty would be to tax people less as they are nearer to the poverty line and tax people more as they are further from the poverty line. In other words, if we want to solve poverty by getting all poor people above the poverty line, we will need to set aside more tax revenue to address this social problem.

Eighth, as we solve the problem of poverty with the input of both capitalism and government, we should also see a decline in the severity of other social problems that are influenced by poverty, such as selling drugs to make money to survive in poverty, engaging in prostitution, burglarizing homes or businesses, robbing people or businesses, and using drugs or drinking alcohol as a way of escaping the reality of one's poverty with the result that one is less capable of getting out of poverty. All of these social problems—drug sales, prostitution, crime, and addiction—are exacerbated by the existence of poverty in people's lives. Consequently, as we solve poverty in our country, we should also see a decline in these other social problems.

Ninth, given that solving poverty will help us solve or decrease other social problems, it may be prudent to focus on poverty as one of the first social problems we address. That way, we get more bang for our invested buck. It is at least something to consider, given that we have many social problems but only a limited amount of resources to apply to these problems.

What Can We Do?

What can we do? There are a number of actions we can take to solve the problem of poverty. In this section of the chapter, we discuss a number of steps we can take that are realistic and humane and will not cause people to sacrifice a lot of their resources, although some of us who are not poor will need to sacrifice some of our resources for the benefit of lifting poor people out of poverty. As I suggest various policies, see whether you think these policies will get our poor people out of poverty and be as little sacrifice as is possible on those of us who are not poor.

Note that these solutions will not give poor people a middle-class lifestyle, but they will help them to live better lives than they do now. The solutions that could get our American poor out of their poverty are the following:

- Raise the minimum wage and tie it to yearly inflation
- Increase the child care subsidy so that parents of children who want to work, and are physically able to work, can work
- Increase the earned income tax credit (discussed more fully later in the chapter) to make up for the gap between the minimum wage and the poverty line
- Decrease the income tax, Social Security tax, and sales tax on the poor, near poor, and working poor so that they have more take-home pay
- Increase unemployment compensation, provide more and better job training, and create more effective job placement services in a capitalistic economy in which people lose their jobs due to corporations moving to other countries or going out of business
- Give corporations tax incentives to create new jobs in our country
- Create a guaranteed minimum income that will help to keep people above the poverty line when our economy does not produce enough jobs
- Improve the housing subsidies for poor people so that they can live in adequate housing
- Create more public transportation facilities so that poor people, who cannot afford cars, can get to where jobs are

- Provide adequate health care for the poor, the near poor, the working poor, and other people who do not have health care
- Provide good public schools so that poor children have a better chance of getting out of poverty than they now have
- Provide the elderly who are poor with a prescription drug subsidy so that they can spend their Social Security and retirement incomes on everyday expenses, or provide a more comprehensive health care system that covers the cost of prescription drugs
- Provide the preceding combination of subsidies and services to help those who are not capable of having jobs, such as the elderly and the severely disabled, to support themselves and live above the poverty line

If our country could carry out these social policies, we could go a long way toward solving the problem of poverty and also toward addressing other social problems that are related to poverty. Let us now elaborate on each social policy in turn.

Raise the Minimum Wage and Tie It to Yearly Inflation

The minimum wage was $5.15 per hour and had been that amount from 1997 to 2006 (U.S. Department of Labor, n.d.). In 2006, Congress passed a law stating that the minimum wage would increase by 70 cents each year for the years 2007, 2008, and 2009 ("Waitress lauds wage increase in radio show," 2007). In the summer of 2009, the minimum wage increased its third and final time to $7.25 per hour. It has now been over 6 years since the minimum wage has been increased.

Under the minimum wage of $7.25 per hour, if a mother of two children gets a minimum wage job and works 40 hours per week for 52 weeks per year, she will earn $290 per week or $15,080 per year. The problem is that this yearly income does not lift her family out of poverty; she and her children are still below the poverty line of $19,790 (U.S. Department of Health and Human Services, 2015) by $4,710, that is, $19,790 − $15,080 = $4,710.

If Congress raises the minimum wage, this will help poor people who have a minimum wage job get closer to getting out of poverty. Hence, this is one means that our society can use to decrease poverty. Raising the minimum wage is not without problems, however. There are at least three problems that we need to be aware of when we raise the minimum wage. First, not all poor people have minimum wage jobs—they have no jobs at all (recall that in December 2009, 10% of Americans were out of work and looking for jobs and by February 2015, although the unemployment rate had declined significantly, 5.5% of Americans were still out of work and looking for jobs). Also, other poor people are elderly, children, or disabled who cannot work as a way to get out of their poverty. So, raising the minimum wage helps some poor people who have low-wage jobs, but it does not help other poor people who have no jobs or who are not able to have jobs. Consequently, although this method of helping poor people does have some positive effects, it is less efficient than we might like it to be.

A second problem with raising the minimum wage is that it increases the labor costs of employers. Employers either have to decrease their number of employees, which can lead to more poverty for those employees who have lost their jobs, or make less profit.

Finally, a third problem of raising the minimum wage is that it can be inflationary, that is, prices of goods and services increase faster than people's wages. Whenever any employees (factory workers, teachers, nurses, government employees, and so on) ask for and get a raise, this can contribute to inflation. You and your family want a raise each year to keep up with or even exceed the rate of inflation, so that you can have the same or exceed the standard of living you have had in the past. Most Americans would like to get a raise each year in order to maintain their current standard of living or increase it. But these raises, along with the raises of millions of other Americans, are inflationary. But then, do we raise your or my wages as employees in order to maintain or increase our standard of living but not do the same for the wages of poor people?

What then should we do? There are problems with raising the minimum wage, but we live in a society where there is usually 2% to 3% inflation per year. Consequently, if we do not raise our wages, we stand to lose 2% to 3% of our standard of living per year. Almost no one wants to lose their standard of living year after year, including poor people with minimum wage jobs. Yet, given the average loss of standard of living if no wages are increased each year, this means that workers on the minimum wage have lost somewhere around 17% of their standard of living in the last 6 years since the last minimum wage was raised to $7.25 per hour (2.83% average inflation per year × the last 6 years of minimum wage remaining at $7.25 per hour = 16.98% or around 17% loss in their standard of living). Would you like to have had your standard of living decrease by 17% in the last 6 years? Probably not. Americans want to hold on to their standard of living and, if possible, increase it.

Knowing that raising the minimum wage does not help all poor people, that it raises labor costs for employers, and that it is inflationary, what can we do? We can make a compromise. In order to help the poor in a more consistent way, instead of raising the minimum wage inconsistently every 5 to 10 years, we could raise the minimum wage to, say, 80% of the poverty level and tie this level to yearly inflation. That way, Congress does not have to periodically revisit this problem of the minimum wage and employers do not get hurt as much as they do if Congress raises the minimum wage to 100% of the poverty level and then ties the poverty level to yearly inflation. The policy of raising the minimum wage to a percentage of poverty level, although somewhat inflationary, would not be as inflationary as raising the minimum wage to 100% of the poverty level.

This is not a perfect solution to solving poverty, but it can help poor people in minimum wage jobs get closer to getting out of poverty and yet keep inflation and labor costs at lower levels.

Whatever gap that remains between poor people's wages and the poverty level could be filled by having the earned income tax credit make up the difference. The earned income tax credit, discussed later in the chapter, could be money given by the government to people who have below-poverty-level jobs to make up the gap between their incomes from their minimum wage jobs and the poverty level. This way, incomes do not get so low in a capitalistic economy.

Increase the Child Care Subsidy

How do we get a mother and her children out of poverty when she is already working full time? This mother will, in all likelihood, need to pay someone to take care of her children while she is at work. Typically, this will cost a minimum of $50 to $100 per child per week. This cost for child care for a woman with a minimum wage job will decrease the weekly income she brings home; for example, at the minimum wage of $7.25 per hour, she will earn $290 per week if she works 40 hours per week, minus $100 a week for day care for two children (only $50 per child), leaving her with $190 per week. As you know, trying to keep together a family of three with $190 per week to pay for rent, food, gasoline, water bill, electric bill, car insurance, house insurance, health insurance, and many other expenses (shoes, clothing, school supplies, maybe eating out at a McDonald's every 2 to 3 weeks, etc.) will be extremely difficult—if not impossible. Rent alone can eat up one half of the $190 after child care is paid for. Is it no wonder that families living at this level of existence face many problems that those of us who are not poor do not face?

Our state governments and the federal government have recognized the problem of the cost of child care for low-income parents and have provided funds to help pay a portion of child care costs. This help with child care expense gives mothers on welfare an added incentive to go to work, especially at a minimum wage job. The problem, however, is that with the downturn in the economy during recent years, state governments have needed to hold the line on what they can give out in child care subsidies. For example, the State of Kentucky has had a waiting list of 2,700 parents who have applied for child care funding, but the state is unable to satisfy their requests.[2] This lack of funding makes it harder for these parents to get off of welfare and hold a minimum wage job and, furthermore, to continue to work without returning to welfare.

This raises the following question: Do we provide more funding for child care for parents who have minimum wage jobs? This question raises a difficult dilemma for all of us in our country because our federal government is currently spending more than it receives in taxes and therefore getting further into debt. Moreover, President George W. Bush successfully got a tax cut through Congress that will result in less tax money coming in to the federal government to pay for things such as child care subsidies for parents earning the minimum wage.

This situation raises more questions. Do we provide more poor and near-poor families with child care subsidies even though it means paying more taxes? Do we maintain current spending for child care subsidies and leave a lot of low-income parents without child care subsidies, which acts as an incentive to be on welfare and a disincentive to work at a minimum wage job? Do we decrease child care funding even though we know that the consequences will be that more poor parents will need to give up their minimum wage jobs and return to welfare? If more parents return to welfare, then more of our tax money will go to pay for welfare. Does it make more sense to pay more for child care subsidies than to pay more for people returning to welfare? Does it make more sense to get people to want to work than to be on welfare? If so, then do we increase our allocation for child care subsidies? These are difficult questions that we need to answer as an American people.

If we want to solve the problem of poverty in our country, it seems that we will need to continue to provide, and even increase, child care subsidies to include more parents who want to get off of welfare, get a job, and get out of poverty. Helping poor people who have minimum wage or near-minimum wage jobs with their child care expenses seems to be a key element in helping poor Americans get out of their poverty.

Increase the Earned Income Tax Credit

In addition to increasing the minimum wage, is there any way that a mother with two children can have enough money for her family to be close to, at, or even above the poverty line? Yes, there is a way. When she files her income tax return, she can apply for what is known as an *earned income tax credit* (TaxCreditResources.org, n.d.b). This is money that the federal government and some states[3] give to people who work but still have below-poverty-level incomes. The purpose of the earned income tax credit is to help get poor working people closer to the poverty line and give them "added incentives to work" (TaxCreditResources.org, n.d.b).

The earned income tax credit was created in 1975 by Congress and was expanded in 1986, 1990, and 1993. It expanded during the 1980s and 1990s under two Republican presidents and one Democratic president: Ronald Reagan, George H. W. Bush, and Bill Clinton (Wilson, 1997, p. 222). One source asserted, "EITC [earned income tax credit] lifts more working families above the poverty line than any other federal program."[4] Wilson (1997) noted that these increases in the earned income tax credit "reflected a recognition that wages for low-paying work have eroded and that other policies to aid the working poor—for example, the minimum wage—have become weaker" (p. 222). Even with increases in the earned income tax credit during the mid-1990s, it still fell short of making up for "the sharp drop in the value of the minimum wage and the marked reductions in AFDC [Aid to Families with Dependent Children (welfare)] benefits to low-income working families since the early 1970s" (p. 222). Even when food stamps were added, workers' incomes still fell below the poverty line during the mid-to-late 1990s (p. 222).

If we want to solve the poverty problem in the United States, we could make sure that those workers who have minimum wage jobs receive an earned income tax credit as a way to put them above the poverty line. As we discussed in a preceding section, we could tie the minimum wage to the rate of inflation and then make the subsequent adjustment to the earned income tax credit so that all working people who are still poor could rise above the poverty line, thereby getting many Americans out of poverty.

Decrease the Income Tax, Social Security Tax, and Sales Tax on the Poor

We can give poor people more take-home pay each week by decreasing the taxes that they pay. One way to decrease taxes on the poor is to make our income tax, Social Security tax, and sales tax more progressive, where poor people pay less in taxes and rich people pay more in taxes. Let us take the Social Security tax as an example. Currently, Americans who are employees and who make $118,500 per year or less pay 6.2% of their income in tax. People who make more than $118,500 in income do not pay any Social Security tax on the amount over $118,500. We could change this tax to make it a progressive tax. For example, the poor pay 1% in Social Security tax, and the rich pay, say, 8%. If the poor pay only 1% instead of 6.2%, they would increase their take-home pay by 5.2%, thereby helping them come closer to getting out of their poverty.

We could also decrease the state sales tax for poor people. For example, the sales tax in Indiana rose from 6% to 7% (In.Gov, 2009). A poor family of four needs the same amount of toothpaste, toilet paper, shampoo, and soap as does a rich family of four. When these two families go to the store to purchase these items, they both pay the same amount of sales tax. This sales tax takes a larger proportion of money out of the income of the poor family than it does out of the income of the rich family. We could pay a sales tax based upon the income we make. That is, the less income we make, the less sales tax we pay; the more income we make, the more sales tax we pay. The sales tax would become more progressive and help poor people to get out of poverty.[5]

We currently have somewhat of a progressive tax in place with respect to the income tax we pay. We could make the income tax more progressive, that is, poor people pay a lower percentage of their incomes in tax, and rich people pay a higher percentage of their incomes in tax. Taken together, if we make the income tax, the Social Security tax, and the sales tax more progressive, we could provide more money for poor people to help them get out of poverty.

As you can see, to change the way we tax people can be a major method of helping people get out of their poverty. Typically, we do not connect taxes to poverty, but we need to be conscious of this connection. Also, we need to continually remind ourselves that we humans in general, and we Americans in particular, socially construct all kinds of things—norms, laws, ideologies, values, beliefs—and taxes. Given that we created these things, we can change these things, knowing that changing these things will make life more humane. One of the things we can change is our tax system as a way to help people get out of their poverty.

Improve Unemployment Compensation, Job Training, and Job Placement Services

In any capitalistic economy, a number of people will lose their jobs through no fault of their own. For example, corporations move out of a community or out of the country. A company adds robots instead of workers. A company is taken over by another company and a number of people lose their jobs. Life is like that in capitalism. In capitalism, there is no guarantee of keeping one's job. In capitalism, corporations put their survival and profits ahead of the welfare of their workers. As a consequence, people, from time to time, will lose their jobs and fall into poverty. Given this situation, as long as there is capitalism and unemployment, we will need to take steps to help those people who are out of work. Here are some steps we can take.

Unemployment Compensation

As soon as people lose their jobs through no fault of their own and they drop into poverty, we need to provide them with certain services. One service we could provide is enough money for them to pay their daily, weekly, and monthly bills. Currently, we have unemployment compensation for people when they lose their jobs. This program was established in 1935 with the passage of the Social Security Act, through which workers who lose their jobs "through no fault of their own" (Cornell Law School, n.d.) receive a percentage of their individual earnings within 2 weeks of filing for benefits. These benefits can last up to 26 weeks. However, during periods of high unemployment, when workers have used up these 26 weeks, extended benefits can go into effect for an additional 13 weeks.[6] The weekly benefit that the unemployed worker is supposed to receive is between 50% and 70% of the worker's previous wage. However, data show that in actuality "the national average weekly benefit amount as a percent of the average weekly covered wage was only 35 percent" (Almanac of Policy Issues, n.d.).

This raises the following question: Can people live on 35% of their former income and pay their monthly bills and not fall into poverty? One way to help people stay out of poverty is to provide enough unemployment compensation to keep them above poverty.

Job Training

Another service that we can provide is to get people connected to retraining schools to help them learn new skills that are in demand in the current economy. As you probably know, a capitalistic economy is continually changing, with some jobs decreasing in demand and other jobs increasing in demand. As a consequence, our job training programs need to change and adjust as our economy changes.

People can take different paths in getting retrained. They can go to vocational schools that teach specific skills; they can go to employers who will train them; or they can go to a college or university to get a broader education in the form of a bachelor's degree to prepare them for professional careers such as lawyers, doctors, professors, engineers, and so on.

Local administrators of these job training programs can make recommendations as to how we can have more effective training programs. We can also make these services more visible and more known through radio, television, and newspaper advertisements that inform poor and unemployed people as to how and where they can get job training. Moreover, our schools can do a better job of teaching high school students how to write a résumé, how to search for a job, how to apply for a job, and how to interview for a job (Almanac of Policy Issues, n.d.). That is, high schools could be more interrelated with state job training and placement services so that high school graduates could more quickly and easily find the training, education, and jobs that they want.

Job Placement

We currently have in the United States various kinds of placement services that help people get jobs. For example, in Indiana, Transition Resources helps migrant and seasonal workers get connected to jobs (Almanac of Policy Issues, n.d.). Older workers who are looking for jobs can get help from a service called Experienced Workers (Almanac of Policy Issues, n.d.). There are job matching services that match people to local jobs or to jobs that are available statewide. More recently, a national service called America's Job Bank helps to give people access to jobs at the national level (Almanac of Policy Issues, n.d.).

So, to get people out of poverty more quickly, we could increase the amount of unemployment compensation while they are unemployed; we could work to get unemployed people into job training programs and make sure that these training programs are changing along with changes in the economy; and we could work to improve local, state, and national job placement services. The improvements that we could make in these three areas could help newly unemployed people who have fallen into poverty or other people who have been in poverty for a longer period of time to get out of poverty more quickly. This quicker turnaround time from unemployment to employment will also mean that we, who are not poor, will pay less in taxes that go toward providing for unemployment compensation.

Give Corporations Tax Incentives to Create New Jobs

Even though people are trained and are looking for jobs via placement services, we need to find ways to create more jobs for the many Americans who are unemployed. One important way to do this is to give corporations incentives to create jobs in the United States. Corporations are in business to make profits. If they do not make profits, they will be out of business quickly. So, if corporate managers think that creating more jobs in our country will increase their profits, they will create more jobs.

One way to stimulate job creation by corporations is to decrease the taxes on corporations and to make up for this tax loss by making the income tax more progressive. The wealthy would pay more in taxes, with regard to their income and the wealth they own, and the poor and working classes would pay less in taxes. Local, state, and federal governments could give more tax breaks to corporations in exchange for corporations providing a certain number of jobs in the United States.

Likewise, we could create disincentives by taxing corporations more when they move plants and jobs to other countries. This is probably a more controversial policy, but it is one that could be investigated, discussed, and considered. We need to continually consider new and creative ideas as to how to create jobs for Americans.

Provide a Guaranteed Minimum Income

If we find that the economy cannot provide enough jobs for all Americans who want them, we might need to consider giving some kind of income to people so that they can survive and stay above the poverty line. Capitalism has cycles of more or less unemployment. During the Great Depression of the 1930s, the unemployment rate rose to more than 20%. During the boom years of the 1990s, unemployment was at times less than 4% (University of Texas, n.d.). Starting in 2000, our economy began to take a nosedive. By July 2003, the unemployment rate had reached 6.4%. During our recent recession, the unemployment rate rose to 10% by late 2009. As you can see, a capitalistic economy such as ours can result in millions of Americans having no means to survive unless they qualify for food stamps and a little bit of welfare money to keep them afloat—for awhile.

What do we do when people cannot get jobs? Gans (1995) discussed the economy, jobs, and poverty in *The War Against the Poor* and asserted that we might need to face the fact that our capitalistic economy will not produce enough decent-paying jobs for all who want or need them. He stated that because of the loss of factory jobs to other countries, the use of robots and computers in place of human workers, and corporate downsizing of mid-level jobs, we face a big challenge of producing enough jobs for everyone (p. 133). As a result, we might need to consider other alternatives if we wish to lift the poor out of their poverty.

If, in such a scenario, the government did not respond with some type of safety net of both income and services, poor people could not get out of poverty and could feel a sense of despair and anger, especially in a country such as the United States, where we emphasize upward mobility. Moreover, the poor could question the legitimacy of the prevailing social system, form various kinds of conflict groups, and promote conflict in some way (this is a good example of where our theory of conflict and social change and the accompanying causal model outlined in Chapter 1 can be applied).[7] Thus, the stability of the country depends, in part, on matching the ideology of upward mobility with real opportunities for people to be upwardly mobile. If jobs are not forthcoming, we might need to rely on the government to provide some sort of safety net of income and services.

One safety net that we could provide is a guaranteed minimum income that puts people above the poverty line when, through no fault of their own, they cannot find jobs and need money to pay their bills. Possibly, a guaranteed minimum income could begin at the point when people have tried to get jobs and their unemployment compensation has run out.

We could construct the guaranteed minimum income in such a way that it is more in people's vested interests to find work than to remain on the guaranteed minimum income. In other words, when they find work, they make more money at their new jobs than they would if they remained on the guaranteed minimum income. This could be one of the methods that we use to get people out of poverty if the other methods we have discussed do not totally solve the problem of poverty.

The guaranteed minimum income has been suggested by conservatives as well as liberals. At first thought, you might think that this is "just another liberal idea" that recommends that we, as taxpayers, need to pay more in taxes to provide for yet another government program. However, the conservative economist Milton Friedman, in his book *Capitalism and Freedom,* supported this idea (Friedman, 1962, pp. 190–195). Friedman (1962) asserted that there are a number of advantages to having a guaranteed minimum income. First, it would be "directed specifically at the problem of poverty" (pp. 191–192). Second, it could act "as a substitute for the present rag bag of measures directed at the same end" (p. 192). Third, it "could be far less costly in money" (p. 193). As a conservative who did not like big government and many government programs and the waste and overlap that these programs can bring, Friedman concluded that the guaranteed minimum income is the best way to address poverty. Also, former President Richard Nixon, a Republican conservative, suggested in the late 1960s and early 1970s that we implement guaranteed minimum income. Finally, Harold Kerbo, a researcher in the study of social stratification, noted, "The United States is the only industrial nation that does not have a basic guaranteed income program for all families below the poverty level" (Kerbo, 2009, p. 39).

If we implement the guaranteed minimum income, this is how it could work. We, the American people, would decide how much of our tax money we want to give to lift poor people above the poverty level. Let us say, for example, that a mother of two children was laid off from her minimum wage job at which she was making $15,080 per year. The poverty level for her and her two children was $19,790 (again, 2015 figures). She received unemployment compensation, but her time on this has been exhausted. She could, at this point, receive a guaranteed minimum income—for example, $20,000—which puts her and her children just above the poverty line. If she finds a part-time job that gives her $1,000 in income, we would not take away the equivalent amount of $1,000 from the guaranteed minimum income because then she might have no incentive to work. To give her an incentive to work, when she earned $1,000, we would take, for example, only $500 away from the $20,000 guaranteed minimum income. As a result, she would get $19,500 of guaranteed minimum income and $1,000 from her job and would now make $20,500. That is, she would make more money working than she would not working. If she was able to work more and made another $1,000, again only $500 would be subtracted from her guaranteed minimum income, and she would now make $19,000 from guaranteed minimum income plus $2,000 from her job, to give her a total income of $21,000. In other words, she always makes more money the more she works—thus, giving her more incentive to work than not to work.

If our capitalistic economy cannot provide enough jobs for everyone, we might someday be in the position that Gans (1995) predicted. Should we, as a society, consider the guaranteed minimum income as an option for getting Americans out of poverty? This is an option to which we will need to give serious thought and discussion. It could solve our poverty problem, especially if we find in the future that our economy does not provide enough jobs for Americans who want and need them—especially if the trends of deindustrialization, robotization, and downsizing continue and the number of new jobs created does not offset the number of jobs lost.

Improve Housing Subsidies

What should we do for people who live in dilapidated housing or have no housing? Even if we raise the incomes of poor people to a little above the poverty line, in many instances they still will not have enough money to live in adequate housing.

During the Depression of the 1930s, when many people were out of work and had a difficult time in finding decent housing, the government began to build housing for people as a way not only to provide housing but also to provide jobs for people and therefore stimulate the economy. Slum housing was cleared, and 114,000 low-rent units were built (Palen, 1997, p. 320).

Although this program ended during World War II, it was successful in that it built housing that poor people could afford.

With the Housing Act of 1934, which created the Federal Housing Administration (FHA) and the Veterans Administration (VA), both of which insured home loans, banks began to loan more money to people who were starting to improve financially and could move out of public housing. The people getting these loans began to move to new homes being built in the suburbs. The FHA and VA, however, discouraged giving loans to African Americans; this would ensure, they believed, that White people buying new homes in the suburbs would have their property values protected.

The results of these loans and discriminatory policies were as follows. First, White families who were improving their financial situations moved out of public housing and into the suburbs. Second, Black families who could afford to buy homes in the suburbs had no option to borrow money and build new homes. Thus, they had no chance, like White families, to own new homes, build equity, that is, ownership in their homes, and hence use the building of equity as a way to build wealth. Third, the people who were left in the public housing units were less likely to be financially successful, with the result that lower-income people became more physically concentrated in public housing. Fourth, the children who remained in public housing saw fewer and fewer successful role models who were making their way up and out of poverty through legitimate means (versus through illegitimate means such as robbery, selling drugs, and prostitution). Fifth, the general public in the United States began to take a more negative view of public housing as the very poorest of the poor began to make up the vast majority of residents of public housing, thereby giving public housing in the United States a negative stigma compared with public housing in Europe, where many working-class and middle-class people lived. Sixth, White families were given a tax break on the interest they paid on their mortgages (home loans), whereas Black families who could afford to own homes but were discriminated against in being denied home loans were not able to take advantage of this tax break. Together (1) the home loans (mortgages) along with (2) the tax break on interest paid to banks on these home loans allowed White families to begin to build wealth in the United States but denied African American families to build wealth this way. This, by the way, is another example of how discrimination, of some kind, can cause wealth inequality between two groups of people—regardless of how good, honest, and hardworking the group is that is being discriminated against.

More recently, our country has provided vouchers to poor people so that they can go to privately owned apartment buildings, get an apartment, and pay 30% of their income toward rent. The federal government pays the landlord the rest of the rent. This program is called Section 8. The advantages of Section 8 are as follows. First, poor people can choose various places to live, thereby giving them some freedom of choice of apartments and geographic location. Second, given more freedom of choice of geographic location, poor people no longer need to be physically concentrated in one area and hence have more choice of neighborhoods and schools. Third, poor people now have a chance to live closer to their jobs. Fourth, the federal government does not need to be in the business of building and running a housing program.

Currently, giving poor people vouchers via the Section 8 program could be the best answer for helping poor people to attain adequate housing. However, because 5 million families still live in inadequate housing,[8] we could expand this program so that more poor people could have adequate housing. If we do not provide enough Section 8 funding for poor people, it seems that the only other alternative that will provide enough adequate housing for poor people is for the government to get back in the business of building low-income housing. The problems with this are that the government adds more bureaucracy in building and maintaining such housing while the poor end up living in areas of the government's choosing. Thus, there are higher concentrations of poor people in such housing and fewer chances for employment. Given these problems, the Section 8 program seems to be a better idea—both for poor people and for the government.

Create More Public Transportation

Section 8 vouchers provide people with choices as to where to live. These vouchers also help the poor, who cannot afford to own cars, to rent homes near public transportation, thus providing the poor with better access to jobs.

How do people in large and medium-sized cities get to their jobs, grocery stores, and other places they need to go, for example, doctor appointments and dentist appointments? If they cannot afford a car, what do they do? Ideally, they live close enough to walk to jobs, grocery stores, schools, hospitals, and banks. But in the spread-out fashion of our contemporary cities, where services many times are miles apart, transportation for poor people becomes a major challenge. Public transportation helps to solve this problem.

Consequently, one way for poor people to have greater access not only to jobs but also to services to meet family needs (for example, groceries, hospitals, food pantries, child care services) is to expand the public transportation system. For example, during recent years, San Francisco has created a subway and train system and has continued to expand both systems to take care of the transportation needs of more and more people and, thus, allow more people to get to jobs and services more cheaply and more easily in other parts of the San Francisco Bay Area. The extension of these public transportation systems should be especially helpful for poor people in getting to and from jobs and services.

These public transportation systems have another potential benefit that can address one of our other social problems that we will address later—the environment. These public transportation systems also allow many people who are not poor to use these services and hence decrease the use of cars that cause air pollution in our country. So, this partial solution to poverty can also work to partially solve our environmental problems (see Chapter 13 for a discussion of our environmental problems).

What can we do in smaller cities and rural areas? One program that has been implemented in southeastern Indiana, called "Catch-a-Ride" and covering a five-county area, offers transportation for poor people who need to get to work (personal interview with M. Hueseman, Catch-a-Ride, Lifetime Resources, August 31, 2003). We could design a national program, based on the Catch-a-Ride model, that covers smaller cities and rural areas to help both poor and nonpoor travel to their places of work and get to the services they need.

Provide Adequate Health Care for the Poor, Near Poor, and Working Poor

Even after much discussion by President Bill Clinton during the early to mid-1990s about the need to provide all Americans with some form of adequate health care, by 1999, our country still had 44.3 million Americans who did not have health insurance (Pear, 1999). By 2009, we had around 50 million Americans who did not have health insurance—about one out of six Americans (Zaldivar & Espo, 2009). Many Americans fall into a crisis situation if their family members get seriously ill or have a serious accident. The illness or accident can cost the family thousands or hundreds of thousands of dollars. Many of these families without health insurance have been poor, near poor, or working poor because the jobs the parents have had do not provide health insurance benefits. They have a job but no health insurance. Many other people in our country (hopefully, you someday, if you are currently a college student) have a job, have health insurance from the job, and a retirement plan from the job. Because a number of poor and near-poor people have jobs that do not provide health insurance, given their below-poverty level wages or near-poverty level wages, they cannot afford to buy health insurance on their own. So, until the Affordable Care Act was passed (March, 2010), approximately 50 million poor and near-poor

Americans did not have health insurance and therefore tended to put off going to the doctor or dentist simply because they could not afford to pay for the medical service. Toothaches, broken bones, and diseases were left untreated. With the passage of the Affordable Care Act, we now have millions of more Americans who have health insurance.

Our country is the only industrialized country that does not have a "national health program meeting the medical needs of all families" (Kerbo, 2009, p. 39). Providing health care for all Americans could be another partial solution to helping poor people get out of poverty. Moreover, providing health care for all Americans would address three social problems discussed in this book: money inequality, poverty, and no health care for one sixth of all Americans (see Chapter 10 for an in-depth discussion of what we can do to provide health care for all Americans and, in doing so, help more of our poor get out of their poverty).

Create Good Public Schools

To give poor children a chance to get out of their poverty, we could make sure that we create good public schools for them. By *good schools,* I mean a number of things. First, I mean that children are in a safe environment when they are at school. Second, I mean that all public schools are well maintained and have up-to-date facilities and equipment so that students get a very good education (and can also be proud of their schools).

Third, I also mean that all of the teachers are well qualified by being certified in the areas they teach. Moreover, these schools have low student-to-teacher ratios so that teachers can give more specialized time per student. For example, schools in poverty neighborhoods could have lower student-to-teacher ratios of 10 to 1, where teachers can concentrate on bringing each child up to his or her full potential. With such a low student-to-teacher ratio, the teacher can spend more time with each student individually. This is especially important for poor children since they are more likely to be from one-parent families where they cannot get as much help at home from their parent since the one parent is more likely to be at work. Also, the parents of poor children are more likely to be less educated and therefore less able to help their children with homework. Moreover, if the parent of a poor child is less educated, possibly not having even graduated from high school, the parent may not have as great of an appreciation for being able to get a high school and college education as middle- or upper-middle-class parents who realize how much their high school, college, and even graduate-school education helped them get higher-paying jobs and a more comfortable standard of living.

In other words, the child born in a poor family starts out life at a considerable disadvantage compared with a child born in a middle- or upper-middle-class family. If we, in our society, can offset this disadvantage to some degree, by giving a poor child a good education that gives that child the means to make a good life on his or her own, then we can make progress toward helping poor children eventually make their way out of poverty.

In such a quality educational atmosphere, children from poor families will get a good education, which will, in time, help them go on to college or trade school or better prepare them to work right after high school. To provide schools that are safe, well maintained, have up-to-date equipment, have well-qualified teachers, and have low student-to-teacher ratios will mean that we invest more money in our public school system.

If we want to work at getting rid of poverty, we will need to create a better public school system for poor children. Creating such a system will be a major way to help poor children acquire the proper education and skills to get out of poverty and make a good life for themselves.

Give the Elderly a Prescription Drug Subsidy

A group of poor people who will not be helped with an increase in the minimum wage, a larger child care subsidy, or better quality schools is the elderly who are poor. We need to create other ways to get them out of poverty so that they can live a decent lifestyle.

A number of things could be done to help the elderly poor get out of their poverty. Many of the elderly poor have Social Security income that helps but might not keep them out of poverty. Medicare, a health insurance program provided by the federal government, is a great help in providing the elderly with health care. Yet the prescription drugs that the elderly must pay for can take a substantial chunk out of their monthly incomes. With the passage of the Affordable Care Act, the elderly will pay less and less for prescription drugs until 2020 when their prescription drug costs will be fully covered ("The Final Bill at a Glance," March 23, 2010, p. A4).

Concluding On an Optimistic Note

If we want to do so, we can decrease poverty in our country. The reason I say this is that Western European countries have already done so. While the poverty rates in countries such as Germany, France, Belgium, Denmark, The Netherlands, and Sweden are roughly the same as our poverty rate (as measured by income below 50% of median income in a nation), *all* of these countries' poverty rates declined to 5% to 7% levels after they added income and services provided by the government, whereas our country's poverty rate remained much higher at 19% (Kerbo, 2009, p. 268). If European countries can do this, we can do it, too. This brings us to the following question: Are we willing to get rid of poverty in our country? As we pointed out in this chapter, we can do this.

Questions for Discussion

1. Should we increase the minimum wage?

2. Should we increase the child care subsidy?

3. Should we increase the earned income tax credit to get poor people above the poverty line?

4. Should we tax the poor less in terms of income tax, Social Security tax, and sales tax while we tax the rich more?

5. Should we tax corporations less to give them incentives to stay in the United States and provide more jobs for American workers and tax corporations more when they move jobs out of the country?

6. What should we do about unemployment compensation, job training, and job placement?

7. If our economy cannot provide enough jobs for all Americans who want jobs, should we have a guaranteed minimum income?

8. What combination of the previously discussed measures could best eliminate poverty?

9. Which of the solutions discussed in this chapter will be tried, and which will not? Why?

10. If you were asked to eliminate poverty, what would you do?

5

How Can We Solve the Problem of Racial/Ethnic Inequality?

The year was 1954. I had just turned 10 years old. My aunt, uncle, and cousin had been to Miami Beach, Florida, the summer before and were excited about vacationing in Florida again and wanted our family (my mother, father, older brother, and me) to go this summer. My father was not sure that he could afford the trip (recall that at that time many families adhered to the traditional gender roles where the father worked at a job, and the mother stayed home to work at cooking, cleaning, doing the laundry, grocery shopping, and doing the endless ironing that I remember seeing my mother do in the kitchen). With just one income, and that income being a high school teacher's income, we were not poor, but we did not have much left over after paying the monthly bills. My father finally decided that with the money he earned being the secretary of the Kiwanis Club and taking wedding pictures during the summer (he was a wedding photographer during the summer to make ends meet), and saving a little bit here and there, we could go to Florida. To say the least, as a 10-year-old boy who had never been out of Indiana, I was overjoyed! On the drive down to Florida, I would get to see a big river called the Ohio River, I would get to see what mountains really looked like when we went through the Smoky Mountains, and I would get to see my first Civil War battle site on top of Lookout Mountain in Tennessee. When we got to our destination, I would get to stay in a motel (motels were something new at that time), play on the beach, dive into the waves, and swim in the ocean.

I was so excited to see and experience all of these things. What I did not realize at the time, nor did anyone else in my family, was that I was to have an experience that would leave an indelible mark on me for the rest of my life. We were on our way in the family car (very few people went on vacations by planes in those days), and we had already driven over the Ohio River into Kentucky and had seen the Smoky Mountains and the Civil War battle site. We were now in the middle of Georgia, in peach tree country, where on both sides of the road were endless fields of peach trees and you could smell the aroma of peaches in the air. This is where, unbeknownst to me at the time, I had my life-changing experience.

We stopped along the roadside (nearly all roads had just two lanes at that time because there was no such thing as the interstate system) to get some gasoline at a small gas station and use the restroom. I got out of the car and went toward the restroom. The signs said, "White Men" and "White Women." There was a third sign that said, "Colored," and an accompanying arrow that pointed to behind the station. I went to the "White Men" restroom (I am White). On leaving the restroom, my curiosity got the better of me because I wanted to see what the "Colored" restroom was like. I walked behind the station and discovered that there was no restroom—just a field.

I was shocked. I ran to my mother and father, who were near the car, and exclaimed in an upset way, "The colored people do not have a restroom! Why is that?" My parents, I am sure, were somewhat taken aback and really did not know what to say. I recall my mother saying, "Honey, let's get in the car, and we'll talk about this later." A few minutes later, because I was so upset that I felt people were not being treated equally and fairly, my parents tried to change the subject to calm me down. I eventually calmed down and resumed thinking about the beach, the ocean, the waves, and so on.

However, I never forgot that moment. I would not fully understand that moment and what was to transpire in my life until years later as an adult. Let me explain to you, using our sociological perspective, what happened in my life since then.

My parents were loving and caring and were considerate and respectful of all people. My father, unlike many other White people at the time, spoke to, knew, and talked with Black people in my hometown and always did so with a spirit of dignity and respect. When he was away from them, he never talked down or against them. I grew up in this atmosphere thinking, "That is the way you treat everyone—with dignity and respect." Recall from Chapter 1 the theoretical idea of differential association. My association was with my parents, who taught me to treat all people one way. Others, as I was to later find out, were taught to treat some people, especially those of another skin color, another way. One sociological insight here is that differential association can be, and usually is, much more influential on us than we realize. This idea also hearkens back to the idea by the great French sociologist, Emile Durkheim, who said, as you may recall from Chapter 1, that society is external to us and yet coercive on us. That is, as you and I are born, society is outside of us in the form of norms, values, laws, beliefs, and customs. All of these socially constructed things are eventually taught into us and hence begin to influence how we think, believe, feel, and act. Most of the time, we are not conscious of this process, but it happens to all of us. We call this process *socialization.* Typically, parents have the most influence on us via socialization, especially when we are young. Others, such as teachers, coaches, and religious leaders, will later play a role in socializing us and therefore have increasing influence on us as we grow older.

What happened to me that day was that, sociologically speaking, I began to be conscious of racial inequality for the first time in my life. In an abrupt and unexpected way, I learned about the existence of one kind of inequality, namely racial inequality. I saw it with my own eyes. No one could tell me differently. I learned that colored people were treated differently and unequally from White people. In that moment, two things happened: (1) I became conscious of racial inequality and (2) I became concerned about it. I became concerned because what I saw went against everything that I had been taught—at home, in school, and in my church—that all humans are to be treated with dignity and respect.

I was to have a number of experiences thereafter that only reinforced what I had unexpectedly seen and experienced on that day decades ago. Over the years, I was to learn that, even in my hometown in Indiana, Blacks lived in only two neighborhoods of the city. They never went swimming at the public swimming pool; they were not in my church but rather had their own churches. I never saw them in a restaurant. They were not members of the Kiwanis Club, the Lions Club, or country clubs. They did not stay in the motel down in Florida, walk along the beach, or swim in the ocean, but they did work at the motel maintaining the air conditioning, trimming the shrubs, and so on.

As I matured, I began to see and realize what these things meant. I observed many instances of *segregation,* meaning that the minority population is separated from the majority population in many different ways by the informal norms, customs, and laws at the time. At that time, I did not realize it, but I was beginning to look at life in a sociological way. I was not aware of the discipline called *sociology* that focused on the study of why we act and believe the way we do due to the social conditions we grow up in and how we are socialized.

During my sophomore year in college, I took an introductory sociology course as a way to fulfill a requirement for the bachelor's degree. Again, I did not realize what would soon happen to me. The professor began to say, "We are going to study the society for the next 16 weeks, and among the things we are going to study are poverty, racial prejudice and discrimination, and . . ." I was immediately hooked. Those were topics that I had wanted to know more about all of my life—or at least since I was 10 years old when I had the experience at the gas station in Georgia. No other course had ever taught me about these subjects. I had been curious about these issues for years but did not know that there was an entire discipline devoted to the study of them. I was curious and had an insatiable desire to know as much as I could about social phenomena such as racial prejudice and discrimination—what caused these things to happen, why they exist in a society where we are supposed to love one another, what all the consequences of prejudice and discrimination are, what will happen in the future, and what can be done.

Not too long after this, after taking a few more courses in sociology, I realized that this was what I wanted to do: study sociology, teach it, and share it with others. So, in a rather circuitous route that spanned a number of years, I found my calling. In looking back, I saw that I had become conscious and concerned on a summer day in Georgia years before. Later, I was to realize how curious I was about the study of social phenomena in general and racial inequality in particular and also realize that I had found my calling. This was how I got into sociology.

I tell this personal story with the use of sociological concepts and theoretical ideas as a lead-in to address how we can solve the social problem of racial/ethnic inequality. Let us now discuss where we currently are in our society and where we could go.

Now, and Where to Next?

Recall our theory of conflict and social change and the theoretical propositions and causal model in Chapter 1. During the mid-1900s, African Americans became increasingly conscious of and troubled by the racial prejudice and discrimination they had to face daily. More and more, they communicated with each other about their dilemma and were eventually led by a charismatic leader by the name of Martin Luther King, Jr. They formed a conflict group and began to have peaceful protests in the form of marches, demonstrations, boycotts, and sit-ins. They put pressure on presidents Eisenhower, Kennedy, and Johnson and members of Congress to pass civil rights laws that would allow all minority groups to use any public accommodations (for example, restaurants, department stores, and motels), vote, hold public office, work at any job for which they were qualified, and live in any house and neighborhood they could afford. They sought to be able to join private clubs in which they were interested (country clubs, tennis clubs, Kiwanis Club, Lions Club, Rotary Club, and the like). They wanted to be able to travel anywhere in the United States and have accessible restrooms and drinking fountains. They wanted to visit state and national parks and go hiking and camping. They wanted to visit theme parks like Disneyland and Disney World. They wanted to stay in motels and hotels and receive the same food and lodging accommodations that Whites received. They wanted to have the same chance as Whites to play college and professional sports and earn college scholarships and professional salaries. That is, they wanted to be treated the same as White Americans.

African Americans did not make much progress in their attempt to gain racial equality until, as the theory of conflict and social change shows, they became conscious of their unequal situation, they saw the unfairness of this situation, they questioned the legitimacy of their unequal situation, they formed conflict groups, and they carried out peaceful conflict in the form of what is now known as the civil rights movement. Over time, as the theory predicts, African Americans were able to bring about a new social construction of reality. For example, in 1954, the U.S. Supreme Court (*Brown v. Board of Education* [1954]) directed that all public schools in the United States no longer be racially segregated and unequal (for example, unequal facilities and unequal teacher salaries) and become racially integrated and equal. Throughout the latter 1950s and throughout the 1960s, various laws were passed by Congress that further decreased the inequality between Black and White Americans. For example, the following began to be desegregated: buses; city halls (Black Americans could work in city halls and hold political offices such as mayor and city councilperson); county courthouses (again, Black Americans could become a sheriff or sheriff's deputy or be elected as auditor or treasurer or county commissioner); colleges and universities (Black Americans could be students and be professors and administrators at these schools), and sports at colleges and universities (Black Americans could be athletes or coaches).

All of these social changes created a new social structure in the United States—new informal norms, new laws, new ideologies—a new way of living not only for Black Americans but also for White Americans. As the theory of conflict and social change predicts, over time, prejudice and discrimination decreased, inequality in the form of money, power, and prestige decreased, and a more humane and just society began to develop.

There has been substantial structural change since the 1950s in the form of new informal norms, including how we treat each other in everyday interactions; new desegregation laws (for example, desegregation of schools, offices, motels, hotels, restaurants, parks, and the military); and laws to allow Black Americans in particular and minorities in general to vote, hold public office, and buy homes and live in neighborhoods they can afford. These changes brought about new ways to apply the main values of our country, such as equal opportunity, justice, and freedom, to minorities and not just to the majority population of White Americans. So, the result has been substantial social change for African Americans in particular and for minorities in general. Females, Latino Americans, Native Americans, homosexuals, the elderly, and the disabled are other minorities whose members have benefited from structural change (that is, change in laws, informal norms, values, beliefs, and ideologies) and change in our consciousness that grew out of the civil rights movement by African Americans. The civil rights movement of the 1950s and 1960s was meant to create more equality for Black Americans, but it had the latent function, as sociologists would say, of providing a model for other groups (women, gays, the elderly, and so on) to seek social change and gain more equality.

Where are we now? Although our country has made great strides in moving toward more equality for many different minority groups, we still have some distance to travel before we can say that minority Americans of all kinds have the same equality as do majority Americans. This raises the following question: Where can we go from here? That is, how can we move further in the direction of more racial/ethnic equality during the 21st century? In the coming pages, I make a number of suggestions that can take us in that direction.

What Might Racial/Ethnic Equality Mean?

What might we mean by achieving racial/ethnic equality? Such equality could include some of the following changes. There will no longer be racial/ethnic *prejudice*, meaning a negative attitude by one group of people that prejudges another group of people. There will no longer be *discrimination*, meaning unequal treatment by one group of people toward another group of people. There will no longer be institutional discrimination, in which the traditional way of doing things works to the disadvantage of minorities. For example, we, as Americans, pay for our public schools through local property taxes. This puts minority people at a disadvantage because they are more likely to live in poverty-laden areas that cannot collect as much tax revenue from property taxes as do White areas and therefore cannot afford to have as good-quality public schools as Whites. In this instance, racial/ethnic equality would mean that there will be good-quality public schools for both White and Black Americans. Attaining racial/ethnic equality would mean that there are the same or similar proportions of minorities in each social class as there are Whites. For example, in 2011, the median income for White Americans was $69,829, while the median income for Black Americans was $40,495, 58% of White income (Macionis, 2015, p. 357). As you can see, Black American families make $29,000 less than White American families. Moreover, Black American children are more likely to be born in poverty than White American children. While 6.1% of White American children are born to White American couples who are poor, 16% of Black American children are born to Black American couples who are poor (Macionis, 2015, p. 233). So, Black American children are two and one half times more likely than White American children to start out their lives in poverty. However, when we see that White and Black Americans have the same percentages of poverty, the same median incomes, and the same amounts of wealth, we will be more confident in saying that we have reached racial equality in the United States.

So, there are a number of empirical measures that we can use to see when we would achieve racial and ethnic equality or to see that we are at least moving in the direction of more equality. When we achieve all of these kinds of equalities together, it will be a sign that our country has finally reached racial/ethnic equality. Realistically, it may take a while, possibly some time into the 21st century, to achieve all of these equalities.

What More Can We Do?

I suggest two general ways to solve, or at least greatly decrease, racial/ethnic inequality. The first deals with what we can do to decrease racial/ethnic inequality directly; the second deals with what we can do to decrease this type of inequality indirectly.

Direct Measures to Solve or Greatly Decrease Racial/Ethnic Inequality

Teach More Tolerance and Acceptance

Schools, Teachers, and Teaching. To address racial/ethnic prejudice and discrimination directly, we can increase the effort to teach tolerance and acceptance of other races and ethnic groups in schools. Teachers can emphasize the need for all Americans to act on some of the core values and beliefs of our society, such as equal opportunity, fairness, justice, and freedom. Teachers can devise various techniques to teach children that all Americans—not just Whites, middle-class people, or males—deserve to have these values and beliefs fully applied to them. The more students continually hear this message from kindergarten on into elementary, middle, and high school, the more a consistent type of socialization is taught and firmly established in the minds of young people, the more likely this type of socialization will be accepted, internalized, and promoted, and the more likely that the socialization of intolerance from the home environment or elsewhere will be discouraged and will continually diminish over time.

Government. One way to address racial prejudice and discrimination is for the government to sponsor public service messages of tolerance and inclusiveness of all races and ethnicities on television and radio and in newspapers and magazines and on highway billboards and on the Internet. By taking such steps, the government can communicate clearly and visibly to the American people that such a stance represents the will of the American people. In other words, to hearken back to our theory of conflict and social change, the government establishes a new legitimacy; that is, it is seen as right to act in a tolerant and accepting way toward all Americans, regardless of race or ethnicity.

Private Organizations. Private organizations can sponsor activities with the intent of teaching tolerance and acceptance. We already have numerous organizations that help groups of people, such as Big Brothers and Big Sisters, Habitat for Humanity, the Salvation Army, Boys & Girls Clubs, and the YMCA. Many of these organizations already teach tolerance and acceptance and have for many years. These organizations, in cooperation with each other and their local communities, can brainstorm ways that they can work together to present a common, visible, and intentional theme of tolerance and acceptance. So, these organizations could be role models that could lead their respective local communities in promoting more tolerance and acceptance.

We as Individuals. We as individuals can be alert to opportunities that we have each day to say or do something that promotes racial/ethnic tolerance and acceptance. An easy step for all of us to take is to treat every person we meet each day with dignity and respect. This is a simple act that each person can do on a daily basis. As individuals, we can serve as daily role models of tolerance, acceptance, dignity, and respect. Everywhere we go in our daily lives—the post office, the barber shop, the grocery store, the gas station, the restaurant, the gym, the church, the school, the family, the dorm, the fraternity/sorority, the workplace—everywhere, we as individuals can carry with us a certain "way about us" that says to others, "I give dignity and respect to all human beings."

Redress Grievances

We can continue to enforce the existing laws against racial/ethnic discrimination so that minority Americans can go to court to have racial/ethnic transgressions redressed. This option can be made more well known by teaching about it in schools and by the government's incorporating such information into its public service messages.

Accept More Interracial and Interethnic Dating and Marriage

Up to and including the 1950s, there was a strong norm or taboo against Whites and Blacks dating and marrying. For example, Richard Loving, a White man, and Mildred Loving, a Black woman, had been married just 5 weeks in 1958 when the county sheriff and two deputies "burst into their bedroom" (Page, 2008, p. H-1) and "shined flashlights in their eyes" (p. H-1). The Lovings were told that their marriage license was no good in Virginia; they were immediately arrested and sent to jail (p. H-1). A few people, like the Lovings, did marry, but most parents, friends, and others strongly advised against interracial dating and marriage. Given such an atmosphere of informal norms and strong social pressure, most Blacks and Whites (and other combinations of minorities such as Whites and Mexican Americans or Whites and Native Americans) did not venture into dating. They might have seen and been around someone of another racial/ethnic group to whom they were attracted, but they knew that their parents "would have a fit" if they even brought up the subject. So, for most people, the social structure of informal norms and customs and family and community social pressure were, as Durkheim would put it, external to and yet coercive on anyone who might even consider dating someone of a different racial/ethnic group or a different religious group (during the 1950s, there was still a strong norm among many families that Catholics did not date or marry Protestants and vice versa, and "heaven forbid" dating Jews, agnostics, atheists, or anyone else who did not have the "right" faith).

During the 21st century, we see more and more interracial/interethnic dating and marriage. In shopping malls, restaurants, movie theaters, and other public places, we see mixed couples. In schools, we see students who are of different shades and colors, representing mothers and fathers from different racial backgrounds. So, we are in the process of seeing and accepting couples of mixed racial/ethnic and religious backgrounds.

As our society in general and as we as individuals get used to and accept interracial/interethnic dating and marriage, this process will, over time, work to promote more racial/ethnic equality. We will get used to seeing and interacting with people of different combinations of races and ethnicities and will come to see this as less and less of a "big deal." Such interracial/interethnic dating and marriage and procreation of offspring will, I hypothesize, continue to break down barriers between people of different skin color, and there will be increasing tolerance and acceptance. To put it in Merton's (1967) terms, interracial dating and marriage will act as a *latent function*, that is, it will act as an unintended consequence that will increase the survival of minorities; as there is more interracial/interethnic dating and marriage, minorities will be more accepted; will be more upwardly mobile; will attain more money, power, and prestige; and will become more fully integrated within the American society.

Promote a New Kind of Affirmative Action

The U.S. Supreme Court affirmed affirmative action in college admissions, to a degree, during the summer of 2003 (Greenhouse, 2003). In a 5-to-4 decision, the justices stated that race can be considered as one factor in admission to law school. The intent of the Supreme Court is that although admissions offices cannot use quotas with regard to race, they can use race as a factor in achieving diversity of a student body "because such policies promote cross-racial understanding and break down racial stereotypes" (p. A4). *Stereotypes* are oversimplified generalizations about a group of people that are many times unfavorable.

Although affirmative action helps minority students gain admission to undergraduate and graduate schools, helps to give them more opportunity to get ahead, and creates a more diverse student body that allows for more interracial/interethnic interaction and understanding, there are major criticisms of this method of attempting to solve racial/ethnic inequality.[1] First, it can leave out well-qualified White students who earn higher academic grades and national test scores and have more extracurricular experiences than do minority applicants, thereby polarizing society with accusations of reverse discrimination against Whites.[2] Second, it can help middle- and upper-middle-class minorities who might not need the help, given their higher social class situation. Rather, lower-income minorities and Whites are the ones who need help in having a chance to get ahead.

Many people in our country have thought that we needed to go through a time of having affirmative action in college and graduate school admissions and in hiring for jobs because there was so much prejudice and discrimination that pervaded every aspect of our society (for example, hospitals, restrooms, drinking fountains, movie theaters, restaurants, motels, hotels, churches, neighborhoods, voluntary organizations, department stores, bus stations, high schools, colleges, universities, factories, pro baseball, basketball, and football teams, the movie industry, politics, unions, many different kinds of jobs, and—even cemeteries!).[3] In other words, we needed to take strong measures to break these many barriers so that minorities could get a chance to go to college and get decent-paying jobs.

It seems that a number of African Americans have benefited from affirmative action and have joined the middle class, as indicated by their incomes and middle-class occupations. The children of these families will, like children of White middle- and upper-middle-class families, have sufficient resources to attend good schools, go to college and graduate school, and get good jobs without any assistance from affirmative action programs.

However, minorities who are still left out of the chance for upward mobility in our country, especially African Americans, Latino Americans, and Native Americans, are those who come from poor families and low-income neighborhoods, regions, or reservations that have high unemployment, high poverty, and poor-quality public schools. Given these challenging social conditions that these minorities grow up in, problems continue to persist among these poor minority Americans.

In other words, we can reformulate affirmative action that is for the poor—poor minorities and poor Whites.[4] This type of affirmative action would be more acceptable to most Americans because they would be more sympathetic to anyone who is poor—regardless of skin color—Black, White, brown, red, or yellow.[5]

Get More Minorities Into the Middle Class or Higher Classes

The more we can get minorities into the middle class or higher classes, the less racial/ethnic prejudice and discrimination there will be, because there will be more interaction and understanding between minorities and Whites as well as acceptance of minorities by Whites and acceptance of Whites by minorities. Blacks and Whites will live in the same neighborhoods; they will have similar kinds of occupations; they will join similar voluntary associations; their children will go to the same schools and be on the same teams, choirs, bands, student governments, and other extracurricular activities. All of these commonalities together will help minorities and

Whites to understand and accept each other as fellow Americans and fellow human beings.

Indirect Measures to Solve or Greatly Decrease Racial/Ethnic Inequality

To get more minorities into middle or higher social classes, we can also carry out a number of indirect measures: (1) develop good-quality public schools for all Americans, (2) create more decent-paying jobs, (3) build a tax system that takes less money from the poor and near-poor (minorities and Whites), and (4) provide social services such as health care and child care. All of these measures together will create the social structural conditions for poor minorities (and poor Whites) to move into higher social classes, thereby creating more racial/ethnic equality.

Develop Good-Quality Public Schools

One indirect way we can create more racial/ethnic equality is to create good-quality public schools for all children in the United States (see Chapter 7 on unequal public education). Currently, we have unequal public education in our country, and this, in turn, perpetuates racial/ethnic inequality.

The main reason for educational inequality is the way that schools are funded. Public schools in our country are funded mainly through people paying taxes on the property they own. These local property taxes pay for the building and maintenance of school buildings, teacher salaries, and books, computers, and other materials. The problem is that a disproportionate percentage of African American, Latino American, and Native American schoolchildren live in poverty areas where not as much property tax can be collected for each child. As a result, these children, along with poor White children, frequently do not have the quality of schools that middle- and upper-middle-class children have. Consequently, these students are many times not academically prepared for trade school or college and therefore are not as able to get good-paying jobs. Thus, they are more likely to end up in below-poverty level, minimum wage jobs that typically have no health care or retirement benefits (remember a minimum wage job of $7.25 an hour will earn a worker $15,080 a year if he or she works all 52 weeks per year, but he or she will still be $8,770 below the poverty level, which is $23,850 for a family of four).

In other words, to have the chance to be upwardly mobile in our society by having a good job, young people today, more than ever before, need to get a good education. Otherwise, they are more likely to earn minimum wage jobs that put them thousands of dollars below the poverty line—even when they work full time, all year long.

As you know, we have lost many good-paying unskilled factory jobs to other countries (called *deindustrialization*) because corporations can pay factory workers in other countries lower wages, with no health or retirement benefits, and hence can make a larger profit. From the mid-1800s to the mid-1900s, our country had many decent-paying unskilled factory jobs that provided sufficient incomes for many American families. However, starting in the 1970s and continuing into the 21st century, there are fewer of these kinds of jobs and more of the lower-paying kinds of service jobs.

So, if we want to help poor African Americans, Latino Americans, and Native Americans—as well as poor Whites—to have a chance at getting ahead and have a chance at getting good jobs with good salaries, one major step our country can take is to create good-quality public schools so that poor minorities and poor Whites have a chance to get a good education. By the way, it is in our vested interests as a country to create such schools for all American children, so that these young people will be prepared to take the many new skilled jobs that our economy is creating, such as those in the computer field, engineering, and medical technology.

Providing for such schools means that we, as a country, will need to invest more money in our public school systems from kindergarten through the 12th grade. With more money invested, we can hire more teachers and more qualified teachers, meaning teachers who are certified in the areas they teach (for example, a biology teacher has a major in biology in college and has ample educational background to know how to teach biology). Many poor minority children in particular are not taught by certified teachers. Also, there might not be enough certified teachers to fill all of the positions in all public schools in our country. A key reason why there are not enough certified teachers is that many people who go to college do not want to become teachers because they believe that teachers do not make enough money. So, unfortunately, we do not always get "the best and brightest" to go into teaching. A number of excellent college students could potentially love teaching, but they want to make more money and therefore choose medicine, engineering, and other more lucrative fields. Even if enough certified teachers are available, these teachers still may not want to teach because a number of schools have overcrowded classrooms, do not have enough equipment, do not have well-maintained buildings, and are located in dangerous neighborhoods. The result of all this is that children, especially poor minority children and poor White children, do not get the excellent education that they could get.

With more money for public education (better salaries, better equipment, and better buildings), we can motivate more people to go into teaching and provide children with enough certified teachers. With enough money, we can build well-maintained school buildings for all children. With enough money, we can provide enough books, computers, and other materials for teachers to be able to do a good job and for students to be able to learn to the best of their ability and prepare themselves for college, trade schools, and graduate schools so that they can get better paying jobs with health and retirement benefits and jobs that can sufficiently provide for their families. So, a major key to racial/ethnic equality is to create excellent public schools for all children in the United States. These types of schools will provide poor minority children and poor White children with a greater chance to be upwardly mobile and be prepared to work at better-paying jobs and therefore attain middle-class lifestyles.

This raises the following question: Where will the money come from? Currently, I see two possibilities that will help us to improve our public schools. One possibility is that we can make the federal income tax more progressive, where lower-middle class, working class, and poorer people pay lower taxes and richer people pay higher taxes. Also, we could tax the wealth of rich people more, for example, have a higher tax on inherited wealth and a higher tax when people make a lot of money in stock. A more progressive income tax, a higher tax on wealth, and more tax on gains in stock could supply the money needed for good-quality public schools for all children in the United States.

The problem, as you might suspect, is that the wealthy will not want their incomes, their wealth, and their gains in stock taxed more. Moreover, they have disproportionate influence in local, state, and national governments to resist any increase in taxes. Yet, of all the places to get additional tax revenue to pay for schools, these places would take away some money of the very rich, but the rich would still be able to retain most of their money and still maintain their extremely high lifestyles.

Create More Decent-Paying Jobs

We need to find some way to have a strong and vibrant economy that provides enough good-paying jobs for all of the Americans who want them. If we do not create enough jobs, and especially if we do not create enough good-paying jobs, Americans, even those with good educations and well-developed skills, will be unable to get jobs appropriate for their educational and skill levels. So, this leads to the following crucial question: How do we create enough good-paying jobs in a capitalistic economy that does not provide enough jobs and enough decent-paying jobs?

One key method is to invest more money in *research and development,* with the intent of finding more ways to create good-paying jobs. That is, governments, corporations, colleges and universities, private foundations, and "think tanks" invest money to hire people to do the following work that can eventually increase the number of good-paying jobs in our country:

- Invent new products and thus give new or existing businesses reasons to expand their plants and hire more people to produce these new products
- Invent new services that people want to receive and thus create a new demand for jobs
- Invent new ways to make a profit by recycling existing products
- Invent new industries, for example, the solar, wind, and water power industries that are increasing the demand for such new products such as solar panels and wind turbines and creating new jobs for people who produce and install these products
- Fund research to see how American companies can sell more goods and services to people in other countries
- Expand current services to meet the needs of people and, by so doing, create more jobs in the service sector; for example, expand the child care subsidy, which creates more jobs for child care workers

A second key way to create more decent-paying jobs is to have less tax on corporate earnings and more tax on personal income and wealth. The reason for decreasing corporate taxes is that corporations will have more incentive to remain in the United States, and our country will, in turn, retain more good-paying jobs. So, the way we can restructure our tax system can be related to our desire to create jobs, thus allowing poor minority and poor White people a chance to attain decent-paying jobs.

Build a New Tax System

Another area where our country could create more racial/ethnic equality is the way we tax people (again, recall our discussion in Chapter 3 on decreasing inequality). African Americans, Latino Americans, and Native Americans are disproportionately poor. During the last 30 years of the 20th century, these three groups typically had poverty rates of approximately 30% of their respective populations, whereas Whites had poverty rates of approximately 10%. Given that these racial/ethnic minorities are three times more likely to be poor, we could decrease various taxes on poor people, the near poor, and the working poor. This tax cut would help the poor, near poor, and working poor keep more of their take-home pay and hence help them to get out of poverty. This action would be a step forward for many African American, Native American, and Latino American minorities who are poor, near poor, or working poor.

Another way we could change the tax system so that poor minorities and poor Whites could become more equal to nonpoor Americans would be to change the way we tax people for Social Security. As we discussed in Chapter 4 on poverty, people who have jobs pay 6.2% of their wages in Social Security tax if they earn $118,500 or less per year. However, people who earn more than $118,500 do not pay any Social Security tax on the money they make above this amount. If they make $150,000, $200,000, $300,000, $500,000, $1 million, or even more, they do not pay any more Social Security tax. We could create more racial/ethnic equality by having a progressive Social Security tax through which poor, near-poor, and working-poor Americans pay a lower percentage of their income in Social Security tax (while people with much higher incomes continue to pay into Social Security, rather than stop at $118,500). Because a higher proportion of minorities have poverty and near-poverty incomes, they will have more take-home pay and hence not have to live so close to subsistence. As a result, we, as a country, will have more racial/ethnic equality.

Another way to create more racial/ethnic equality is to provide a larger earned income tax credit, through which the federal government gives additional money to people whose incomes are below the poverty line. We could continue to do this and increase this amount so that poor people who are racial/ethnic minorities, as well as poor Whites, receive enough money to move them above the poverty line. Gans (1995) predicted that our country might need to provide more income for people in this way if our economy does not provide enough jobs for everyone or does not provide enough income from the jobs they do have. Because African Americans, Latino Americans, and Native Americans are disproportionately poor, increasing the earned income tax credit would increase their incomes and help our country to achieve more racial/ethnic equality.

Provide More Social Services

If our country could provide more funding in areas such as (1) Section 8 subsidized housing for the poor or near poor (recall our discussion of Section 8 in Chapter 4 on poverty), (2) more public transportation to allow many of the poor who cannot afford personal transportation to get to jobs (also, recall our discussion on this matter in Chapter 4 on poverty), and (3) more subsidized health care (see Chapter 10 for an extended discussion), these services, along with others, would help minority groups to move in the direction of more racial/ethnic equality. In addition to helping our country achieve more racial and ethnic equality, these kinds of services would greatly help poor White Americans, too.

In other words, any way we can help poor Americans to increase their standard of living, and hence create less inequality in our country overall, will also help minority Americans to have a higher standard of living and thus create more racial/ethnic equality. We all know that increasing funding for these social services will mean that we will need to collect more taxes to pay for these services. And this means that some people will need to be taxed more to pay for these programs. As I stated previously, the least sacrifice would occur if we increased taxes on those with the highest incomes and the most wealth. Those Americans with the highest incomes and the most wealth would still retain much of their incomes and wealth and hence would still enjoy a very high standard of living.

Final Comments

I conclude this chapter with the following thoughts. Our American history has been filled with much prejudice and discrimination, for example, slavery, extreme segregation in all areas of life for African Americans, and the taking away of lands and ways of life of Native Americans and the forced placing of them on reservations that changed their entire way of living. There is still leftover prejudice and discrimination within some Americans even today. Institutional discrimination, such as the policy of local property taxes funding public schools and the policy of "last hired, first fired," continues to work to the disadvantage of minorities. The effects of 200 to 300 years of prejudice and discrimination have resulted in minorities, even to this day, living disproportionately in geographic areas of high unemployment; leading to higher rates of poverty, homelessness, and stress in the family; and living in neighborhoods with higher crime rates.

Although our ancestors socially constructed this racial and ethnic inequality with tragic consequences on minority Americans for hundreds of years, we have begun to move in a more humane, just, and equal direction with such actions as (1) Supreme Court decisions (for example, the 1954 decision that stopped the 100-year tradition of segregated schools where Black and White students attended separate and unequal schools); (2) the passage of civil rights laws that allowed minorities to go to any place serving the public, allowed them to vote and thus have influence in the political process and even to hold public office, and allowed them to buy homes in any neighborhood that they could afford; (3) the development of a greater awareness by Whites and their greater sympathy for the plight of their fellow Americans who were members of various minorities; (4) steps taken by each of us as individual Americans in our day-to-day lives to carry out small acts that create more equality;

and (5) the election of our first African American president when millions of White Americans voted for him. So, even though our ancestors' past actions created long-term consequences that proved to be a daunting challenge, our more recent actions have moved our society in a more humane and just direction. As Dr. King stated on a warm August day in 1963 on the steps of the Lincoln Memorial, we Americans will no longer judge others by the color of their skin but by the content of their character (Washington, 1986, p. 219).

Questions for Discussion

1. Should race/ethnicity continue to be used as one of the variables that undergraduate and graduate schools use in making admission decisions?

2. What variable or variables should be used to decide who gets admitted to a college or a graduate school? For example, should any of the following be considered as a legitimate variable: if one is an athlete, if one is the son or daughter of an alumnus, if one is a male or female, if one plays a band instrument or is a singer, if one is an artist, if one comes from a family whose members have given a lot of money to the school, or if one is a bright student?

3. Where could our country go from here in terms of achieving racial/ethnic equality?

4. Where do you think our country should go in terms of achieving racial/ethnic equality?

5. What do you predict will happen with racial/ethnic inequality during the next 10 to 20 years? What is your reasoning?

6. Which do you think will be better for our country in terms of promoting more unity: Should we promote more interracial marriages, or should we promote more racial/ethnic groups marrying within their respective groups?

7. How would you characterize the current racial/ethnic inequality in our country?

8. Which suggestions in this chapter do you predict will be tried, and which ones will not? Why?

9. What are your predictions for groups such as the Ku Klux Klan that are primarily organized to be prejudiced against and discriminate against racial or ethnic minorities? Do you see these kinds of groups increasing or decreasing in numbers and influence in the United States and why?

10. What are the short-term and long-term consequences on racial and ethnic equality of electing Barack Obama as president of the United States?

6

How Can We Solve the Problem of Gender Inequality?

The year was 1848. The place was the west-central part of the state of New York, in a small town named Seneca Falls. Horse-drawn wagons were approaching the small town from all directions on those warm summer days in the middle of July. There was an air of excitement. A battle was brewing. There were no canons or rifles. It was not that kind of battle. It was a battle that was to begin and would last even to this day. The wagons approaching the small town that day had mainly women in them but some men. They were traveling to a convention that was, eventually, to change the world as humans knew it. The participants were gathering to discuss, decide, proclaim, and attempt to carry out the ideal that women should be equal to men. In fact, they concluded, "We hold these truths to be self-evident that all men and women are created equal" (Evans, 1989, p. 95). Wow! For that time and in those social-historical conditions, that was a radical thing to declare—equality for women? "No way," was probably the knee-jerk response for most Americans at the time. In this small town in west-central New York, what appeared to be a rather insignificant meeting of a relatively few American women and men was, in fact, the beginning of a long and difficult and, at times, seemingly impossible march toward a new way of human beings living with and among each other: women and men seeing each other and treating each other as equals.

More than 165 years have come and gone since that convention. What has happened since then? Well, a lot of things have happened. Some women, such as Elizabeth Cady Stanton and Susan B. Anthony, became famous for their tireless efforts to achieve the goal of what we now call *gender equality*. Many of the early founders of this movement, such as Stanton and Anthony, did not live to see much if any change for women. But over time and with a lot of effort and a lot of patience, change did indeed come. Stanton and Anthony had both passed away by the early 1900s. However, by 1920, the Nineteenth Amendment to the U.S. Constitution was passed, giving women the right to vote. During World War II, in the early 1940s, many women throughout our country worked in all kinds of factory jobs that had previously been filled only by men, showing everyone at the time that women could do these jobs, too—if given a chance. Being able to do all kinds of jobs and earn a good income became attractive for many women. This new situation gave them a sense of accomplishment and a sense of independence. What can we say has happened in the past 50 years or so?

With respect to income equality, women have made substantial gains since the middle of the 20th century. For example, during the early 1960s, "women earned about 59 cents for every dollar men earned" (Armas, 2004, p. A1). By 2007, however, women's median income rose to 81.5% of men's income (Mishel, Bernstein, & Shierholz, 2009, p. 178). In education, in 1970, 43.1% of all college graduates were women (Rosser, 2005, p. 42), but in recent years, women are earning more college degrees than men—59% to 41% (Macionis, 2015, p. 313). For the first time in American history, on January 4, 2007, we had a female Speaker of the House of Representatives, Nancy Pelosi, thus far, the highest office attained in our national government. In the 1990s, for the first time in American history, we had our first female secretary of state, Madeleine Albright, and have since had two more women as secretaries of state, Condoleezza Rice and Hillary Rodham Clinton. In the 1980s, again for the first time in American history, a women, Sandra Day O'Connor, was appointed to the Supreme Court and then in the 1990s, Ruth Bader Ginsburg, who also happened to be Jewish, was appointed to the Supreme Court. In 2009, we confirmed the third woman to the Supreme Court, Sonia Sotomayor, a Latin American woman who grew up in poverty in the projects in New York City. In confirming Judge Sotomayor, Eugene Robinson, columnist for the *Washington Post*, stated that "The nation continues to take major steps toward fulfilling the promise of its noblest ideals" (Robinson, 2009, p. A5).

In many areas of society, women are making progress. There are now many women presidents of colleges and universities in the United States. We have seen a substantial increase in women's participation in sports. In the 1950s, there was little chance for girls to play high school sports—there were few or no teams for high school girls. By the early 21st century, more than 3 million girls were playing high school sports on many different kinds of teams (Eitzen & Sage, 2009, p. 327). Likewise, in intercollegiate sports, compared to the 1950s, there are now many different kinds of teams, thousands of women playing, and thousands of women receiving athletic scholarships to play college sports. For example, one successful girls' high school basketball coach in Indiana reported that she garnered more than $4 million in scholarship money for her former athletes (Cheatham, 2009). This means that compared to the 1950s and 1960s, many young, gifted female athletes are now able to get full athletic scholarships, go to college, become college-educated, and broaden their selection of all kinds of better-paying occupations. Also, in the realm of politics, women have made substantial advances. In the 1960 U.S. Congress, women made up 3.7% of the membership (History, Art & Archives, U.S. House of Representatives, Office of the Historian, Women in Congress, 1917–2006, 2007). Whereas, in the 2015 U.S. Congress, 20% of the U.S. Senate and 19% of the U.S. House of Representatives are women—five times more women than 50 years ago ("Congress by the Numbers," 2015).

As you can see, in a number of different dimensions, our country has been moving in the direction of more gender equality. We have not reached full equality by any means, but the general direction is toward more equality, and, moreover, the pace of the movement has picked up substantially since the 1960s, when the modern women's movement grew much stronger and made the rest of us in society much more aware of the existing inequalities between women and men.

What Can We Do?

If we want our society to move toward the goal of gender equality, through which women have equal opportunities with men; have the ability to get a wide variety of jobs for which they are prepared; have equal chances with men for promotion and upward mobility; and have the chance to gain the same amounts of money, power, and prestige as do men, there are a number of actions we can take. These actions are by no means exhaustive, that is, they do not cover all of the actions that we can take, but they consist of a number of important steps that we can take to move even closer to gender equality. Some examples of the action we can take include the following:

- We can socialize or teach girls and boys to treat others more equally.
- We can subsidize more child care to make sure that women who care for children have a chance to earn decent incomes and have the careers they wish to have.
- We can elect more women to political positions so that their viewpoints and vested interests will be included in the making of laws and carrying out of social policy.

- We can ensure that girls and women have good public schools and colleges and universities to attend so that they will be prepared to earn the money that they want to earn and have the careers that they want to have.
- We can change the way we tax women (and men) of lower incomes so that they have more income with which to live.
- We can provide affordable and good quality health care for women (and men) so they are not forced to spend much, most, or all of their earned income on health care at the expense of paying for food, shelter, and other needs.
- We can provide for more paid maternity leave for mothers so that they can have sufficient time to develop happier and physically and mentally healthy babies.
- We can provide other kinds of social services as needed for girls, women, and mothers to flourish; we can increase the minimum wage so that women (and men) have enough income to live a decent life.
- We can teach boys and men to view girls and women as fellow human beings who are made up of many dimensions of their personalities and are not just seen as sexual objects to be used for boys' and men's sexual satisfaction.
- We can work to decrease violence and abuse against girls and women; and we can pass the Equal Rights Amendment to make sure that all boys and girls and men and women are treated equally and seen as equals.

Socialize Girls and Boys More Similarly

One of the most important actions we can take is to socialize children at home and in school to treat both boys and girls equally. For example, by socialization in the home (with *socialization* being defined as people learning the ways of a society, for example, norms, values, and beliefs), parents can socialize their daughters to play sports, play with mechanical things, play with toys such as bulldozers and trucks along with playing with dolls, read about girls and boys doing a variety of jobs, and watch television shows that portray girls and boys as well as men and women being active, making decisions, and doing a variety of activities. To the degree that parents socialize their children in this manner, children will think that it is natural for both girls and boys to do a wide variety of activities.

Recall in our theory of conflict and social change (see Chapter 1) that we, as humans, socially construct our norms, values, beliefs, and traditions. These social patterns can take on the additional power of religious support such that these humanly constructed social patterns are seen as coming from God or the Gods.

Some of these norms, values, and beliefs have to do with what males and females are expected to do in a particular culture at some point in history. For thousands of years in many cultures, our human ancestors socially constructed the idea that males did certain things and females did certain things. There was some overlap of what males and females did, but, depending on the culture, there was always some variation, and many times a lot of variation, in what males and females did. If a woman or man stepped outside these hundreds of years old or even thousands of years old norms, values, beliefs, and traditions, they could be severely punished by those in power in that respective culture—in all likelihood, the political or religious leaders of that time. The woman or man could even be seen as going against the God or Gods of that particular culture and could face torture, crucifixion, burning at the stake, and eternal damnation. These methods of social control used by those in power in that culture would usually be enough to scare off anyone who would want to change and upset the balance of gender inequality that had been socially constructed and handed down for generations. Hence, the status quo of great gender inequality was maintained for hundreds or even thousands of years.

Probably, for many of you reading this, it is hard to believe, given that you are living in a culture and a time in history where you see change every day and where you see people marching, demonstrating, and standing up for what they believe. However, for most of human history, people could not so easily stand up for what they believed without jeopardizing their lives and the lives of their loved ones. Putting the fear of torture, agonizing death, and eternal damnation in people can usually divert them from trying anything new, such as seeking gender equality. Those in political and religious power have known this for thousands of years and have employed these methods of social control on humans and therefore stopped or greatly slowed all kinds of social change throughout human history, for example, race, gender, age, class, religion, sexual orientation, and so on. Hence, norms, values, beliefs, and traditions of many kinds, such as those pertaining to gender inequality, were perpetuated, for thousands of years. This is indeed hard to believe, but we humans have done this to ourselves in many areas of life—one of which is gender inequality. Hence, for thousands of years, until in the last 50 to 100 years, there has been relatively little social change in so many areas of life. You and I are living at a unique time in history where so much social change is occurring—not so for 99% of our human ancestors who lived before us.

However, since the late 1960s in our country, with the rise of the modern women's movement, we have begun to increase the overlap of what males and females do. As we have gone in this new direction of more gender equality, we have been in the process of changing how we socialize males and females. More and more, we are teaching or socializing males and females to do the same things, such as play sports, get more education, and work in the same kinds of jobs.

Because we are already going in this direction in society, this leads to the following question: How can we teach more parents to socialize their children to create more gender equality? One additional step that our society can take is to develop parenting classes in elementary, middle, and high school that teach students not only how to cook, clean, pay the bills, and feed children nutritious food (for more on this, see Chapter 10 on health care) but also how to give their future children equal opportunities. In other words, a key part of the parenting class would be to teach parents how they can raise girls and boys to have a variety of careers, rather than to teach girls to raise the children, wash the clothes, cook the food, and clean the house and teach boys to seek more education, make the family decisions, and pursue jobs and professional careers.

Schools can do other things to promote more gender equality. For example, teachers can treat boys and girls equally in the classroom. Many teachers are already becoming more aware of how they can treat girls and boys equally. The proportion of times they call on boys or girls, whom they praise and reinforce, and how they praise and reinforce—all of these teacher-controlled actions are ways they can consciously work to make sure they treat both genders equally. Teachers typically have some freedom in picking reading materials for their students. They can intentionally select reading materials that show both men and women being active, making decisions, and working at a variety of jobs, with both men and women occupying leadership positions that create money, power, and prestige. In other words, teachers have the ability to be a major influence in promoting more gender equality.

To teach more gender equality, teachers will need to be trained accordingly. College methods classes in teaching can show future teachers what kinds of methods and techniques they can employ and what kinds of behaviors they can display to promote gender equality. Likewise, college and university professors in courses other than education courses are already becoming more aware of treating both genders equally and are taking steps to promote more gender equality, such as calling on female and male students equally and grading exams blind so that there can be no gender, racial, or other kinds of discrimination. Also, colleges and universities in general are hiring more female professors, promoting them to associate and full professorships, appointing them as department heads and deans of faculties, and choosing them to be college and university presidents.

A very important part of creating an atmosphere of gender equality in elementary, middle, and secondary public school classrooms is to elect members of school boards who are sympathetic to the idea that females and males should be treated equally. Parents' organizations can be influential in helping to elect these kinds of people to school boards and can make their voices heard. The more people in public education (for example, school board members, superintendents, principals, teachers, coaches, counselors) desire to create equal opportunities for female and male students in the public schools, the more likely they will achieve this goal.

In many small communities, one individual (or one group or organization) with strong beliefs about this issue can make this issue visible by making his or her (or its) voice heard at school board meetings and parent–teacher association meetings. In other words, individuals, groups, and organizations can act as external pressures to promote more gender equality in schools. This idea of promoting more gender equality has never been viewed as favorably as it is now. Many Americans are realizing that if we want to fully embrace our cultural value of equal opportunity, we must apply it to both genders.

Otherwise, the custom of "This is the way we have always done things" will continue. The result will be that we will continue to have a social structure that reinforces gender inequality instead of gender equality. The old adage that "the squeaky wheel gets the grease" seems to apply to this situation. If so, this is an instance in which individuals, groups, and organizations can make a difference with respect to this particular social problem in our country.

Subsidize Child Care

To move toward more gender equality in our country, one important thing we could do is to provide child care that is affordable, safe, accessible, and developmental (Crone, 1998). The reason this is important is that, traditionally, women have borne the major responsibility of taking care of children. So, as women get out into the occupational world and seek to have careers in which they have a chance to be as upwardly mobile as men, they will need to have child care available. Otherwise, women with children will continue to be at a disadvantage, compared with men, in developing their careers and being upwardly mobile.

For poor and near-poor mothers who work, not only is finding safe, accessible, and developmental child care important; finding child care that is affordable is a big challenge because paying for child care can take a lot of a mother's wages. One of the key ways for mothers, especially for poor and near-poor working mothers, to have more money is to receive some kind of subsidized child care. Currently, our federal and state governments provide for some subsidized child care, but there are many working mothers who have applied for subsidized child care and have not received any help.[1] This means that many of these working mothers might need to quit their jobs because they cannot afford to pay for child care—sometimes as much as

$200 to $300 per week, which translates into $800 to $1,200 per month, which, in turn, takes up most or all of a woman's income, working at the minimum wage of $7.25 per hour. In other words, if we want poor and near-poor mothers with children to have jobs and survive financially, to get off and stay off of welfare, and to have a chance of being upwardly mobile, we will need to help them with more subsidized child care—especially women who are making at or near the minimum wage. As women can get into the workforce and stay in the workforce, they will make more money and have more chances to be upwardly mobile, thereby creating more gender equality.

This raises the question of how we use our federal tax money and how much tax money we raise. It becomes a political question, but I want you to become aware of this question. Congress and the President decide how much to tax, whom to tax, and how to use the tax revenues the government receives. Should we bring in more or less tax revenue? Should we tax the poor, working, and middle classes more, or should we tax the rich more? Should we spend the tax revenue the government receives more on the military, health care, child care, or some other area? These are the decisions that Congress and the President make—huge, crucial, and extremely important decisions for all of us. So, the question of paying for more subsidized child care must be placed within the larger context of how we will spend our tax money and how much tax money we decide to raise. President Obama, in his State of the Union speech to the Congress in January 2015, urged the congress to provide more subsidized child care (Dionne, 2015). Time will tell what Congress will do in this area of creating more gender equality.

As you recall when we talked about conservatives and liberals in Chapter 2, conservatives tend to want to have less spending on social services and more spending on the military, as the conservative presidencies of Ronald Reagan and George W. Bush demonstrated. Hence, allocating more spending of tax dollars for subsidized child care will probably meet with more resistance from conservatives and with more acceptance from liberals. However, since liberals control the White House and conservatives control both houses of Congress (as of January, 2015), and since Congress decides how much to spend, such as on child care, there may not be more money set aside for subsidized child care for working mothers. We will see in 2015 and 2016 what will actually happen.

Elect More Women to Local, State, and National Public Offices

In all probability, as more women, both liberal and conservative, run for political offices and win local, state, and national offices, their presence in legislative bodies will be a major factor in moving our country toward more gender equality. I include conservative women, especially politically moderate and more educated conservative women, because they will be more insistent that women be paid the same as men for doing the same jobs, that women be given the same opportunities in various careers as men, and that women be given the same chance for upward mobility as men.

If, on the other hand, more extremely conservative women and men, such as fundamentalist Christian conservatives, get elected to political offices, the idea of gender equality in general and of child care subsidies in particular will probably not expand much and could even diminish because more fundamentalist Christian conservatives would be less enthusiastic about women getting a lot of education and having professional careers where they spend much time outside the home and away from the family. For example, a leader of the Mormon church at a 2-day conference in Salt Lake City, Utah, urged that "having women at home remains an essential part of society" and that "he cautioned against blurring feminine and masculine differences" (McCombs, 2013). Typically, fundamentalist Christian conservatives want a woman to be primarily a wife and mother in a more traditional gender role of more gender inequality where the husband and father is the head of the household, the main decision maker, and the one who is the sole or primary job holder and maker of money outside the home. If a woman is successfully socialized in this type of social situation, she is less likely to learn to want to obtain a lot of education, have a professional career, make administrative decisions, and be independent. During the coming years, while wearing your "sociological hat," you might analyze the relationship among fundamentalist conservatives, moderate conservatives, and liberals and how they address the social problem of gender inequality.

Ensure Good-Quality Public Schools

A key factor in achieving more gender equality in our country is to have good-quality public schools. Such schools will allow all Americans to be better prepared to go to college or trade schools and get better-paying jobs. Currently, a number of students go to public schools that do not adequately prepare them to go to college or trade schools. They are more likely to end up taking minimum wage jobs that leave them below the poverty level and with little chance of being upwardly mobile. Women in general and female heads of households in particular who are poor and have little education and few skills are less likely to be upwardly mobile. To work toward more gender equality, we will need to get all children (female and male) better educated so that they can have a better chance for more upward mobility. Consequently, excellent public education and training will not only allow Americans in general to be more upwardly mobile but will also allow more females to develop the educational tools to get ahead, thereby promoting more gender equality (see Chapter 7 on how we can create a better public education system).

Make Women's Labor Indispensable to Society

To move toward more gender equality, it seems imperative, according to Rae Lesser Blumberg (1984), that we take steps to make sure that women become more indispensable to the workplace, to the economy, and to our society in general.[2] As women become indispensable in the workplace, they will be in greater demand as members of the workforce. With this greater demand for their skills, they will have more economic and political power. With more economic and political power, they will have more influence over the creation of laws and social policies that will work to their vested interests. For example, women will have more influence over laws regarding their rights in marriage and divorce, their rights in deciding whether or not they want to have children, and their rights in deciding when they want to have children via laws that allow for the use of the birth control pill and the "morning after" pill, the right to have an abortion, and other kinds of technologies that give women more decision-making power over their lives.

In the past, under the more traditional gender roles by which both men and women were expected to abide, women had little or no power over the conditions under which they could have sexual relations, have children, and the number of children they could have. As women have gained in economic and political power, however, they have been able to influence the passing of laws that implement social policies that work to their vested interests and hence move our society toward more gender equality.

Good-quality education for females and more child care subsidies for working women will be needed as initial steps for making women's labor indispensable to society, giving women more economic and political power and, in turn, helping them to pass laws and create social policies that will create more gender equality.

Change Tax Policies to Promote Gender Equality

As we have discussed previously, if we tax lower-income people less, they will have more money left over from their paychecks to pay their bills, allow their children to go to school to get more education and training, and enable their children to be more upwardly mobile in our society. If we, for instance, lowered the income tax rate on lower-income people and lowered the Social Security tax on them as well (and at the same time raised the income tax rate and Social Security tax on, say the wealthiest 1%, 5%, or 10% of the people in our country), lower-income people in general and lower-income female heads of households in particular would have more income. There would be less income inequality in our country in general, and there would be more income for poorer women in particular, moving lower-income women in the direction of more gender equality.

Provide Affordable Health Care

Providing health care, at first thought, might not appear to be related to achieving more gender equality. On further reflection, however, one realizes that adequate health care can be of great help to women gaining more gender equality (for more details, see Chapter 10 on health care). Currently, the United States is the only industrialized country that does not have a health care system for all of its citizens (Kerbo, 2009, p. 39) although the Affordable Care Act passed by the U.S. Congress and signed into law by President Obama in 2010 is allowing millions of more Americans to finally have health insurance—over 10 million in 2014 and over 11 million in 2015 (O'Donnell and Ungar, 2015, p. 1B; Rudavsky, 2015, p. A9). If we had a health care system for all Americans, this would greatly benefit lower-income female heads of households. Lower-income female heads of households would, in a sense, have higher incomes because they could spend the money they earned from their jobs for other things besides health care. Providing affordable health care, along with lowering income and Social Security taxes on lower-income people, would help female heads of households, especially poor and working-class female heads of households, to move in the direction of more gender equality.

Provide Paid Maternity and Sick Leaves

A key factor related to providing health care that could move our country toward more gender equality is paid maternity and sick leave for women. Currently, American women can take 3 months off from work, but these maternity leaves are unpaid, unlike the policies in many European countries that provide paid maternity leaves.[3] In President Obama's 2015 state of the union speech (Korte, 2015, p. 3B; Marcus, 2015, p. A-15; Groppe & King, 2015, p. A-4), he proposed paid sick leave, which would especially help women of lower to moderate incomes and women who are single heads of households to take time off from work when they are sick or ready to have a baby. Women who are married and their husbands are working and bringing home money to pay the monthly bills are more able to take time off work from work when they are sick or ready to have a baby. However, many American women of moderate and lower incomes cannot afford to take maternity leave that is unpaid. Providing paid maternity leave for women would especially help poor, near-poor, and working-class women who could then take maternity leaves and hence provide better care for their babies. These paid leaves would also mean that our society is considerate of the needs of mothers in the workplace. Mothers returning to work following these paid leaves would be able to retain their incomes and work statuses in their jobs, thereby allowing them to be as upwardly mobile as men. Providing paid maternity and sick leave for women in the United States would move our country in the direction of more gender equality.

Provide Social Services

As a side note, you should be aware that usually when there are more social services for Americans in general, such as Social Security for the elderly, health care for all Americans, child care subsidies for poor and working families, good-quality public education for all children, and paid maternity and sick leave for all Americans, these social services, taken together, mean that there will also be more services for women. As women have access to more social services, our country will move in the direction of more gender equality.

Increase the Minimum Wage

Another way for women to move toward more gender equality is for the United States to increase the minimum wage. Many mothers in the United States work full time for $7.25 per hour and are still thousands of dollars below the poverty line (recall that the poverty line for a family of four in 2015 is $23,850 while the minimum wage of $7.25 per hour will mean that she will make $15,080 in a year if she works 40 hours per week for all 52 weeks in the year, resulting in her making $8,770 less than the poverty line). So, as we have noted before, people in the United States, women in particular, can work full time all year round and still be thousands of dollars below the poverty line. In other words, being a full-time worker in the United States does not mean that the worker will be out of poverty. Christopher (2004) noted, specifically with respect to women,

> When working full time (at least 35 hours per week), about one-third of U.S. women and more than 40 percent of U.S. single mothers earn wages too low to

free their families from poverty. In other Western nations, particularly Sweden, The Netherlands, and the United Kingdom, working full time pulls the vast majority of women (including single mothers) and their families above the poverty line. (p. 108)

As you can see, raising the minimum wage in our country would be especially helpful for one third of all the working women in our country. With such an increase in the minimum wage, these women might earn at least poverty-level wages instead of wages that are now only 63% of the federal poverty level ($15,080/$23,850 = 63%). Yes, this may result in some job losses if companies are not able to increase wages for all employees, but based on the 1990 to 1991 and the 1996 to 1997 minimum wage increases, the job losses would not be "significant" (Christopher, 2004, p. 111).[4] If we want one third of all working women in the United States to move toward more gender equality, we can do this by increasing the minimum wage.

Decrease Violence Against and Abuse of Women

Historically, the use of violence against women in the home has been a barrier that has kept women "in their place" and hence has perpetuated gender inequality. As our society can decrease violence against women in the home, these women will be more comfortable in speaking up for what they think is right and speaking up for their vested interests. A consequence of women being able to speak up more will be to move our society toward gender equality.

Ways to decrease violence in the home are varied. Socialization in public schools via parenting classes, where boys are socialized to be husbands and fathers who use discussion and negotiation rather than physical force as methods of interacting with wives and children, is one way (for more details, see Chapter 11 on families). Another way to decrease violence against women is to make safe houses and shelters available for women and children to go to whenever violence occurs in the home. Also, the option for women to take their violent husbands to court to get restraining orders against them and to get their violent husbands to serve jail time are other methods that can serve to deter violence against women. Also, as women take more positions within the criminal justice system (for example, police officers, probation officers, prosecuting attorneys, defense attorneys, and judges), women will have more understanding and support from the criminal justice system than they did in the past when men made up the entire criminal justice process and were not as understanding or supportive. This social change will promote more gender equality in our society.

Teach Men to View Women in Multidimensional Ways

Likewise, our country can change the way we socialize boys and men. Instead of women being portrayed as sex objects in ads, movies, and television shows viewed by boys and men, women can be seen in other ways. Currently, we are somewhat conscious of working toward the goal of seeing and treating women in other ways. However, a quick look at current ads on television, in magazines, along highways, and on the Internet suggests that we have a long way to go. As we socialize boys and men to treat girls and women in what we might call *multidimensional* ways (that is, boys and men are taught to see girls and women in many different ways, rather than seeing them only as sex objects), we should see a subsequent decline in rape and sexual harassment against women. As teachers treat both boys and girls as multidimensional individuals, as schoolbooks portray boys and girls in multidimensional ways, and as parenting classes teach future husbands and wives to treat each other as multidimensional persons, we will begin to create new generations of males and females who see each other in many ways and not just in a one-dimensional, sexual object type of way. During the last 30 years of the 20th century, we began to be conscious that males in our culture were being taught to see women mainly as sex objects, and we began to change this perception, but we will need to continue to work on this during the 21st century as we move toward more gender equality.

We will face a number of dilemmas as we move toward a society in which women are seen in a multitude of ways. Do we ban pornography—in other words, censor what adults can watch? Do we ban ads that use sexual attraction of males toward females as a way to sell products? Do we ban women from dressing scantily and showing parts of their breasts, buttocks, and midsections? Do we socialize women not to flirt with men? Do we socialize boys and men to get them not to think sexual thoughts so often? To what degree can and should we socialize sexual thoughts out of males, and to what degree should we confront biological limits of suppressing sexual desire in men? There is a need for further inquiry, research, and discussion with regard to these questions.

Currently, our culture is sending mixed messages. On the one hand, we are trying to move toward seeing women in multidimensional ways. On the other hand, we are still putting emphasis on women as sex objects in ads, television shows, movies, and online. So, as a society, we still have a way to go before we have solved this aspect of gender inequality.

Pass the Equal Rights Amendment

Another way we can move toward gender equality in our country is to pass the Equal Rights Amendment, which states that people cannot be discriminated against based on their gender. Congress passed this amendment during the early 1970s, but not enough state legislatures ratified it. A number of people might question whether an amendment to the U.S. Constitution is needed when we already have a number of laws and U.S. Supreme Court decisions favoring more equality for women, including the Nineteenth Amendment to the U.S. Constitution in 1920, through which women received the right to vote (Eitzen & Zinn, 2003, p. 262); the Equal Pay Act of 1963, which prohibited employers from paying women less than what men are paid for doing the same job; the Civil Rights Act of 1964, which "banned racial, ethnic, and sexual discrimination in employment and union membership" (Farley, 1995, p. 306) and "prohibited discrimination by privately owned businesses providing public accommodations" (p. 306); Title IX Educational Amendments Act of 1972, which required "schools that receive federal funds to provide equal opportunities for males and females" (Eitzen & Sage, 2009, p. 327); and the 1973 decision of the U.S. Supreme Court in *Roe v. Wade,* which allowed women to decide whether or not to have abortions. So, why have a constitutional amendment when so many of the rights of women already seem to be covered?

There are two reasons. One is that there still might be areas of discrimination that the existing laws do not cover. An Equal Rights Amendment to the Constitution would give women the legal right to go to the courts to seek a redress of grievances if there was unequal treatment based on a person's gender. A second reason is the symbolic value that such an amendment would give. That is, such an amendment would state, in a very clear and visible way, that our country treats women and men equally.

Concluding Thoughts

A concluding note is that as more women are given equal opportunity, our society will receive more of the fruits of the contributions of women. As a result, our society will become more efficient as more Americans are able to live up to their potential. Adding each individual contribution to the whole of the society will make for much more contribution to society.

Yes, the level of competition will rise as more women get a chance to "throw their hats into the ring." And yes, a number of men will lose out to women who are better qualified and have higher skill levels. These consequences will occur whenever a society gives equal opportunity to a new group of people, as we have seen, for example, in the case of African Americans in sports. Such is the nature of a society where everyone is given equal opportunity and people are allowed to compete on a level playing field.

There is a good chance that many, if not all, of the suggestions I have discussed for creating more gender equality will eventually be implemented. The reason I say this is that since the 1950s, with the onset of the civil rights movement by African Americans followed by social movements of women, Native Americans, gay and lesbian Americans, disabled Americans, and elderly Americans, there has increasingly become in our society a spirit and a consciousness of moving toward more equality along a number of dimensions of life. It seems that we have created a momentum that will continue to move our society in the general direction of overall equality and in the specific direction of gender equality.

There is a statue in the Capitol building in Washington, DC, that has three figures. Two of the figures are of Elizabeth Cady Stanton and Susan B. Anthony. The third figure has yet to be sculpted—that of the first woman President of the United States. In recent years, we have had our first African American president. You and I are living in a historical time in human history. Quite possibly, the third figure of that statue will be sculpted and take human form, in all likelihood, in the not too distant future.

Questions for Discussion

1. In addition to what we discussed in this chapter, what else can we do to move toward more gender equality in our country?

2. What do you predict for the next 5, 10, and 20 years with respect to gender inequality in our country? What is your reasoning?

3. What will be key barriers in our moving toward more gender equality?

4. What steps can we take to overcome these barriers?

5. What are various indicators that favor our country moving toward more gender equality?

6. Will we have a woman as president? If so, when? What is your reasoning?

7. Should women serve on the front lines in battle in the military? What is your reasoning?

8. If we had an amendment to the U.S. Constitution concerning gender equality, what might be some consequences of this amendment?

9. What do you predict will be done at the world level with respect to gender equality in the next 5, 10, or 25 years?

10. What do you think should be done at the world level concerning gender equality?

7

How Can We Solve the Problem of Unequal Education?

A number of elementary, middle, and high school students in our country go to very good schools. They have well-qualified teachers, decent-sized classes, good facilities, and a safe environment. They are getting the kind of educational experience that we hope all children in the United States get. However, as you no doubt know, many children in our country do not go to these kinds of good schools. Kozol (1991), in his book *Savage Inequalities,* documented some of the deplorable conditions that a number of our American children must endure in school. Moreover, with the economy being in bad shape in the early 2000s until around 2014 and with the local, state, and national governments having difficulty in paying their debts, money for schools is tighter. Once money gets tighter for schools, class sizes tend to go up, positions such as counselors and teacher assistants can be cut, art and music programs can be cut, teacher salaries rise more slowly, and school facilities are not as well-maintained or upgraded (Rodriguez, 2003).

In this chapter we discuss some things we could do to make excellent schools available for all American children. Given that public educational systems depend on the tax money coming in to local communities and to the entire state, how much tax revenue can be collected has a major influence on how much we can improve our public schools. Governments, local and state especially with respect to public education, have to stretch the tax revenues they receive from citizens of a particular community or state in many ways. Local and state governments have to pay for streets and highways; water and sewage systems; police and fire protection; public health facilities and personnel; local and state parks and the people who work at these parks and protect these parks; and—yes, pay for public elementary, middle school, high school, and universities and the facilities and people (teachers, professors, counselors, teacher aides, secretaries, principals, superintendents, custodians, bus drivers, and nurses) who work in these educational facilities. So, local and state governments are constantly struggling to decide how to pay for all of these services and not slight any service and give each service what is needed to satisfactorily carry out its respective function. Probably, if we could ask local and state governmental officials what is the toughest aspect of their jobs, they most likely would say how to decide how much to give to each of these services with a limited amount of tax revenue to spend. Citizens want good roads, good schools, good police and fire protection, good water and sewage systems. But local and state governments typically do not have enough money collected from taxes to do everything well. So, public school systems must be placed within the larger context of one of a number of services that local and state governments provide. With this in mind, let us discuss some specific actions we can take to improve our public education system in our country.

What Can We Do?

Hire Certified Teachers

We can hire only teachers who are certified to teach in the subject areas they are hired to teach. Currently, school systems, especially when they do not have enough money, hire people who are not certified to teach the subjects areas they are assigned to teach. As a result, students who have these teachers are at a disadvantage compared with those who are taught by certified teachers.[1] Also, at times, even certified teachers are required to teach in areas in which they are not certified. This hurts teachers' morale and their enthusiasm.[2] They spend years preparing to teach one subject but end up teaching another subject. So, hiring teachers who are not certified or placing teachers in areas other than their certification hurts both students and teachers.[3]

To make available more qualified teachers who are certified in specific areas to teach and to have enough of these teachers for all public schools from Grade 1 through Grade 12, we will need to carry out two measures. First, we will need to have more stringent requirements as to who can teach. Schools cannot always find certified teachers to fill certain positions, so they temporarily "fill in" with people who are not certified to teach the subjects they were hired to teach. They may be conscientious, smart, and good people, but they do not know the subject matter in much depth (if in any depth at all). For example, a school might need a certified teacher in biology. However, the school cannot find such a teacher, so it does the best it can and hires, for example, a college graduate who has never taken any biology courses in college or maybe has taken one or two such courses. Even when this person does the best he or she can, this teacher not only does not have the depth of understanding of the subject matter but also does not have the love of the subject matter. Furthermore, this person has no grounding in teaching methods. In other words, these teachers do not have the depth for the subject matter, the love for the subject matter, and the methods of how to teach the subject matter. The students who have these kinds of teachers are at a considerable disadvantage in their education and hence in their future chances for upward mobility compared with students who have well-qualified teachers.

One way to get more certified teachers is to pay teachers more money. Many people who might be excellent teachers will not even consider going into the field of teaching because it pays lower salaries than what they can earn in other occupations. Higher pay will attract more people into teaching and make available more certified teachers for our public schools.[4] Once we get more certified teachers, we can fill our classrooms with well-qualified teachers and greatly improve our educational system.

Reduce Class Sizes

A second measure we can take is to reduce class size.[5] When classes are smaller, the teacher can give more individual attention to each student. This tends to result in better test scores.[6] Research suggests that smaller classes help students not only to complete high school but also to graduate on time and graduate with honors.[7] The National Education Association (NEA), a group that promotes better public education for American children, supports a class size of 15 students in regular programs and an even smaller class size in programs for students with exceptional needs. This makes sense in that teachers with small classes can spend more time and energy helping each child to succeed. Smaller classes also increase safety, discipline, and order in the classroom. When qualified teachers teach smaller classes, kids learn more. The research strongly indicates that smaller class sizes work to increase student achievement.[8]

A low teacher-to-student ratio is especially important to kids who have not had a chance to get much help from their low-income families. Typically, they have not had the chance to travel; visit museums; have books, magazines, and newspapers around the house to read and stimulate their imagination; own and use a computer; or learn about college from their parents because their parents are less likely to have had a college education.[9] In all likelihood, low-income children, more than middle- and upper-middle-class children, will therefore need more personal attention in the classroom to make up for what they do not get from their family environments.

Provide Up-to-Date Facilities and Equipment

To have excellent public schools, we need to have good, up-to-date facilities and equipment.[10] Children who study using out-of-date facilities and equipment are at a disadvantage in this increasingly technologically oriented society.[11] Different parts of the school, such as restrooms and labs, may be run-down and not work. Paint may be falling off the walls, and the school might not be a place where students (and teachers) are proud to attend. Students might not have running tracks, football fields, gyms, choir rooms, or band rooms where they can practice or play. They might not have microscopes, band instruments, band uniforms, computers, textbooks, chalk, and paper, all of which are needed in the contemporary school to give students a full education.[12] Jonathan Kozol observed the following about the schools in East St. Louis: In the boys' bathroom, four of the six toilets did not work, there was no toilet paper, and there were no toilet seats (Kozol, 1991, p. 34); a history teacher had 110 students but only 26 textbooks (p. 35); there were windows without glass, and there were dark hallways because there were no light bulbs in the sockets or light bulbs had burned out (p. 36); certain classrooms were so cold in the winter that students needed to wear their coats (p. 37); the physics lab had no equipment (p. 30); the high school had no videocassette recorders (VCRs) (p. 29); the biology lab had no lab tables (p. 28); there were few dissecting kits, and even the ones available were incomplete (p. 28); chemical supplies, even in a city that had two chemical plants, were scarce (p. 28); "I need more microscopes," said a teacher (p. 28); and so on.

With such deplorable facilities and equipment, it comes as no surprise that the children in the East St. Louis schools were not well prepared to get jobs or go to vocational school or college. These public schools, consequently, did not prepare the children to become independent adults. It therefore seems likely that these children (and other children in similar social conditions throughout the United States) will have higher rates of unemployment, poverty, homelessness, and crime. Hence, the social structure of inadequate schools will lead to other unfortunate consequences for those neighborhoods and cities.

This situation is a good example of the application of the concept, *sociological imagination,* where the larger social structure in which people live causes them to have personal troubles (Mills, 1959). For example, students going to inadequate public schools (larger social structure) will have more personal troubles (having fewer choices of jobs, being less qualified to attend vocational school or college, which, in turn, can lead to lower-skilled jobs and temporary jobs and, hence, lower income and more unemployment, which could potentially lead to committing more crime and spending more time in prison). Once we can begin to connect the larger social structure (public school systems) with the personal troubles of people (lower-income jobs, more unemployment, and even more crime), we can begin to see how the larger social structure can play a significant role in the lives of individuals— many times without these individuals or the rest of society comprehending the effects of the social structure on the individual. So, if we, as a society want to decrease these personal troubles in people's lives (see Chapters 8 and 9 on crime and drugs, respectively), one important step we can take is to create better public schools for all students so that they can get better jobs, make higher incomes, and live more independent lives.

Build Smaller and Safer Schools

To have excellent public schools means that the schools are safe to attend.[13] Part of having safer schools is having more teachers, as discussed previously. Also, part of having safer schools is having smaller schools[14] so that each student is seen as "somebody" who is more likely to feel integrated within the school.[15] With fewer students, a higher percentage of people at the school can be on teams, in choirs, in bands, in clubs, and so on. A smaller school means that a higher percentage of students are able to find their "niche" within the daily offerings of activities that the school has to offer. As a higher percentage of students become more involved and committed to the school via its various activities, there will be less likelihood of these students losing interest in school, becoming indifferent to the school, and even poten-tially gravitating toward illegitimate activities both in and out of school. So, having smaller schools and various activities available to students so that they feel that they are a part of the school will keep them more engaged in school and, in turn, prepare them for vocational school or college and for a better life in the future.

Problems That Prevent Us From Having Excellent Public Schools

To have smaller schools, we will need to build more schools. And, of course, we will need to spend more money on education. Most Americans would like to have all American children have a chance to get a good public education.

Yet, at the same time, many of these Americans feel as though they are taxed enough and therefore do not want to create a better public education system if it means paying more taxes. Moreover, because much public education (Grades 1–12) is paid for by local property taxes, there is little desire by many people to pay more property tax to pay for better public schools when they already pay many other taxes (for example, federal income tax, state income tax, and state sales tax).

Another problem is that some people choose to pay extra money to send their children to private-religious or private-secular schools. They do not want to pay any more property tax that goes to pay for public schools when they send their kids to these private schools. Their thinking may be that so long as their own children are taken care of educationally, why should they need to pay for the education of other people's children?

A third barrier to creating excellent public schools is that the federal government and state governments are currently having financial problems. After running surpluses during the late 1990s, in 2009, during the depth of the recent recession, the federal government spent more than it received in tax money (called *deficit spending*). Moreover, 44 of the 50 states were having major financial problems (National Education Association [NEA], n.d.b).

So, as we discussed at the beginning of this chapter, good public schools depend on more money being invested in them.

Tax Money for Schools

To have good-quality schools, we will need to invest more money in our public schools to get more certified teachers, have smaller classes, and have smaller schools that are well maintained and have the needed facilities and equipment. It follows that we need to have more of our tax revenues funneled toward our public schools. Fruchter (1998) asserted that to achieve this, we need to reform "the way we fund public education" (pp. 15–16).

Instead of placing this added tax burden on property owners, a more humane and realistic way to fund our schools could be to create a more progressive federal income tax, whereby the wealthiest Americans, say the wealthiest 1% to 10%, pay more federal income tax. Because the wealthiest 1% of the people in our country have 34.3% of all the wealth, and the wealthiest 10% of Americans control 71.2% of all the wealth (Kerbo, 2012, p. 35), these wealthy Americans are the most able to pay more tax and still live an outstanding lifestyle.

The tax money that is collected by the federal government from the wealthiest 10% of people in our country could be distributed to local school districts with the stipulation that the administrators of these local districts use this money in four areas:

1. To hire only certified teachers to teach in their certified areas.

2. To hire more certified teachers to reduce class size to 15 or fewer students in low-income school districts.

3. To build and maintain facilities such as band rooms, choir rooms, libraries, auditoriums, gyms, tracks, and fields and also buy the needed equipment such as microscopes, band instruments, choir music, pianos and organs, computers, and books.

4. To build more schools in order to create smaller schools so that a larger percentage of the student body can participate in various activities and thus feel like they are a part of their school community.

By spending tax money in these kinds of ways, we can more fully ensure that all school districts will create good-quality schools.

Local school districts and local school superintendents, school boards, principals, teachers, and citizens of the district will still decide whom to hire as certified teachers, where to put kids and in what classes, what classes are required, what overall curricula are created, what books to order, how to build the facilities and what the facilities will look like, when the school year starts and ends, what holidays will be taken, and what specific equipment to buy. In other words, local people will still have much freedom to decide how they want to run their schools, as long as they hire certified teachers, hire more certified teachers, have smaller class sizes, have smaller schools, and have well-maintained schools with up-to-date equipment.

Positive Consequences

If and when we create a better school system in our country, numerous positive consequences will follow. When we can provide an excellent education for all American children, these children will be more prepared to be upwardly mobile in our society. As young people are more prepared to be upwardly mobile, they will experience less frustration in a society that exhorts them to be upwardly mobile and yet does not give them the means to be so.[16] Consequently, with a good education, young people will have a chance to move up in the society using legitimate means.

When young people can be upwardly mobile via legitimate means, they are less likely to resort to illegitimate means. Merton (1968) discussed this process in his article titled "Social Structure and Anomie." Merton noted that if a social structure is created that blocks opportunities and does not allow people to be upwardly mobile through legitimate means, people are more likely to use illegitimate means such as robbery, burglary, selling illegal drugs, and prostitution to earn money.

As we give all young Americans a good education, we will give them the capacity to be upwardly mobile through legitimate means. As a result, we should see fewer people resorting to illegal means to get ahead and thus should see a decrease in certain kinds of crime (the focus of Chapter 8). We should also see decreases in the costs related to crime, such as the need for fewer police, less prison space, less prison personnel to look after prisoners, and less cost in court time. We can then reallocate the tax money that went to pay for more police, prisons, and prison personnel to other purposes.

Moreover, if students who are poor receive a good education, they have more of a chance to climb out of poverty. The result will be that we, as a country, will not need to spend as much tax money on poverty programs (for example, food stamps, welfare, and Medicaid) to help people survive, because they will be able to survive on their own. Also, poor and near-poor children will have more hope that they, too, can get ahead in this world. They will go to safer schools, and this will lead to a more fulfilling educational experience for them as well as be a great relief to their parents.

Another positive consequence of providing good schools for all American children will be that the reality of giving people an opportunity will come closer to matching our ideology that says that every American should have an equal opportunity to succeed. Some people think that we already have equal opportunity in our country for all young Americans. However, we know that a person's race, social class, sexual orientation, and/or gender still play a role—sometimes a major role—in who has more or less opportunity in our country. With a good-quality education for all American children, regardless of their race, class, sexual orientation, or gender, our country will not only come closer to living up to its ideology of providing equal opportunity for all Americans but will also diminish the influence of these variables on who does and does not get ahead in the United States.

What Will Not Work If We Want Excellent Public Education: The Voucher System

Former President George W. Bush's voucher plan will not create good-quality public education for all American children. With the voucher plan, a child can go to a public school outside of his or her community or to a private school, and that school will receive a voucher—a certain amount of money (for example, $3,000)—to pay for that child coming to the school.[17] The intent is to give children, especially poor children going to deplorable public schools, the chance to go to good private secular or religious schools.

There are specific problems and more general problems with this policy. As for the specific problems, just because a poor child may want to go to a school outside of his or her district does not mean that the other school wants that child as a student or has room for that child even if the school officials are willing to accept that child and other children like him or her.[18] Ask yourself this question: If you were a school official and you were faced with 10, 20, 50, 100, or 200 children who wanted to come to your school as new students, and they were poor and minority children who were behind the current students in your school in reading, writing, and math abilities and therefore needed considerable attention by your current teachers and staff to help these children catch up, and your school was a predominantly middle-class or upper-middle-class school with nearly all White kids who had parents who paid extra money to have their children go to a high quality private school, would you want to take on more students who are likely to be ill prepared and from a lower social class?

Probably, a number of you would ideally say "Yes" in that you believe it is the right thing to do to give all kids a chance at a good education. But the reality is that this situation creates a disincentive for many school officials to accept more children if a school is already filled or nearly filled and if the children applying to the school will require disproportionately more attention from the current teaching staff.[19] This means that the current teaching staff, facilities, and equipment will be stretched further. Also, what about the potential problem of racism and problems between White kids and Black kids in the school? And what about the potential problem of different social classes not understanding or accepting each other?

These are questions that will be considered by many private school officials at the school to which low-income kids are applying. Ideally, private schools using vouchers will accept all children—including low-income children, minority children, and ill-prepared children. In reality, I predict that a number of school officials, once they consider the consequences of accepting these new students, will turn down a number of them. As a result, this policy of a voucher system will help some low-income kids but will leave out most of them.[20] I predict that most low-income students will continue to go to the deplorable public schools they are currently attending and that our public education system will not change much. Most of these low-income kids will still go to inadequate public schools, get a poor-quality education, will not have the chance to be upwardly mobile in their lives, and will instead end up working part time or full time at minimum wage jobs with few or no health or retirement benefits or using illegitimate means to make money and therefore having a greater proclivity of ending up in jail or prison.

With respect to the voucher system, there is also the problem of using the taxpayers' money to subsidize children who go to private religious schools.[21] A number of people in our country are upset about this.[22] Because 85% of the private schools in our country are religious, there is a high probability that when a child uses a voucher (public tax payer money) to attend a private school, the school will be of a certain religious persuasion. Hence, we will use public funds to support private and religious education—a potential problem in keeping the church and the state separate (NEA, n.d.e).

In a more general way, the voucher system will not solve many problems of the public school system. First, it does not do anything about dealing with the current problem of making sure that public schools have only certified teachers who teach in their certified areas. Second, the voucher system does not do anything about hiring more certified teachers in schools located in low-income neighborhoods that need these kinds of teachers even more. Third, the voucher system does not do anything about directing more tax money into inadequate public schools; rather, it directs less public tax money to these schools, making them potentially even more inadequate. Fourth, the voucher system does not do anything about providing low-income public schools with excellent facilities and equipment to allow certified teachers to teach well. Fifth, the voucher system does not do anything about creating smaller public schools so that a higher percentage of kids in a given school have a chance to take part in choirs, bands, clubs, and teams and therefore will feel more a part of their schools, thereby decreasing the chances of their resorting to illegitimate activities. None of these five conditions is changed by using the voucher system. We still have many poor students taught by uncertified teachers in public schools that have poor facilities and inadequate equipment, and we still have public schools that are large, impersonal, and unsafe. In other words, the voucher system of using public tax payer money for private and mainly private religious schools does not solve the problems of our public schools. In order to solve the problems of our public schools, we need to invest more public tax payer money into public schools. Otherwise, the public school systems of our country, who serve most of the students of our country, will not change the quality of education. So, the voucher system will help some poor students, but it will not help most poor students who will still remain in the public school system.

Moreover, the voucher system can be mainly a subsidy for middle-class and upper-middle-class parents who send their children to private schools.[23] For example, instead of parents paying $7,000 to send their child to a private school, the voucher could knock $3,000 off the cost and allow the parents to pay only $4,000. The intent of the voucher plan is not to subsidize middle-class and upper-middle class parents to send their children to private schools, but to a degree that is probably what will happen. Because the voucher system might enable wealthier children to go to private schools at less expense to their parents, the result could be the unintended consequence of segregating lower-class children from middle-class and upper-middle-class children even more and segregating White children from Black children more.

As for how the American public feels about the voucher system, "Most Americans oppose voucher programs" (Carroll, 2003, p. A9). Based on a national poll by Phi Delta Kappa International and Gallup, Carroll reported, "Support for a program that allows students and parents to choose a private school to attend at public expense dropped to 38 percent from 46 percent" (p. A9).

All in all, the voucher system will help some kids get a better education, but it will not help many students who really need the help and will therefore not create a good public education system for all students in our country. As Gutmann (2000) noted,

> There is no evidence that vouchers will produce good schools for the vast majority of children who need them most. This democracy—if it is to be worthy of the name—needs public action to create the schools that all our children deserve. (p. 24)

Questions for Discussion

1. How important is it that we have certified teachers teaching in our schools?

2. How important is it to increase salaries for teachers to get more quality people to go into teaching? How could or should we pay for higher salaries?

3. What do you predict will happen with unequal public education in our country during the next 5, 10, and 20 years? Will it become more equal, stay about as it is now, or become more unequal? What is your reasoning?

4. If we had a national goal of making all public education of good quality, where could and should we get the money to pay for this?

5. How can the federal government help?

6. Should the federal government help?

7. What do you think should be the responsibility of local school districts and school boards in comparison with that of state governments and the federal government regarding education?

8. How would you improve our public schools?

9. How do you think we should pay for improving our schools?

10. What might be a totally new way of looking at education that could provide an excellent education for all students in the United States?

8

How Can We Solve the Problem of Crime?

You may think as we begin this chapter that I am going to suggest building more prisons and adding more police, investigators, judges, courtrooms, and probation and parole officers. No, I do not go in that direction to recommend ways to decrease the crime we have in our country. I go in another direction of ways to decrease our crime, and I will say more about this shortly.

You also may think that I am going to address all crime. No, I do not do that. I focus on the crimes that have social causes, versus psychological causes, and that are related to the influences of poverty, inequality, and racial/ethnic and gender discrimination (refer back to Chapters 3 through 6 as a lead-in to helping us understand the kinds of crime I address). In other words, how might the existence and perpetuation of poverty, inequality, and racial/ethnic and gender discrimination lead to certain kinds of crimes, and what can we do about these crimes?

I focus on crimes that are more likely to occur in our society because of no opportunities, few opportunities, or blocked opportunities in our social structure. By this, I mean that there is something about the social structure of our society, either now or in the past, that has stopped or greatly hindered people from using legal means of surviving, making a living, and getting ahead in American society. For example, from the early 1600s to the mid-1800s, our country had slavery. This was a social structure, that is, a social pattern of laws, informal norms, beliefs, values, statuses, and roles that were interrelated and persisted over time. As I emphasized in the theory of conflict and social change in Chapter 1, humans create social structures. And yet, as Marx pointed out, these social structures can control humans to such an extent that humans are not able to survive, make a living, or get ahead (Marx, [1844]1964, [1845]1967; Marx & Engels, [1848]1992).

In the social structure of slavery, for example, African Americans, no matter how smart, creative, and hardworking they might have been in 1750 on a plantation in South Carolina, had few or no opportunities to own their own farms, move about freely from town to town, vote, hold office, have control over their own families, set up businesses, go to school, go to college, and so on. In other words, the social structure of slavery did not allow African Americans to control their own lives. Rather, their lives were largely, if not totally, controlled by the social structure of slavery. The social structure of slavery is a good example of what Durkheim ([1895]1966) was talking about when he said that social phenomena are external to us and yet coercive upon us. That is, many times these humanly created social phenomena, such as the social structure of slavery, influence us more than we realize.

Because of the great prejudice and discrimination toward African Americans as a result of slavery for 200 years (from the 1660s through the 1860s) and great prejudice and discrimination as a result of legalized segregation and informal segregation for another 100 years (from the 1860s through the 1960s), African Americans, compared with White Americans, generally speaking, could not get ahead, had few choices in life, and could not live life the way they wanted to live because their destiny was largely, if not totally, determined by the existing external and coercive social structure.[1] To be disadvantaged in life for over 300 years or 10 generations of family life has been a travesty for an entire group of people in our country.

The example of slavery and African Americans is just one example of a social structure that has given little or no opportunities to a group of people. Another example is the placing of Native Americans on reservations. They were restricted in where they could live and how they could make a living. For example, many Native American nations had been hunters and gatherers, agriculturalists, or some combination of the two.[2] In a number of instances, they were moved from areas where there were plenty of animals to hunt, berries to pick, and fertile land to farm to areas that had few animals, few berries, and less fertile land. As a result of this forced migration, they were placed in physical environments that provided them with fewer means of survival.[3] This, too, has been a travesty for another group of people in our country.

If we want to decrease the kind of crime that is caused by social structures that limit opportunities for people, we will need to give people more opportunities, specifically more *legal* opportunities. Otherwise, just to survive, people may, for example, rob other people, burglarize houses, steal cars, sell illegal drugs, engage in prostitution, become pimps, or use violence to protect their territory in a neighborhood to continue to make money selling drugs. These kinds of crimes are more likely to occur when people have few legal opportunities to get ahead.

A good theoretical analysis of these types of crimes can be found in Merton's (1968) article, "Social Structure and Anomie" (recall our theoretical discussion in Chapter 1).[4] In a nutshell, Merton stated that when people have legitimate opportunities to get ahead, most of them will use these legal channels to get ahead. However, if we create social structures, such as the social structure of racial/ethnic prejudice and discrimination, that do not allow people to get ahead; the social structure of poverty, in which people live in neighborhoods of high unemployment and hence have few legitimate means to get ahead; and the social structure of deplorable schools, which greatly limits what people can do, would like to do, and are capable of doing, we should predict more crime—more stealing (cars and other goods), burglaries, robberies, selling of drugs, prostitution, and so on.

However, if we give people more legal opportunities to earn money, they are less likely to resort to illegal means to get ahead, and hence we should see a decrease in crime. These thoughts raise the following question: How can we give people more legal opportunities? Answering this question leads us to ideas about what we can do to solve or greatly decrease the kinds of crimes based on few or no opportunities.

What Can We Do?

There are a number of actions we can take to change our social structure in order to give people more legal opportunities and, in doing so, decrease crime. For example, we can improve public education to create more legal opportunities, we can change social policies to create more job opportunities, we can provide more unemployment compensation, job training, and job placement, we can improve trade schools, we can decrease inequality and increase the standard of living, we can provide health care to more Americans, we can register and license all guns in the United States, we can invest in what I call "the front-end" of preventing crime (which I will explain later), we can provide more job training and job placement opportunities to prisoners serving their time in prison and then are subsequently released as citizens to become legal wage earners, and we can place increasing emphasis on "the front-end" measures of preventing crime. In the following paragraphs, I discuss these steps in more detail.

Improve Public Education and Create More Opportunities

One step that we can take to give people more legal opportunities is to give them an excellent public education from Grade 1 through Grade 12. In Chapter 7 on unequal public education, I stated that we could have a much better public education system by hiring only certified teachers and having them teach in their certified areas, hiring more teachers so that class sizes are smaller (especially for low-income children who need extra help because they are less likely to get help from home compared with middle- and upper-middle class families), creating smaller schools so that a higher proportion of students in the school can take part in extracurricular activities and therefore feel that they are a part of the school community, making sure that we have well-maintained schools, and making sure that the teachers and students have the equipment—such as enough chalk, pencils, paper, textbooks, microscopes, computers, and band instruments—they need to do a good job. As more children get to attend good-quality public schools and get a firm academic grounding during the first 12 years of their educational careers, they will be more prepared to pursue legal opportunities and less likely to resort to illegal opportunities, thereby reducing crime.

Change Social Policies and Taxes to Create Jobs and Opportunities

If people have more legal opportunities, they have a greater chance of securing legal jobs and therefore are less likely to feel the need to resort to crime to survive. Consequently, if we want to decrease crime, we will need to provide more legal jobs for people. As I mentioned in Chapter 4 on poverty, during the first few years of the 21st century, the United States had an overall unemployment rate of between 5% and 6%. But by 2009, given the recession, the overall unemployment rate rose to 10%, meaning 1 out of 10 Americans were out of work and were trying to find jobs (U.S. Unemployment Rate, 2009). People living in low-income, minority areas of our country, for example, inner-city neighborhoods, rural areas, and reservations, experienced even higher rates of unemployment. By 2015, the economy had picked up with the Dow Jones average rising above 18,000 where it was three times higher than what it was in 2009 (Shell, 2015, p. 4B), the unemployment rate fell from 10% in 2009 when President Obama took office to 5.5% in early 2015 (Waggoner, 2015, p. 1B), and the economy produced over 2.3 million jobs in 2014 (Shell, 2015, 4B). How do we continue to create more jobs so that more and more people have legal opportunities to live life and not have to resort to crime?

There are a number of things we can do to connect people to legitimate jobs. One action we can take is to provide child care subsidies for poor people, especially single mothers, so that they can work outside the home. Without child care subsidies, many mothers will not make enough money, especially at minimum wage jobs, to afford child care and be able to keep these jobs. The child care subsidy, plus a minimum wage job, allows single mothers to get legitimate jobs rather than seek out illegitimate activities such as engaging in prostitution, selling drugs, and shoplifting. In other words, if we want to decrease crime, we need to give single mothers legal options that pay better than illegal options.

Another step we can take via jobs and opportunities is to raise the minimum wage so that there is more of an incentive to work at legal jobs than to become involved in illegal activities. If after working 40 hours per week, people do not have enough money to pay their rent, pay for food, and pay for other necessary expenses and are still thousands of dollars below the poverty line, they will have greater incentives to consider illegal options as a way to survive and get ahead. In addition to increasing the minimum wage, we can also increase the earned income tax credit to make up for the gap between the new minimum wage and the poverty line, for example, the minimum wage as of 2015 will provide an income of $15,080 per year, but the poverty line for a family of four is $23,850, $8,770 below the poverty line. President Obama has proposed increasing the minimum wage to $10.10, which would give a worker $21,008 (Davidson, December 29, 2014, 5B). That would still be $2,842 below the poverty line for a family of four ($23,850 − $21,008 = $2,842). However, with an earned income tax credit of $2,842, that would help a family of four get right at the poverty level. Moreover, we could decrease income taxes and Social Security taxes on poor and lower-income Americans to get them a little bit above poverty. So, an increase in the minimum wage, additional help with an earned income tax credit, and a decrease in income and Social Security taxes could help get many poor Americans above poverty and give them less incentive to commit crime.[5]

Another action that our country can take is to decrease taxes on corporations in exchange for creating more jobs in the United States. A drop in corporate taxes can create more of an incentive for corporations to remain in the United States and provide more jobs for Americans. As this happens, there will be more job opportunities for people and less likelihood of people choosing illegal opportunities, thus acting to decrease crime. In essence, a change in tax policy can lead to more jobs, which can cause less crime.

In other words, we can increase child care subsidies to attract women to more legal jobs, we can increase the minimum wage to attract men and women to more legal jobs, we can increase the earned income tax credit so that people who have legal but low-paying jobs can receive enough tax credit to be at or a little above poverty and hence give these people more incentive to get and stay in legal jobs, and we can decrease taxes on corporations in exchange for their staying in this country and providing more legal jobs. All of these incentives will lead to more legal jobs and, in turn, lead to less crime in our country.

Provide Unemployment Compensation, Job Training, and Job Placement

We can also increase unemployment compensation for people who have lost their jobs so that they are less likely to resort to crime to survive while they are out of work. We can provide better job training and retraining so that people who have lost their jobs can more quickly find new legal avenues of employment and feel hope that they can take this route rather than the illegal crime route. Furthermore, we can get better at placing people in jobs that open up, so that they believe they have a good chance to get a legal job, again increasing the incentive to get legal jobs while decreasing the incentive to commit crime. As we increase and improve our unemployment compensation program, our job training programs, and our job placement programs, we will develop a better social service network that allows Americans to choose legal opportunities over illegal opportunities, thereby decreasing crime.

Remember, in a capitalistic economy, there is no guarantee that every adult who desires a job will get a job (moreover, in a capitalistic economy, even if an adult gets a job, he or she may still be thousands of dollars below the poverty line). Even during good years, there is usually some unemployment. For example, during the mid-to-late 1990s, we had unemployment— in the 3% to 4% range (University of Texas, n.d.). Yet, during the recession of 2008 to 2011, we had a rate of 10% unemployment. Consequently, under the conditions of capitalism where (1) there are not enough jobs and (2) there are not enough decent-paying jobs, providing unemployment compensation, job training, and job placement services are imperative—if we wish to decrease crime.

Improve Skills Training in Public and Trade Schools

Another action we can take in our country to decrease crime is to place more emphasis on skilled trades in our public high schools. Besides providing better quality public schools in general, which will help all students prepare for better jobs, providing better trade schools in particular, as one part of the improvement in the public school system, will give a number of high school students who do not want to go to college, or who are not capable of going to college, an avenue that will provide them with skills that could give them good-paying legal jobs, hence decreasing their incentive to opt for criminal careers.

Decrease Inequality and Increase the Standard of Living

We can also take steps to decrease the overall wealth inequality in our society so that more poor and near-poor people have a decent standard of living. So long as many Americans live considerably below the poverty line and many others live near the poverty line, there is an incentive for these Americans to find illegal means to survive. If they can have a decent standard of living via legitimate jobs that pay above the poverty line, they will have less incentive to commit crime. So, if we want to have less crime, it is in our vested interests as a country that we attempt to decrease inequality by redistributing resources somewhat (recall our discussion in Chapter 3 on what we could do to decrease inequality in our country).[6]

It is also in the vested interests of Americans who are not poor to want less inequality so that they will be less likely to be the victims of crimes such as burglary, robbery, and car theft. So, in addition to having less crime, our society will be safer if we create a more equal or less unequal society in which the needs of poor and near-poor Americans are met. As I suggested in Chapter 3 on the problem of rising inequality, we can create a more progressive income tax and Social Security tax and decrease the sales tax so that poor and near-poor people will pay less tax and hence have more money left over from their paychecks to meet their family needs. Having more money left over each week (after less tax has been taken from their paychecks) will reduce people's incentive to commit crime.

Provide Better Health Care to Reduce Crime

A national health care system can provide health care for many poor and working-class people who otherwise have no health care (for more details, see Chapter 10 on health care). As we mentioned in Chapter 4, before the Affordable Care Act (popularly known as *Obamacare*) was passed and implemented, approximately 50 million Americans or one out of six Americans had no health care coverage (Zaldivar & Espo, 2009). This was the largest number of any industrialized country in the world. In fact, "the United States is the only major nation that does not ensure health care for all its citizens" (Kerbo, 2012, p. 41). The Affordable Care Act is beginning to remedy this situation to some degree. For example, during the sign-up period ending in mid-February, 2015, it was estimated that approximately 10 million people would sign up for health insurance (O'Donnell, February 5, 2015, p. 3B; O'Donnell and Ungar, February 12, 2015, p. 3B), and as of the deadline date of mid-February, 11.4 million people signed up—8.6 million through the federal system and 2.8 million through state-sponsored systems (O'Donnell and Ungar, February 19, 2015, p. 1B). By the way, 10 million people signed up for health insurance in 2014 (Rudavsky, 2015, p. A-9). These sign-ups will help poor and working-class Americans and their families finally get health insurance. So, we are moving in the direction of helping more Americans have health care—though we are still not like other industrialized countries that cover all of their citizens.

A comprehensive health care system that covers all Americans would do at least two things. First, it would decrease inequality of health care in our country. Second, it would mean that people, especially people with lower incomes, would not have to spend so much of their income on health care expenses and could instead use their income to pay for food, shelter, and other necessities, thereby decreasing their incentive to resort to crime as a way to subsist.

In the past few paragraphs I have suggested that changes in the way we tax ourselves and the kinds and amounts of social services we provide can lift up poor and near-poor people in our country and create disincentives for them to commit crime, thereby decreasing crime overall. Although it might seem unrelated at first, upon further reflection, we can begin to realize the following: (1) the way we tax people (for example, income, Social Security, and sales taxes) and (2) the social services we provide people (for example, health care and child care subsidies) are key factors that influence crime. The way we tax people and the services that we provide them can increase the incomes of poor and working-class Americans and can therefore decrease the incentive to commit crime.

As you can see, I have focused on changing the way we tax Americans, on social policies and programs, on the creation and retaining of jobs, and on providing more legal opportunities. In other words, if we change the social structure and create a social structure that gives people more legal opportunities to have a decent standard of living, this more humane social structure, in turn, lowers the tendency for people to commit crime. As David Brooks notes in his book *The Road to Character*, we work "toward the goal of creating a society in which it is easier for people to be good" (2015, pp. 89–90). The more that we can change the social structure in the following ways: (1) to give people more legal opportunities in the form of skills, education, and decent-paying jobs; (2) to give people more income via lower taxes; and (3) to offer people more needed services that provide a base for all Americans to live decently, the less likely they will commit crime.

Register Guns

Another factor that we might consider is the registering and licensing of all guns in the United States. Although this action does not relate to the main thrust of the preceding paragraphs, which emphasizes giving people more legal opportunities to earn money, it can help to reduce crime in two ways. One way is by decreasing homicides in the United States. For example, although the U.S. population is twice the size of Japan's population (Population Reference Bureau, 2014), the number of homicides from the use of guns has been hundreds of times more in the United States than in Japan (Booth, 2007, p. 207). More specifically, with respect to children and gun violence, "the rate of firearm deaths among children under age 15 is far higher in the United States than in 25 other industrialized countries combined" (Eitzen, Zinn, & Smith, 2009, p. 353).

Besides decreasing the homicide rate in the United States, the registering and licensing of all guns in the country could help by making it more difficult for people who intend to commit crime to obtain guns. This is not foolproof; people can still get firearms in illegal ways. However, we can make it more difficult for these people to get firearms. Less access to guns should therefore not only decrease the very high homicide rate in our country but also decrease our very high violent crime rate; the United States has the highest violent crime rate (murder, rape, assault, and robbery) of any industrialized country (Eitzen, 2007, p. 198).

Making guns less available ties into one of our previous points on opportunity. If we can decrease the incentive to resort to illegal opportunities by making guns less available to those who want to commit crime and, at the same time, increase the incentive to opt for legal opportunities by providing more education, jobs, and services, we will create a social structure in which people will not want to commit crime in general and violent crime in particular.

Invest in the "Front-End" of Crime

I have focused mainly on what our society can do so that people will be less likely to commit crime in the first place. In other words, if we invest a lot of effort and money in preventing crime, our investment should eventually pay off. If I am right, we would not need to invest as heavily in police, courts, and prisons that become more needed *after* people have committed crime. For example, once people have committed crime, we need more police to catch suspects. We need more lawyers, judges, and courts to try and convict defendants. We need more prisons and prison personnel to hold the convicted criminals. So, it is extremely expensive for our society to pay for all the crime that we have.

If we, as a society, can invest more in the "front-end" of this process where people have less incentive to commit crime in the first place, we can spend less on the "back-end" of this process, that is, the police, courts, and prisons. There will still be a need for police, courts, and prisons, but the need should be less as we invest more in the "front-end" of society by giving legal opportunities to more Americans.

Provide Job Training and Job Placement in Prisons

Speaking of investment in the back end of this process, another action we could take is to provide more and better job training in prisons and more job placement for men and women who have finished their prison terms. Many men and women who have completed their time in prison are let out of prison with nowhere to go and no jobs to help them stay legal. If our prisons could train people to become carpenters, electricians, plumbers, machinists, repair technicians (for example, cars, appliances, televisions, computers), and other kinds of skilled and semiskilled workers, these men and women leaving the prison system would have a better chance to find legal jobs and hence more incentive to "go straight," that is, to remain engaged in legal opportunities. Moreover, if the prison system had an effective job placement system, then men and women leaving the prison system would have a much better chance of getting legal jobs and "going straight" in their lives. By implementing such a combination of job training and job placement programs in our prison system, we could take another step toward decreasing crime.

The job training and job placement programs both are a part of the larger idea of rehabilitating people in prisons rather than only punishing them. In the past in the United States, our prisons were mainly a place of punishment, offering little or no rehabilitation. If we want to decrease crime, especially the rate of recidivism, that is, the rate at which former prisoners return to prison due to new crimes they commit, it makes sense that we increase rehabilitation, especially in the form of providing job training and job placement. In other words, if we can rehabilitate people leaving prison by giving them job skills and then place them in jobs, former prisoners will have the opportunity to make a decent living in a legal manner, thereby decreasing crime.

Moreover, if people leaving prisons have, while in prison, gone through job training and job placement for months or even years, they have had a chance to think about the possibility and to anticipate and plan for the day when they will be free and have legal and decent-paying jobs. This set of social conditions will help them to go through what sociologists call *anticipatory socialization,* where people in prison will have thought about what it will be like to be free and work in legal, decent-paying jobs. Once they are working at their new jobs, they will be members of new reference groups (recall our discussion in Chapter 1) that will help them get connected with other people who are working at legal jobs. It would seem, therefore, that this combination of providing job training, job placement, and new reference groups will increase the probability of people who are leaving prison going straight and decrease the probability of their returning to crime, thereby decreasing crime.

Ideally, if we could get people who are leaving prison into an entirely new social environment, where the effects of differential association (recall our theoretical discussion in Chapter 1) with former friends and acquaintances who had helped them to commit acts of crime in the past were no longer a problem, the chances for crime and hence recidivism would diminish. By coming out of prison, having a new job skill, working in a decent-paying job, being a member of a new reference group at work, and being in a new social environment separated from the former reference group that promoted and reinforced their acts of crime, people leaving prison would be less likely to commit crimes. These new social conditions that create legal opportunities would be much more conducive to reducing crime.

So that former prisoners can move to another geographic location where they no longer interact with their former colleagues in crime, we might need to provide them with some kind of incentive, such as a certain amount of money per month for a while as a way to cover their moving expenses and to set up a new living situation. Former prisoners, with their new decent-paying jobs and new reference groups (and, it is hoped, new friends and legal role models), will have established a new legal way to live life.

The policies I have suggested, both front-end and back-end, will require creative ways of thinking about crime and require new ways to invest money and expertise. The actions we take at the front-end—better education, training, child care subsidies, more decent-paying jobs, a higher minimum wage, and lower taxes on poor and near-poor Americans—and the actions we take at the back-end—job training, job placement with new, legal reference groups and role models, and new geographic locations away from old, illegal reference groups and role models—together should decrease crime in our society.

Put More Emphasis on the Front End

As you can see, my suggestions for decreasing crime are a little different from those suggested by others, in that I put more emphasis on changing the front end of the process by providing more legal opportunities for people so that they have the incentive to do legal work and remain legal. The more we can invest in these front-end policies, the less we will need to invest in the back-end policies.

Other people may emphasize adding more police, more patrol cars, more police walking neighborhood beats, more surveillance cameras, more harsh punishment, and more prisons. We can go this way and put the money we invest into decreasing crime in doing these kinds of things. I am sure that these kinds of things will reduce crime somewhat because they will increase the certainty that someone committing a crime will get caught and be punished. Research suggests that certainty of punishment adds to the deterrence of crimes (Paternoster, 1989). This is all well and good, and I think that these kinds of actions will be effective to a degree.

However, given the limited resources our society has to work with, investing in expanding the legal opportunities for Americans not only will address the causes of crime but also will create the type of social structure that will reduce crime year after year and decade after decade. Also, investing in more front-end measures will go along with the values of our society where we believe in giving people opportunity to get ahead, as long as they do their part in being honest and hardworking. Most Americans have always thought that if people are honest and hardworking, they should have the chance to live a decent life. Investing more in these front-end ideas will create such a social structure where more Americans have the means to actually live such a decent life.

A Dilemma: Capitalism and Crime

A dilemma that we, as Americans, need to face and deal with in some way is the dilemma of capitalism and its relation to the emphasis on materialism and consumerism and crime. As Merton (1968) noted, one of the main reasons that people break the norms of the society to gain money and material things is the emphasis our society puts on these things. Merton noted that in our society, these are the things people think are "worth striving for" (p. 187). He added,

> The cultural emphasis placed upon certain goals varies independently of the degree of emphasis upon institutionalized means. There may develop a very heavy, at times a virtually exclusive, stress upon the value of particular goals,

involving comparatively little concern with the institutionally prescribed means of striving toward these goals. (p. 187)

So, when "there is an exceptionally strong emphasis upon specific goals" (Merton, 1968, p. 188), such as the importance we in our society have placed on making money and having many material things (for example, homes, things in our homes, and cars), we should predict that a number of people will use illegal means to get these things.

In the society in which we currently live, we turn on the television and see advertisements every few minutes urging us to buy certain products or services. Hence, during a typical 2 hours of watching television, we will be bombarded with 40 to 50 commercials telling us to buy this or that. We pick up a magazine and see many advertisements in it as we thumb through the pages. We read a newspaper and see as many as five advertisements on one page. We drive along highways and see numerous signs telling us to buy all kinds of products and services. We use a computer and see ads among our e-mails or when we use the Internet. We attend sporting events and see ads nearly everywhere we look in the stadium, park, field, or field house. Ads are even fixed on restroom walls for us to look at and reflect on as we take care of our biological needs! As you can see, we are literally surrounded in our culture with the emphasis on consuming (Ritzer, 2005).

It will therefore not be surprising to you that a certain amount of crime is related to the emphasis on consuming. Why is there such an emphasis? The nature of capitalism helps us to understand why. As you know, capitalism is based on owners of the means of production producing products and services and selling these products and services to make a profit. Consequently, the more products and services that can be sold, the more profit that can be made. This is where advertising and commercials come into the picture. Advertising and commercials try to get us to want to buy all kinds of products and services.

So, back to the dilemma that I mentioned a few moments ago. On the one hand, most of us in the society want to decrease crime. Yet on the other hand, as Merton (1968) pointed out, if "there is an exceptionally strong emphasis upon specific goals without a corresponding emphasis upon institutional procedures" (p. 188), people are more likely to commit crime. So, what do we do in a society that emphasizes the goal of obtaining many material things but does not provide enough institutionalized means to legally attain these things, for example, enough jobs and enough decent-paying jobs?

Do we decrease the cultural emphasis on the goals, that is, decrease the emphasis on obtaining material things? We could do that by banning many kinds of advertising and try to emphasize a less materialistic lifestyle. However, it is hard to imagine that we could do this in our society, for a number of reasons. First, our people are accustomed to having materialistic lifestyles. It is hard to imagine our giving up such a lifestyle. Second, it is hard to imagine in capitalism that corporations would accept not being able to advertise their products and services. If this scenario is accurate, for the foreseeable future we will need to work at decreasing crime within a social structure that has, as Merton put it, an extreme emphasis on having a lot of things.

Given such a social structure, it appears that we will need to work to change the social structure by institutionalizing ways for people to have access to the material things via legal means. This brings us back to our discussion earlier in this chapter regarding the need to provide more legal opportunities for people—providing better public schools, teaching people trades so that people can earn good incomes, creating more decent-paying jobs, and so on. So, even though it is not realistic, for the time being, to decrease the emphasis on obtaining material things as a way of decreasing crime, it does seem realistic to increase the legal opportunities for people as a way to decrease crime.

Questions for Discussion

1. In addition to the points discussed in this chapter, what else can we do to decrease crime in the United States?

2. What should we do in our country? What is your reasoning?

3. What do you predict will be done in our country during the next 5, 10, and 15 years to decrease crime? Why?

4. Should we hire more police and build more prisons? Why?

5. Is it possible to decrease the emphasis on material goods and consumerism in our country? What is your reasoning?

6. If you were poor, why might you commit crime?

7. If you were rich, why might you commit crime?

8. What one thing could be done in society to greatly decrease crime?

9. If there are not enough jobs for people and we want to decrease crime, what can we do?

10. If you were stealing cars, selling drugs, or working as a prostitute, what do you think would give you the incentive to have a legal job?

9

How Can We Solve
the Problem of Drugs?

There are strongly held, opposing views in the United States on what we should do about our drug problem. Many Americans believe that the current policy of keeping certain drugs illegal—for example, marijuana, cocaine, heroin, and methamphetamines—is the best policy, even though a number of users manage to get and take these drugs, and still others manage to sell them at a profit. So, even though the current policy is far from fool-proof, many Americans believe that keeping certain drugs illegal is still the best policy.

Other Americans are of the opinion that our current drug policy is wrong because it does not allow adults (defined as people who are at least 18 years old and can therefore vote, serve in the military and possibly die in a war, marry, have children, hold down full-time jobs, and live independently) the freedom to decide for themselves whether or not they want to take a certain drug. They believe in giving Americans as much freedom as possible vis-à-vis the choice of drugs. So, in this social problem of drugs, a key issue is deciding how much freedom adults should be able to have in choosing which drugs they want to use and whether these drugs should be legal. Currently, there is much disagreement over this issue.

Because Americans disagree, it is not surprising that our current drug policy is inconsistent. For example, nicotine, the drug in cigarettes, cigars, and pipe tobacco, is legal to use, and yet it kills more than 480,000 Americans per year (U.S. Department of Health and Human Services, 2015). Alcohol, the drug in beer, wine, and whiskey, is also legal; it kills 100,000 people per year

(Eitzen, Zinn, & Smith, 2009) and therefore kills "25 times as many as all illegal drugs combined" (p. 397).[1] In other words, all the illegal drugs combined kill less than 1% of the two legal drugs, nicotine and alcohol.

What should we, as a country, do about the drug problem? Should we continue the current policy of keeping a number of drugs illegal even though we know that a lot of people still use and sell these drugs, and we know that we spend a lot of money trying to stop people from taking these drugs and trying to stop people from bringing these drugs into our country? Should we keep nicotine and alcohol legal even though they cause more deaths than all illegal drugs combined? Should we continue to be inconsistent with our drug policy where some drugs are legal and highly promoted—for example, beer ads on television—while other drugs are illegal and are publicly scorned? Should we be consistent in our drug policy? That is, should we become consistent and either make marijuana, cocaine, heroin, and methamphetamines legal or make alcohol and nicotine illegal? Or should it not matter that we are inconsistent in our drug policy? Should we let adults decide what drugs they can use legally, or should we not let them decide? These are important and yet very difficult questions that our country needs to answer if we want to solve our drug problem.

So, what can we say to help us solve this social problem? Let us consider the advantages and disadvantages of going one of three ways and see what you think: (1) maintain the current and inconsistent policy of keeping alcohol and nicotine legal and keeping marijuana, cocaine, heroin, methamphetamines, and other drugs illegal; (2) change the current policy to legalize drugs for people who are 18 years old or over; or (3) take a step-by-step approach by legalizing one drug at a time to see what happens; for example, first legalize marijuana, see what happens, and then go from there.

Keep the Current Policy

Advantages

One advantage to keeping the current policy is that by keeping marijuana, cocaine, heroin, methamphetamines, and other drugs illegal and harder to get than they would be if they were made legal, the fact that these drugs are defined by the general society as illegal and bad will no doubt deter a number of people from using them and potentially abusing them. A number of children will be taught, "These drugs are bad for you; so, don't use them." This admonition from parents, teachers, other adult leaders, and fellow playmates sends a strong message to many children that will deter many of them from using illegal drugs. To the degree that this admonition works, these young people will not use these drugs and hence will not be in the situation of becoming addicted and having problems with these drugs.

A second advantage of keeping such drugs illegal is that the greater difficulty of obtaining the drugs, their cost, and the unknowns of what is actually in the drugs one is buying will deter many people from ever trying and using these drugs. These deterring factors will prevent many people from having drug-related problems in their lives, for example, with their health, with their jobs, and with their families.

A third advantage to maintaining the current policy of keeping certain drugs illegal is that, given that there will be less drug use, abuse, and addiction, there will be less cost in maintaining drug rehab centers. Not as many people will become addicted. Hence, not as many rehab centers—and the costs that go with them—will be needed.

Disadvantages

There are a number of disadvantages to continuing to carry out the current policy of keeping certain drugs illegal. For example, we are beginning to see a pattern of people robbing drugstores not for the money but rather for the drugs kept at the drugstores. Some people will go to extremes to get their drug of choice to use or sell. This means that pharmacists and others who work in drugstores will be working in an atmosphere that is less safe. Also, potential robberies of drugstores for the drugs will cause drugstores to need to spend more money for security precautions and to pay more for insurance policies insuring the products and people in the drugstores, hence increasing the cost of doing business.

Another problem with the current policy is that we still have millions of Americans using illegal drugs, but our current law enforcement system is not adequate to handle them. For example, although data show that for 2012, 309,100 prisoners were in prison for drug-related crimes (Carson, 2014), survey research suggests that 24.6 million Americans reported illegal drug use in the previous month (SAMHSA, 2014). In other words, only 1.3% of illegal drug users have gone to prison, while 98.7% of illegal drug users have not. Moreover, of the 24.6 million Americans who use illegal drugs, 80% of them were illegal users of marijuana (SAMHSA, 2014, p. 15).

Another problem with the current policy is that because a number of drugs are illegal, their illegal status promotes drug-related crime such as violence, gang warfare, and organized crime. Individuals, gangs, and criminal organizations sell illegal drugs to make money, that is, they are in business, an illegal business, to make a profit. Becker (2001) noted that the world market value of illegal drugs is "at several hundred billions of dollars—in the same league as the markets for cigarettes and alcohol" (p. 32). In other words, selling illegal drugs is a profitable business. To protect their profit, sellers resort to violence to keep rival sellers out of their market.[2] Hence, there are threats, fights, shootings, stabbings, and murders to protect the business, that is, to maintain their monopoly in certain neighborhoods, cities, or regions of the country. Consequently, as a result of keeping drugs illegal, there will be more illegal business and more violence. This situation is especially unfortunate for poor, inner-city neighborhoods where many gangs sell drugs and make the surrounding neighborhood a dangerous place to live.

Another problem with the current policy of keeping drugs illegal is that it costs billions of dollars in taxes to enforce. It costs American taxpayers $1 billion per week to try to stop the flow of illegal drugs into the country and to have the criminal justice system try, convict, and jail illegal users and sellers (Zeese, 2006). Because of the policy of jailing illegal drug users and sellers, more than 60% of all federal prisoners and 22% of all state prisoners are in prison for drug offenses (Myers, 2001, p. 237). Taken together, 26% of all state and federal prisoners in our country are in jail for drug-related offenses (p. 237). Each new prison cell costs $80,000 to build, and each new prisoner costs the state or federal government approximately $25,000 per year to house (Eitzen, Zinn, & Smith, 2011, p. 381). With all this investment of taxpayer money, "we have not stopped the supply; we have only dented it and made the drugs that enter the United States more expensive" (Eitzen, Zinn, & Smith, 2009, p. 403).

Our current drug policy also causes our government to be involved in the domestic politics of other countries by trying to get these other countries to destroy their coca and opium crops. Our government's action raises the following ethical question: How much right or authority do we have in destroying farmers' crops in other countries? Although our current policy may decrease the quantity of drugs smuggled into our country, it does not endear us to these countries and their farmers when we want them to destroy their major means of economic survival.

Another disadvantage to keeping drugs illegal is that it takes not only considerable taxpayer money (recall that we spend $1 billion per week) but also considerable police time to try to stop illegal drug activity. As a consequence, the more time police spend at trying to stop illegal drug activity, the less time they spend focusing on other crimes such as murder, robbery, rape, burglary, and corporate crime (for example, tax evasion, false advertising, and stealing retirement funds from employees). As a result, many Americans may not realize how our current drug policy affects how police spend their time.

Another disadvantage to keeping a number of drugs illegal in the United States is that as alleged sellers and users are arrested and brought to trial, the result is an increase in time and expense in our court system. For example, judges need to spend more time on drug-related trials, and more judges are needed to preside over the many drug-related trials (remember, 26% of all prisoners are in jail for drug-related crimes). Also, more courtrooms, court personnel, and prosecuting attorneys are needed, resulting in more expense for the taxpayers who pay for the new courtrooms and salaries of these additional governmental officials. In a nutshell, more court time and taxpayer expense go to address one kind of crime: drug crime.

A consequence of keeping drugs illegal is that they cost more to buy (Becker, 2001, p. 32). Yet as Becker (2001) noted, "The fact remains that most illegal drugs remain popular and available, regardless of price" (p. 32). People who do not have the money to buy these drugs are more likely to commit other kinds of crime, such as shoplifting, burglary, robbery, and prostitution, to get the money to buy the drugs. So, although we do not intend for our current drug policy to cause an increase in other kinds of crime, our policy makes these drugs cost more and this, in turn, results in users who do not have enough money to buy these drugs committing more crime to be able to purchase the drugs. Hence, our current drug policy unintentionally acts as a latent dysfunction (that is, has the unintended consequence of decreasing the survival of a group of people) by increasing other kinds of crime (recall our discussion in Chapter 1 on functional theory and the idea of latent dysfunctions).

Another major disadvantage of the current policy of keeping certain drugs illegal is that the users do not know what they are getting when they purchase the drugs (Nadelmann, 1988, pp. 20–21). That is, when they buy drugs off the street, they do not know how pure the drugs are and what else might be contained in the drugs. So, the users, not knowing how the contents of their purchases will affect them, take a chance on serious, unintended medical consequences when they use the drugs.

Another disadvantage of the current policy is that users can be labeled as deviants, addicts, and criminals, and these labels can work to keep them from getting legal jobs. They can be stigmatized and hence have a harder time living and working in the legal world. Consequently, this negative labeling process acts as a latent dysfunction for their survival. When someone is given a label that defines that person almost totally, and we do not see them in any other way, sociologists use the term *master status*. Sometimes, the master status that a person has is seen as positive, such as those who love to watch or play basketball may be seen by others as "a great basketball player." But in the case of a drug user, being seen in a negative way, the person who uses drugs is seen as a deviant will be at a disadvantage in our society, for example, in trying to find jobs.

Finally, another disadvantage of the current policy is that it does not give adults the freedom to decide for themselves whether or not they want to consume certain drugs. This is especially upsetting to people who have a libertarian philosophy and believe that "drug use is a personal matter in which the state has no business" (Fine & Shulman, 2003, p. 60). Szasz (1972) asserts, "It is none of the government's business what idea a man puts into his mind; likewise it should be none of the government's business what drug he puts into his body" (p. 75).

In our country, we believe in giving people a lot of freedom. However, in the area of drug use, we have decided that adults should not have this freedom. They are allowed to use nicotine and alcohol, but they are not allowed to use marijuana, cocaine, and heroin (although some states have recently legalized marijuana). This raises the following question: Should adults (18 and over) be free or not free to decide what drugs to use?

Legalize Drugs for Adults

As in the current policy of keeping certain drugs illegal, there are also advantages and disadvantages to legalizing drugs. Let us consider these advantages and disadvantages.

Advantages

If we legalize drugs such as marijuana, cocaine, heroin, and methamphetamines, as well as other drugs that are now illegal, one advantage is that we should observe less crime. When these drugs can be obtained legally, say in drugstores, the drugs will be cheaper in cost because the supply will be greater; for example, farmers in other countries and our country will not have their crops burned, and there will be no stopping of drugs at our country's borders. People who have lower incomes will not need to commit as much crime—stealing, burglary, robbery, prostitution, and so on—to buy drugs. Consequently, in addition to decreasing drug crime, other kinds of crime will decrease.[3] Other kinds of crime, such as gang violence and gang warfare, could decrease as well because if there will not be drugs to sell, there will not be as much territorial fighting and violence to keep other gangs that sell drugs out of a certain neighborhood.[4] People instead will be able to go to a local drugstore to purchase drugs at a lower cost, thereby knocking out, or at least seriously damaging, the drug market by gangs. Finally, we should see a decline in organized crime because the legal selling of drugs will hurt the market for drugs sold through organized crime networks.[5] In fact, it is not in the vested interests of gangs and organized crime to see drugs legalized, because customers will be able to buy them in a legal and less costly way and will know the purity and contents of the drugs they are purchasing, thus resulting in a substantial decline in the purchase of drugs through gangs and organized crime. Hence, the legalization of drugs would be dysfunctional for the survival of gangs and organized crime. So, it is ironic to think that gangs and organized crime would not want drugs legalized because that would be against their vested interests of making money.

With a decline in various kinds of crime, with a decline in gang violence and gang warfare, and with a decline in organized crime, we will not need to spend as much of our tax money on trying to stop crime. There will not be as many police officers needed because buying and using drugs will no longer be crimes. There will not need to be as many prosecuting attorneys, judges, and courtrooms, and this will in turn mean less taxpayer money going to these expenses. Also, there will not need to be as many prisons and prison personnel, because there will not be people being convicted of buying and selling illegal drugs if the drugs are legal to buy (recall that approximately 26% of all state and federal prisoners are in prison for drug-related crimes) (Myers, 2001, p. 237). So, our taxes could go down as a result of the decrease in these costs. Or we could take the tax money that was spent on crime prevention and use it to address other social problems.

Legalizing drugs will allow police to spend more of their time and attention on other kinds of crime—such as burglary, robbery, rape, murder, and corporate crime—and this greater expenditure of time will, in turn, help us to solve and deter these crimes. Police will also not need to be stretched so thin, needing to develop so many skills and so much knowledge about areas of drug crime. The more police can specialize in fewer areas of crime, the more effective they can be at catching criminals and decreasing crime.

Also, there can be less police corruption. Police officers do not make high salaries. They can therefore be tempted to supplement their incomes by receiving payoffs from drug dealers. Nadelmann (1988) noted,

> What makes drug enforcement especially vulnerable to corruption are the tremendous amounts of money involved in the business. Today, many law enforcement officials believe that police corruption is more pervasive than at any time since Prohibition. Repealing the drug prohibition laws would dramatically reduce police corruption. (pp. 19–20)

Another advantage to legalizing drugs is that it gives adults in our country more freedom to choose whether or not to take drugs and what drugs to take.[6] Rather than the government deciding for them, individual adults can choose whether or not to use marijuana, cocaine, heroin, and other drugs. As we mentioned in the previous section, it may be fruitful for our country to have a national discussion on whether or not adults should have freedom to choose to use drugs.

Another advantage of legalizing drugs is that there will be less negative labeling of the users of drugs. Right now, people who use illegal drugs are many times labeled as deviant. This label makes it harder for these people to live normal lives. If drugs are legalized, the stigma of a drug user could lessen and hence the effects of this stigma could be less in drug users' lives. Users would be less likely to be discriminated against and more likely to be able to get and keep legal jobs, pay their bills, and interact with people who have legal jobs, thereby making users more likely to engage in legitimate activities in various areas of their lives and less likely to commit crime.

Another major advantage of legalizing drugs is that the government will be able to tax the sale of these drugs.[7] This could be a major source of new tax revenue badly needed for local, state, and federal governments. Given that all levels of government need more revenue, taxing the sale of marijuana, cocaine, heroin, and other drugs would be beneficial for the government and, at the same time, take some of the pressure off of other taxpayers as their taxes decrease.

Another key advantage of legalizing drugs is that it will create new legal jobs. For example, farmers growing plants in other countries that produce marijuana, cocaine, and heroin will not be stigmatized and will not have their governments and our own government working against them to grow these crops. This will, in turn, bring in more revenue for these countries and their governments and for the farmers and middle people who process the crops into the drugs and transport them to countries that consume the drugs. Legalization will also create new agricultural jobs in our country in that farmers will be able to grow plants that produce marijuana, cocaine, and heroin. We will need more people in our country to process the plants, check for purity, transport the drugs, and sell the drugs at local drugstores. So, legalizing these drugs would create more jobs in our country and especially would give a stimulus to people who work in agriculture and related jobs.

Finally, users will have information about the purity of the drug and what else is contained in the products they purchase. Right now, when people buy illegal drugs, they have no idea what else is contained in the drug. Hence, legalizing drugs will protect the health of the users more than the current policy does.

As you can see, there are many advantages to legalizing drugs—probably more than most Americans realize. Now let us consider the disadvantages to legalizing drugs.

Disadvantages

One of the main disadvantages is that we will probably see a certain amount of drug addiction increase if we legalize drugs such as marijuana, cocaine, and heroin. This is understandable, given that these drugs will be more accessible in drugstores and will be lower in cost. As a result, people will be able to buy these drugs more easily, as they do now with alcohol and nicotine.

Before we fully accept the idea that there will be an increase in the use and addiction of these new legal drugs, let us make a few cautionary statements. Nadelmann (1988) noted that decriminalization of marijuana in a dozen states during the 1970s "did not lead to increases in marijuana consumption" (p. 29). Also, the Netherlands decriminalized marijuana and saw its consumption decrease. Moreover, research indicates that during the late 19th century, when there were no drug laws, drug use was roughly the same as it is today, even with all of our drug laws and regulations (p. 29). So, although there may be an increase in the use and abuse of these newly legalized drugs because they are cheaper to get and easier to buy, this is not a certainty.

If there is more addiction, we, as a society, will need to be ready for this. This would mean, for example, that we will need more drug rehabilitation facilities and personnel than we have now. As a consequence, some of the tax money that we receive with the sale of these drugs and that we save in needing fewer police, judges, prosecutors, trials, and prison cells will need to be set aside and redirected to pay for additional facilities and personnel who will help those users who abuse drugs.

With this increase in addiction, there will probably be some increase in people being absent from their jobs, doing lower-quality work, and having family problems. We should predict and expect these kinds of consequences if people have the choice of taking these drugs. With problems of more absenteeism, lower-quality work, and family problems, we will need to have counseling and rehabilitation facilities to address these consequences.

So, although we should see a decrease in time required of and expenses incurred by police, courts, and prisons because the criminal justice system will not be involved in trying to catch, try, convict, and jail people who use illegal drugs, other expenses will be incurred. Which way will be more expensive? No one knows for sure, but I would predict that it will be much lower in cost to provide rehabilitation centers and counseling personnel than to have police spend 18% of their time investigating drug-related activities, have the court systems devote court time to drug-related crimes, use tax revenues to pay for prison space for 26% of all state and federal prisoners imprisoned for drug-related offenses, and have federal law enforcement spend billions of dollars trying to shut down drug operations in other countries in an attempt to slow down the flow of illegal drugs into our country. All in all, I predict that we would find a moderate to large difference between the expense of keeping certain drugs illegal versus the expense of making them legal.

Finally, even if we legalize drugs, I predict that nicotine and alcohol will continue to be the two main drugs of choice for most Americans and will therefore continue to be the two most abused drugs in our society. The reason I say this is that Americans are already accustomed to using these two drugs at parties, at bars, and in their homes. These two drugs have been an accepted part of our culture for more than 75 years. Moreover, there are powerful corporations that have strong vested interests in continuing to make high profits by keeping these two drugs as the drugs of choice for Americans. If I am correct, the continued use of alcohol and nicotine will tend to temper the increase in the use of these other drugs. However, if corporations can advertise these new legal drugs on television, on the Internet, on billboards along highways, and in newspapers and magazines, the use of these new legal drugs could rise sharply. So, the increase in use of these new, legalized drugs would therefore depend on the regulations we put on these drugs, for example, whether or not they can be advertised.

Take a Step-by-Step Approach by Legalizing One Drug at a Time

There is a third approach that could be labeled as a "middle-of-the-road" approach. As a compromise between the two policies of keeping certain drugs either illegal or legal, we could experiment with legalizing one drug and see how this goes. We could legalize it, sell it in drugstores, see how it affects our society, and then assess where we want to go next.[8] For example, we could legalize marijuana and see what happens in our society.[9] Does it hurt our society too much or not very much? That is, is it better to legalize it and deal with the problems this causes, or is it better to keep it illegal and deal with the problems this causes? We might not know the answers to these questions unless we experiment by legalizing marijuana and then see which way we, as a society, would rather have it—legal or illegal.

I suggest that we experiment first with marijuana rather than with cocaine or heroin because the public sees marijuana as the least harmful in that it is not as powerful and not as harmfully addicting. If it were legalized, it could be regulated like alcohol and nicotine; adults would be allowed to buy it at drugstores or at privately owned shops that are regulated and taxed.

Currently, marijuana is legal in four states: Alaska, Washington, Oregon, and Colorado where there has been a 74% increase in the market from 2013 to 2014 and "at least 10 states are already considering legalizing recreational marijuana in the next two years through ballot measures or state legislatures" (Ferner, 2015). Let us discuss the advantages and disadvantages of using this middle-of-the-road, or step-by-step, approach by using the example of legalizing marijuana since it is currently being debated in state legislatures in a number of states.

Advantages

One advantage would be that we could tax the legal sale of marijuana, and this would help our society address our government debts and deficits. We also know that we will be able to tell users what the marijuana contains and how pure it is. That way, people will know precisely what they are getting and how it will affect them.

Another advantage will be that our prison population will decrease to the degree that it is made up of people convicted of selling or using marijuana. This decrease in the prison population will take the pressure off our crowded prisons and decrease the need to build costly new prisons.[10] Also, we will no longer need to use police and court time to catch and try alleged sellers and users. All of these things—less use of police time, less use of court time, and a decline in the prison population—will mean that we will not need to use as much tax money on crime prevention and punishment.

Another advantage of this step-by-step policy will be to give more freedom to adults who feel that they should have the right to decide for themselves whether or not to use marijuana. Those Americans who have a more libertarian philosophy will appreciate being able to have this additional freedom in their lives.

Even before it began to become legal in some states in recent years, it was already one of the largest cash crops in our country (Fine & Shulman, 2003, p. 58). For example, Nadelmann, even in 1988 noted that marijuana production in our country was believed to be "a multi-billion-dollar industry" (1988, p. 9). If marijuana was legalized, it could help a number of farmers in our country to have another legal crop with which to make a profit and survive in the profession of agriculture. Also, we could export it, thereby helping us with our balance of trade deficit. Furthermore, growing it, transporting it, processing it, and selling it would mean that we could create more jobs, thereby helping our economy, which, though improving to only 5.5% unemployment from 10% unemployment of the 2008 and 2009 recession, is in need of more legal jobs.

Disadvantages

There are also disadvantages to legalizing marijuana. More people could get addicted to marijuana because it would be more easily available to those who want to use it (Marcus, 2014, p.A-23). If this happened, we as a society would need to spend more tax and insurance money to rehabilitate people who are addicted.

When people drive under the influence of marijuana, their reaction time slows down, and they are more likely to make misjudgments and cause more car accidents, the same as when they drive under the influence of alcohol. We always hope that people under the influence of a drug will use good judgment and not drive. Many people use good judgment. However, we all know that some people do not use good judgment, and some of these people cause car accidents that can be tragic for themselves and others—as we have seen over the years with drinking alcohol and driving. Here the problem is not so much the use of the drug in and of itself as it is the use of the drug in a situation that could cause harm to the user and other people. Consequently, if marijuana were legalized, we should predict that there will be at least some rise in car accidents and in more material costs that accompany these accidents.

Where to Go From Here?

So, what should we do in our society with respect to illegal drugs? As you know, I as a sociologist cannot answer a "should" question. Sociology cannot tell the society what it should do. I, as a sociologist, have pointed out advantages and disadvantages to keeping drugs illegal, to legalizing drugs, or to taking a step-by-step approach to legalizing drugs.

There are many opinions as to what we should do. With other social problems, most people want to decrease poverty, decrease crime, decrease various forms of prejudice and discrimination, and decrease pollution. As for drugs, however, there is, at this time in our country, no clear direction as to which way we want to go.

To make matters more difficult, this issue can also become a hot issue that politicians use against their opponents by trying to get voters to react emotionally rather than to have voters calmly and objectively look at the pros and cons of taking each approach. As a result, candidates often fear raising the issue of legalizing drugs in a campaign. Consequently, we have not had much of an open and objective discussion on this issue in our country.

As to where we are and where we need to go in the United States, it seems to me that it could be fruitful for our country to have an honest, open, and objective[11] national discussion and lay out the advantages and disadvantages of going each way. We, in sociology, along with other disciplines of psychology, political science, economics, anthropology, history, biology, and chemistry, could add our research findings about drugs and their effects on the body, drugs in history, or drugs in other cultures so that we could have the most informed discussion possible.

Given such a national discussion, we could grow in our awareness, knowledge, and understanding of how drugs fit within the larger social structure of our society.[12] Also, as a result of such a discussion, we would be in a better situation to make a decision as to which direction we want to go in our country.

Questions for Discussion

1. Are we spending too much money trying to stop people from using or selling illegal drugs and trying to stop others from bringing illegal drugs into our country? If so, what should we do?

2. Should we be consistent in our drug policy, that is, either make alcohol and nicotine illegal or make marijuana, cocaine, heroin, and methamphetamines legal? What is your reasoning?

3. Should adults have the freedom to use the drug they would like to use? What is your reasoning?

4. If we legalized drugs that are currently illegal, what kinds of laws would we need to create?

5. If marijuana were legalized throughout the country, what would be the consequences in our country?

6. Should marijuana be legalized? What is your reasoning?

7. Should we experiment with marijuana and legalize it in certain cities or geographic areas and then see how it works and what the consequences are?

8. Should we try a step-by-step approach to legalizing drugs, that is, legalize one drug and see whether that goes okay, and then legalize another drug and see whether that goes okay? What is your reasoning?

9. Should we legalize all illegal drugs? What is your reasoning?

10. What do you predict will occur with respect to the legalization of illegal drugs in your lifetime? What is your reasoning?

10

How Can We Solve the Problem of Health Care?

H ealth care is an immensely difficult problem in our society. Every industrialized country except the United States provides national health care for all of its citizens (Kerbo, 2012). Until the passage of the Affordable Health Care Act, there were 50 million American citizens, that is, roughly 1 of every 6 Americans, who had no health care insurance coverage.[1] So, this means that when people who did not have health care insurance became sick or had a toothache, it would cost them a lot more money to see a doctor or dentist than it would cost those people who do have health care insurance. As a result, they would be more likely to put off going to the doctor or dentist or not get any medical help at all.[2]

Employers that helped pay health care costs for their employees were finding that, because of rising health care costs, they were less competitive than (1) U.S. companies that did not provide coverage and (2) foreign companies that did not provide health care benefits (Durbin, 2005; Maynard, 2006; Reid, 2009). Because the costs of health care insurance have been increasing, more and more employers have been finding that they cannot afford to provide health care coverage for their employees (Reid, 2009). As a consequence, all through the late 20th century and into the 21st century, employees have been having a harder time finding and paying for their health care.

Until the Affordable Care Act was passed, many retired people living on moderate to lower incomes needed to use more and more of their retirement incomes to pay for prescription drugs (Carroll, 2003). Also, another problem we have had is that poor people who were on Medicaid (the government health care program for the poor) still might not receive health care due to low reimbursement rates provided to doctors. (Yetter, 2005).

In short, we have had many problems with our past health care system. Let us look at our past problems, then see where we are today, and then see where we could go in the future to create an excellent health care system for all Americans.

Consequences of Our Problem

For many decades, our country has resisted going to a health care system that includes all Americans, beginning with President Harry Truman who tried and failed to create such a health care system (Espo, 2009). The result has been that millions of Americans have gone without any health insurance and hence have put off going to doctors and dentists until their situations were so serious that they could not do so any longer. The consequences for these sick individuals have been that (1) they were in much worse health, (2) they endured needless pain and discomfort, and (3) many of them, over 20,000 Americans, died each year from treatable diseases but had no health insurance and therefore could not afford to go to the doctor (Reid, 2009). Adults missed work and lost pay while their employers lost profit. Students of all ages missed school days, were in danger of getting lower grades, and could not participate in school activities. A sad example of this occurred in the state of Kentucky in 2005 where 338,000 Kentucky children never saw a dentist that year (Yetter, 2005, pp. A1–A2).

There are a number of reasons why these children did not receive dental care. First, more than half of the dentists in Kentucky did not treat people who were on Medicaid because the dentists believed that they did not get reimbursed enough from Medicaid to cover their expenses (Yetter, 2005). Second, because parents on Medicaid are poor, many times they did not have the means of transportation to get to those dentists who are willing to treat their children (Yetter, 2005). Third, many parents worked at jobs in which it was difficult to get time off from work, or they were not permitted to leave work in order to take their children to the dentist (Yetter, 2005). Fourth, even in those cases where parents were allowed to take time off from work, many times they would lose pay that they could not afford to lose, especially when they made low wages (Yetter, 2005).

Without a health care system that covers all Americans, there have also been negative consequences for the elderly in our country. The elderly, especially those who had moderate to lower incomes, needed to use a considerable portion of what little Social Security income and retirement income they had to pay for monthly prescription drugs, which meant that they had less money left over to pay for food, rent, transportation, and other expenses (Carroll, 2003). Due to the high cost of drugs in the United States, a number of Americans have purchased drugs from Canada through Internet sites.[3] As you can see, there has been a serious conflict of vested interests (see our theory and causal model in Chapter 1) between the elderly who need prescription drugs at lower prices because these prices take so much of their retirement incomes and the drug companies who argue that they need to charge higher prices because of the cost of doing research on new drugs.[4]

There have also been consequences for many U.S. companies due to our lack of a comprehensive health care system that covered all Americans. By paying for health coverage of their employees, companies have had to add on to the prices of their products, making their products less competitive in the marketplace, especially compared with foreign companies that did not have to pay for health insurance because their governments paid for such coverage.[5] For example, it was estimated that General Motors needed to add $1,500 to the price of each car to pay for its employees' health care coverage.[6] Also, because of rapidly rising health care costs, American corporations had to cut back jobs. For example, General Motors announced in November 2005 that it was cutting 30,000 jobs in North America by 2008 (Durbin, 2005; Maynard, 2006). The result has been that American corporations have been less competitive, and American workers have lost jobs due, in part, to health insurance costs. Consequently, for a number of different groups in our society—the poor, children of the poor, the elderly with moderate to lower retirement incomes, employees in companies with no health care, and corporations who have tried to provide health care—there have been many unfortunate consequences of our health care system.

There has also been, as you might well predict, a relationship among one's income, one's health, and one's health care coverage. Kerbo (2012) asserted that "good health is to some degree unequally distributed through the stratification system" because "adequate health care is unequally distributed" (p. 40).[7] Once again, we see how one social problem, such as much inequality of money, power, and prestige (see Chapter 3) is connected to another social problem such as little or no access to health care. As we can find ways to decrease the social problem of much inequality, we can also address another social problem such as the health care of people.

A final consequence of the health care system of the 20th and early 21st century was that Americans faced the constant pressure of rising health care costs. Although this affected everyone, it affected Americans with less

income more harshly. For example, from 2004 through 2009, yearly
health care costs always increased more than the yearly rate of inflation
(see Table 10.1). Notice that in column 3, yearly health insurance premiums (what people pay for health insurance) always rose faster than column 2, yearly inflation rates. Also, notice in column 4 that the premiums
increased from at least 1.2 times the inflation rate to 9.9 times the inflation. So, the health insurance companies were always increasing their
prices more than the inflation rate. With regard to the implementation of
the Affordable Care Act, by 2014, the exchanges were up and running.
Data in Table 10.1 suggests that, in 2014, the yearly premiums were
increasing at a rate of only 3%; so, the premiums were only 1.9 times the
inflation rate for that year. This is data for only one year, but if these statistics continue, then the rise in premiums could be less as the Affordable
Care Act gets more established.

Table 10.1   Health Insurance Premium Increases Always Higher Than
Yearly Inflation Rates (2004–2014)

Year	Inflation Rate (%)	Yearly Premium (%)	Times the Premiums Are More Than Inflation Rates
2004	2.68%	9.7%	3.6 times
2005	3.39%	9.3%	2.7 times
2006	3.24%	5.5%	1.7 times
2007	2.85%	5.5%	1.9 times
2008	3.85%	4.7%	1.2 times
2009	–.62%	5.5%	9.9 times
2010	1.6%	3.0%	1.9 times
2011	3.2%	9.5%	3.0 times
2012	2.1%	4.5%	2.1 times
2013	1.5%	3.8%	2.5 times
2014	1.6%	3.0%	1.9 times

Source: Compiled from "Current U.S. Inflation Rates: 2005–2015" (2015) and "Premiums and
Worker Contributions Among Workers Covered by Employer Sponsored Coverage, 1999–
2014" (2015).

Why Don't We Have a Health Care System That Covers All Citizens Like All Other Industrial Nations?

There are a number of reasons why we do not have a health care system for all Americans. The main reasons seem to boil down to the following: (a) the vested interests of maintaining the current health system, (b) the desire to maintain political power, (c) the ideology of individualism that we have created in our country (again, refer back to our theory and causal model of conflict and social change in Chapter 1), (d) the fact that many Americans currently have access to excellent health care, and (e) the fact that most Americans do not know much about possible alternatives to our current system.

Vested Interests

Doctors, dentists, drug companies, hospitals, and health insurance companies want to make money. The current health care system results in doctors and dentists earning high incomes and health insurance companies, drug companies, and hospitals making profit. Vested interests—that is, what benefits a certain group of people—can be an extremely strong barrier to almost any kind of social change. T. R. Reid (2009) notes, "The vested interests that are doing well in the health business now—insurance companies, hospital chains, pharmaceutical companies—have blocked significant restructuring of our system" (p. 22). Or, as Daniels, Light, and Caplan (1996) put it, "The failure of national health care lies in the fact that comprehensive reform threatens powerful, wealthy interests" (p. 17).[8]

Let us take the example of drug companies versus the elderly and the price of prescription drugs. Due to the high cost of drugs produced in the United States, more and more Americans have been buying their drugs from Canadian companies. Moreover, a national poll found that 70% of respondents agreed that "it should be legal for Americans to buy prescription drugs outside the United States" (Lester, 2003, p. A5). U.S. drug companies have been fighting to keep the importation of prescription drugs from other countries illegal, arguing that U.S. drug companies need to recover the costs of doing research to create new drugs, and that drugs from other countries could be "unsafe" (Carroll, 2003, p. A7). The "unsafe" argument is probably not a valid one given that "Canadian authorities subject all drugs sold in the country, including those made in the United States, to testing similar to that conducted by the FDA [U.S. Food and Drug Administration]" (p. A7). As you might expect, there is disagreement over whether and how much money drug companies need to be able to do research on new drugs and how much profit they make. The drug companies say that the average cost to do research on a drug is $800 million (Carroll, 2003). Hence, they say they need the higher prices on their drugs to make up for expensive research. Anne Northup, a former Republican congresswoman from Kentucky who supported the importation of prescription drugs to decrease drug costs for Americans said that, on the contrary, drug companies are making 18% profit after paying their taxes—"a breathtaking amount of profit" (Carroll, 2003, p. A7). From a profit point of view, why would drug companies want to change the American health care system as long as they are making that much money?[9]

Assuming that this situation is a key barrier to any change in the health care system, we will need to address this impediment in some kind of equitable and fair way such as decrease the costs for drugs but provide reasonable compensation to drug companies.

In addition to the profit concerns of drug companies, the income concerns of doctors under a possible national health care system would also need to be addressed. For example, evidence from a study conducted on Canadian physicians found that when these physicians are paid well, they are less resistant to a national health care system (Globerman, 1990). Reaching an equitable and fair situation with doctors will also require considerable national discussion in our country. Most Americans highly regard doctors and dentists and medical personnel in general because of their years of training and education, their expertise, and their ability to decrease the pain and suffering in the rest of us and the ability to cure many of us. So, for most Americans, we want to compensate these medical personnel appropriately.

Another huge vested interest has to do with American health insurance companies. They are for-profit companies that make a lot of money selling health insurance to the rest of us. Consequently, they have a huge vested interest in not wanting the American health care system to change if it means that health insurance companies no longer get to make big profits. Furthermore, they definitely do not want to have a health care system that provides health care for all Americans but is run and paid for by the government through taxes, which would cut them out altogether from being in business and making a profit. So, either a government run or a nonprofit insurance company run health care system could be much cheaper and could include all Americans; this would cut out profit making for insurance companies. Hence, the health insurance companies would not want such a change. Moreover, given that they can give a lot of money to members of the U.S. Congress to vote against any health care system that becomes a nonprofit system and given that they can spend millions of dollars on television and newspaper ads being against any government-run or nonprofit run health care system, this means, or has meant so far, that the alternatives of either a government-run system or a nonprofit-run insurance system have not been considered (for an extended discussion, see Brill, 2015).

Political Power

Fear of losing one's political power is another barrier to creating a comprehensive health care system for all Americans. Presidents and members of Congress attain their positions of power in government, in part, through the large contributions of wealthy and powerful health insurance and drug companies. As you might predict, the more this relationship occurs, the less these politicians want to "bite the hand that feeds them," that is, the less they want to risk losing contributions and therefore risk losing their political office (again, see Brill, 2015, for an extended discussion of the politics and political power that go into the making of an American health care system).

People who want to be in Congress or be President or members of Congress who want to remain in Congress need lots of money to get elected and re-elected. As Weber ([1914]1968) and Marx and Engels ([1848]1992) noted, more than 100 to 150 years ago, money and power tend to be closely related. In the cases of Congress and the President (as well as state offices such as the governor, state senator, and state representative offices), substantial money is needed to gain and retain office and therefore political power. Some of the people and organizations with a lot of money in our country are doctors, dentists, drug companies, hospitals, and health insurance companies. Doctors and dentists can make $300,000, $400,000, and $500,000 per year and drug companies, hospitals, and health insurance companies can make millions of dollars, hundreds of millions of dollars, or even billions of dollars per year. Hence, these individuals and organizations can have a big influence on who gets to be in political positions and have political power in our country. Hence, they influence legislation that is favorable to their vested interests. As a result, money, political power, and the kinds of laws and social policies that we have can be, and many times are, closely tied to each other— that is, money, leading to political power, leading to certain laws and certain social policy.

Ideology

To understand the third reason why we do not have a health care system for all Americans—ideology—we need to refer back to the beginning of our country. Historically, our early American ancestors did not want monarchies to rule us, they did not want governments to grow too big and intrude into our lives, and they did not want a feudal caste system in which people could not move up and down the social class system (however, our country did institutionalize such a caste system for African Americans in the form of slavery and later in the form of legalized segregation and discrimination, and we also accepted many traditions of Europe where males ruled and did not allow women to be upwardly mobile). Our ancestors began to construct a new social reality[10] that tended to emphasize more individualism, getting ahead, having the chance to be upwardly mobile, being more industrialized, being more urban, and being a more capitalistic nation. Such a view of life has meant that we have been slower to accept government programs and services than have people in European countries. This belief system where we emphasize more individualism and less reliance on the government has been a significant barrier to our having a health care system for everyone. People in European countries and elsewhere have grown up relying more on their respective governments and therefore have more easily accepted and viewed some kind of a national health care system as normal and to be taken for granted. We can therefore see how ideology can play a significant role in creating laws and social policy and, hence, in solving our social problems.

Excellent Care

A fourth reason we do not have a health care system that covers every American is that many Americans already have health care. Many of us have nice homes and cars, we live in nice neighborhoods, we send our children to good schools, we take nice vacations, we have enough money to pay our bills, we have plenty of food, we have all kinds of options for recreation and leisure activities, we can go to shopping malls that are filled with all kinds of things to buy, we can purchase new technological innovations that are continually coming onto the consumer market, and so on. In other words, many Americans live a very good lifestyle. Moreover, many of us have excellent health care coverage provided by our employers and our own monthly payments. Given such an ideal situation, why would we be concerned about health care? We have excellent health care. Like other problems, if we are not personally bothered by them, we tend to take less interest in them—whether the problem is poverty, inequality, discrimination, or lack of health care.

Lack of Knowledge

Finally, a fifth reason we do not have health care for everyone is a lack of knowledge. That is, we Americans do not know much about how health care systems work in other industrialized countries. Other than hearing a little about Canada having lower prices on prescription drugs than the United States, we know little or nothing about other health care systems with which to compare and discuss various options. Many times, when people do not know much about something, they fear the unknown. Instead of being able to seriously consider various health care options based on knowledge, we base our decision making on how we benefit from our healthcare system but do not know how we might benefit from other healthcare systems, for example, being accepted for health care even if we have a pre-existing health condition, always having access to health care even when we move from one job to another job or have no job or regardless of how serious and expensive our illness is, we do not go into debt—all of these benefits that people in other industrialized countries have had, but we in America have not had.

If Americans can acquire knowledge about elements of health care systems from other industrialized countries, such as Germany, Canada, and Great Britain, and then can discuss the pros and cons of these elements, we would have knowledge that could relieve our fears about the unknown, and this knowledge could help us consider new ways of having a more comprehensive and yet less costly health care system. Until we have this knowledge, we will be ambivalent about trying anything new and different and hence will conclude, "It is better to stay with the known"—even though the known may not be the best for us.

In short, the vested interests of wanting to make much money, the desire to maintain political power, the ideology of individualism and the belief that we should not rely on the government (or should rely on it as little as possible), the fact that many Americans already have excellent health care, and limited knowledge about other ways we could have a health care system together present formidable barriers to our having a good health care system for all Americans. However, if we can overcome these barriers, we may have a chance to create a health care system that covers all Americans and yet is less costly.

Criteria for Health Care System for All Americans

No one knows exactly what an American health care system that covers all Americans would look like. Assuming that we create such a system, it would be unique. It could take on elements from other countries, such as Germany, Canada, and Great Britain (more about these countries later). Because these nations are also democratic, are predominantly capitalistic, and have high standards of living, and because they already have health care systems that cover all of their citizens, we could borrow various elements of their health care systems to create our own unique system.

Although no one knows what such a health care system would look like, we can develop criteria that we might want in a new system and discuss how we might implement these criteria:

1. Americans will receive health care based on their health care *needs* instead of their *ability to pay* for health care.[11]

2. All Americans will be covered by this new health care system.[12]

3. All Americans will receive good-quality care.

4. All Americans will receive care in a timely way.

5. An integral part of the health care system will be an emphasis on preventing illness by creating incentives and providing education for people to live healthier day-to-day lives, thereby decreasing the cost of the health care system.[13]

6. An integral part of the health care system will be an emphasis on preventing illness by providing periodic checkups so that potential illnesses can be caught early, thereby decreasing the cost of the health care system.

7. Americans live not only healthier day-to-day lives but also happier day-to-day lives.

8. Doctors, dentists, nurses, and other health care personnel are reasonably paid for their education, training, and expertise.

9. Drug companies are reasonably paid for their products and the research required to create these products.

10. Health insurance companies that could be harmed by the loss of business resulting from a new health care system will be reasonably compensated so that they can move into other areas of insurance or other areas of business.[14]

11. For-profit hospitals and hospital chains can choose to run their hospitals for a reasonable amount of compensation from the government or to sell their hospitals to the government for a reasonable amount of compensation.

12. Americans create a health care system where the costs are comparable to the costs that occur in other industrialized countries.

How We Could Implement These Criteria

Given the preceding criteria that we would want to have in a health care system that meets the health care needs of all Americans, let us now discuss how we might implement these criteria.

Buy in Bulk and Use Competitive Bidding

One element of our current health care system that could be used nation-wide is what the Department of Veterans Affairs (VA) is currently doing with millions of American veterans of military service (Pear & Bogdanich, 2003; Weigel, 2006). The VA saves a lot of money in buying its drugs for our veterans "through bulk purchasing arrangements—using generic drugs where possible—and competitive bidding" (Pear & Bogdanich, 2003, p. A7). That is, instead of veterans buying drugs at high prices in drugstores, the VA has drug companies bid on which companies will provide particular drugs at the lowest prices. The VA buys these drugs at much lower prices and, in turn, provides these drugs to the veterans who "pay just $7 for up to a 30-day prescription" (Pear & Bogdanich, 2003,). If we used this same strategy for all Americans where the federal government (1) bought drugs in bulk, (2) used generic drugs where possible, and (3) had the drug companies bid on drug contracts, the costs to the federal government would be less and taxes would be less. The drug companies selling the drugs would still make a profit—although not as much profit as they do in the current health care system. By using this strategy, we could satisfy some of our criteria, such as (Criterion 9) allowing drug companies to earn a reasonable profit and yet (Criterion 12) decrease the cost of our health care system.

Create Social Conditions That Promote Healthy Lives

Another key element of an effective health care system is to get people to live healthier lives. This alone could save taxpayers a lot of money in that there would not be as much expense for chronic or emergency care, hence addressing Criterion 12 of lowering the cost of our health care system and addressing Criteria 5, 6, and 7 of living both healthier and happier lives.

One way to promote healthier lifestyles is to give Americans tax breaks if they achieve certain health care goals throughout the year. For example, if, on examination, people are designated as being overweight, they can get an increasing tax break as they lose a certain amount of weight. The same principle could be applied to people who have high levels of cholesterol and blood pressure and other measurable indicators of health. Also, if we could invent a way to measure the amount of exercise people do over the course of a year, we could give people a higher or lower tax break depending on how much exercise they did in a year. Likewise, if we could measure and report the healthy intake of food (for example, fruits, vegetables, grains) and measure the amount of rest needed for good health, these measurements could also be factors going into decreasing people's taxes. Such a system could address Criterion 5: prevent illness by educating people to live healthier lives; Criterion 7: help Americans live healthier and happier lives; and Criterion 12: decrease the cost of our health care system.

A second way to promote healthy lifestyles is to provide early education and more education on how to live a healthy lifestyle. From the first grade onward, students can be taught about eating the right kinds of foods and getting sufficient exercise and rest. Part of a health care system would be to allocate more money to school systems to teach children about living healthier lifestyles and to mandate that all public schools provide only food that is part of a healthy diet and that any unhealthy food (for example, soda, pizza, burgers, fries) cannot be provided at the schools. Such early education about how to live a healthy lifestyle would address Criterion 5 of preventing illness through education and Criterion 12 of decreasing the cost of our health care system.

This health care system could provide for all Americans to have periodic exams—medical and dental. There are a number of reasons for these exams. First, any problems will be discovered early so that there is a better chance to cure people. Second, early detection and cure will mean that Americans will endure fewer catastrophic illnesses that are so costly, thereby decreasing the costs of our health care system. Third, the early detection and cure will mean that people will be in less pain for a shorter amount of time. Periodic exams will therefore satisfy Criterion 6 (prevent illness through periodic checkups), Criterion 7 (people live happier lifestyles), and Criterion 12 (decrease the overall cost of our health care system).

Besides these direct measures that will help people live healthier lifestyles, an indirect action that will help people live healthier lives is decreasing economic inequality in our society (see Chapter 3 on how we can decrease inequality). Budrys (2003) noted that there is a correlation between one's social class and one's health. She reported, "Accumulated evidence tells us that social class must be a more important factor than anyone previously realized" (p. 211). She adds, "The association between social inequality and poor health is consistent and powerful" (p. 211). She concludes that if we want to have better health in our country, we need to decrease inequality. Hence, as we work to decrease inequality, we will also help to decrease the health problems in our country and, in so doing, decrease our health care costs (Criterion 12).

Institute a Progressive Federal Income Tax to Pay for the New Health Care System

To have a health care system that covers all Americans (Criterion 2) with good-quality care (Criterion 3) in a timely way (Criterion 4), we will need enough money to pay for it. Because the new health care system could be one national system, probably the most realistic way of procuring the money in the United States would be to get the money at the federal level via a progressive income tax.

The additional money needed might not be that much more and may even be less than we are currently spending for health care. Currently, we are paying taxes for Medicare to help retired people have health care and for Medicaid to help poor people have health care. We are also paying taxes to pay the health care system for our veterans. Besides these three government programs, there are many employers paying insurance companies to insure many of us who work. Finally, most of us, who have health insurance plans with our employers, also contribute from our salaries and wages to our health insurance plans. As we would change to one health care system, we could abolish Medicare, Medicaid, the Veterans system, employer costs, and employee costs and instead pay one cost through our income taxes to the federal government.

Which system—our current system of many systems or one new health care system—will cost us more? I do not know. We would need to have experts consider all of the variables and analyze how the costs of the current and new systems compare. We could find that once we subtract (a) the costs of Medicare, (b) the costs of Medicaid, (c) the costs of the Veterans system, (d) the costs of more than 50 bureaucracies that serve Medicare, Medicaid, and Veterans programs, (e) the costs to employers to insure their employees, (f) the costs to employers that lose business because they are less competitive in the marketplace, and (g) the costs to employees to help pay for their own health insurance, the difference between the costs of the current system of many programs and many bureaucracies and the costs of one comprehensive system may be substantial. Other countries have fewer systems or one system, and their health care costs are lower (Reid, 2009). Given that all other industrialized countries are able to cover all of their citizens and yet pay for health care at less of a cost—sometimes almost one half the cost—compared to what we pay in our country (Reid, 2009), it seems that considering one health care system that covers all Americans could be in order.

By having a progressive income tax that brings in sufficient revenue to pay for our health care system, we will be able to pay doctors, dentists, and other health care professionals reasonably (Criterion 8), pay drug companies reasonably (Criterion 9), compensate health insurance companies and hospitals sufficiently (Criteria 10 and 11), and decrease the overall cost of our health care system (Criterion 12) and yet serve all Americans (Criterion 2). Such a strategy would help to reduce the opposition of health care professionals, drug companies, and health insurance companies that have vested interests in the current health care system.

Institute One Health Care System

In Canada, although each province and territory creates its own health care system, each system must meet minimum standards set by the federal government (Health Canada, n.d.b). Both the federal and provincial governments contribute to paying for their health care system with both federal and provincial taxes. We, in the United States, could go in the same direction, but because our states are strapped for raising tax revenue, we might choose to have the federal government pay for the health care system and have one system that is standard throughout the country. Some advantages of this kind of system is that when people move to other areas of the country, as many Americans do, they would not need to go through the process of dropping one system and signing up for another system, they would not need to fulfill any waiting period for being on the new system,[15] and they would know what the specific benefits are because the benefits would not change from state to state. If we went in the direction of having one national system, we would know that not only all citizens would be covered but also all citizens would be covered all of the time (Criterion 2).

Ensure That Medical Care Is Geographically Dispersed

The new health care system would need to make sure that all Americans can get to medical care within a reasonable amount of time (Criterion 4). We need to ask, "Is there reasonable access to medical care in rural areas of our society, in inner cities, and on reservations?" If not, we would need to plan our new health care system to achieve not only Criterion 3 (good-quality care) but also Criterion 4 (receive care in a timely way). The problem of geographic access is a bigger problem for poor people because they are less likely to have their own means of transportation[16] to get to medical care. To provide access to all Americans, we may need to give doctors, dentists, and nurses financial incentives to live in geographic areas where there are currently disproportionately fewer medical personnel.

Use Public Education: Teach Diet, Cooking, and Exercise

The public school system, from kindergarten through the twelfth grade, can be given sufficient funding to teach students (a) what food to eat and not eat, (b) how to cook nutritious food to make it taste delicious, and (c) how to get healthy exercise.

To achieve these three goals, we could create a new major in college, called *healthy lifestyles*. A student who majors in healthy lifestyles would learn how to have the best diet possible, how to cook the most nutritious meals possible, and how to get the healthiest exercise possible. Once students in this major learn these three areas, they would then learn how to teach these three areas of healthy living to others, especially elementary, middle, and high school students. Public schools would incorporate these new kinds of teachers and courses into their classrooms. Also, corporations could be given tax breaks if they hired people who have degrees in healthy lifestyles to teach courses to employees.

As a part of this action, public school systems could be required to serve only nutritious food and could be prohibited from serving food that has high saturated fat, a lot of sodium, high cholesterol, many calories, and high sugar content.[17] Foods such as pizza, burgers, fries, cake, cookies, and soft drinks would not be served. Diets at the schools would be made up of foods such as fresh fruit and vegetables; baked and grilled chicken, turkey, and fish; and water, low-fat milk, and tea.

Carrying out this recommendation will address Criterion 5 (providing education for people to live healthy day-to-day lifestyles) and Criterion 7 (living healthier lifestyles that lead to more enjoyable day-to-day lives). By having such an educational system in place, we would prevent many serious illnesses from occurring (Criterion 5) and would cut the overall costs of our health care system (Criterion 12). By instituting such a health care system in our country, we will (1) be proactive with respect to our health, (2) live healthier and happier lives, and (3) decrease the cost of our health care system.

Try Out the New Health Care System in a Select Number of States

Before we switch the entire country to a new health care system that covers all Americans, we could select a few states that would like to be a part of this initial stage to carry out the new system. By doing this, we could benefit in two ways. First, we could "work out the bugs" before we went nationwide with the new health care system. Second, we could show the rest of the nation that the system could work and how it could work. Canada unintentionally did this during the late 1940s and early 1950s, when four provinces began health care plans, thereby demonstrating to the rest of the Canadian population that, yes, such a system could work in Canada (Graig, 1999, p. 125). If a few states showed the American people that such a comprehensive health care system could work and how it could work, Americans who were dubious might be more inclined to give such a system a try.

Before we go to the next section of this chapter, I want to mention a few historical points. First, as far back as 1916, Congressman Meyer London of New York called for a national health care system (Walker, 1969, p. 299). A few years before his call, labor unions, state legislatures, the American Medical Association, the American Pharmaceutical Association, and the American Hospital Association voiced concerns over the lack of health care in our country and called for and carried out various studies. At the time, there were a number of state legislatures that were seriously considering creating state health care plans. So, consideration of a comprehensive health care system has been around in our country for nearly 100 years. Once we get used to the pros and cons of the Affordable Care Act, we may want to take the next step of creating one excellent health care system that covers all Americans, is less costly than the multiple systems we have now, and addresses all of the criteria discussed above.

Advantages of Health Care for all Americans

There will be a number of advantages if and when we have one comprehensive health care system that meets the criteria outlined. One advantage is that many poor people who were on Medicaid but will be on the new health care system will finally be treated by all doctors and all hospitals. As we noted previously, currently a number of doctors will not treat poor people on Medicaid because they believe that they do not get paid enough from Medicaid to cover the expense of treatment. Likewise, hospitals do not always get reimbursed for the services they provide because the people who are served either cannot pay for the medical services or are on Medicaid and Medicaid, which do not always reimburse hospitals enough to cover their costs (Daniels et al., 1996, p. 5). One comprehensive health care system would provide health care to poor people and reimburse doctors and hospitals sufficiently to cover their expenses.

The working poor, who have no coverage through their employers but who are not poor enough to be eligible for Medicaid, will also benefit from one health care system that includes all Americans. This would mean that up to 50 million people in the United States who have not had health coverage would finally get coverage (Zaldivar & Espo, 2009). Once the working poor could get access to health care, they would not only live healthier lives but would also experience less absenteeism from work where it has been estimated that they would make 10% to 30% more income per year and thereby increase tax revenues to various levels of government (Budrys, 2003, p. 233). So, having a healthier workforce would help both corporate profits and government revenues.

The elderly, by having access to a national health care system, will immediately have a higher standard of living because they will not need to use portions of their Social Security and retirement incomes to pay for prescription drugs. Hence, they would no longer need to choose between paying for their pills and paying for their food. They could live a healthier and happier lifestyle.

In addition to helping the preceding groups, corporations would benefit. Corporations would benefit because they would no longer need to pay for health coverage for their employees. This would immediately make American businesses more competitive in the world marketplace. For example, General Motors reported that it had to add $1,500 to the cost of each car just to pay for the health care coverage of its current and former employees.[18] Even though foreign car companies also pay health insurance premiums, "because those foreign health care systems cost so much less to run than ours, foreign competitors pay far less for health coverage than American companies do" (Reid, 2009, p. 25), thus putting American companies at a competitive disadvantage. One comprehensive health care system could immediately cut the costs for American companies and therefore put these companies in a much better competitive situation relative to companies in other countries. This change alone could prove to be a major stimulus to our economy or what sociologists call a latent function, that is, a consequence that is not intended but unintentionally increases the survival of a social system.

Another key benefit that would come from having health care for all Americans is that there could be just one bureaucracy administering this system versus the many bureaucracies administering the current health care systems. Currently, we have one bureaucracy administering the Medicare system for the elderly and 50 state bureaucracies administering the Medicaid system for the poor.[19] We also have a completely different health care system and bureaucracy for veterans. Then we have many health insurance companies with their respective bureaucracies for people who get their health insurance from their employers. Moreover, if a person changes jobs, then he or she has to join a new health care system and new bureaucracy. So, as you can readily see, we have many health insurance systems with many bureaucracies with many different rules. All of this is very complicated and really not needed. But that is what we have in this country, so far.

If we had one health care system for all Americans administered by one bureaucracy with one set of rules, we could get rid of more than 50 bureaucracies (states, veterans, Medicare, Medicaid, and employers) with different sets of rules and create a system with one bureaucracy with one set of rules that would benefit all Americans. One bureaucracy focusing on one health care system with one set of rules would be (1) more efficient, (2) less costly than many bureaucracies constantly creating different rules and procedures, and (3) more understandable for American citizens. Having one system with one set of rules that makes things much more understandable for the everyday American citizen—this alone would be a huge improvement in our country.

Moreover, although libertarians wish to have hardly any government (except for the defense of the country),[20] and conservatives do not want big government with many bureaucracies (Fine & Shulman, 2003, pp. 9–11), it would seem that most libertarians and conservatives would opt for one system that has one bureaucracy and one set of rules versus the current fifty-some government bureaucracies with fifty-some sets of rules. Also, one system with one bureaucracy that would be more organized could cut costs of health care—another advantage that almost all Americans—libertarians, conservatives, and liberals would like. As Reid (2009) asserted, "In fact, a better-organized system, covering everybody, would almost certainly cut our health care costs—after all, every other rich nation's health care system is cheaper than ours" (p. 25).

A related advantage to having one government bureaucracy is the fact that doctors and dentists, under one health care system would not have "the huge cost and time burden of processing insurance forms and negotiating with insurers regarding clinical decisions for their patients" (Daniels et al., 1996, p. 5). Doctors and dentists would deal with one bureaucracy rather than fifty-some bureaucracies and one set of rules versus many sets of rules. This should greatly relieve the headaches of office personnel in doctors' and dentists' offices who currently need to work with all of these bureaucratic entities. More simplicity, more efficiency, less cost, and more understanding of one system would all be a part of this one system.

Another advantage of having one health care system that serves all Americans is that wherever people move in the United States and whether or not they have a job, they will still be covered. Currently, as Americans move from one job to another job, they typically do not have health insurance that moves with them. So, once they get to their new job, they have to sign up for new and different health insurance with new and different rules and regulations. Also, as Americans get laid off from their jobs or get downsized, they lose their health coverage, putting all members of their families at risk. With one health care system covering all Americans, wherever they live in the United States and whatever their circumstance—job, no job, new job, elderly, poor, and so on—they will be covered. People will also know what their benefits are. Their benefits will not change from job to job. Such a situation will take away much stress that occurs now when people lose their jobs or move to other parts of the country. They will no longer need to worry about the health care part of their lives. It will be constant, consistent, and much clearer than past and current health care systems.

Another advantage of having one comprehensive health care system that covers all Americans has to do with the current situation of health maintenance organizations (HMOs) that provide health coverage for people. HMOs charge a flat fee to those who join. The people joining HMOs know that they do not need to pay any more money to receive health care. That sounds good for these people. There are, however, two problems with this system. HMOs, knowing that they will get a flat fee, will want to include only healthy people in their plans so that health care costs will remain low, and the HMOs will make more profit. They will not want to sign up people who have serious illnesses that will cost a huge amount of money to treat and that will decrease the profit the HMOs make.[21] So, seriously ill people or typically healthy people who have had to have medical care in the recent past can be turned down for coverage by HMOs. So, HMOs do not provide coverage for all Americans.

A second problem with the HMO system is that HMOs are not required to disclose the treatments they offer and the conditions under which they are offered, consequently making it next to impossible for people to know whether or not they will receive coverage. On the other hand, a comprehensive health care system would include all Americans (Criterion 2) and spell out specifically what kind of care they will receive (Criteria 3 and 4).

Disadvantages of Health Care for All Americans

One disadvantage of health care for all Americans would affect the executives of companies. In many current situations, executives of companies currently pay the same premiums for health care coverage as do their employees. Although the premiums can take a considerable chunk of employees' wages and salaries, they take a much smaller fraction from the salaries of executives. In essence, the current system of paying monthly premiums is regressive on employees. That is, employees pay a higher proportion of their incomes on health care coverage than do executives. In this way, the past and current systems work to the advantage of executives. In 1990, the ratio of worker pay to top corporate executive pay was 40 to 1, but by 1998, the ratio increased to 419 to 1 (Kerbo, 2009, p. 23). With executive pay increasing disproportionately to worker pay, this means that the monthly health insurance premiums that workers pay have become more regressive than ever.

However, if a health care system for all Americans was put in place, it could be that the way to pay for this new system would be through a more progressive income tax. That is, as people make more money, they pay more tax, and as people make less money, they pay less tax. If such a tax were instituted to pay for the new health care system, executives who paid rather a small part of their salaries to pay for health care would pay more for their health care. So, a new health care system that included all Americans and was paid for by a progressive tax system would be a disadvantage to corporate executives.

On the other hand, if the new health care system was paid for via a more progressive tax, the executives of various companies would benefit in that their respective companies would no longer have to pay for company health care systems, which, as we have noted before, would place companies in a better competitive position vis-à-vis their foreign competitors. So, even though individual executives would be at a disadvantage by paying a higher progressive income tax, their respective companies would be in a better competitive situation relative to their foreign competitors, hence making for greater survival and more profit for these American companies.

Another disadvantage will affect the drug and insurance companies. If the federal government will request competitive bids from these companies to see which companies can offer the lowest prices on drugs and services and purchase drugs and services in bulk, these companies will not make as much profit as they are currently making. Consequently, their executive salaries and employee wages will not be as much as they are now. These companies will still make reasonable profits and compensation, but they might not make the 18% profits that have been previously reported. And as you and I might predict, drug and insurance companies will attempt to discredit a health care system for all Americans if they believe they will make less profit. Given that the drug and insurance companies have "deep pockets" with which to mount a negative campaign against a health care system for all Americans that results in their making smaller profits, we, as sociologists, would predict that there is a high likelihood of advertisements on television and in newspapers and magazines and on the internet vilifying a health care system that covers all Americans. We should also predict that some members of Congress who receive significant amounts of campaign contributions from these companies will wax indignant about the perils of going down the path toward a "socialistic system." Such terms and phrases as *socialism, communism, not a real American, not the American way*, and so on would be a key part of the advertising in opposition to a health care system for all Americans.

Consequently, we, as sociologists, should predict that drug and insurance companies will, in all likelihood, succeed at slowing down the progress toward a health care system that includes all Americans. Whether their efforts result in halting or even stopping the movement toward a comprehensive health care system or whether they merely slow down the process, we should predict that a major barrier to getting such a health care system will be the actions of the drug and insurance companies—unless these companies can be assured of reasonable profits and compensation within the new system. As we mentioned before under criteria for a health care system that includes all Americans, drug companies (Criterion 9) and insurance companies (Criterion 10) would be reasonably paid and compensated.

What Other Countries Include in Their National Health Care Systems

Before we conclude this chapter, let us see what other industrialized countries—Germany, Canada, Great Britain, and Japan—include in their health care systems so that we can get an idea of what we in the United States could do. As T. R. Reid (2009) notes, "If we could import these common principles from the other rich countries, our health care system would work better for patients, providers, payers, and the American economy" (p. 23). We could take the best from each of these health care systems and create our own excellent system.

Germany

Germany was the first country to have a national health care system, which was created during the late 1800s by Otto Von Bismarck. Graig (1999) notes that the German health care system "is among the most comprehensive in the world" (p. 50); the German system covers the following areas:

> Medical, dental, in-patient hospital care, prescription drugs, preventive care, and even rehabilitative treatments at health spas are covered. Patients do not pay deductibles, though there are minimal copayments for eyeglasses, dentures, prescription drugs, and the first fourteen days of a hospital stay. . . . Another measure of the breadth of German national health insurance is in the area of income replacement. Generous maternity benefits provide full pay during the period six weeks before birth through eight weeks after birth. (p. 50)

People below a certain income must be a part of this system (this includes approximately 75% of the population), and those above this income can choose to be a part of this system (Graig, 1999). Two thirds of the people who are above this income level and who have a choice as to whether or not to be part of the national health care program choose to be a part of it (Graig, 1999). This means that another 17% along with 75%, or altogether about 92%, of all Germans are included or choose to be within this system.

The German health care system, though expensive, is still cheaper than the American system (the American system is the most expensive in the world spending 15.3% of GDP—gross domestic product— whereas the German system is two thirds that of the American system, spending 10.7% of GDP [Reid, 2009]). Reid (2009) notes the following differences between the German and American health care systems:

> First and foremost, the sickness funds are nonprofit entities; they exist to pay people's medical bills, not to pay dividends to shareholders. Thus, they don't have the same incentive that the U.S. insurance industry has to limit the people they cover or deny claims; in fact, the German insurance plans are required to accept all applicants and to pay any claims submitted by a recognized doctor or hospital. They don't have to pad their premiums to pay for a claims-review bureaucracy or to allow for profit. The result: The sickness funds have about one-third the administrative expenses that are normal in American health insurance. That makes the whole German insurance system much cheaper. (p. 75)

Moreover, when German workers lose their jobs, they do not lose their health coverage, because the government unemployment benefits will cover the workers—another key difference between the German and the American health care systems (Reid, 2009, p. 75).

To pay for the German health care system, employers and employees pay an equivalent amount into the system, based on the employees' incomes (Graig, 1999). The German system provides "the same benefits to the unemployed as to the employed" (Graig, 1999, p. 53). Unlike the current U.S. system, if German workers lose their jobs, they are still covered (Graig, 1999). Patients can choose the doctors they want (Graig, 1999). Doctors get paid based on negotiations between doctors' associations and the associations that run the national health care system.[22]

Canada

The idea of a national health care system in Canada began to take hold during the 1940s when a Gallup poll found that 80% of Canadians favored a national health care system, and that the Canadian Medical Association, representing the doctors in Canada, also supported the creation of such a system (Graig, 1999). Canada's health care system is actually 12 systems representing 10 provinces and 2 territories (Graig, 1999). Doctors have private independent practices and are paid fees for their services each month, but these fees have already been negotiated between the government and the doctors. Hospitals are mainly private nonprofit organizations (Graig, 1999). Each provincial and territorial health care system needs to meet four criteria set down by the federal government. First, each plan is comprehensive, so that many services are offered. Second, each plan is administered publicly, that is, by an agency of the provincial government. Third, each plan is available to all people in the province; so, there are no pre-existing conditions that prevent patients from getting care. Fourth, people from one province, when visiting another province, can get medical service (called *portability*) (Graig, 1999). In the process, a province can even buy out private health insurance buildings, computers, and employees (Graig, 1999). Hospitals have remained private nonprofit organizations, but instead of being reimbursed by an insurance company, they are reimbursed by the government. Consequently, Canadian citizens, instead of paying doctors and hospitals directly or paying insurance companies to pay the doctors and hospitals, pay taxes to the government, which pays the doctors and hospitals (Graig, 1999), which is about one half of what Americans pay in premiums to private insurance companies in the United States (Reid, 2009). Graig (1999) described the Canadian system this way:

> Preventing a two-tier system of health care made up of those who could pay and those who could not was a high priority. The federal government determined that the best way to avoid such a two-tier system was to take the dramatic step of outlawing private insurance coverage for any services covered under the provincial plans. Provincial universal hospital and medical plans thus took the place of all the various forms of insurance—private, not-for-profit, and public—that had existed up to that point. The provincial governments became the single purchasers of publicly insured hospital and medical care services. . . . By the mid-1970's, 95 percent of all costs of hospital and medical care services were paid through the provincial health plans and 0 percent of the population had private comprehensive health insurance coverage. (p. 128)

Graig (1999) also pointed out that Canadians go to the doctors of their choice and present a health card. As such, they do not need to fill out any forms, pay any copayments, or pay a deductible. A *deductible* is a certain amount of money that the patient needs to pay for health care first before the rest is paid for by the patient's insurance.

As you might predict, there has been and continues to be conflict between the doctors' associations and the provincial governments as to how much doctors will be paid for the services they render. A number of Canadian doctors feel that they are not paid enough. They are paid about one half of what American doctors are paid (Reid, 2009). Hence, there is not as much financial incentive for Canadians to become doctors. As a consequence, Canadians feel that their health care system is "underdoctored," which leads to the problem of longer waiting times to see doctors as compared to the United States. Provincial governments try to hold down rising medical costs, whereas doctors want to get a higher return on the services they provide. Hence, the negotiations are continually difficult. Some doctors—approximately 1%—have left Canada as a result of these contentious disagreements (Graig, 1999).

As you can see, even with a national health care system, there will be built-in conflicts of interest. So, even if we go to one comprehensive health care system in the United States and achieve the goal of meeting everyone's medical needs, our system, like other national health care systems in other countries, will, in all probability, be in a continual process of conflict, negotiation, and change. These are the kinds of conflicts that will need to be hammered out if we in the United States go toward a health care system that covers all Americans.

It seems that the people of Canada, all in all, are glad to have their health care system. As Reid (2009) notes, the Canadian National Health Insurance system "records high levels of satisfaction" (p. 127). Reid adds that it is Canada's "most popular social program" (p. 127). Canadians like the fact that all Canadians can get care regardless of income. So, no one can be denied because of pre-existing conditions, and no one can go bankrupt due to excessive medical expenses, such as has occurred in the United States. Canada comes out ahead of the United States on longer life expectancy and lower rates of infant mortality and yet costs about half that of the U.S. system. The key complaint of the Canadian system, however, is the long wait for care in nonurgent situations. Reid notes that "if your medical problem is not urgent enough to require immediate treatment, Canada will almost always keep you waiting" (p. 128). This is one area in which Canadians would like to improve their system.

Great Britain

Great Britain has what is called the National Health Service (NHS), which "the entire British population depends on" (Graig, 1999, p. 151) for its health care needs. The central government plays the key role, more so than in the United States, Germany, Canada, or Japan. That is, the government finances and runs the health care system (Graig, 1999). When people who are against government health care systems such as Medicare, Medicaid, and Veterans Affairs, and call all of these kinds of health care systems "socialism," they are often thinking of the British health care system (Reid, 2009). The British health care system "provides essentially cradle-to-grave care, regardless of one's ability to pay, and is free to the patient at the point of service" (p. 154). The phrase "free to the patient" means that patients do not pay money when they go to the doctor, but they pay the federal government in taxes and the government, in turn, pays doctors and hospitals. In 1997, the government spent 6.7% of gross domestic product (GDP) on health care, whereas the United States spent 13.6% of GDP (or roughly twice as much money) on health care, yet various health indicators, such as infant mortality and life expectancy rates, were similar in the two countries.

The British health care system costs less than half what the American system costs, but the British system has two key problems that the American system does not: longer waiting lists to get medical service and shortages in technology (Graig, 1999). Until the Affordable Care Act was passed, 1 out of 6 Americans did not have health care coverage, whereas all citizens of Great Britain have been covered. Prescription drugs, which have been a political "hot potato" in the United States and have been and are very costly, are nearly free in Great Britain. That is, some people need to give copayments, but 80% of prescribed drugs are dispensed free of charge (Graig, 1999). Yet, Reid (2009) suggests that, all in all, "the people who provide care in the NHS are enormously proud of their system and . . . the people who receive care from the NHS are among the most satisfied medical customers on earth" (p. 104).

Any health care system seems to struggle with the problem of keeping costs down as new technologies increase costs and as vested interests, such as doctors who want higher incomes, work to increase costs. Reid (2009) suggests that the British health care system does an excellent job of keeping down costs and "is a model for any country that wants to provide quality care at low cost" (p. 112).

With any national health care system in any country, there will be conflicts of vested interests, continual desire for more or less of something depending on the interest groups, and so on. Great Britain is no different. Although Great Britain has been able to keep its health care costs relatively low, the British people want more services (Graig, 1999). Also, the British population, like the American population, is aging, and hence there will be more elderly people requiring more services. Also, although the waiting time to see a doctor or get medical service has not increased in Great Britain since the 1960s, the number of people on waiting lists has increased (Graig, 1999). So, an aging population, a demand for more services, more people on waiting lists, and an ever-changing economy make for continual change within the British health care system. Vested interests of patients, taxpayers, doctors, hospitals, and the government all work to put pressures on any national health care system. So, we in the United States, like the people in Great Britain and other countries, whatever health care system we could eventually create, will need to change our health care system as different variables change. This seems to be what happens in other countries and will probably happen in our country.

Japan

Except for the United States, as in other countries, Japan's insurance companies are nonprofit companies. Unlike American insurance companies, the Japanese health insurance companies "exist to pay medical bills, not to earn a profit for investors" (Reid, 2009, p. 90). This is a key reason why the Japanese health care system is one half the cost of the American system. Another reason that the Japanese health care system is much cheaper than the American one—the American cost is 15.3% of GDP while the Japanese cost is 8% of GDP (Reid, 2009)—is that the government under the Ministry of Health and Welfare negotiates with doctors and hospitals, and the results of these negotiations apply to all doctors and hospitals in Japan (Reid, 2009). These negotiations mean that "the system squeezes cost by sharply limiting the income of medical providers—doctors, nurses, hospitals, labs, drug makers" (Reid, 2009, p. 86). This is unheard of in the United States where many doctors make $300,000 a year or more, hospitals make millions of dollars, and drug companies and insurance companies make profit of millions, hundreds of millions, or even billions. Another way of keeping costs down is that every Japanese citizen is required to sign up for health care through his or her employer; the premium is split between the employer and employee (Reid, 2009). That way, the cost is spread over many people. For those who are unemployed or too poor to pay a premium, local governments cover their health care costs, with the result that "coverage never lapses" (Reid, 2009, p. 88).

The Japanese health care system has a number of advantages for patients. Japanese patients pick their doctors and hospitals. The insurance plans in Japan must accept people with pre-existing conditions—unlike the U.S. system until the Affordable Care Act was passed. The insurance plans "must pay every bill submitted by a physician or a hospital" (Reid, 2009). Also, the Japanese system has little or no waiting to get to see a doctor, and yet Japanese patients go to the doctor three times more often than Americans do (Reid, 2009). Also, Japanese doctors make house calls, something long gone in the United States.

The Future: What Could Happen?

No one knows what will happen in the near future.[23] However, I have some ideas given recent trends in our country. The recent trends are that health care costs have increased substantially, making more people aware of this growing problem. Another trend is that more corporations and nonprofit organizations are decreasing or eliminating coverage for their employees because health insurance costs so much. For example, 69% of American corporations provided health care coverage for their employees in 2000, but only 60% provided coverage in 2006. One implication of this decrease in coverage is that members of the middle class have been threatened with a decrease or loss of health care coverage (Beauchamp, 1996). Such a trend will get the influential middle class more concerned about the problem of health care in our country. Another trend has been that prescription drug costs have continued to climb at such a rate that elderly people must use more and more of their Social Security and retirement incomes to buy the prescription drugs that they need. This has decreased their standard of living to the point that many retirees have experienced more financial stress during their retirement years. Another trend that occurred in the late 1990s and early 2000s was that the number of uninsured in our country increased from 44 million in 1999 to 46 million in 2006 to 50 million in 2009.[24] Another trend that has occurred is that Medicare for the elderly and Medicaid for poor people were being cut back, making it more difficult for the elderly and poor people to get health care.[25] Another trend that has occurred, especially in the 2000s is that the health care problem has continually been in the news, with the result that Americans have become more aware of this problem and have wanted to do something about it. For example, a front-page article titled "Support Swells for Universal Health Care" in the *Louisville Courier–Journal* on January 30, 2006, was typical for readers wanting to learn more about the health care problem (Unger, 2006). A few weeks later, an editorial titled "Ailing Health System Needs More Than a Few Band-Aids" in the *Indianapolis Star* on February 21, 2006, was another early example (Feldman, 2006). Since 2006, there has been a growing number of newspaper articles and editorials; in the spring, summer, and fall of 2009, news articles and editorials appeared almost daily in the newspapers as numerous committees in Congress worked on a new health care system and President Obama pushed hard for a new system (see for example, Elliott, 2009; Hiatt, 2009; Marcus, 2009; Werner, 2009b, ; Zaldivar, 2009b; Zaldivar & Espo, 2009).

Consequently, we are focusing more and more on this problem. This leads me to predict that unless something unforeseen happens, such as another war or natural catastrophe that would divert our attention and resources, we, as Americans, will increasingly work to improve our health care system. As to where this process will eventually end, I do not know, but let me share with you what happened in our country prior to our passing the Affordable Care Act, or as some people call it, *Obamacare*.

Summer and Fall 2009 and Winter 2010: Finally, Serious Debate

More than 65 years ago, President Harry Truman began the preliminary discussion on health care for Americans (Reid, 2009, p. 11). Discussion over this issue has come and gone, but nothing comprehensive has been done for all Americans. Partial steps have been taken, however. Medicare and Medicaid were created in 1965; Medicare protected people over 65 (Reid, 2009, p. 38) while Medicaid protected those who were poor. As of 2005, Medicare covered 40 million Americans or 14% of the U.S. population, while Medicaid covered 38 million Americans or 13% of the population (Macionis, 2008, p. 560). Yet, by 2005, 47 million Americans still had no health insurance or approximately one out of six Americans; moreover, most of these 47 million Americans (78%) were working, but their employers did not provide health coverage (Macionis, 2008, p. 561).

As of winter, 2010, 1 of 6 Americans still did not have health insurance to protect them when they became sick or needed checkups or preventive care. There were three main reasons why these Americans had no health insurance. One reason was that employers could not afford to provide health care for their employees. A second reason was that many of these uninsured Americans could not afford to buy health insurance on their own—it was too expensive relative to the low incomes that they had. A third reason was that if someone already had an illness, called a "pre-existing condition," the insurance companies did not have to insure these people. So, they typically did not insure these people because they would lose profit on these individuals. Many of these people with pre-existing conditions who could not get health insurance could not pay the huge costs of treating their illnesses on their own; so, they would either go without treatment and therefore live lives filled with pain and continued sickness or die sooner since they had no treatment (Reid, 2009, pp. 1–3). If they chose to get treatment and paid thousands, hundreds of thousands, or even millions of dollars, they and their families would typically lose their life savings, any investments that they had, their homes, and would end up living in poverty for years, and in many instances, for the rest of their lives. Reid (2009) asked a revealing question:

How many people went bankrupt (due to medical bills) in other countries compared to how many people went bankrupt due to medical bills in the United States?

> In Britain, zero. In France, zero. In Japan, Germany, the Netherlands, Canada, Switzerland: zero. In the United States, according to a joint study by Harvard Law School and Harvard Medical School, the annual figure is around 700,000. (Reid, 2009, p. 31)

In the spring of 2009, Congress, at the behest of President Obama, once again took up the issue of health care in America. When President Obama was elected in November 2008, there was an air of seriousness about addressing our health care problems. Polls conducted during the 2008 election found that 79% of those polled wanted either "'fundamental change' or 'a complete overhaul'" (Reid, 2009, pp. 10–11). The President, the Congress, and the American people, it appeared, were finally ready to move toward a better health care system.

Many things occurred in the summer, fall, and early winter of 2009. In a sense, it was a raucous time for our Congress. Three committees in the House of Representatives and two committees in the Senate began to formulate plans for health care reform. It seemed that all summer and all fall and even to the end of 2009, the Congress and many American people were concentrating on this one issue and were even "caught up" in this whole affair.

August is a time that the Congress takes the month off for vacation. But many members of Congress went back to their home states and congressional districts and held what are known as "town halls," that is, meetings where citizens could air their views (Gerth and Rose, 2009). In many of these town hall meetings, there was considerable tension between more conservative citizens who did not want the government to take over the health care system because, from their perspective, they did not want more "big government" and more taxes and liberals, who on the other hand, believed that the state of affairs in our country with respect to health care was, to say the least, deplorable (Adams, 2009). They noted that unlike any other industrialized nation, our country did not cover the health care of all of it citizens. Moreover, many Americans were not allowed to get health care coverage because they had pre-existing health problems and therefore, health insurance companies, who were in business to make profit, did not accept these people who would be a great expense to the insurance companies. So, as you might expect, there were different views expressed at these town hall meetings where moments of tensions arose.

By the time the Congress reconvened in September, the main issues of the health care debate were coming more clearly into focus (Alonso-Zaldivar, 2009a; Highlights of the Plan, 2009). Yes, there were huge differences in philosophy (Groppe, 2009). Conservatives were generally of the opinion that small government, low taxes, and private enterprise should take care of health care, while liberals were generally of the opinion that all Americans should be covered, pre-existing conditions should not be allowed as a criterion for not providing coverage, and competition should be introduced into health care by creating a public option (that is, a government health care option, as a means of introducing competition into the market, with the intent of controlling spiraling health care costs caused by private health insurance companies that are in business to make profit). Given this large gap in philosophy, as you might predict, politics entered into the debate (Milbank, 2009; Obama's Chance to Recast Debate, 2009). The Republicans did not want the newly elected Democratic president, Barack Obama, to have a big victory by passing health care reform (Babington, 2009). Likewise, the Democrats wanted a big victory for their new president. Hence, all through the summer, the fall, and into December 2009, differences in philosophy and the playing of politics took center stage during the health care debate (Alonso-Zaldivar, 2009b; Zaldivar, 2009a). As you might suspect, such conditions made for a highly emotional time, with daily displays of drama, innuendo, and outright accusations.

Finally, in November and December, the Democratically controlled House passed a health care bill that included a public option while the Senate, also Democratically controlled, passed a bill without a public option (Alonso-Zaldivar, 2009c; Babington & Loven, 2009; Werner, 2009a). In winter 2010, members of the House and the Senate met to "iron out" differences in their respective bills to see if they could create a health care bill that would be voted on by both houses of Congress and sent to President Obama to sign.

There were many questions to be answered at that time. Will the final bill include a public option that will create more competition and hence control health care costs? Will insurance companies have to insure people who have pre-existing conditions? Will insurance companies accept people with pre-existing conditions but charge a lot more for their health insurance? How many more Americans out of the 45 to 50 million who were not insured will actually end up getting health care coverage? And if the bill passes and is signed into law by President Obama, when will it take effect— immediately or 1, 2, 3, or 4 years from now? Will the United States no longer be *the only* industrialized country in the world not to provide health care for all of its citizens, or will we continue to be the only industrialized country not to cover all of its citizens? In other words, are we on the road to solving this social problem of 50 million Americans not having health care and the United States having the most expensive health care system in the world, or are we not?

March 21, 2010: Health Care Reform Passes Congress

The setting: the House of Representatives of the United States Congress. The date and time: Sunday, March 21, 2010, at 10:30 p.m. Individual Republican and Democratic members have been speaking for or against the bill all day and well into this evening. Finally, the last person to speak about the bill is Nancy Pelosi, the Speaker of the House. She notes that our country has discussed the problem of lack of health care for Americans for over 100 years. She states further that we are now about to make history by finally providing the American people with health care. She finishes her speech and is applauded loudly with a standing ovation by her fellow Democrats while the Republicans sit and watch. Within minutes, the gavel goes down, and the voting begins. Everything comes down to this moment. Will we finally have health care for more Americans or will we not?

For the next 15 minutes, voting takes place. National television networks cover this extraordinary session; so, millions of Americans are watching this event unfold. All Republicans vote no. Some Democrats vote no. But the vote, yes, for health care reform begins to mount. What is needed are 216 yes votes—a majority in the House. Slowly, over the next 15 minutes, the yes vote begins to grow. Now, it is 180—now, 190. Will the House reach 216 votes and pass health care reform or not? It is 10:43 p.m., and the count is up to 210. Can the Democrats get the last 6 votes? At this moment, it is very suspenseful both in the House chamber and for many Americans watching on television. I looked at my watch and at 10:45 p.m., the 216th vote was cast, and a loud and joyous sound burst out in the chamber. Health care reform, in the United States—after 100 years of serious consideration—passed.

In essence, what did this mean? What changed? In a nutshell, this is what happened:

1. An additional 32 million people will be insured. This will mean that about 94 percent of all Americans will be insured.

2. Insurance companies can no longer deny Americans with pre-existing conditions.

3. Insurance companies can no longer cancel a policy once one of their clients gets sick.

4. Insurance companies can no longer place a lifetime limit on an insured person.

5. Insurance companies can no longer deny children with pre-existing conditions.

6. Insurance companies can no longer charge women more for insurance.

7. To pay for the added obligations for insurance companies, people "with incomes above the federal poverty level must enroll in coverage or face a penalty" (O'Donnell and Ungar, February 2, 2015, 1B) and the penalty for 2014 is $95 per person or 1% of household income, whichever is higher and the penalty for 2015 is $325 per person or 2% of household income, whichever is higher and the penalty for 2016 is $696 per person or 2.5% of household income, whichever is higher (O'Donnell and Ungar, February 2, 2015, p. 1B).

8. Medicaid will be expanded to cover more lower-income people.

9. For people who make money from investing and for individuals who make $200,000 or more per year, they will be taxed more to help pay for health care reform.

10. The so-called "donut hole" (where people on Medicare are covered, then not covered, and then covered again, for the cost of their prescription drugs) will decrease each year and will disappear by 2020 where all of their prescription drugs will be paid for, eliminating the "donut hole," thus making life more financially stable for the elderly.

11. Small companies, the self-employed, and the uninsured can choose an insurance plan from what will be called "exchanges" where a number of insurance companies will offer plans, increasing the competition and thus containing costs.

12. There is no government run health care program (known as the "public option"). For-profit health insurance companies will still be where most Americans (except for the poor on Medicaid, the elderly on Medicare, and veterans on veterans health care) will choose their health care.

13. Any government taxes cannot be used to pay for abortion. Furthermore, no health care plan is required to offer abortion insurance. Also, in health care plans where abortion insurance is offered, policyholders will have to pay for this insurance separately. Finally, states can ban abortion coverage in insurance plans.

14. The new health care reform will mainly begin in 2014 but some changes will begin immediately such as (1) people with pre-existing conditions can now buy insurance, (2) sick children cannot now be denied coverage, (3) insurance companies now no longer have a lifetime limit on what they pay, (4) there are now no co-payments for preventive care and vaccines, (5) parents can now cover their children up to age 26 (was 23), and (6) the

donut hole will start to be closed with a $2.50 tax rebate to those on Medicare (phone communication with the office of Congressman Baron Hill, March 22, 2010).

("The Final Bill at a Glance," Louisville Courier–Journal, March 23, 2010, p. A4 [Numbers 1–6 and 8–13]):

So, with the passage of this bill in the Senate and in the House and with the signing of this bill by President Obama, we in the United States came closer to providing health care for all Americans. Although we did not provide all Americans with health care, we did provide millions of more Americans with health coverage with the expansion of Medicaid to cover more lower-income Americans and with 10 million Americans signing up for health insurance in 2014 and 11.4 million signing up in 2015 (O'Donnell and Ungar, February 19, 2015; Rudavsky, January 15, 2015).

Where we go next in our country is unknown. Many Republicans want to do away with the law and have introduced many bills in Congress to do just that. All have failed so far. Many Democrats want to keep the new law, which allows millions of more Americans to have access to health care, either through expanded Medicaid for low-income people or through exchanges that provide people some choice as to how much they can afford to pay. Still others hope that we will go further and finally provide health care for all Americans at a more reasonable cost by either having nonprofit insurance companies provide care and cut out the cost of making a profit or taxing Americans and having the government manage health care at probably one half the cost of what it is today. Republicans and conservatives, due to their philosophical beliefs, typically do not want another government program even though it would cover all Americans and cost less. So, this is where we are today. With the Affordable Care Act, or as some call it, *Obamacare*, we are closer to having health care for all Americans but not there yet. The final chapter of this social problem is yet to be written—possibly during the lifetime of those college students who are reading this.

Questions for Discussion

1. Should we have a health care system based on people's *ability to pay* for health care or on their *need* for health care?

2. If we created a health care system for all Americans, what, in addition to the things discussed in this chapter, would you put in an American health care system? Why?

3. What suggestions in this chapter would you drop? Why?

4. If the American people had a chance to read this chapter, what do you think their thoughts would be? Where would they agree, and where would they disagree? Why?

5. Will we someday have a health care system that covers all Americans and is not so expensive? Why, or why not?

6. How could we move toward a more preventive philosophy in health care?

7. Are we becoming a healthier or unhealthier society? What is your reasoning?

8. What one step do you think Americans could take to have much healthier lifestyles?

9. How healthy are the lifestyles of college students? Why is this the case?

10. How could college students live healthier lifestyles?

11

How Can We Solve the Problems of Families?

You might ask why I put the chapter on solving the problems of families after all of these other chapters. I did this for a specific reason. If we can solve or decrease many of the social problems that we have just discussed, we can go a long way toward solving the problems of American families. Let me show you how solving or ameliorating these social problems will greatly help our families.

Decreasing Inequality to Help Families

As we discussed in Chapter 3, the United States has the most inequality of any industrialized country, and our inequality continues to widen. As you recall, we mentioned that our chief executive officers earn the largest salaries of any such executives in the world, whereas our workers earn some of the lowest wages of workers in other industrialized nations.[1] For example, in the last 35 years (since around 1980), CEO pay in our largest corporations has increased 900% while worker pay has increased only 10% (Quigley, 2014). Hence, the ratio of CEO pay to average worker pay was 30 to 1, but now it is 296 to 1 (Quigley, 2014). So, average worker pay has not increased very much over the last 35 to 40 years, in large part due to many companies moving to other countries to pay lower wages, known as deindustrialization, which, in turn, caused U.S. worker pay to stagnate for years. Moreover, so many of our workers make minimum wage, which is $8,770 below the poverty line **for a family of four,** making it difficult for these families to survive. Our country is the only industrialized country that does not have a health care system for all of its citizens although more Americans have health insurance, due to the Affordable Care Act (also, known as Obamacare). Other countries provide paid leave that can last more than a year for pregnancy, whereas the United States provides leave, but it is unpaid and for just 3 months. Other countries offer more extensive child care subsidies than we do. As you can see, low-income parents in other countries are helped much more than low-income parents in our country. In fact, as we pointed out in Chapter 4 on poverty, we have long waiting lists of low-income families waiting to get child care subsidies. All of these indicators suggest that we have more inequality than any other industrialized nation, translating into more hardship on American families. As families have fewer resources with which to survive, we should predict that these families will experience more problems such as stress, abuse, and divorce.

Given all of this inequality, a key way to help American families is to decrease the great economic inequality so that more American families have enough money not only to survive but also to have a decent standard of living. Dr. Martin Luther King, Jr., noted this back in the late 1960s when he pointed out that we need to realize the connection between economic inequality and other problems in our society such as race, substandard housing, and substandard education (Robinson, 2015). One optimistic sign is that the federal government and a number of states plan to increase the minimum wage; so, to the degree this happens in the next few years, more than 2 million workers will come closer to being near the poverty level and possibly above it (Davidson, 2014). As we can decrease the inequality in our country by implementing a more progressive income tax (through which poorer people pay less in tax[2] and richer people pay more in tax), providing health care for everyone, and offering more child care subsidies and rent subsidies for housing, these measures can work together to decrease the stress on many low-income families and families just above poverty. This decrease in stress will create the social conditions to have more stable and happier families.

Decreasing Poverty to Help Families

Getting families who are in poverty out of poverty is a solution to one social problem that could have a big influence on American families. Probably no one variable does more to hurt families and put more stress on them than poverty. If families do not know how they are going to pay next month's rent, do not have enough money to buy food for the whole month, and do not have decent clothes for their children to wear to school, these financial burdens can put great stress on poor and near-poor families, leading to lower self-esteem for the parents, to more arguing about finances, to more spouse abuse or child abuse, to greater strains on marriages, and to more divorces.

Although the factor of poverty is not the only factor that causes these unfortunate consequences, it no doubt plays a key role in decreasing the unity, stability, and happiness of families. If we, in our country, seriously work to get our poor people out of poverty (see Chapter 4 for a number of specific suggestions), we can go a long way toward helping our poor families live more stable, secure, and happier family lives. As we discussed in Chapter 4, various European countries have reduced their poverty substantially in two ways: (1) by how they tax people and (2) by the services they provide. If other countries can get most of their poor out of poverty, we should be able to do this, too.[3]

Creating Enough Jobs and Enough Decent-Paying Jobs to Help Families

I could have put the following discussion in the preceding section about decreasing poverty, but I want to emphasize the importance of decent-paying jobs to the solving of problems of American families. As we discussed in Chapter 4 on poverty, there are two problems with the job structure within a capitalistic economy that hurt many American families. First, a capitalistic economy does not create enough jobs. For example, we have been coming out of a severe recession that had 10% unemployment peaking in October of 2009, but we still have 5.5% unemployment 6 years later—even as many jobs are being created and the economy has picked up considerably (Waggoner, 2015). Second, a capitalistic economy not only does not create enough jobs, but it also does not create enough decent-paying jobs so that all American families can live decent lifestyles. Remember, just because you have a job—and a full-time job—in a capitalistic economy does not mean you are no longer poor. Recall that the minimum wage of $7.25 per hour will give you a yearly income of $15,080 (working 40 hours a week, all 52 weeks of the year), but the poverty level for a family of four is $23,850. So, a full-time job at the minimum wage will mean that you are $8,770 below the poverty level or to put it another way, you are at 63% of the poverty level. So, when people say, "Get a job!" they do not realize that many people have jobs and full-time jobs and yet are considerably below the poverty level.

So, it is not that they do not have jobs, and it is not that they are lazy; it is because their jobs pay way below the poverty level.

When families cannot earn enough money to pay their bills, they will continually be under stress, resulting in greater chances for spouse abuse, child abuse, child neglect, and divorce. Hence, the kind of economy we have, a capitalistic economy, is directly related to the problems our families have. As I mentioned previously, our capitalistic economy will not change soon; that leaves us with what we can do *within* a capitalistic economy to create enough jobs for families to have decent lifestyles. Maybe a goal for our country could be not to get every family to a middle-class lifestyle but to get every family at least at the poverty level and possibly a little bit above the poverty level.

As we discussed previously, creating a progressive income tax system that takes pressure off low-income families by allowing them to keep what little take-home pay that they receive and developing a social service system that meets the needs of many people will greatly alleviate the stress on many families. Consequently, the combination of (1) less tax on low-income families, (2) more social services (for example, affordable and quality health care for all American families, child care subsidies so that mothers can work, Section 8 housing subsidies, and college student loans), and (3) enough jobs and enough decent-paying jobs (such as jobs that pay at least the poverty level or above) would act to greatly enhance the livelihood of American families, and this, in turn, would decrease family stress and thereby decrease the chances for divorce, child abuse, child neglect, and overall unhappiness of the family.

Creating Racial and Ethnic Equality to Help Families

As long as we have racial and ethnic prejudice and discrimination (whether it be at the individual, group, or institutional levels), we will have racial and ethnic inequality. Prejudice and discrimination, historically and even to this present day, have been major causes of inequality in societies. Unfortunately, this has been the case in our society, too. These social conditions lead to a number of families in our society not having the same opportunities as other families have. These families do not receive as good an education, do not get the chance to be as upwardly mobile, and do not get to be in occupations with more money, power, and prestige. As a result, these families do not have as much income to buy homes and accumulate wealth, are not able to have a number of material goods in their homes, are not able to pay their bills as easily, are not able to send their children to good schools, and are less likely to take vacations or be able to afford other leisure activities, such as going out to nice restaurants and attending sporting events, plays, or concerts. In other words, prejudice and discrimination result in these families having fewer life chances.

Moreover, the families that have to endure prejudice and discrimination, in all probability, face much more stress and many more self-esteem problems. First, they experience the stress of not having enough money to pay their bills. Second, the inability to pay bills can affect the parents' self-esteem. As the sociologist Charles Horton Cooley noted with his concept of the looking glass self (Cooley, 1964), we look to others (for example, our parents, our friends, our teachers, our coaches) to see how they see and judge us, and we tend to see and judge ourselves based on how others see and judge us. With respect to parents who experience prejudice and discrimination, it would not be surprising to find their self-esteem is affected along with that of their children.

The stress of money problems alone can put great strain on families. In his classic work *Tally's Corner*, Liebow (1967) discovered that many African American men of the early 1960s living in Washington, DC, could not find decent-paying steady jobs. Not having the opportunity to obtain decent-paying jobs caused many men not to want to marry, because they knew they could not support their families; or if they did marry and had every intention of having lasting, stable, and happy marriages, they found that they could not get decent-paying steady jobs to keep their marriages together. In other words, Liebow found that the social structure of prejudice and discrimination had a huge effect on African American families. For example, he noted,

> In general, the menial job lies outside the job hierarchy and promises to offer no more tomorrow than it does today. The Negro menial worker remains a menial worker so that, after one or two or three years of marriage and as many children, the man who could not support his family from the very beginning is even less able to support it as time goes on. The longer he works, the longer he is unable to live on what he makes. (p. 211)

As we discussed in Chapter 5 on racial/ethnic inequality, we have made progress in decreasing discrimination in our society by creating and enforcing civil rights laws so that any American can go to a restaurant, park, stadium, or concert; can vote; hold political office; get a bank loan (called a *mortgage*) to buy or build a home; get loans or grants to go to college; play on sports teams and earn an athletic scholarship; can go to graduate school, law school, or medical school; and can become a doctor, lawyer, professor, or so on. We have made considerable progress in decreasing discrimination and, in doing so, we have increased opportunities for African American, Native American, Hispanic American, and other American minorities. To the degree that we have made this progress, especially since 1950, we have helped American families from various minority groups to increase their opportunities and increase their chances for upward mobility; hence they have the chance to have more stable, secure, and happier family lives. Consequently, as we continue to work to decrease discrimination in our society, we should observe a positive effect on minority families in terms of a decrease in stress, spouse abuse, child abuse, child neglect, and divorce. Consequently, our solving or greatly ameliorating one social problem, racial and ethnic prejudice and discrimination, will be a key factor in helping solve another social problem, the problems of our families.

Creating Gender Equality to Help Families

As more females get good-quality educations, they can have more chances at being upwardly mobile and hence earn more money. If they become single mothers, they will have decent incomes that will provide for more secure and stable family life. With the high divorce rate, leaving many mothers on their own to take care of themselves and their children, it is more imperative than ever before that women have good educations or training so that they will be prepared for the life of a single parent, if need be. Hence, if we want to help female heads of families, our society will need to continue to work toward more gender equality.

Including Gay and Lesbian Couples to Help Families

During recent years, we have had a lot of discussion in our country about whether or not gay and lesbian couples should be allowed to marry. One question we could ask about this issue is, "How can we help families become happier and more stable?" What could we do to achieve these two goals: (1) more happiness and (2) more stability?

We know that some American males and females—2.8% of adult males and 1.4% of adult females—are same-sex oriented (Laumann, Gagnon, Michael, & Michaels, 1994, p. 297). Thus, assuming an American population of approximately 300 million, one-half male and one-half female, we can predict that approximately 4.2 million American males and 2.1 million American females, or about 6.3 million Americans, are same-sex oriented. Although some homosexual Americans have been socialized to be homosexual (Kinsey, Pomeroy, & Martin, 1948; Kinsey, Pomeroy, Martin, & Gebhard, 1953; Roughgarden, 2004; Stone, 1985), evidence suggests that most people, both heterosexuals and homosexuals, are born with a particular sexual orientation.[4] So, sexual orientation is not easy to change. Those of us who are attracted to the opposite sex will probably be that way all of our lives. Likewise, those of us who are attracted to the same sex will probably be that way all of our lives. Consequently, given that heterosexuals are mostly born their way and homosexuals are mostly born their way, one of the first steps our society could take to achieve the goals of creating happier and more stable families is to acknowledge that most Americans, whether heterosexual or homosexual, have specific sexual orientations that are strong, enduring, and highly resistant to change—regardless of what other people feel or believe about homosexuality or how they have been socialized regarding homosexuality or what religious beliefs they have been taught relative to homosexuality.

The next step we can take is to accept gays and lesbians as they are and include them more in our society rather than exclude them by discriminating against them. Note that even though I talk about same-sex individuals as if they were one uniform group of people, research has shown that homosexuals and heterosexuals fall along a continuum of sexual orientation: a number of Americans are exclusively heterosexual; other Americans are mainly heterosexual with some same-sex interest; still other Americans are oriented somewhat equally in heterosexual and same-sex ways; other Americans are mainly same-sex with some heterosexual orientation; and, finally, still other Americans are exclusively same-sex oriented.[5] In reality, there is much more sexual variation among Americans (and among humans in general) than many Americans realize (or want to admit); for example, a 1994 study showed that 75% of male and female heterosexual Americans have practiced oral sex while 25% practice it as a current activity (Laumann et al., 1994, p. 101), and 25% of men and 20% of women heterosexuals have had anal sex (Laumann et al., 1994, p. 107).[6]

As we discussed in Chapter 5 on racial and ethnic inequality and in Chapter 6 on gender inequality, when we are prejudiced and discriminate against a group of people, we exclude these people from different aspects of society (informal conversation, parties, clubs, churches, various jobs, and so on), with the result that they experience negative consequences such as a more narrow range of opportunities, lower income, less upward mobility, lower self-esteem, anger, hurt, rage, and hopelessness. If, on the other hand, we work to accept homosexual persons as they are and work to include them fully in all aspects of American society, this means that we will need to create social conditions that let them live up to their potential. How can we do this?

In addition to passing and enforcing laws that give homosexual Americans equal opportunities to get jobs, be promoted, and obtain housing, our society can also take steps to help homosexual couples have more enduring relationships. For example, we can enact laws that allow them to be legally married. Currently, 59% percent of Americans support same-sex marriage or what is popularly called gay marriage (Roberts & Roberts, 2015; Wolf, 2014). Also, as of February, 2015, 37 states and the District of Columbia allow gay marriage (Wolf, 2015). The U.S. Supreme Court, however, ruled on June 26, 2015, that same-sex marriage is legal throughout the country in all 50 states (Wang, 2015). This decision will create a more firm social structure for homosexually oriented Americans to have more stable marriages like heterosexually oriented Americans. When they have legal marriages, like heterosexually married couples, they can share health care insurance coverage, own homes together, sign for loans together, visit each other in hospitals, and inherit wealth from a surviving partner. With such legal rights like heterosexually married couples, they can have more stable relationships with less stress and hence more happiness.

Although these legal rights will not guarantee that they will have everlasting relationships just as these legal rights do not ensure that heterosexual couples will have everlasting relationships, these rights will certainly decrease the stress that homosexual couples have had to face. Until homosexual couples are under the same legal conditions with respect to marriage as heterosexual couples, homosexual couples will experience more stress, uncertainty, and instability.

The legal ability to have more stable relationships will allow homosexual couples to build more stable and secure families for children. Whether through adoption or through one of the partners contributing his sperm or her eggs, they will be able to create more secure and stable environments within which to raise children. These new legal conditions will make for more stable and happy families.

It seems that as we have changed our society to include more Americans who were at one time excluded, for example, African Americans, Native Americans, Hispanic Americans, women, disabled Americans, and homosexual Americans, we give these Americans more of a chance to flourish. Once given this chance, they are able to make all kinds of contributions to our society and to humanity that they were not able to do previously.

Decreasing Crime to Help Families

Crime affects our society financially in that tax money needs to be set aside to pay for more police, judges, courts, and prisons; prisons alone can cost taxpayers $25,000 per year per prisoner, above and beyond the costs of building prisons (Macionis, 2008). Crime also affects how much people fear being possible victims of crime. Moreover, crime affects families, in that when a parent is sent away to prison, families suffer not only from the lack of emotional support but also from the lack of financial support. Consequently, higher crime rates mean that more American families are disrupted in various ways for long periods of time.

If we can work to decrease crime in our society (see Chapter 8 on specific steps we can take to decrease crime), we can keep more parents out of prison and in their homes so that they can provide for their families both emotionally and financially. As you recall from Chapter 8, we can provide more legal opportunities[7] for Americans by providing excellent public schools and trade schools and by providing more student loans to low-income students so that they have the chance to further their education. More educational opportunities will result in Americans having a better chance to be upwardly mobile, to earn decent incomes, and to know that they can get ahead in life.[8] The more that we can create social conditions in which all Americans can make ends meet by legal means, the less incentive they will have to make ends meet by illegal means. With less incentive to commit crime, more families will remain intact and hence be more stable and happy.

Changing the Way We Deal With Drugs to Help Families

Currently in the United States, possessing and selling drugs such as marijuana, cocaine, heroin, and methamphetamines is a crime. If users and sellers of drugs are caught and convicted, they are given prison sentences. Many times, those found guilty are parents who are sent off to prison for a number of years. This creates havoc for these families. In Chapter 9 on drugs, I suggested that we could take an intermediate step of legalizing the use and sale of marijuana (recall that marijuana was legal for the first 161 years of our nation's history—until 1937—and has been illegal since then). Making marijuana legal would cut back on the parents who currently go to jail for possessing or selling marijuana. The benefit for these families would be that the parents would still be at home raising their children and making money to make ends meet for their families. Instead of sending these parents off to jail and putting great financial stress on these families as they try to pay their bills, by legalizing the use and sale of marijuana we would allow more parents to remain with their families and hence would create a more stable financial environment for these families.

In recent years, various states have begun to legalize marijuana and allow the sale of it. As we noted in Chapter 9 on drugs, marijuana is legal in four states: Colorado, Washington, Alaska, and Oregon and has seen a 74% increase in the market from 2013 to 2014 and "at least 10 states are already considering legalizing recreational marijuana in the next two years through ballot measures or state legislatures" (Ferner, January 26, 2015). Consequently, in the next 5 to 10 years, we should get a clearer picture of just how many states will allow the sale and consumption of marijuana and what all the intended and unintended effects of such an action are. This, and how it could affect our families, is something our society still has to work out. While it will keep a number of parents out of prison who would have gone to prison before marijuana was legalized, are there other factors such as increased addiction and spending of family income toward the buying of marijuana that could work against the stability and happiness of families? We will need to do thorough and comprehensive research in order to find out all of the effects of the legalization of marijuana on the family.

In the case of drugs such as cocaine, heroin, and methamphetamines, even if we did not make them legal, instead of simply sending parents off to prison, our society could provide more counseling, rehabilitation, education, training, and job placement options. If we moved in the direction of a balance among counseling, rehabilitation, education, training, and job placement, on the one hand, and going to prison, on the other, we could decrease the number of parents who serve long prison sentences and therefore decrease the number of families that are devastated emotionally and financially by the imprisonment of a parent. So, to help American families, we could change our drug policy somewhat as a way to keep more American families together.

Creating a National Health Care System to Help Families

The Affordable Care Act has helped millions of American families finally get health care coverage. This new health care program has been a major step in helping the 50 million Americans and their families get health care. Many of these families will now be able to get health care due to the Affordable Care

Act. As we noted in the health care chapter, 10 million Americans in 2014 and 11.5 million Americans in 2015 signed up for health insurance (O'Donnell and Ungar, 2015; Rudavsky, 2015). These millions of Americans signed up for health insurance through insurance exchanges where there are a number of health insurance companies who bid to be the insurance service for the customers. This competition among these insurance companies should make the cost of health care more reasonable for Americans. Also, with the passage of the Affordable Care Act, more poor and near-poor Americans were eligible to be included in Medicaid, the health care program for poor and near-poor families. Thus, with the expansion of Medicaid and with the creation of competitive exchanges, millions of Americans are now able to have health insurance and consequently receive health care when they need it.

As a result of the expansion of Medicaid for poor and near-poor families and the creation of health insurance exchanges for nonpoor families, the stress that has existed for years when someone in a family has gotten ill but the family could not afford health care coverage and therefore could not go to see a doctor or dentist or not go to the hospital—this stress, worry, and anxiety about how to help their family member and how to pay for any medical bills is greatly diminished. Hence, having a more comprehensive health care system that covers more Americans than ever before in our country's history and having such a system at a more reasonable cost should help many American families.

For many moms and dads throughout the country, the stress of money problems is a major stress on American families. In fact, it is one of the major reasons for divorce. If we as a country can relieve that stress due to the lack of money, we are helping our American families considerably. One of the ways we can decrease the money problem is to provide for more affordable health care.

We by no means, through the Affordable Care Act, provide all Americans health care that all Americans can reasonably afford. Under the Affordable Care Act, we have come closer to this goal, but we still have a way to go. Someday, if we can reach the point where all Americans have good health care without the stress of having to pay so much for health care, such as occurs in other industrialized nations, then we will be able to reduce the stress on families even further and thus create more stable and happy families.

Creating Good-Quality Education for All Students to Help Families

Although many American children get good-quality education (in the form of small classes, certified teachers, and up-to-date facilities), there are many other children who sit in large classes, have uncertified teachers teaching subjects they know little about, go to schools that do not have well-maintained buildings, and do not have enough textbooks, microscopes, band instruments, and art equipment (Kozol, 1991). In the latter situation, these school environments do not prepare children to get ahead in our society.

Because of many families' racial/ethnic backgrounds and their financial conditions, they live in areas that have lower-quality schools; because the property taxes in their areas are lower, there is less tax revenue collected that can pay for good-quality schools. As we decrease the prejudice and discrimination in society, we can help the financial conditions of these families so that they can move to areas that have better school systems.

As we discussed in Chapter 7 on education, we can take a number of steps to increase the quality of education in the schools where many minority families are currently sending their children. We can increase the quality of education by providing more money (1) to hire more teachers to decrease the student-to-teacher ratio so that students receive more one-on-one instruction, (2) to hire certified teachers who teach in their certified areas so that students get well-qualified teachers, and (3) to provide up-to-date technology and facilities so that students are receiving an up-to-date education that will prepare them for jobs and careers in the 21st century.

One key way to get more money for schools that will be the least hurtful to the American people is to create a more progressive income tax system, through which the richest people in our country pay more in taxes. Currently, 1% of Americans own 34% of all the wealth in our country, and 10% of Americans own 71% of all the wealth in our country (Kerbo, 2012). These Americans who have benefitted the most from our capitalistic way of life could be taxed a little more, via a more progressive income tax, to provide for a better education for all Americans—and yet they would still retain most of their wealth.

Educating Students to Help Families

Most American children in Grades 1 through 12 attend our public school system. Given such attendance, the public schools can be a venue for teaching children how to be better spouses and parents. It seems possible that we could create a curriculum that could be offered in elementary, middle, and high schools that would present and discuss essential information on how to be better spouses and parents. Either a national committee of experts or a committee of experts created from each of the 50 states could develop such a curriculum—or both. Curricular topics that could be created and discussed in class include how to treat one's spouse, how to make decisions with one's spouse, how spouses can manage money, how to cook and how to cook nutritious foods, how spouses can please each other sexually, how to treat children, how to raise children, and how to manage time. These are universal to all families where all families could get help in these areas.

Marriage and family experts could arrive at a commonly agreed-on curriculum that could be used in all public schools; the depth of knowledge presented would progress as children advanced from elementary school, to middle school, to high school. Consequently, by the time students were 16 years old or had reached the mid-high school years, they would be better prepared to become both husbands and wives and mothers and fathers than previous generations of students had been.

These courses will not guarantee that all marriages and families will be successful. But these courses will give students a knowledge base and reference points with which to make more informed decisions, thereby moving future husbands and wives and mothers and fathers in the direction of experiencing more stable, secure, and happier home environments.

This course could be a part of the same course that we talked about in Chapter 10 on health care that would teach students how to pick nutritious foods to eat, how to cook these foods, how to get healthy exercise, and how to live a healthy lifestyle overall. Such a course could therefore not only increase the physical health of students but also prepare them to be better future husbands and wives and moms and dads.

Some students are already taught in their homes how to pick and cook healthy foods and how to get appropriate exercise. They are also taught how to be good spouses and parents because their own parents model such excellent behavior each day. However, we know that not all students grow up in such ideal social environments. This course would help to fill the gap that these students missed as they were growing up. In doing so, we will help create more stable and happier families.

Educating Parents to Help Families

We could also set up adult classes for people to learn how to be better spouses and parents. These classes could be offered by public school systems, public health departments, or local governments to give adults information and advice if they are thinking about becoming spouses or parents or if they are already spouses or parents and feel that they need more help or advice. As an incentive for spouses and parents to take these courses, we could create some kind of tax deduction. Also, if spouses or parents have come before the criminal justice system because of spousal abuse, child abuse, or child neglect, they could be required to take adult spouse and parenting courses as a part of the rehabilitative sentencing handed down by judges.

Summary of What We Can Do to Help Families

As you can see, how well families do in our society depends on how well we solve other social problems, such as decreasing inequality in general, decreasing poverty in particular, decreasing racial/ethnic and gender inequality, increasing the quality of public education, and providing health care for all Americans. Solving or addressing each of these social problems will go a long way toward helping American families to become and remain stable and happy. So, the more we can solve other social problems, the more we can help our American families.

We can also take steps to decrease the problems of families, such as educating children in how to be better spouses and parents, educating spouses and parents in how to be better partners and heads of families, and working to create laws and social policies that include homosexual partners and homosexual families so that all families have a better chance of living more stable, secure, and happier lives.

No other chapter in this book demonstrates so clearly how social problems are interrelated as this chapter does. Consequently, as we successfully address the other social problems that we have discussed, we will, at the same time, take a major step in solving the problems of our families.

Questions for Discussion

1. How much will our addressing the other social problems we have discussed help us to solve the problems of families?

2. In addition to what was discussed in this chapter, what else can we do to help families in our country?

3. What else can we do to decrease stress in American families?

4. What else can we do to decrease spousal abuse in American families?

5. What else can we do to decrease child abuse and child neglect in American families?

6. What else can we do to increase the happiness and stability in families so that there will be a lower divorce rate?

7. What would you do to solve problems in gay and lesbian partnerships and families, given the existing discrimination against such families?

8. How will legalized homosexual marriages help their marriages?

9. Of all the social problems discussed in the previous chapters, which problem do you think, if solved, would help families the most?

10. What do you predict about our solving problems in American families in the next 10 to 20 years?

12

How Can We Solve the World's Population Problem?

W e, as humans, have a big problem. We are increasing our world's population very quickly and have been doing so for the past 100 years. Our world's population is doubling at a rate of every 58 years.[1] This would not be so bad if we had just a few million people on Earth. Instead, we have more than 7 billion people!

If we continue at the current rate of doubling the world's population, we could have 14 billion people by around 2072; if you happen to be a 20-year-old college student, this means that by the time you are 78 years old, we could have another 7 billion people on Earth. These growth rates raise a number of important questions. Can our Earth support an additional 7 billion people? Will we develop new technologies that provide enough food, water, and shelter for these people? Will we have enough fertile land? Will we have enough fresh water? Will we have enough housing? Will there be enough jobs for people to make money to survive? Will there be continual outbreaks of disease? Will many people be malnourished? Will many people starve to death? Will people rise up and incite revolutions because they do not have enough food and water to survive?

These are important questions, yet we cannot answer these questions with certainty. To say the least, these questions are disturbing and even scary. We need to begin arriving at answers to these questions sooner rather than later. Again, if you happen to be a college student, your generation will need to have or begin to create answers to these questions. Even if the rate of population growth would happen to slow down and we would add 5 billion people instead of 7 billion people during the next 58 years, the preceding questions remain relevant because we would need to find some way to house, feed, and have enough water for 12 billion people. Even now, with 7 billion people, we do not have enough clean water for every human being, and many people do not have enough food to eat.

Unlike the social problems we have covered in previous chapters of this book, where we, in the United States, can take specific steps to remedy the problems we have in our own country (for example, our own poverty problem or our own problems of prejudice and discrimination or our own health care problem), the solution to the world's population problem will require many countries to work together.

With these initial thoughts in mind, let us first discuss the causes of the population problem, which may give us insight into how to solve this problem. There are two main causes on which I focus: the growing population of the world and the unequal distribution of resources both within and among countries of the world.

Causes of the World's Population Problem

The Growing Population of the World

Birth Rate and Death Rate

With respect to the first cause of the world's population problem, we need to consider two variables: the *birth rate*, which is the number of births per 1,000 people per year, and the *death rate*, which is the number of deaths per 1,000 people per year. If the two rates are roughly the same, that is, as many people are dying as are being born, then the population will neither increase nor decrease. Actually, in the past 100 years, the death rate decreased quite a bit, but the birth rate decreased more slowly. The result has been that each year a lot more people were being born than were dying, leading to a big increase in the world's population.

The death rate decreased for various reasons. We started enclosing our sewage systems within pipes so that the sewage could not spread disease to people. We started growing more grain (which could be stored and used when we needed it) and this meant that people had better and more consistent diets and therefore did not die so early in their lives. We invented more medicines and vaccines, and this meant that people were not dying of diseases so often.

The birth rate also decreased, more so in some countries than in others, but not as fast overall as the death rate; hence the rise in the world's population. The reason why the birth rate decreased was that as countries industrialized, the people in those countries began to move to cities to work in factories. As families moved to cities, children were not economic contributors to the family so much as they were in the rural setting on farms where the children could help out planting and harvesting and taking care of farm animals such as cattle, sheep, goats, and hogs. It therefore became more expensive to raise children in cities where they were not as able to be economic contributors to their families. Over time, as having children became more of an economic liability, families began to have fewer children. This process, as you might predict, happened more in industrialized and urbanized countries than in rural countries. Consequently, in industrializing countries that were becoming more urbanized, the birth rate went down faster than it went down in countries that were still mainly rural where more children were needed to help with the farming.

The overall result of this process of a large decline in the death rate and a more moderate decline in the birth rate was that the world's population began to increase more rapidly. This is the problem that we face in today's world. The world's population is currently doubling every 58 years, and we either have to slow down this increase or greatly increase the supply of drinkable water, increase the food production, and housing, health care, and jobs for all of these additional people—or do a combination of decreasing the rate of population growth and increasing these other factors. Whatever we do will be a gargantuan task for the human race.

Unequal Distribution of Resources Both Within and Among Countries

A second major cause of our population problem is the unequal distribution of resources within and among countries, resulting in people being unable to have enough resources to sustain themselves. I will first discuss this unequal distribution within countries and then discuss the unequal distribution among countries.

Unequal Distribution Within Countries

Two factors stand out about the unequal distribution of resources within a particular country: the unequal distribution of resources because of who owns the land and the unequal distribution of resources because of discrimination by the political leaders.

Unequal Land Distribution. With respect to unequal land distribution, the problem is that in a number of countries, a few people own most of the land and therefore have control over who gets to use the land and how it is used. For example, the Gini index for land inequality, which measures how much land ownership is concentrated within a few people in a country, shows that countries in Latin America such as Nicaragua, Peru, Brazil, Argentina, and Columbia have much higher concentrations of land distribution in a few hands than do other countries in the world (Kerbo, 2012). In fact, Kerbo (2006) noted, "In some Latin American countries, 10 percent of the people own about 90 percent of all the land" (pp. 33–34).

The result of this situation is that many people in these countries do not have land of their own to grow food such as rice, beans, and potatoes for their families, making it difficult for them to survive. To make matters worse, the relatively few people who own most of the land will use their land to grow cash crops such as coffee and sugar, which will be traded to developed nations. In fact, these rich landowners, especially in Central and South America, "are tied to world agriculture markets and big agribusiness firms in the rich countries, often keeping both landowners and agribusiness firms rich at the expense of landless peasants" (Kerbo, 2012, p. 482). Although these landowners make a lot of profit, their fellow citizens do not have access to land as a means to survive. As these landless people have more children, many times due to the lack of access to effective birth control (largely because of the power of the Catholic church in Central and South America being against various kinds of birth control), they are not able to provide enough food for their families. The consequences for these families are higher rates of malnutrition, disease, and starvation. In addition to the consequences on landless families, there are consequences for the respective countries. Cities in these countries experience increased instability when landless, rural people move to cities in search of economic survival and these cities do not have enough jobs, let alone enough housing, water, and sewage facilities. In a nutshell, the situation of a few people owning much of the land; large capitalistic businesses wanting to make profit with cash crops such as sugar, bananas, and coffee instead of food crops such as beans, rice, and potatoes; and restrictions of the Catholic church not allowing the use of more effective methods of birth control result in many poor, landless families not having enough food and shelter to survive.

Political Discrimination and Subsequent Unequal Distribution of Resources. Another factor that contributes to the growing number of people in a number of countries is that one racial/ethnic group controls the government of that country and discriminates against other racial/ethnic groups by not providing them with land, water, food, and other resources with which to survive.[2] In these situations, as these groups grow in numbers, they cannot increase their resources accordingly. The result usually is some combination of malnutrition, disease, and starvation.

Consequently, when a growing population of a country is combined with either unequal land distribution or political discrimination of resources or both, the increase in the population becomes a problem, with probable consequences of malnutrition, disease, and starvation to follow. If, on the other hand, there is a population increase and there is a corresponding redistribution of resources to meet the increasing demand of more people, we will not have a population problem—at least not at that time. However, because countries have a finite amount of resources, at least in the short term, until they can discover or produce more resources, an increase in the population will mean fewer resources per person in those countries, even if they are distributed equally (and that is very rare).

Unequal Distribution Among Countries

Another problem related to the world's population problem is the inequality of resources among countries. Developed countries such as the United States, Canada, Western European countries, Japan, and Australia have more resources and can therefore provide for their people more easily than can poor countries such as Liberia, which has a per capita income of $790 per year, and Burundi, which has a per capita income of $820 per year (in contrast to the United States, which has a per capita income of $53,960 per year, and Norway, which has a per capita income of $66,520 per year) (Population Reference Bureau, 2014).

The poorer countries of the world frequently do not have enough resources to allow their people to live decently. This situation of having the bare minimum is further aggravated when the birth rates in these poorer countries are much higher than the death rates, resulting in quick increases in the population but not corresponding increases in resources such as fertile land, fresh water, food, shelter, and jobs. If the resources of the world were redistributed more equitably, from richer countries to poorer countries, the increase in population of these poorer countries would not be a problem or would not be as much of a problem. As of now, there is no world plan to redistribute resources somewhat—let alone equally. Consequently, the growing population in the poorer countries, where most of the population growth is occurring (Population Reference Bureau, 2014), leads to growing poverty and stress on the people of these countries.

As you are probably beginning to see, the three important variables of birth rate, death rate, and access to resources influence whether or not we have a population problem. If one or some combination of these three variables gets out of whack, we have a problem. For example, if birth rates are much higher than death rates, but the amount of resources remains the same, we will have too many people for the existing resources. If death rates plummet due to vaccines to stop disease, but birth rates remain the same, there will be many more people and possibly not enough resources to take care of these people. If one group in a country keeps most of the resources and discriminates against other groups, the other groups will not have enough resources to live or to live decently. Moreover, if these other groups grow in population, they will have an even more difficult time surviving. If some countries have many resources and other countries have few resources, the people in countries with fewer resources will have a harder time surviving. As you can see, the mixture of birth rate, death rate, and unequal distribution of resources can be the recipe for disaster for many people on Earth.

I know that the phrase "recipe for disaster" is strong, but as a sociologist, I predict that under the current social conditions—more births relative to deaths, when resources of food, water, and shelter and access to farm land and access to jobs are not growing in proportion to the increase in population—there will be fewer and fewer resources for each person to use. Therefore, we should see more people in developing countries experience more unemployment, poverty, malnutrition, and starvation. As sociologists, we should also predict that these social conditions should create more political instability (demonstrations, riots, attempted coups, civil wars, and revolutions) as people find it harder and harder to survive.

What Can We Do?

There are a number of things that we, as citizens of this world, can do to solve or decrease the problem of rising population. We will find, however, that whatever solution we suggest, there will be people who will be against that solution. So, the problem with solving the population problem of our world will be due not to a lack of answers but rather to the vested interests, values, and beliefs of certain groups or countries that will act as barriers to solving this problem.

Decrease the Birth Rate

A key answer to solving the population problem of our world is to decrease the birth rate of many countries. In many countries that are also struggling with poverty, mothers are bearing five, six, or seven children.[3] With a birth rate that high, so many people are being born that the country cannot provide enough food, shelter, schooling, and other basic services such as clean water and efficient sewage systems to support the population. When, 15 to 20 years later, these children are looking for jobs, there will not be enough jobs available. So, a major solution to the population problem is to decrease the birth rate to one, two, or three children per family. It has been estimated that "half of the married women in developing countries do not want more children but do not have access to effective methods of birth control" (Eitzen, Zinn, & Smith, 2009, p. 64). Part of the answer, then, is to provide women with birth control so that they can have only the number of children they want to have.

Even if countries provide more birth control, there are other challenges to decreasing the birth rate, such as overcoming vested interests and differences in values and beliefs. First, let us look at the problem of vested interests. Parents in many poor countries rely on their children in two ways to survive. First, these parents live in rural settings and need extra hands to help with the planting and harvesting of crops. Hence, they see children as economic assets that help with the crops and tend to the care of various animals such as sheep, goats, cattle, and chickens. Second, when these parents are too old to farm the land, their children serve as a form of social security for the parents by continuing to farm the land, tending to the animals, and taking care of their parents. For these two reasons—help with the farming and being a means of social security—it is in the parents' vested interests to have more children.

In addition to the influence of vested interests, let us also look at the problem of values and beliefs. In a number of cultures, having children shows the rest of the community that the man of the household is a "real man." When he has children, he gains prestige. Likewise, when a woman shows that she can bear a number of children, she is seen as a "real woman" by having the ability of to carry out her role of bearing children.

As you can see, vested interests and values and beliefs can combine to cause parents to have five, six, or seven children. Also, parents believe that, because of diseases that children can contract, parents need to have more children in case some of their children die during infancy or childhood.

This leads to the following question: How can we decrease the birth rate in countries where these conditions exist? This is a challenging question. At the individual family level, it is functional for families to have more children to help in farming, to serve as a form of social security, and to have enough children in case some of the children die in childhood. However, at the societal level, it is dysfunctional for the country to have more mouths to feed and more resources to use up when the country is already strapped for food and resources. Moreover, at both the national and worldwide levels, more children mean more depletion of resources and more pollution.

These depletion and pollution problems are even more pronounced in developed countries where each additional child will use more resources. For example, a child in a developed country is likely to use more gasoline for a car and use more electricity for showers, lights, and heating, resulting in more depletion of resources such as coal, oil, and natural gas and resulting in more pollution compared with a child in a developing country. As a result, one estimate suggested that having one person in a developed country is equal to having 55 persons in a developing country (McKee & Robertson, 1975, p. 68). So, whereas parents in poorer, rural countries have vested interests in economic survival by having more children, children in more developed countries have vested interests in living a higher material lifestyle that depletes resources and pollutes the environment much more so than children in developing countries.

We, as a world community, are coming to realize that we need to decrease the birth rate—given so many more people and using up of our land, water, and other resources and the continued and increasing pollution of our planet. What do we do? Let us discuss some actions we can take to decrease the birth rate.

Increase Funding for Birth Control

We in developed countries can increase the amount of money we provide for birth control throughout the world. We know that many married women in the world do not want more children. Many of these women desire to use birth control but do not have access to it. Governments and countries that contribute money to make birth control more accessible but do not want to use their contributions to fund abortions can stipulate that their contributed funds go only for birth control. This money would go for purchasing birth control devices, for training people to teach others how to use these birth control devices, and for providing transportation to get birth control devices to people who live in mountains, deserts, or jungles. In other words, the goal would be to provide access to birth control to every woman in the world who wants to use it. This allows individual families to decide how many children they want, giving them freedom in their family planning.[4]

It has been estimated that it would take $8 billion per year to provide birth control for all of the women in the world who want it (Eitzen, Zinn, and Smith, 2011). Some extremely rich individuals have made more money than that in one year. If some individuals make this much money in one year, it seems well within the realm of possibility that the citizens and countries of the world could raise this much money for one of the world's most pressing social problems. The administrations of President George H. W. Bush and President George W. Bush withheld funding for global birth control programs, whereas the administrations of President Bill Clinton and that of President Barack Obama provided funding for global birth control programs.[5] So, even in our own country, there are political vested interests that work against providing enough money for the women of the world to have access to birth control.

Along with having access to birth control, people could be taught that if certain kinds of birth control (for example, the condom) were used, HIV/AIDS transmission rates could be decreased, but that would not happen if other methods (for example, the rhythm method, the pill, the intrauterine device, the diaphragm) were used (Rosenfield, 2000). The distribution of condoms could be of great help for the people in many southern African countries that have been experiencing horrendous rates of AIDS. For example, 18% of the adults (between the ages of 15 and 49) in South Africa, 23% of the adults in Lesotho, 26% of the adults in Swaziland, and 24% of the adults in Botswana contacted AIDS (Population Reference Bureau, 2009). So, in 2009, nearly 1 in 5 adults in southern Africa contacted AIDS.

Provide More Education for Women

Another way to decrease the population is to educate women. When women go to school and stay in school longer, they tend to have fewer children. The reasons for this are twofold. First, as women go to school longer, they begin to be more interested in careers, and this usually means that they have fewer children. Second, as women go to school longer, they tend to marry later and bear fewer children. So, as we promote more education for women in particular and more gender equality for women in general, it is likely that women will have fewer children, thus helping us to address, in an indirect way, the world's population problem.

In cultures that are industrialized or industrializing, women are already getting much more education than 50 or 100 years ago and are having many kinds of careers that they are able to choose from and, as a result, find a lot of fulfillment in their lives via their careers. The ideologies, values, beliefs, laws, and informal norms of these societies have changed to the degree that women are not only allowed but many times encouraged to get a lot more education and to seek careers that will last much of their adult lives. As a result of this new set of social conditions, women are having fewer children.

However, in cultures that are less industrialized, many of these cultures are still quite patriarchal where women are discouraged from going to school, discouraged from getting a lot of education, and discouraged from having careers. In these cultures, the social conditions of religious and secular ideologies, values, beliefs, laws, and informal norms all work to keep women at home and socialize women to see motherhood as the prime if not the only role that they should play. No going off to school for years at a time and being outside the home and away from the family. No thinking about and considering all kinds of careers. This is not right. This is not good. Furthermore, this may even be against the religion and the God of that culture. So, in this set of social conditions, women are more likely to stay at home and have more children.

The challenge for humanity in the 21st century is how to come to some kind of compromise in the patriarchal cultures where women could decrease their birth rates to some degree. Does this mean changing that culture's ideology, values, and beliefs? Does it mean changing their traditions? Probably, from the perspective of people from many Western cultures where patriarchal traditions are on the way out and gender equality is on the way in, they might say, "Of course, you [traditional cultures] must change." In reality, this is easier said than done, especially if the gender inequality is closely tied to and reaffirmed by the religion of that culture. In reality, this will have to be discussed, worked out, and have many compromises along the way as we humans not only attempt to address the social problem of gender inequality in general but also attempt to address the social problem of too many people in particular. Once again, we see how two social problems are related and hence, addressing one may help address the other.

Since gender inequality is such a passionate concern for many women (and men, too) in the world of today, there will probably be more progress made on moving our world toward more gender equality as the 21st century proceeds. Given that this process occurs, the movement toward more gender equality will also help decrease the world's birth rates, which will, in turn, help address our population problem. So, over the process of this century, we may very well, in an indirect way and in a way that turns out to be a latent function, observe that the world's population problem also is addressed. We will see.

Provide Social Security for the Elderly of Poorer Countries

To possibly address the issue in many developing countries of children serving as a means of social security for their parents, developed countries could provide foreign aid that would act as a partial replacement for children acting as a means of social security. This policy could be both expensive and controversial for developed countries, but providing such aid could be a key incentive for farming parents in developing countries to decrease family size. Such a program could take some of the pressure to provide social services off cities that receive so many people from the countryside; this, in turn, could decrease the potential for political instability in developing countries, disruption in trade, the takeover of foreign corporations by insurgents within these unstable countries, and the use of foreign troops to quell uprisings in developing countries. It could thus be in the vested interests of developed countries to provide such a social security program in return for uninterrupted trade, protection of foreign investments, and reduced need to send troops to those countries.

Forgive or Decrease Debt

A partial solution that is also controversial would be for developed countries to forgive or decrease developing countries' debt in return for the developing countries agreeing to decrease their birth rates. The forgiving or decreasing of developing countries' debt would give the governments of the developing countries an incentive to decrease their birth rates. This action would be costly to developed nations in the short term, but, over time, better relations between developing and developed nations could be created;[6] developing nations would have the chance to get out of debt, increase their standard of living, and eventually could be potential markets for developed nations (Stoltenberg, 1989). Also, getting developing nations out of debt would help to create more political stability, stabilize trade relations, and protect the developed countries' investment interests. Furthermore, as developing countries have a chance to develop economically as a result of debt reduction, they tend to decrease their birth rates (Epstein, 1998, p. 8).

A number of people believe that it is morally appropriate to give poorer countries a chance to get out of their relentless poverty. That is, forgiving or decreasing the debt of developing countries not only would be a way to decrease the birth rate and eventually create new markets for developed countries but also would be "the right thing to do."

Redistribute Land

Another policy that could be carried out might not decrease population growth directly but could allow people to survive. This policy would redistribute land in developing countries to some degree. As a result, many farming people could have their own land and could grow their own food to sustain themselves. Without land, especially in agricultural societies, people are highly vulnerable to the actions of landowners, for example, "rich landowners in Latin America especially are tied to the world agricultural markets and big agribusiness firms in the rich countries, often keeping both landowners and agribusiness firms rich at the expense of landless peasants" (Kerbo, 2009, p. 482). Such a social policy of redistributing land would be a controversial policy among the wealthy few who own most of the land. Remember, in some Latin American countries, "10 percent of the people own about 90 percent of all the land" (Kerbo, 2006, p. 34). On one hand, from the wealthy people's perspective, it would be in their vested interests not to give up the land so that they can continue to make profit by growing cash crops on their land. However, on the other hand, if there is an increasing tendency for political unrest, coups, civil wars, and revolutions because of so much inequality in these countries, it could be in the long-term vested interests of these landowners to give up some of their land in return for more political and social stability.

Where Are We?

As you can see, we have a problem that will not be easy to solve. Recall our theory of conflict and social change from Chapter 1, and consider how we can apply that theory to this social problem, especially with regard to values and beliefs, vested interests, and inequality. For example, part of the problem of trying to solve the world's population problem has to do with cultural, religious, and political values and beliefs that hinder or even prohibit the use of effective means of birth control and hence inhibit a country's ability to decrease its birth rate and therefore stabilize its population. Another variable in our theory is how vested interests play a key role in who receives resources and who does not receive resources. A third variable of inequality—the inequality of resources within a country between rich landowners and the many rural poor who have no land to survive and the inequality of resources between rich and poor countries—plays a crucial role in the population problem. Moreover, if the population increases, but the available resources do not increase proportionately, over time there will be fewer resources per person with dire consequences.

Even though this is going to be a very difficult social problem to solve, we as citizens of the world need to face this problem and discuss what we can do to solve it. We have dealt with other problems and have overcome some of them, such as decreasing certain diseases and decreasing the severity of certain social problems such as racial/ethnic and gender inequalities. We have also made progress in establishing world organizations, such as the United Nations, as a means to address world social problems. As you will recall from our theory of conflict and social change in Chapter 1, two key variables of solving a social problem are our awareness that we have a problem and our ability to communicate with others about this problem. At this point in history, we are aware and communicating about the problem of increasing global population. As we further raise awareness among more people and have more discussions, it seems that there will be a greater chance that we can solve or at least substantially address this problem, sometime during the 21st century.

Questions for Discussion

1. What could developing countries do to decrease their high birth rates?

2. What should developing countries do to decrease their high birth rates?

3. What could developed countries do to help developing countries to decrease their high birth rates?

4. What should developed countries do to help developing countries to decrease their high birth rates?

5. What do you predict will happen during the 21st century with respect to our growing population problem? What is your reasoning?

6. As our world's population continues to grow, what will be the consequences for developing countries?

7. As our world's population continues to grow, what will be the consequences for developed countries?

8. What consequences will there be for your own life as the world's population continues to grow during the next 10, 20, and 30 years?

9. What do you think are the possibilities for land redistribution in Latin American countries?

10. What do you think are the possibilities for rich countries forgiving or decreasing the debt of poor countries?

13

How Can We Solve the World's Environmental Problem?

We have a big environmental problem. We have been polluting our planet's air, water, and land; depleting its resources; and accumulating a lot of waste for which we need to find places to store. Why have we been doing these things? There are four major reasons. One major reason was discussed in Chapter 12: We have over 7.2 billion people on Earth today (Population Reference Bureau, 2014), and all of these people need food, water, clothing, and shelter. In addition to these minimal needs to survive, millions of people in developed nations have cars, large homes, air conditioning, heated houses, washers, dryers, heated water for bathing, refrigerators, stoves, and so on. Hence, having over 7 billion people on Earth, compared to 5.2 billion people just 24 years ago (Population Reference Bureau, 1990), and having many people with a high standard of living, means that we humans will, in the foreseeable future, pollute a lot, deplete a lot, and build up huge amounts of waste that need to be stored.

A second major reason why we have a big problem of polluting, depleting, and storing of waste is that during the past 200 years, we have gone from an agricultural way of life to an industrial way of life. Instead of "living off the land," growing grain to eat, and tending to farm animals, we built factories and machines and created a new status called the *factory worker* to produce all kinds of products to consume—as a stroll through a typical shopping mall will clearly show. To create these consumer products, we use a lot of resources and pollute the air, land, and sources of water.

The key to this industrializing, and hence polluting and depleting, has been the creation and development of modern capitalism. Simply stated, capitalism produces products to make profit. Thus, to make more profit, owners of capital—that is, factory and business owners—need to produce and sell more products. It is therefore in the vested interests of those who own factories and businesses to produce and sell as much as they can so as to make as much profit as they can. The very nature of this process has resulted in substantial depletion and pollution.

As of this point in human history, although capitalism has helped to create the highest material standard of living that the world has ever seen, it has, at the same time, increased the rate at which we pollute, deplete, and have problems storing waste (recall our discussion of latent dysfunction in Chapter 1). As former Vice President Al Gore (2000) concluded in his book *Earth in the Balance,* "Human civilization is now the dominant cause of change in the global environment."[1]

A third major factor that has caused our environmental problems is that we have created an ideology within capitalistic, developed nations—one that is spreading more and more to developing nations due to television, computers, e-mail, and the Internet—that people in both developed and developing nations want an ever-higher material standard of living (Eitzen & Zinn, 2000; Ritzer, 2005). A higher material standard of living means producing more material goods—cars, houses, washers, dryers, refrigerators, stoves, water heaters, heating and air conditioning systems for homes and offices, and so on. All of this means that we need to use more resources to produce more products, resulting in the further depletion of many resources. As we produce and consume these products, we pollute more and have more waste left over.

People in developed nations have become accustomed to ever-higher standards of living. For example, we in the United States at the beginning of this new century made up 4.5% of the world's population, but we consumed 25% of all the oil, coal, and natural gas being consumed in the world (Eitzen & Leedham, 2001). So, our country alone used up a lot of the world's resources in order to have and maintain our high material standard of living. To have such a high material lifestyle, our country has also discharged a disproportionate amount of pollution. By 2012, we became 4.3% of the world's population, but we added 14% of the carbon dioxide produced by humans to the world's air, producing what has become known as the "greenhouse effect," which scientific evidence indicates is warming up the Earth and starting to produce climate change (Population Reference Bureau, 2014). Consequently, although we in the United States enjoy a high standard of living, we must realize that we disproportionately deplete and pollute huge amounts in order to enjoy that lifestyle. This raises an important question: Should we, as Americans, be more responsible for solving the problems of depletion and pollution since we pollute and deplete disproportionately more—four to five times our population?

The fourth major cause of our environmental problem is that, increasingly, people in developing nations are noticing how well people in developed nations are living and want to have some or many of the same amenities as do people in developed nations. They too want washers and dryers, air conditioning, televisions, cars, computers, cell phones, good roads, good hospitals, nice schools, good universities, bigger and nicer homes, and so on. The result has been increased depletion of resources, increased pollution, and increased accumulation of waste in these countries as well.[2] For example, carbon dioxide emissions, a key factor in global warming, have increased considerably for the world from 6,127 million tons in 1990 to 9,667 million tons in 2012 (Population Reference Bureau, 2014). So, even though various world leaders and organizations want our world to decrease CO2 emissions, we have increased emissions one and one half times. While developed countries have *decreased* their emissions from 3,813 million tons in 1990 to 3,606 million in 2012, developing countries have *increased* their emissions from 2,029 million tons to 5,510 million tons (Population Reference Bureau, 2014). For example, while a developed country like Germany decreased their emissions from 276.4 million tons to 199.7 million tons, China, which has been industrializing and developing greatly in the last 20 years, has substantially increased their emissions from 671.1 million tons in 1990 to 2,625.7 million tons in 2012—that is, they have increased their CO2 emissions by 3.9 times. As you can see, as there is a desire to have a higher standard of living, there is the tendency (so far) to use more coal, oil, and natural gas, which results in pollution in the form of CO2 emissions.

We are currently creating a new worldwide ideology through which people in increasing numbers want and expect higher material lifestyles. So, it appears that the increasing pressure to produce more goods and services to create a higher material standard of living for the 6 billion people currently living in less developed countries (Population Reference Bureau, 2014) will mean that our world will continue to face environmental problems now and in the foreseeable future.

Consequences

One of the most dangerous consequences of polluting the environment is that we add huge amounts of carbon dioxide to the atmosphere as the result of burning fossil fuels, such as coal, oil, and natural gas by industries and automobiles. The result is the warming of our planet and the possible change of Earth's climate, which could wreak havoc for the growing seasons, the amount of rainfall needed for crops, the rising level of the oceans,[3] with the endangerment of many coastal cities throughout the world, and other problems.[4] Data reported by Al Gore, former vice president of the United States and someone who has been concerned about the environment since he was a college student, found that "the 12 warmest years in the 140-year record have all occurred since 1983" (Gore, 2000, pp. xiii–xiv). Those data were collected in the late 20th century. This trend has continued into the 21st century. Data collected by the National Oceanic and Atmospheric Administration (NOAA) and National Aeronautics and Space Administration (NASA) show that "in 2014 the world had its hottest year in 135 years of record-keeping" (Borenstein, 2015, p. A1). Moreover, "Nine of the 10 hottest years in NOAA global records have occurred since 2000" (Borenstein, 2015, p. A6). Professor Michael Mann of Penn State University states, "We are witnessing, before our eyes, the effect of human-caused climate change" (Borenstein, 2015, p. A6). Because we humans have caused this problem (recall our theory of conflict and social change in Chapter 1 and how we socially construct the social conditions in which we live), we need to find a way to get out of this potentially life-threatening situation.

Climate change will cause certain areas of the world that had produced enough food to produce less food, leading to malnutrition and starvation. For example, scientific evidence now suggests that the spewing of sulfur dioxide in the air by industries from the United States, Canada, Europe, and Asia caused the decrease in rainfall in Africa, creating malnutrition, starvation, and famine (Verrengia, 2002). This condition creates the incentive for people to move to find places to grow enough food. Hence, as we see more global warming, it is probable that we will not only see more starvation and malnutrition in certain areas of the world, but we will also see more people from these areas migrating in search of a way to feed themselves (Gore, 2000; Intergovernmental Panel on Climate Change, 2001).

Moreover, with the rise of global temperatures because of more carbon dioxide in the air, the ocean levels will rise. One third of the world's population lives near coastlines (Gore, 2000; see also Hunter, 2001). The cities these people live in will be in danger of being flooded. The result will be that many people will have to migrate inland from the coastlines. Consequently, such migration will cause the stretching of resources wherever these people go. These migrating people will need housing, land, and access to drinking water. To tie this migration process, due to climate change and rising ocean levels, to the rapid rise in the world's population is to make us ponder how we, as global citizens, will respond.

Also, a tie between our world's population problem (see Chapter 12) and the world's environmental problem is that as there are more people on Earth, there will be more carbon dioxide that is exhaled (Gore, 2000). Instead of a few million people exhaling carbon dioxide (as was the case more than 100,000 years ago) or even 1 billion people exhaling carbon dioxide (as was the case 100 years ago), we have more than 7 billion people exhaling carbon dioxide today. So, the increase in Earth's population is another factor that could cause a major change in Earth's climate—a change we do not want to occur.

We have also polluted a lot of the fresh water on Earth, with the result that more than 1.7 billion people do not have safe drinking water (Gore, 2000; see also Pimentel et al., 1998). That is, at least 25% of all the people on Earth do not have good drinking water—something that many of us Americans cannot imagine with our available drinking fountains, bottles of fresh, clean water that we can buy at the store, or water we can readily turn on from the water taps of our homes! Moreover, many people in the world are in danger of using contaminated water because human waste is not properly treated before it is dumped into rivers because they cannot afford to have sewage systems. As you might predict, one consequence of untreated sewage is the rise in diseases such as cholera and typhoid (Gore, 2000). Industry has also caused water pollution because many industries have discharged their wastes into rivers. In a number of instances, factory owners do not take responsibility for the waste they produce while they make their products in order to make more profit. Consequently, more profit is made at the expense of the environment in general and at the expense of fresh water in particular. Moreover, as more developing countries industrialize, they too will have problems of not having enough fresh water if their industries do not take responsibility for the pollution they produce.

Another environmental issue is the continual destroying of the rainforests of the world. The rising populations of developing countries have created a need for more agricultural land to grow crops to sustain the population. Also, governments of debt-ridden developing countries try to pay off their debts or at the very least pay the interest on the debts they owe by cutting down trees from their rainforests to sell as lumber (Brown, 2009). Yet these rainforests produce oxygen and fresh water and consume carbon dioxide that humans create when they burn fossil fuels such as coal, oil, and natural gas or simply breathe (Brown, 2009).

Another potentially dangerous consequence of our cutting down the rainforests of the world is the loss of thousands—even millions—of species of plants, animals, and insects. As yet, we do not know all of the consequences on the environment of the loss of these species. Ehrlich, Daily, Daily, Myers, and Salzman (1997) made a good point when they stated, "Until science can say which species are essential in the long term, we exterminate any at our peril" (p. 101).

In the capitalistic industrial world that we now live in and with 7.2 billion people—more and more of whom want a higher material standard of living and have been socialized by advertisements to want an ever higher standard of living—we have come to the point where we have created a lot of waste and do not know what to do with it all (Gore, 2000). Landfills (used to be called "junkyards") are piling up. States are trying to send their waste, junk, or garbage to other states. Along with this consequence of a huge buildup of waste is that it is usually stored on the cheapest land, typically near where poorer people and minorities live (p. 149). Hence, poorer people and minorities are the ones who, more often than not, have ended up living nearest these waste sites—another unintended consequence of our modern, materialistic way of living—or what sociologists call a latent dysfunction for the people having to live near these sites.

What Can We Do?

Before I get into specific actions we can take to solve the environmental problem, I say some general things about how we need to view the problem.

General Points to Make

Our society and our world have largely emphasized short-term gains, especially in a capitalistic economy in which we emphasize profit and keeping costs to a minimum (and hence not wanting to include the costs of pollution and waste storage) rather than considering long-term costs such as climate change, depletion of our resources (such as fresh, clean water), and pollution of our planet (air, land, and water). In considering our environmental problem, we need to think more in long-term ways rather than only in short-term ways (Marchetti, 1986). If we think in the short term only, we are more likely to think mainly of our own vested interests—our profit, our convenience, and our standard of living. If we think about ourselves and our vested interests only, we will not think about the good of our world now and in the future.[5] By thinking short term, we will be less likely to think about what is good for our various communities, local, national, and global. However, by thinking more long term, we will think about what is good for these communities. Consequently, we will be much more likely to think about our environmental problems—how they currently affect us and how they will affect us in the future, if we do not address them. By also thinking long term, we will consider future human beings and their time on Earth in addition to just considering our time on Earth (Gore, 2000; Jan, 1995; Brown, 2009).

More and more people are coming to the realization that we must consider the long term, what is good for the global community, and what is good for future generations if we want to survive as a species. This will require us to think, plan, sacrifice, and change our ways of living. As our theory of conflict and social change points out (see Chapter 1), since we humans socially construct this social world (laws, norms, values, beliefs [secular and religious], organizations, institutions, and ideologies), it is up to us to socially reconstruct our social world—if we humans want to survive by solving our environmental problem.

One step we will need to take is to become more educated about our environmental problem (Gore, 2000). Many people in our country, and throughout the world, do not realize the seriousness of our environmental problem. Hence, part of the solution is to make Americans more aware of the problem and to educate them about the problem (recall our theory in Chapter 1 of conflict and social change, the accompanying causal model, and the important part that awareness plays).

Along with those individuals who do not know about the problem and need to be educated are those who do know but want to deny the existence of the problem or the seriousness of its effects (Gore, 2000). Many times, they will have vested interests at stake such as profit, short-term gain, or their jobs. These are the people who will many times put up roadblocks when the rest of us create more education about the environmental problem and create social policy to address the problem. We must find ways to give these people incentives so that they want to address the environmental problem or at least accept the notion that we must address this problem, regardless of their vested interests. The environmental problem will not go away by denying its existence or by denying that it is becoming an ever bigger problem.

The oceans and the air are common property that we all share. If air and water pollution stayed only in the country that produced it, the nation producing this pollution could take the initiative and responsibility to clean up the pollution it produced. But air and water pollution does not stop at state boundaries. Such pollution spreads throughout the world. We, as citizens of this world, not just citizens of a nation, will need to work together to clean up our oceans and air. As Murshed (1993) stated, "We could view the environment—the oceans, the atmosphere—as global common property (public good), and then the problem would be to prevent excessive use or misuse of the global common, which would once again require international cooperation" (p. 43).

Probably, we will eventually need to agree on some worldwide goals for the planet. We have been moving in this direction by attempting to decrease carbon dioxide and chlorofluorocarbon emissions. We will probably need to make saving our environment one of the main goals of our world community. Within this goal, we will need to agree on more specific goals such as decreasing carbon dioxide, sulfur dioxide, and chlorofluorocarbons; increasing the amount of rainforest; finding new, better, and safer ways of storing hazardous waste; and producing more energy without polluting more, depleting more, and creating more waste.

In addition to agreeing on goals, we will need to negotiate agreements among nations as to what we want to do and how we want to accomplish our goals. This will not be easy. As you might predict, national vested interests will collide with international environmental policy. For example, President George W. Bush backed out of the Kyoto Protocol, an agreement among nations to decrease carbon dioxide emissions ("Out of Denial," 2002). Because the United States produces 14% of all the carbon dioxide (while being only 4.3% of the world's population) and is the wealthiest and most powerful nation in the world, when it backs out of an agreement, the original agreement can be hurt considerably. For international agreements to work successfully, rich and powerful nations, like the United States, will need to be part of these agreements.[6]

Creating common environmental goals and reaching international agreements will be helped along greatly when more leaders of various countries begin to take our worldwide environmental problems seriously. This will not be easy for many leaders of nations. To remain popular and get reelected, they first focus more on their nations' immediate and urgent problems. For example, problems of internal political unrest will greatly distract leaders from focusing on the environment. Also, wars and conflicts with other countries will deter leaders from focusing on the environment. Their current economic situations of poverty and unemployment will take priority. Moreover, it will not be easy to get leaders of nations to focus on something that seems, to them, to be distant and therefore not so urgent. But the mounting evidence of environmental degradation will increasingly confront national leaders with the harsh reality that something must be done. We, as a world community, cannot keep putting this off. Also, the more we put this off, the harder it will be to correct it.

At this point, serious goal making and agreement making are good places to start.[7] One factor that could speed up this process is if national leaders from the more powerful countries, such as the United States, China, Russia, Great Britain, France, Germany, Japan, Canada, Australia, and India, promote the environment as part of their overall national and international policy. These national leaders from these influential countries could make substantial progress toward (1) creating world environmental goals, (2) arriving at international agreements, and (3) beginning to figure out how to carry out these goals and agreements.

In thinking about what we can do, key factors to keep in mind in all of the social problems that we face are that we will need to (1) plan ahead, (2) consider the consequences, (3) experiment with new social policy, and (4) carry out social policy that is effective.[8] If we, as humans, do not do these things, we invite chaos by not taking charge of our own destiny. For example, recall the utter chaos that occurred after Hurricane Katrina hit New Orleans, Louisiana, and the surrounding area in August 2005.[9] More than ever, we humans need to plan ahead, do research, and consider all the consequences. With 7.2 billion people on Earth (versus thousands of humans scattered over the Earth a few million years ago) and with the possibilities of huge and destructive wars, with the threat of nuclear wars, with the lack of enough fresh and clean water for people of the world, with the great poverty and inequality that we have in our world, with not enough jobs to provide for the economic survival for millions if not billions of human beings, and with the continual religious wars and terrorism that plague our contemporary world where one group of human beings believes its religion is the one true religion and therefore it believes it has the right to force the rest of us human beings to convert and believe in that religion or else be killed—as fellow humans living in this type of world—we, more than ever before in the history of human beings, need to be very careful in what we do.

With respect to our environmental problem, each day, each month, and each year, this problem gets worse. Because the environment is a problem that is less visible than other social problems, we are less likely to realize its effect, for example, more carbon dioxide in the air causing more global warming or more chlorofluorocarbons in the air causing a larger hole in the ozone layer and allowing more cancer-producing ultraviolet rays to bombard Earth. Hence, we are less likely to feel a sense of urgency about this problem than with other problems we see more visibly.

Also, as the environmental problem grows, there could be a point where the environment gets so bad that we are not able to take enough action to reverse the problem in time for humans to survive. Consequently, the sooner we take action on this problem, the more likely we can control it and solve it. The one thing that we cannot afford to do is to put off facing the environmental problem. This problem and its consequences can only get worse, with the worst scenario being that we can no longer control it.

In thinking about our environment and what we need to do in order to survive on Earth, we need to address and solve three problems: (1) pollution of the air, land, and water; (2) depletion of our resources; and (3) what to do with all the waste we produce. By "we," I mean two groups of people. First, we as citizens of the world need to address these problems. Second, we as citizens of the United States need to address these problems. The reason why I distinguish between these two groups is that we in the United States, along with people in other developed countries, have a special obligation to address these problems because we contribute to them disproportionately. We in developed nations especially need to contribute to solving these environmental problems because we contribute more to them relative to our national populations. Also, those of us in developed nations, given our greater wealth, have a greater capacity to do something about the environment.

As one partial solution to our environmental problems, we could stabilize the population of the world (Boeker & Van Grondelle, 2000; Brown, 2009). Given the current set of social conditions, as we have more people on Earth, we will have more pollution, depletion, and buildup of wastes. This is a good example of where one social problem (increasing population) contributes to another social problem (increasing environmental problem). Consequently, if we can solve one social problem (stabilize or even decrease the world's population), we can, at the same time, help solve another social problem (stabilize and begin to solve our environmental problem).

Specific Actions We Can Take

Depletion: What We Can Do

As we create a higher material standard of living, we use up oil, coal, wood, metals, land, and other natural resources. With more people on Earth and more industrialization to produce more goods to have a higher standard of living, we use more and more natural resources to turn them into the goods we want. One of the problems with this is that we can run out of a number of these resources.

One answer to this problem is to recycle the resources we have already used and to use them over and over. The trick is to know how we can do this and then make it profitable, if possible, for companies to want to be part of the recycling process. As a way to make this happen, the government can do more research to find new ways to recycle and reuse our resources. Also, we can give tax incentives to new businesses that want to go into the recycling business as a way to make money. Thus, we use the profit motive and the creativity that it can awaken to help solve our depletion problem.

An additional way to solve the problem of depletion is to use different resources in place of the resources we are currently using. For example, instead of relying on coal and oil to produce much of our energy, we could do more research to find more and better ways to use solar, water, and air power that would not put carbon dioxide and sulfur dioxide in the air. These kinds of energies of the sun, the wind, and water power are not used up, can be used over and over, and do not hurt the environment. Currently, only about 4% of all of our energy is produced from solar and wind power while coal produces 37% of the nation's electricity (Star Editorial Board Opinion, June 8, 2014, p. A17). In terms of which states are the most coal-dependent, West Virginia is at 95%, Kentucky at 90%, Wyoming at 85%, and Indiana at 84% (Star Editorial Board Opinion, June 8, 2014, p. A17). Yet, in recent years due to fracking, which frees up underground natural gas, natural gas has been increasingly used at power plants because of its lower costs and being a cleaner energy source than coal (Star Editorial Board Opinion, June 3, 2014, A11).

If we especially want to address the problems of global warming and acid rain, we will need to use less oil and coal and more solar, water, and wind power. As evidence that we are already beginning to shift to more wind power, a car trip through Kansas, Nebraska, and other states will provide the traveler with visible evidence of windmills cropping up seemingly everywhere in what are historically miles and miles of wheat fields and grasslands. As a result, these lands are not only producing wheat but also generating electricity that neither pollutes nor depletes.

How can we decrease our use of coal and oil and increase our use of solar, wind, and water power? Boeker and Van Grondelle (2000) state, "The present period should be used to introduce renewables on a large scale, both by stimulating research and development and by adapting the energy infrastructure" (p. 80). In addition to stimulating research, we can also have local, state, and federal governments create tax incentives for business, industry, and homeowners to use these kinds of energy sources. For example, currently the federal government gives a 30% tax credit to people who install solar panels on their homes (Sanburn, 2015). This tax credit provides an incentive to use solar energy and in doing so helps to decrease the use of coal and oil and hence decreases carbon dioxide emissions. Also, currently, the State of Kentucky has a $500 tax credit, but the state of Indiana does not have such a tax credit. So, various states can add an additional incentive for people to use power sources that do not pollute. Right now, coal plants emit

75% of all the carbon dioxide produced by power plants in the United States, "the largest source of the nation's carbon pollution" (Koch and Kelly, 2014, p. 1B).

A big problem that will stand in the way of using more solar, water, and wind power is the potential loss in profits by coal and oil companies and the potential loss of jobs these industries provide people. For example, it is estimated that the coal industry could lose 35,000 jobs by 2030 (Koch and Kelly, 2014), not so much by solar, wind, and water power but by coal-burning plants changing to natural gas, due to its lower cost (Bruggers, 2014). As a remedy for this and as a way of diffusing opposition by the coal and oil industries, we could give these industries tax incentives to create a profit-making industry based on the selling of solar, wind, and water power and hence create a whole new area of jobs, producing and installing solar panels and wind mills (Darst, 2014). In other words, these coal and oil industries could begin to switch over to new kinds of power to market. This process is already occurring; the oil company known as BP has invested $2.9 billion in wind, solar, and biofuels as a way to make profit through these new energy sources. If there were employees who lost their jobs as we cut back on coal and oil production, the government could help these people train for and find new jobs.

Because the use of coal and oil causes problems for our environment, we need to become more serious about using nonpolluting and nondepleting sources of energy. If the climate and overall environment were not affected so much, we could continue to go on as we have been doing. But that is not the case. We are fooling ourselves if we think that there is not much wrong with the environment and that we can go on as we have been doing. Germany already provides about 25% of its energy by using solar panels (Holy, 2014). We could become more serious like Germany and make considerable progress in three areas: (1) decrease our carbon emissions, (2) decrease our depletion, and (3) create new jobs in the production, installation, and maintenance of solar, wind, and water kinds of energy systems.

A third partial solution to help control the depletion of resources, especially the cutting down of rainforests for wood, is to redistribute land in developing countries to poor people who have little or no land. If more poor people in developing countries had enough land to farm to grow enough food to sustain themselves, the pressure to cut down the rainforests would be less.

If land redistribution could occur, there would also be less malnutrition, less starvation, and less disease, because people could grow their own food, have better diets, and (as a result) be healthier. As you might predict, land redistribution, as a partial solution to the problems of depletion of rainforests and lack of food, is very difficult. It would require the wealthy people of these countries to give up a certain amount of their land. Even though the wealthy people could still keep a fair portion of their land, they still may not like this solution. As an incentive to get land redistribution to occur, developed countries could agree to decrease or abolish the debt load on these countries. Also, if developed countries would forgive part or all of the debt of these developing countries, these poorer countries would have less pressure to farm mainly cash crops for export that take land away from the production of sustainable crops.

Another important partial solution is that developed countries could provide money for developing countries to plant millions of new trees to replace the trees that have been used up for firewood. As you might already know, as there is a disappearance of trees and entire rainforests, there is less rainfall and hence less fresh water for the people to drink and use in farming. This has happened, for example, in Haiti where many trees have been cut for firewood. As a result, Haiti has had less and less rainfall. With increasing populations in developing countries with decreasing rainfall, this is a recipe for disaster. Hence, we need to plant trees to stop and reverse the process of forest depletion. As an excellent example of what can be done, Wangari Matthai from Kenya created a social movement to plant trees that resulted in the growth of 7 million new trees, helping to stop erosion, create more rain and fresh water, and use up the carbon dioxide in the air (Gore, 2000; Brown, 2009).

Another partial solution to stop the depletion of resources is for our government to be the role model in conserving our resources. For example, local, state, and national governments could use only recycled paper and longer lasting light bulbs such as the new LED bulbs that use a lot less energy. They could establish higher mileage requirements for cars, sport utility vehicles (SUVs), and trucks, slowing down the depletion of oil and at the same time decreasing the carbon dioxide emissions produced in our country (Renner, 2000). Finally, the government could be a key source of funding research that would lead to inventing new ways to deplete less in homes, businesses, and manufacturing plants. In other words, we sponsor research that takes a comprehensive approach to our entire society to see how we can deplete less and in doing so also have the potential for creating all kinds of new businesses and jobs, besides depleting less.

Pollution: What We Can Do

We can continue to write and enforce laws dealing with pollution. This requires that the government be involved in this process. Given the nature of capitalism and the desire to make a profit by keeping down costs, if owners and managers of business and industry are left alone, many times they will not take responsibility on their own to pollute less because doing so means increasing their costs and decreasing their profits. As a result, the government will need to continue to create and enforce antipollution laws and to provide both tax incentives and tax penalties for business and industry to decrease their pollution. This will require us to have an effective Environmental Protection Agency with sufficient funds to carry out any needed enforcement. Ideally, all businesses would take responsibility for the pollution they create. But history has shown that this is not the case. Hence, there needs to be some enforcement mechanism, such as the Environmental Protection Agency, to protect us.

A second way to get business and industry to decrease their pollution is to provide them with money to conduct research on decreasing their pollution (Gore, 2000). Also, other research entities, such as universities and private research organizations, can be given more funding to find new ways to decrease pollution. For example, Romm (1991) pointed out that during recent years, "the cost of wind-generated electricity has dropped by 80 percent, to under seven cents per kilowatt hour, which is competitive with some of today's conventional power sources" (p. 32). Also, the cost of solar energy has decreased to such an extent that it too is becoming more competitive with the cost of using coal and oil (Sanburn, 2015). As universities and private research organizations are given more funds to find new ways to decrease pollution, their new discoveries will provide ways to compete financially with current systems that pollute.

Another way to decrease pollution is to address the carbon dioxide emissions by cars, SUVs, and trucks. Higher standards can be placed on all of these vehicles. The federal government can give tax incentives to car companies to create lower levels of emissions and levy tax penalties on those that do not make any progress. Also, the government can provide funding for research to car, SUV, and truck companies; universities; and independent research institutes to create ways to decrease carbon dioxide and other polluting emissions. Realistic deadlines could be set up for car companies to retool to meet new standards. In other words, tax incentives, tax penalties, and more research can be ways to get these companies to meet these deadlines.

Another way to decrease pollution is to use more mass transportation in the larger cities of our country. Because the cities and states in our country are not in great financial shape, the federal government will need to help in this effort. By having the latest technology applied to creating mass transportation systems throughout the United States, we, as a country, could make a large dent in the amount of carbon dioxide emissions we produce. As we mentioned previously, since our country disproportionately produces more carbon dioxide than other countries, we in the United States have a greater responsibility than other countries to decrease our carbon dioxide emissions. We can look to Japan, Germany, and France as our role models. For example, since the early 1990s, Japan has had a steel-wheel-on-steel-rail train that goes 130 miles per hour (Moberg, 1993). Japan has also applied "maglev" technology, in which magnets are used in place of wheels and a train can go 300 miles per hour (p. 14). Germany and France have trains that can go 200 miles per hour and that will link major European cities (p. 14). We can borrow from the insight and creativity of these other countries as they have found new ways to decrease pollution through new and innovative public transportation systems.

We could also cut carbon dioxide emissions by using more rail transportation to transport goods around the country instead of the thousands of trucks that produce greenhouse emissions. The problem with this is that many of our factories are currently located near interstate highways and have increasingly moved away from rail lines. Although Boeker and Van Grondelle (2000) suggested moving to more rail transportation as a partial solution (p. 85), it does not seem realistic for the United States, as compared with European countries, because so many of our plants are now placed near interstates. We might need to look into this matter more and consider the pros and cons. Given that such a move would put a lot of truck drivers out of work and given that there could be a huge expense in building new rail infrastructure, it might be more logical to build new truck engines that produce little or no greenhouse emissions. More research on the pros and cons of truck use versus rail use needs to be conducted.

We have emphasized cars and interstates so much in our country that we have not given other modes of transportation a chance. If we could look more seriously at other modes of transportation as well as look at what other countries are doing, we might be able to come up with a new transportation system that is much more energy efficient and environmentally friendly. The federal government could give more research money to car companies, universities, and independent research institutes to create a much less pollution-producing and resource-depleting transportation system. We might be closer than many people think; it is already being reported that we could soon see cars that get 200 to 300 miles per gallon ("Good for Us, Good for GM?", 2009). Given that so many cars and trucks get in the range of 15 to 30 miles per gallon of gas, this substantial increase in miles per gallon of gas could mean that our cars and trucks would produce only one seventh to one twentieth the amount of air pollution. This advancement alone would greatly help the United States decrease its carbon emissions. For example, in 1990, the United States produced 1,300 million tons of carbon emissions, while in 2012, it produced 1,397 million tons or just 97 million tons more. However, with such an advancement in miles per gallon to the 200 to 300 miles per gallon range, we could actually begin to decrease our carbon emissions like other countries have done. For example, Germany has decreased from 276 to 200 million tons, France from 109 to 94, and the United Kingdom from 156 to 128 (Population Reference Bureau, 2014).

Another way to address the high carbon dioxide emissions of cars and trucks is to change from the current gasoline-using engines to other kinds of engines. For example, we are beginning to see cars that use a combination of gasoline and electric batteries or cars that are powered only by electric batteries. We are beginning to see cities such as Indianapolis experiment with the rental of electric powered cars where people working in the downtown can move around the city without producing air pollution (Tuohy, 2015). Also, people are starting to buy very small cars that are electrically powered to do their daily in-town driving, going from home to work to the store to back home. So, increasing the miles per gallon of gas, using more electric-powered cars, and getting cities more involved in environmental solutions could turn out to be a great help in cutting our country's carbon dioxide emissions.

Another trend that may continue and that could decrease our air pollution from cars is the trend of working at home. If businesses find that they can continue to cut costs by not having so much office space and can cut costs of salaries, retirement benefits, and health care benefits by not hiring full-time employees, the search for higher profits through lower employee costs could have the unintended consequence of decreasing carbon dioxide emissions. If this trend continues during the coming years, it could be a mixed blessing. We would have lower pollution due to less car transportation from home to work to back home. However, a number of people could have fewer full-time jobs and more temporary jobs with lower salaries, fewer retirement benefits, and fewer health care benefits. We will need to continue to watch how this working-at-home trend continues and what the intended and unintended consequences will be.

At the international level, given increasing evidence of global warming due to increasing amounts of carbon dioxide in the atmosphere, we will need to work as a world community to reduce carbon dioxide emissions. The United States initially agreed to a voluntary agreement, but President George W. Bush rescinded that agreement. However, it now appears that, given the mounting evidence of global warming, we, as a world community, will need to make some type of global agreement.[10] We will need to have a global agreement because while countries like Germany, France, and the United Kingdom are making progress in decreasing their carbon emissions and other countries like the United States have leveled off in their increase of carbon emissions, China has exploded in its carbon emissions going from 671 million tons in 1990 to 2,626 million tons by 2012 (Population Reference Bureau, 2014). China is now producing four times the carbon emissions that it produced 22 years ago and has offset the gains made by other countries that have decreased their carbon emissions. Consequently, in order to decrease the overall carbon emissions in the world, we will need to have the countries of the world agree to decrease their respective carbon emissions. Hopefully, new and better technology such as better scrubbers on coal-burning plants around the world to further decrease carbon emissions and other kinds of technologies such as greater gas mileage for cars, greater use of electric cars, and greater use of public transportation will help all countries, especially China, to substantially decrease their carbon emissions.

In order to decrease our carbon dioxide emissions, President Obama has unveiled a plan to cut carbon dioxide emissions by 30% by 2030 (Koch, 2014). Part of this plan is to retire about one third of the nation's coal-fired plants by 2030 (Koch, 2014). Another part of the plan is to have natural gas and renewable energy such as solar panels and wind turbines play a larger role. For example, due to newer drilling techniques that have decreased the production costs of natural gas, while power plants used 16% of their energy from natural gas in 2000, they used 30% from natural gas by 2012 (Koch, 2014). Likewise, in 2000, 52% of the energy used at these plants was created by coal, but by 2012, only 37% was created by coal, due in large part to the cleaner burning natural gas and its lower costs (Koch, 2014). So, President Obama is working to get a more balanced system of various sources of energy in order to decrease the carbon emissions in our country by 2030.

There are three consequences of President Obama's plan to reduce carbon dioxide, sulfur dioxide, mercury, and other pollutants that are not always discussed. One consequence is in the area of health. With these pollutants in the air at ever higher concentrations, this "increases the risk of heart disease, lung cancer and asthma attacks" (Groppe, 2014, p. A9). The Environmental Protection Agency estimates that due to such high concentrations of air pollutants, more than 1,400 premature deaths occur each year in just the state of Indiana alone (Groppe, 2014, p. A9). A second consequence is in the area of job growth. Analysis by the Environmental Protection Agency suggests that by 2030, although the coal industry could lose 35,000 jobs, "more than 100,000 could be created in the energy efficiency sector" (Koch and Kelly, 2014, p. 1B). A third consequence is in the area of cross-state pollution where as we decrease the air pollutants produced by the power plants of one state, another state that receives the air from the polluting state will benefit by receiving cleaner air, hence having healthier air to breathe—an unintended gift that one state gives to another state (Groppe, 2014).

One of the things that we, as world citizens, need to do is stop the destruction of our rainforests and begin to replenish these forests. This is easier said than done, but we will need to do it for a number of reasons. To decrease the carbon dioxide that is causing the warming of our world, we will need to have more forests to consume more carbon dioxide and produce more oxygen for human breathing. Also, for people to have sufficient water for drinking and water for their crops, we need more rainforests to produce more fresh water. More rain forests could not only help save us from global warming but also help give us fresh water for an increasingly thirsty planet.

At least three things can be done to replenish the rainforests. First, developed countries can provide seedlings to poor nations, such as Haiti and Ethiopia, that have lost much of their forests and hence much of the rain that produces fresh water to drink and grow crops. These poor countries will, in all probability, not be able to afford to purchase these seedlings. Consequently, if developed countries do not help, it will probably not be done.

A second action developed countries can take is to forgive a certain portion of the debt that poor countries have so that they can use what little money they have to dig themselves out of their poverty. With less debt, developing countries can use the money they would have paid for interest on their loans to buy the seedlings themselves or invest in their countries in other ways (Murshed, 1993). Also, with more money available, they will be more likely to use pollution control devices.

A third, more long-term solution is to provide these countries with birth control devices at low cost or no cost, the training on how to use them, and the transportation to get these devices to people living in inaccessible areas. This should begin to slow down population growth and put less pressure on people cutting down more of the rainforests. With less population, there would also not be as much pressure to acquire more land to produce more food and to consume more timber for firewood.

As we have seen before, the solving of one social problem, such as the population problem, can help us solve another social problem, such as the decrease of the rainforests. With less population, we will not need to cut down as many trees, decreasing the negative consequences that this brings (less consumption of carbon dioxide, less production of oxygen, and less production of fresh water). Consequently, we need to be ever alert to how solving one social problem can, unexpectedly, help us solve another social problem.

Storage of Waste: What We Can Do

One of the key actions we can take in the area of decreasing our waste is to connect research entities to business and industry to find profitable ways business and industry can use the waste products they produce. In other words, one way to solve our waste problem is not to have so much waste left over. Another way to decrease our waste is to change the way we produce goods so that we reduce the overall waste and then find new ways to recycle the waste we do produce (Gore, 2000). A good example of this is the German electrical plants that use coal to generate electricity and turn their waste into a marketable product. The process works as follows. As air pollution is created from burning coal, these plants use what are known as *scrubbers* to trap pollutants by spraying a mist of water and limestone over the smoke before it leaves the smokestacks. The resulting waste, known as *sludge,* is then processed to make wallboard for homes and other buildings (Moore, 1995). In other words, the German plant decreases the amount of waste in the production process and then recycles the remaining waste into a new marketable product. So, a new norm, and possibly a new law, could be created that holds that whenever we create a new production process, we need to include within our overall planning of this process what we intend to do with the leftover waste, so as to at least decrease our waste and possibly market it.

The principle is clear. How can we help business and industry to take their waste and decrease it or make something marketable with it? This will require new research on how we can invent new ways to decrease and market waste. If we cannot find a profitable way to market it, how can we at least find ways to decrease the amount of waste and also store it safely? We can give companies tax breaks for doing their own research and can give universities and other research entities funding to do research. Innovation will seldom occur in this area unless we provide incentives for business, industry, universities, and research institutes to do research on these matters. This means that we, as taxpayers, will need to provide tax revenue for more research.

There is a lot of hazardous waste in the form of chemicals produced by business and industry, as well as radioactive waste produced by nuclear power plants, that needs safe storage. A recent solution that has been suggested is to store hazardous waste in underground caves that are fairly inert in their physical stability. This is not a perfect solution, however, because the hazardous material must be transported to the new storage site (Carroll, 2002a). There is a concern that trucks and trains that carry this waste could have accidents (although the evidence indicates that the waste, so far, has been transported safely).[11]

If we use this method, we will be transporting more waste in many more trucks and trains than we used in the past. Hence, there will be a greater chance that accidents could occur. Probably, during the coming years, we will need to see how we can make the transportation process safer if we choose to transport waste to one site. Our government has considered transporting our hazardous waste to caves 1,000 feet underground within Yucca Mountain, located 90 miles north of Las Vegas, Nevada (Carroll, 2002a). The U.S. Senate endorsed using Yucca Mountain as the collection site (Carroll, 2002b), and President George W. Bush signed the congressional bill into law during the summer of 2002 (Associated Press, 2002). As you might predict, however, there have been citizens in Nevada who have not wanted a concentration of hazardous waste in their state. So, this is a potential problem of attempting to concentrate some kind of hazardous waste in a certain locality.

Another potential problem we currently face if we do go ahead and store this waste in these underground caves is that if these substances leak, they could get into the ground water and contaminate the water supply of that region. So, this potential problem calls for additional research into the matter both to come up with safer storage places and make the substances themselves in some way inert, possibly by combining them with other substances. It appears that we need to do more research on the matter.

Another partial solution to the nuclear waste problem is to create fusion reactors. Kahn and Brown (1975) asserted, "The fusion reactor is nearly free of radioactive threats . . . [and] would not leave any radioactive waste to be disposed of directly or indirectly" (p. 334). As you can see, we need to do more research on fusion reactors—their pros and cons and think more "outside the box" and continually be creative in how we address our depletion problem in particular and our overall environmental problem in general.

One of the solutions that our country has been trying more during recent years is that of burning solid waste in incinerators. There are, however, both good and bad consequences of this partial solution to reducing our volume of waste. The good is that we can reduce the volume of waste by 90% (Gore, 2000). The bad is that we create more air pollution by putting into the air a number of poisonous substances such as dioxins, arsenic, and mercury. So, although we may be forced to burn some of the waste in the short term, this is an unsatisfactory solution in the long term because it adds poisonous waste to our air. We, as citizens of the world, will need to do more research on this matter as well.

Conclusion

To carry out the preceding measures will not be easy. As I mentioned in previous chapters, vested interests will play a strong role in preventing or slowing down these solutions. This will happen in the United States as well as in other countries. Even though the Netherlands is seen to have some of the most progressive environmental policies in the world, it too has faced the problem of vested interests of corporations, of making more profit and keeping down costs, and the influence of those who have power in economic matters to hold sway over those who have concern for environmental matters. Barriers will continue to be placed in front of those who seek a healthier environment. Consequently, the general public and those who have economic interests will need to be convinced that these proposed solutions will need to be carried out if we want to improve our environment and have a sustainable place for humans to live.[12]

In concluding this chapter, we might consider what a *New York Times* columnist, Thomas Friedman (2006), said about what we need to do. He said that the "direction in which America needs to go is obvious: toward energy independence" (p. A9). He further added, "We must impose the highest energy efficiency standards on our own automakers and other industries so we force them to be the most innovative" (p. A9). He said that we need to encourage a lot of young people to study math, science, and engineering so that we can "make oil obsolete" (p. A9). So long as we depend so much on oil, the United States and other countries that depend on oil will need to coddle countries that own the oil even though these countries may have unethical dictators and policies that we do not support. He therefore urged that the Congress pass the Energy Freedom Act, where there would be great disincentives to produce SUVs and great incentives to produce energy-efficient cars as a way not only to save our environment but also to save our auto industry (Durbin, 2005; Maynard, 2006). With such incentives, this "will force Detroit to out-innovate Toyota" (p. A9). Considering what we have suggested in this chapter as a way to solve our environmental problems, Friedman's call to seriously address the problems of our environment is timely.

Probably, a key factor, if not *the* key factor, in solving our environmental problem is time. Can we, as a world community, act soon enough to head off environmental trends that could be difficult, if not impossible, to reverse—for example, rising carbon dioxide emissions leading to rising temperatures, melting glaciers, rising sea levels, loss of coast lands, and changing climate patterns throughout the world? Lester Brown (2009) in his book,

Plan B 4.0: Mobilizing to Save Civilization, states that we know "what we need to do" (p. xiii), and he further states, "The challenge is how to do it in the time available" (p. xiii). Time, along with a sense of urgency and proceeding with bold and creative action, are probably the ingredients to solving our environmental problem. The question now for all of us in the 21st century is this: "Will we realize that this is indeed an urgent problem and take bold enough action in sufficient time?" This generation and the next generation of human beings will need to successfully answer this question.

Questions for Discussion

1. What else could we do in our country to improve the environment?

2. What should we do in our country to improve the environment?

3. What do you predict we will do in our country to improve the environment in the next 10 to 20 years? What is your reasoning?

4. What could other developed countries do to improve the environment?

5. What should other developed countries do to improve the environment?

6. What do you predict other developed countries will do to improve the environment during the next 10 to 20 years? Why?

7. What could poor countries do to improve the environment?

8. What should poor countries do to improve the environment?

9. What do you predict poor countries will do with regard to improving the environment? Why?

10. During the next 10 to 20 years, what can you do as a concerned citizen to help solve our environmental social problem?

14

Solving Our Social Problems

Predictions and Conclusions

W hat can we say about the future of solving our social problems, especially from a sociological point of view? Based on what we have discussed in previous chapters, we can make a number of predictions. As we discuss these predictions, keep in mind our theory of conflict and social change, the accompanying theoretical propositions, and the causal model as a way to understand what will happen during the coming years vis-à-vis our social problems and how and to what degree we will solve these social problems.

A Number of Similar Social Conditions

First, many of the social conditions for each of the social problems we have discussed have remained the same. For example, our economy is still capitalistic and continues to globalize. Our political system is still a two-party system with mainly conservatives, moderates, and liberals deciding social policy. Our main values are still the same; that is, most Americans highly value equal opportunity, individual freedom, and justice. Especially with respect to the value of equal opportunity, we are coming closer and closer to actually carrying out this value as we are giving more opportunity to African Americans, women, the handicapped, Native Americans, Latino Americans, and homosexually oriented Americans. We could not say this in the early to mid-1900s as prejudice and discrimination were rampant in our country toward these aforementioned groups. Since the mid-1900s, we have become more conscious of these various kinds of prejudices and discriminations and have worked to create a country closer to having real equal opportunity. Although we have not fully realized this goal, we have made substantial progress. So, having capitalism that is going global more and more, having conservatives and liberals battling each other over what should be social policy in local, state, and national governments and usually coming to some kind of compromise, and continuing to cherish the values of equal opportunity, freedom, and justice—all of these factors continue to make for a similar social structure within which we need to work to solve our social problems.

Defining a Social Condition as a Social Problem

We should see that the defining of what is and is not a social problem will continue to be the key to the origin of a social problem (Blumer, 1971). At times, we will observe a group or an organization bringing what it sees as a social problem to the attention of the general public and political authorities. At other times, we will see a political authority, such as the President or some other highly visible government official, attempt to turn a social condition into a social problem by trying to convince the general public that such a condition is indeed a social problem (Ferrari, 1975). Either way, someone or some group will work to convince the American public that a certain social condition is a social problem.

Legitimation

As a certain social condition gets defined as a social problem, we should observe the process of legitimation, where people communicate with others to try to convince them that a certain social condition is in fact a social problem. Individuals, groups, and organizations will increasingly try to change a social condition into a social problem with the possibility that political authorities will begin to pay more attention to the social condition, deliberate on it, and consider it as a social problem. It is at this point in the process of a social problem that we will notice a filtering process going on, when these political authorities will select a few of the many social conditions capable of being defined as a social problem and dub them "social problems" for reasons we discussed in Chapter 1, such as which social problems are seen as most urgent and serious, which social problems affect the vested interests of the rich and powerful, and which problems get the most media coverage. We should also observe intense competition by various groups and organizations to get "their" social problem accepted as a legitimate social problem in the eyes of the general public and political authorities. Moreover, even if a social condition is given the legitimacy of becoming a social problem, there are just not enough resources to address every social problem. Local, state, and national governments will always have to choose which social problem they will tackle first and how many resources they will direct toward that social problem. This, of course, will get people upset because each group will think that their social problem is the most important to address. But limited resources, even if the social problem is seen as a legitimate problem to address, will cause the focusing of one social problem over another.

Values and Vested Interests

Values and vested interests will play major roles in the life of a social problem. We, as sociologists, will need to ask the following questions for each new social problem:

- What values are being promoted in connection with this social problem? What values are not considered? Why or why not?
- Whose vested interests are at stake? Who is going to gain or lose money, power, and prestige?

Our being aware of the values and vested interests involved in a certain social problem will help us to understand the nature and process of the social problem. We will continually need to look behind appearances, as Berger (1963) stated in his book *Invitation to Sociology*, to discover the values and vested interests that are being promoted.

We, as sociologists, should predict that there will continually be conflicts over values and vested interests. Because of these conflicts, we should predict that there will be compromises. Because no political orientation, such as conservative or liberal, will typically have complete sway over the social policy-making process, we will see elements of both conservative and liberal ideas contained within the compromises that eventually become social policies. Radical social policy, on the other hand, will not, by and large, be accepted, because radical groups will not have the resources or public backing to get support for their views. This is not to say that their proposed social policies are not the best solutions to solve the problems. It just means that these groups will usually not have the power to influence Congress, the White House, or the general public to get their policies accepted.

A new political group that is very conservative, called the Tea Party, has emerged in recent years to win political positions at the local, state, and national levels. They are inclined to not want to compromise at all. As a result, there has been much rancor and disagreement over policy and hence more difficulty in coming to agreement to get things done. This has, in effect, slowed down the policy-making process. If the Tea Party gains even more positions at local, state, and national levels, this will probably mean even more slowing down of local, state, and national governments being able to make timely compromises in order to get laws passed and social policies carried out. If, on the other hand, the Tea Party decreases in its power, then more compromise has a chance to occur, and more laws will be passed, and more social policies will be carried out. It therefore remains to be seen the degree to which the Tea Party will influence our laws and social policies as we move through this new century.

Loss of Control Over the Social Problem

With our sociological perspective, we will observe that the group or organization that made the initial complaint and increased our consciousness about a social problem will many times tend to lose control over how the social problem is defined and what should be done about it as local, state, and federal governments take over responsibility for solving the problem. Probably, most groups that want a certain social condition to be seen as a social problem will not realize that, as they are successful in convincing others (especially governmental officials) of their views, they will lose control over the process they started. Political authorities, with more resources of money, power, prestige, and personnel, will tend to become the key players in further legitimizing a social condition as a social problem and in deciding what should be done, how it should be done, and how fast it should be done.

The health care debate of the winter, spring, summer, and fall of 2009 is a prime example. Numerous individuals, groups, and organizations were interested in how and where our health care policy would go and should go (Brill, 2015). These individuals, groups, and organizations declared the need for health care reform since health care costs continued to rise faster than inflation each year, since people with pre-existing conditions were unable to buy health insurance, since 1 out of 6 Americans had no health insurance, and since the United States continued to be the only country in the industrialized world that did not have a health care system that met the needs of all of its citizens (Kerbo, 2009). By the late fall of 2009 and early 2010, the decision to have a certain kind of health care policy rested more and more with the Congress and President Obama, with various individuals, groups, and organizations that had respective vested interests, values, and beliefs trying to influence the political authorities in creating a final bill. By January, 2010, the Congress and the President were the main players in what would happen with health care reform. So, as the year of 2009 progressed, those who originated the desire to have health care reform would have less and less say over it while the Congress and President Obama had more and more say over it. In all probability, this is what happens with most social problems.

Attention and Resources

We, as sociologists, should also observe that as more attention and more resources are brought to bear on a social problem, the more likely the social problem will be solved or at least improved. However, even after much attention is given and many resources are allocated, we still might not solve the problem, because the social policy that we created is the wrong policy to solve that problem or because other existing social policies might work at cross-purposes with the new social policy. Consequently, we should be conscious of the fact that although attention and resources are required, we also need to have a social policy that will work and will interlock well with existing policies.

Someone Will Be Dissatisfied

We should also predict that someone will always be dissatisfied with nearly any social policy we implement. There are a number of reasons for this. First, the problem and its potential solution can get redefined throughout the process of the social problem. With these different definitions, different groups with different definitions will talk at cross-purposes, resulting in increased dissatisfaction. Dissatisfaction will also arise because different groups will have different values and vested interests that will conflict. For example, conservative fundamentalists and liberals will have a difficult time in agreeing on abortion and gay marriage. A number of rich people will not want to be taxed more to provide health care to Americans who do not have it, to provide child care subsidies for single mothers, or to provide student loans for low-income students. Instead, a number of rich people would rather be taxed less so that they can keep and increase their wealth. In other words, we, as sociologists, should predict that there will be discontent no matter what social policy we try due to individual self-interests and individual values.

Moreover, if anything goes wrong with the implementation of a social policy, we should predict that there will be criticism such as, "See, I told you so; that social policy will never solve this problem!" In other words, built within the process of solving a social problem will be the potential for dissatisfaction and criticism of social policies. Such a conclusion is not very consoling to political officials who must face the wrath of different groups with different values, vested interests, and agendas, but at least these political leaders can take solace in the fact that facing this dissatisfaction and criticism is part of the nature of solving social problems and is not due to them as persons—although others will personally blame them.

Compromise

We should also predict that there will almost always be compromise between conservatives and liberals. As such, the social structure will be slower to change than liberals want and quicker to change than conservatives want, hence making both political groups somewhat dissatisfied. On the other hand, radicals will be totally dissatisfied with whatever social policy is developed because their own version of how to solve the social problem will be ignored and not given a chance. They will therefore lament that the social structure is changing at a snail's pace and conclude, "We will never solve our social problems!" In their frustration, we should observe that they may attempt to carry out some type of partial solution such as create communes, develop their own educational systems, seek new lifestyles through different religions and ways of viewing life, or move to other countries.

With such political freedom in our country, where fundamentalist conservative, moderate conservative, liberal, and radical political orientations all exist simultaneously, there is the built-in potential for disagreement, dissatisfaction, opposition, and conflict. Consequently, we, as Americans, given our diversity of political views, will need to live with a certain level of turmoil. It seems that this is the price we must pay in exchange for living in some semblance of a democratic society.[1]

Becoming Accustomed to Social Change

Given all the social change in the United States since the 1960s—such as the changes in civil rights for African Americans and the changes in laws and informal norms for women, gays and lesbians, the elderly, and the disabled, giving these groups more opportunities than they ever had before—we have become more accustomed to social change as a part of our daily lives.[2] Because we have experienced and become accustomed to more social change, we may be more prepared than were previous generations to make more changes that will help us to solve our social problems.

We may also find that our experiencing so much social change will cause us to pick up the pace in attempting to solve social problems and be more willing to try a greater variety of social policies than previous generations. Picking up the pace and trying a greater variety of social policies could very well result in our solving social problems at a faster rate. The problem that works against this faster rate, however, is the fact that there are millions more Americans now than there were a few generations ago. Hence, we will need more resources and more planning to solve our social problems of today.

Because there has been an increase in opportunities among various minorities and a continued emphasis on getting more education, we should observe a greater number and variety of people in our country who will have the chance to reflect on the social problems of our society. With more reflection by more people from a variety of social and economic backgrounds, resulting in new ways of looking at old social problems, I cannot help but think that we, as a country, and possibly we, as a world community, will develop new and creative ideas to solve our social problems.

Capitalism and Social Problems

What can we say about the future of solving our social problems in relation to capitalism? First, as we discussed in Chapter 1, we should predict that capitalism will, in all probability, be around for a number of years to come because a substantial number of Americans have a good standard of living as a result of living in a capitalistic society. It will continue to be given legitimacy as the best economic system as long as the majority of Americans perceive that they benefit from it. Consequently, for the time being, whatever will be done to solve social problems will be done within the context of capitalism.

Yet, ironically, as we have seen periodically throughout this book, it is capitalism that is a major cause of many of our social problems. For example, capitalism causes much inequality. It causes unemployment, leading to poverty and homelessness. It causes crime because people do not have jobs or have jobs that pay below the poverty line. Corporations illegally dispose of waste to make more profit. Some corporations (or their executive officers) steal retirement funds from their employees to make more profit. Corporations move plants to other countries to make more profit and leave workers and communities behind to fend for themselves. Corporations cut back on retirement and health benefits to make more profit or just to survive (Heilbroner, 1991). As a result of these aspects of capitalism, millions of Americans are left out of the abundance that capitalism provides for other Americans. Knowing this situation, we, as sociologists, will continually need to take into consideration the influence of capitalism on social problems as we attempt to solve our social problems.

Environment, Population, and Standard of Living

Another problem that we, as Americans and as citizens of the world, will need to face is the problem of our environment in light of people wanting an ever-higher material standard of living and in light of our rising world population. Just trying to meet the basic needs of food, shelter, and clothing for more people in the world will cause societies to produce more material goods, resulting in more pollution and more depletion of resources. Given these conditions, we, as sociologists, should predict that the problems of pollution and depletion of resources will continue in the near future and will be a daunting challenge for humans living in the 21st century.

As a partial solution to this situation, Heilbroner (1991) called for providing more services for people instead of providing more material goods. The problem with this solution is that the combination of increasing world population and people's desire for a higher material standard of living may be too strong for services alone to act as a satisfactory replacement for material goods. Possibly, if the population problem can be controlled, and if people are socialized to want fewer material goods, providing services could act as a partial substitute for material goods. For the foreseeable future, however, we should predict that the people of the world will continue to want more material goods, with the result that we will continue to pollute a lot, deplete a lot, and pile up more waste.

If the preceding thoughts hold true, will we someday be forced to alter our values, our lifestyles, and even our economic system? I do not know the answer to this question, but it seems that some things will need to change. Someday, we or our future generations may have no choice but to change our way of living—if we want to survive as a species.

If we need to change, what kind of change might we see? One kind of change that continues nearly daily is technological change. Certain technologies will no doubt solve or lessen some social problems. For example, we might find ways to increase our use of mass transportation or discover ways of continuing to use cars and yet decrease pollution and the depletion of resources. Even when these kinds of technological discoveries are made, we, as sociologists, should predict that these technologies will not be implemented immediately because of the vested interests of those who make a profit in the car and oil industries as they now exist. For example, if we stopped using oil, oil companies and those industries affiliated with the oil companies would lose profit, and workers in these companies would lose jobs.

We should therefore predict that powerful vested interests will fight to stop or at least slow down the implementation of any new technology that would solve or greatly improve the social problems of pollution and the depletion of resources if that technology meant the loss of profit. So, although we might discover new technologies that could help to solve certain social problems, we should predict that other factors, such as power and vested interests, could stop or at least slow down, the use of these technologies. Hence, we should predict that technology alone will never be the complete answer to the solving of social problems because the problem of vested interests will also need to be overcome.

Building a Sustainable Society

Brown (1987), in his book *Building a Sustainable Society*, suggested that we might need to change from a more competitive, growth-oriented, oil-based society to a more cooperative, population-stable, energy-independent type of society. This new way of living is more likely to happen in the future as we realize that we need to change in order to survive. In the meantime, we should predict that there will be huge conflicts over competing vested interests and values that will slow down the change from our current way of living to a more sustainable way of living where (1) we cooperate more within and among societies, (2) we have a population-stable world, and (3) we have an energy-independent society and world.

Someday, we may indeed move to a more sustainable type of society and world but not without considerable turmoil. This is so because although everyone wants to survive, many people do not want to change their values, hurt their vested interests, decrease their standard of living, and, overall, change their current way of living. They have become used to the way they live even though it may not be in the long-term vested interests of humans surviving. We, as sociologists, should therefore predict that moving toward a more sustainable society will be an arduous process. Our short-term interests of wanting to maintain a certain way of life will conflict with our long-term interests of wanting to survive as a species. In many instances, our short-term interests will win out over our long-term interests.

I imagine that what I just stated may give you a sense of pessimism about the solving of our social problems. I do not mean or want to be pessimistic, but as a sociologist I need to look at what I think will happen, not what I want to happen. Yes, personally, I hope that all social problems will be solved—and solved sooner rather than later. But as a sociologist, I must look objectively at the factors that increase or decrease the likelihood of solving our social problems. And when I do that, I cannot help but conclude that there are strong forces such as power, strongly held values and beliefs, and vested interests that will slow down the process of solving our social problems.

Given these strong forces, what we will probably see during the 21st century will be the changing of our society and the world in a disjointed way—sometimes fast and sometimes slow, and sometimes organized and planned, and sometimes disorganized and rather chaotic. Over time, social problems will be solved or greatly improved because more people and leaders will realize the need for solving them and will want them solved, but this trend will not occur overnight just because we wish these social problems were solved. Wishing, however, is at least a step in that direction. Awareness, education, research, understanding, organizing, and taking action are other key steps.

Conclusion

Understand That Life Is Not Always Fair

As you can see, solving a social problem is not easy. African people, from the moment they were put in chains more than 300 years ago, probably thought, "How can we regain our freedom?" Women during the 19th and 20th centuries questioned why they could not vote or hold political office or why they could not become presidents of companies, ministers, or doctors. Poor people of each generation wished they had money and material comforts like other people. Yet possessing the desires for more freedom, equality, and money did not immediately change the social conditions of these people.

Hundreds of years would pass before the descendants of Africans gained some semblance of freedom. Only during the past 30 to 40 years of human history have women been able to participate much more fully in societies.

Poverty, even in the America of today, continues. So, wanting something to change—and feeling deep in one's heart that it should change—does not mean it will change. Many Americans and people in other parts of the world who face, and have faced, various social problems have no doubt wondered and lamented the following:

> Why do we have to go through this? We are not bad people. We are good people. We work hard. We are honest. We treat people fairly and with respect. Why are we treated this way? We are all humans. Why can't we all treat each other as fellow humans?

Whether we have been a part of a larger social problem that has hurt us such as poverty, inequality, or discrimination or whether we have experienced personal turmoil (for example, our parents went through a divorce, and the whole process hurt us deeply), each of us has thought, "This should not happen to me. I did not do anything wrong. I should not have to endure these things!"

This happens to many people throughout the world who are living in dire poverty and do not know where their next meal will come from or how they can make enough money to buy food to survive. This was made clear to me personally when I visited the island country of Haiti and saw immense poverty and extreme deprivation. Everywhere I looked, I saw people with almost nothing and I thought, "How do they survive?" A Haitian woman sits all day on the side of the road in 90 to 100 degree temperatures hoping to sell some used pairs of shoes. A Haitian man puts a mat down on the edge of a busy street and tries to sell some fruit. Someone else works to sell a few pieces of clothing. Many Haitians will start at 4 o'clock in the morning to walk and then ride from their rural mountain homes to get to the city to sell the goods they have to offer and then make the 2- to 4-hour trek back home during the late afternoon and early evening. The same thing is done the next day, and the next day, and so on.

Life is not fair. In fact, life is not fair for many people currently living in many parts of the world, and life has not been fair for many people throughout the course of human history. Not all of us begin our lives with equal opportunities, sufficient food, shelter, and clothing, and freedom from fear and want. For many people, life starts out offering little or no dignity, respect, or means to survive. Life can be cruel to people even when they had nothing to do with their situation. They just happened to be born poor in a poor country. They just happened to be born to a group of people that has been discriminated against and therefore has faced blocked opportunities—possibly for generations. They were not the cause of their situation. It existed before they were born. Yet, they will have to endure their situations all of their lives. They were born. They became little boys or little girls and were naive and innocent and did not understand their situation. But as they lived more years, they began to realize that they were in never-ending situations— and not ones of their making. For most people in these kinds of social conditions, their life situations did not change at all throughout their lives—for example, slaves during the 1700s wanting their freedom, women during the 1800s wanting to vote, and poor people in the inner-city ghettoes of the 1970s wanting good-paying factory jobs when those jobs were disappearing to Mexico, South Korea, China, and elsewhere.

So, life has not been fair for millions of human beings throughout human history, which probably goes back 4 to 5 million years ago. Millions of our fellow human brothers and sisters never experienced equal opportunity, dignity and respect, justice and fairness, enough food, freedom to say what was on their minds, freedom to come and go in life, freedom to not live in fear, freedom to believe in a religion or no religion, and so on. They did not experience any of these things. This is hard to imagine for those of us of today who experience many, if not all of these things. Moreover, many of us take all of these things for granted. Yet, looking back through human history and looking at many of our fellow human beings even of today, we realize that many of our fellow human beings do not live anywhere near the lives that we have been blessed to live.

To become conscious of this about many of our fellow human beings and to have a sense of sympathy for the suffering of our fellow human beings is a key first step by those of us "who have" helping those of us "who do not have." More and more of us are becoming conscious of the inequities and suffering that our fellow human beings experience. With that greater consciousness, I cannot help but think that this will be a key stimulus to the eventual solving of our social problems. Again, consciousness and sympathy will not immediately and miraculously solve our social problems, but consciousness and sympathy will be key first steps in that direction.

Use the Sociological Perspective to Understand More Clearly

As we use a sociological perspective to understand the nature of social problems, what becomes abundantly clear is that the larger social structure—the laws, the informal norms, the daily, monthly, and yearly rituals— both secular and religious, the ideologies, the statuses and roles, the economy, the political system, the inequality of power and money, values and beliefs, and the vested interests that people have—is usually too powerful for one person or a few people to change. The social structure, in a sense, "swallows up" any attempt at change such as having equal opportunity, meeting basic needs, being treated with dignity and respect, and having some amount of redistribution of resources so that people can live decently.

Once something has become a part of the social structure, it is hard to change. As Emile Durkheim, the great French sociologist, pointed out, the social structure is external to us and yet coercive on us (Durkheim, [1895]1966). That is, once we, as humans, create a social structure, whether we realize it or not—and much of the time, we humans do not realize it—it highly influences our thoughts, feelings, beliefs, and actions. It is hard to change the social structure because many people become accustomed to living a certain way of life and because people have vested interests of money, power, and prestige to protect. So long as a certain social structure continues, social problems and the personal problems stemming from this social structure will continue. When we begin to realize how social structures, social problems, and personal troubles are interconnected, we not only develop what Mills ([1959]2000) calls a "sociological imagination," but we also realize how important it is to change the social structures if we want to solve both our social problems and personal troubles. To begin to realize this is to begin to have and to use a sociological perspective to solve our social problems.

Change Parts of the Social Structure

One important conclusion we can make is that if we want to solve or lessen our social problems, we will need to change various parts of the social structure. Those parts could be values, beliefs, laws, informal norms, or some aspects of the economy. With regard to most social problems, we will probably need to change a number of parts of a social structure to solve these problems.

Reflecting on the recent history of the civil rights movement and the women's rights movement, for example, we can say that social change, the decline of a social problem, and the improvement of people's personal lives can indeed occur (see the last parts of our causal model in Chapter 1). Recent history shows that various parts of the social structure need to change if improvement in a social problem is to occur. For example, laws might need to change so that certain categories of people have more opportunity. Once laws are passed, people can resort to the court system to redress wrongs. As a consequence, the court system can be a powerful tool to right the wrongs that people of the past created via the respective social structures they built. Beliefs might need to change. For example, if we begin to believe that all humans should have equal opportunity, we can study and become more aware of the parts of the social structure that hinder this belief. Such consciousness will lead people to come together to form groups, organizations, and social movements to achieve greater equal opportunity (again, refer to our theory in Chapter 1). Informal norms might need to change. In the past, the informal norms may have called for discrimination of certain categories of people. Once the informal norms change, discrimination decreases, allowing more equal opportunity. If the economy is not meeting the survival needs of people, parts of the economy may need to change, or the government may need to step in to meet people's survival needs that the economy, by itself, is unable to meet—for example, when there is considerable unemployment such as occurred throughout the recession of 2008 and 2009 where 1 out of 10 American workers was without a job (Martin, 2009, pp. A1 & A10) or when the jobs that do exist are jobs that pay below the poverty line—recall that the poverty line for a family of four for 2015 is $23,850, but the minimum wage of 40 hours per week for all 52 weeks a year brings in only $15,080 or $8,770 below the poverty level. Hence, one or more aspects of our social structure may need to change if we want to solve our social problems.

Understand the Social Construction of Reality

There is one more point I want you to be aware of about the social structure. We, as humans, created the social structures that have caused the social problems we have today. For example, the early colonists socially constructed the social structure of slavery in colonial America and the legal and informal discrimination of the 1800s and 1900s that resulted in African Americans being at a considerable disadvantage in owning land, starting their own businesses, going to school, going to college, going to graduate school to have the choice of many careers, to have the same opportunities as Whites to be upwardly mobile, to live anywhere they want, and to vote and hold local, state, and national political offices. Early colonists socially constructed social structures that prohibited women from voting, holding political office, owning land, starting businesses, going to college, having all kinds of jobs and careers, and being able to have the same overall opportunities as did men. Since the 1960s, business and industrial owners and managers have socially reconstructed the economic part of our social structure by replacing workers with robots, creating more service-producing industries than goods-producing industries, creating a number of high-wage service jobs and many low-wage service jobs, and moving many factory jobs to other countries, resulting in high unemployment rates for people in inner cities, thus perpetuating poverty, homelessness, higher crime rates, and psychological problems such as stress, low self-esteem, and depression.

Plan a New Social Construction of Reality

We humans have socially constructed social structures throughout history without realizing their negative consequences (Merton, 1967). We created social structures without realizing the havoc they wreaked on society in general or on certain groups of people in particular. Moreover, many groups of people have continued to experience this havoc for hundreds of years. Given that this process of human creation and negative consequences has happened throughout much of human history, it makes sense that we (1) plan the kind of social structures we want given certain criteria that all or nearly all of us could agree on as guides for our future societies and (2) study how new social structures could have more positive consequences and fewer negative consequences for humans.

As for specific criteria we may wish to use in creating future social structures, the following are some we might consider using:

- What social structures are just?
- What social structures are humane?
- What social structures give people equal or near equal opportunity to get ahead?
- What social structures help people to meet their material needs?
- What social structures give people considerable freedom and control over their lives?

Given these criteria, or whatever criteria the people of a society or the world would choose to go by, we could set about to plan and create social structures that satisfy such criteria.

We are at the point in human history at which we realize that we need to be more conscious of the social structures we create. There are too many negative consequences that can happen to people when social structures are created without forethought. Now, more than at any other time in history, we realize that we as humans have created our social structures, and that we can change them.[3] More than ever before in human history, we realize we can have more control over the social structures we create, the consequences these social structures bring about, and thus the way we live our lives. More and more people agree that we have it within our power to create new social structures that will help all of us live more fulfilling lives.

To create social structures based on the criteria we have established, we will need to have (1) research in the area of planning, (2) democratic discussion to get all sides of an issue heard, and (3) testing of our plans before we create new social structures.

We will make mistakes. Although we will try to think of all the positive and negative consequences that may result due to changing our social structures, we will probably not uncover all of the consequences before we create new social structures. We will need to accept that we are not perfect and do not know all and see all. Yet we know that we have past history and contemporary societies to study and enlighten us as well as recent research to rely on to help us uncover many consequences. So, we already have existing wisdom on which to draw.

Realize Hope for the Future

More than ever before in history, we realize the influence that social structures have on humans. We realize that we created these social structures, and that we can change them. We realize that we can create criteria that can act as guides as we plan new social structures not only to meet basic human needs but also to allow humans to flourish. We realize that we have past history and recent research findings to help us plan. We realize that we can test our plans first to "work out the bugs." So, there are many things we realize that can help us to socially construct future social structures that will solve our social problems.

No doubt, social problems are not easy to solve. Yet more than ever before, we understand more fully the workings of society in general and of social problems in particular. We know how many variables relate to each other and what variables cause other variables to change. We realize that we created the social structures within which we live, and that we can change these social structures in order to meet human needs.

Most of us want to solve our social problems and live in a society (and world) that is humane and just. Knowing that we have already made progress in improving a number of our social problems (for example, decreasing poverty among elderly people, decreasing prejudice and discrimination against various minorities, and increasing opportunities for more people), I cannot help but conclude that now, more than ever before in the history of human beings, we can and we will someday solve our social problems.

Questions for Discussion

1. Do you think we will someday create a sustainable society (more cooperative, more population stable, and more energy-independent)? If so, how?

2. Do you think we will someday create a sustainable world? If so, how?

3. Will we solve our current social problems such as poverty, inequality, prejudice, and discrimination? What is your reasoning?

4. How can we solve our social problems in the context of capitalism?

5. What do you think will be the key independent variables, for example, new social structures, different economic systems, different values and beliefs, world versus nation systems, or wise leadership that will help us solve our social problems in the 21st century?

6. What will be the key barriers to the solving of our social problems during the 21st century?

7. Which social problems discussed in this book do you think will be solved, and which ones do you think will not be solved during the 21st century? What is your reasoning?

8. In the future, where will the government fit into the solving of social problems?

9. Do you think that someday all humans will share some common values and beliefs that will help us solve our social problems? If so, what might those values and beliefs be?

10. Where should our own society go from here to solve our social problems?

Notes and References

CHAPTER 1

Notes

1. For additional ideas on the subjective and objective elements of a social problem, see Blumer's (1971) journal article.

2. You might compare my definition with the definitions of other people in the field, including the following. "A social problem is a condition caused by factors built into the social structure of a particular society that systematically disadvantages or harms a specific segment or a significant number of the society's population" (Curran & Renzetti, 2000, p. 3). "A social problem is a social condition that a segment of society views as harmful to members of society and in need of remedy" (Mooney, Knox, & Schact, 2002, p. 3). "When most people in a society agree that a condition exists that threatens the quality of their lives and their most cherished values, and they also agree that something should be done to remedy that condition" (Kornblum & Julian, 2001, p. 4). "Social problems are issues that substantial numbers of the society view as violations of society's social norms or expectations, and about which people believe something can and should be done" (Palen, 2001, p. 10). Parrillo (2002), in his *Contemporary Social Problems*, stated, "We also must know that recognized social problems have the following four components: 1. They cause physical or mental damage to individuals or society; 2. They offend the values or standards of some powerful segment of society; 3. They persist for an extended period of time; and 4. They generate competing proposed solutions because of varying evaluations from groups in different social positions within society, which delays reaching consensus on how to attack the problem" (pp. 4–5). Eitzen and Zinn (2000), in their *Social Problems*, stated that there are "two main types of social problems: (1) acts and conditions that violate the norms and values present in society, and (2) societally induced conditions that cause psychic and material suffering for any segment of the population" (p. 7).

3. For excellent discussions of Comte's life and how he laid the foundation for the beginning of sociology, see Ritzer (1996a) and Turner, Beeghley, and Powers (1995a, 1995e).

4. For excellent discussions of Durkheim's life and work and of how he began the formal discipline of sociology in the academic setting, see Ritzer (1996b) and Turner, Beeghley, and Powers (1995b, 1995f).

5. For excellent discussions of the life and work of Marx, see Ritzer (1996c) and Turner, Beeghley, and Powers (1995c, 1995g).

6. For an excellent discussion on the life and work of Weber, who was the major figure in starting the formal discipline of sociology in Germany during the late 1800s and early 1900s, see Ritzer (1996d) and Turner, Beeghley, and Powers (1995d, 1995h).

7. The sociologists who take this stance use the writings of Weber, the famous German sociologist, who asserted that sociologists need to remain as objective as possible while we are "wearing the hat" of a sociologist. When we are not in our role as sociologists, such as citizens casting our votes or belonging to certain political parties with certain stances on issues, we can and should voice our opinions. See Weber's ([1918]1946) discussion on this topic titled "Science as a Vocation." For example, he asserted, "Politics is out of place in the lecture-room. . . .To take a practical political stand is one thing, and to analyze political structures and party positions is another. When speaking in a political meeting about democracy, one does not hide one's personal standpoint; indeed, to come out clearly and take a stand is one's damned duty. The words one uses in such a meeting are not means of scientific analysis but means of canvassing votes and winning over others. They are not plowshares to loosen the soil of contemplative thought; they are swords against the enemies: such words are weapons. It would be an outrage, however, to use words in this fashion in a lecture or in the lecture-room. . . . Whenever the man of science introduces his personal value judgment, a full understanding of the facts ceases" (pp. 145–146). See also Weber's (1949) discussion titled "'Objectivity' in Social Science and Social Policy," where he maintained that "an empirical science cannot tell anyone what he should do—but rather what he can do" (p. 54).

8. For a more detailed discussion on this matter, see Manis's (1974) journal article.

9. For a more detailed explanation, see Turner's (1998) *The Structure of Sociological Theory*.

10. See a famous book in sociology, Berger and Luckmann's (1967) *The Social Construction of Reality*. In their book, they did an excellent job of showing how humans create all kinds of social phenomena.

11. See Weber ([1914]1968), where he discussed three dimensions of inequality: class or money, party or power, and status or prestige. Sociologists use these three dimensions to measure inequality.

12. See Turner (1998, p. 158), where he reformulated the ideas of Weber in a propositional format. See also Weber ([1914]1968). Turner noted that Weber suggests that if society socializes people to be upwardly mobile and tells them that they have equal opportunity when in fact they do not have equal opportunity, we have created social conditions for these people to question the legitimacy of the existing social conditions.

13. For others who have suggested that there may be a sequence or phases or stages of social problems, see Blumer (1971); Case (1924); Frank (1925); Fuller and Myers (1941); Peyrot (1984); and Spector and Kitsuse (1973).

14. For various theoretical propositions based on Blau's work that I use at various points throughout this book, see Turner (2003).

15. A good place to start to think about what will happen to capitalism and any indicators as to when is to consider the views of Schumpeter (1942).

References

Berger, P. L., & Luckmann, T. (1967). *The social construction of reality.* Garden City, NY: Anchor.

Blau, P. M. (1964). *Exchange and power in social life.* New York, NY: Wiley.

Blumer, H. (1971). Social problems as collective behavior. *Social Problems, 18,* 298–305.

Case, C. M. (1924). What is a social problem? *Journal of Applied Sociology, 8,* 268–273.

Cooley, C. H. (1902). *Human nature and the social order.* New York, NY: Schocken.

Curran, D. J., & Renzetti, C. M. (2000). *Social problems: Society in crisis* (5th ed.). Boston, MA: Allyn & Bacon.

Durkheim, E. ([1895]1938). What is a social fact? In *The rules of sociological method* (pp. 1–13). New York, NY: Free Press.

Eitzen, D. S., & Zinn, M. B. (2000). *Social problems* (8th ed.). Boston, MA: Allyn & Bacon.

Frank, L. K. (1925). Social problems. *American Journal of Sociology, 30,* 462–473.

Fuller, R. C., & Myers, R. R. (1941). The natural history of a social problem. *American Sociological Review, 6,* 320–328.

Gouldner, A. W. (1960). The norm of reciprocity. *American Sociological Review, 25,* 161–178.

Kornblum, W., & Julian, J. (2001). *Social problems* (10th ed.). Upper Saddle River, NJ: Prentice Hall.

Manis, J. G. (1974). Assessing the seriousness of social problems. *Social Problems, 22,* 1–15.

Marx, K. ([1844]1964). Estranged labor. In *The economic and philosophic manuscripts of 1844* (pp. 106–119). New York, NY: International.

Marx, K. ([1845]1972). Theses on Feuerbach. In R. C. Tucker (Ed.), *The Marx–Engels reader.* New York, NY: Norton.

Merton, R. K. (1938). Social structure and anomie. *American Sociological Review, 3,* 672–682.

Merton, R. K. (1967). Manifest and latent functions. In *On theoretical sociology* (pp. 73–138). New York, NY: Free Press.

Merton, R. K. (1968a). Continuities in the theory of reference groups and social structure. In *Social theory and social structure* (enlarged ed., pp. 335–440). New York, NY: Free Press.

Merton, R. K., with Rossi, A. S. (1968b). Contributions to the theory of reference group behavior. In *Social theory and social structure* (enlarged ed., pp. 279–334). New York, NY: Free Press.

Mills, C. W. (1959). *The sociological imagination.* London, UK: Oxford University Press.

Mooney, L., Knox, D., & Schact, C. (2002). *Understanding social problems.* Belmont, CA: Wadsworth/Thomson Learning.

Palen, J. J. (2001). *Social problems for the twenty-first century.* Boston, MA: McGraw–Hill.

Parrillo, V. N. (2002). *Contemporary social problems* (5th ed.). Boston, MA: Allyn & Bacon.

Parsons, T. (1951). *The social system.* New York, NY: Free Press.

Peyrot, M. (1984). Cycles of social problem development: The case of drug abuse. *Sociological Quarterly, 25,* 83–95.

Ritzer, G. (1996a). Auguste Comte. In *Classical sociological theory* (2nd ed., pp. 87–113). New York, NY: McGraw–Hill.

Ritzer, G. (1996b). Emile Durkheim. In *Classical sociological theory* (2nd ed., pp. 183–216). New York, NY: McGraw–Hill.

Ritzer, G. (1996c). Karl Marx. In *Classical sociological theory* (2nd ed., pp. 149–182). New York, NY: McGraw–Hill.

Ritzer, G. (1996d). Max Weber. In *Classical sociological theory* (2nd ed., pp. 217–263). New York, NY: McGraw–Hill.

Schumpeter, J. A. (1942). *Capitalism, socialism, and democracy.* New York, NY: Harper & Row.

Spector, M., & Kitsuse, J. I. (1973). Social problems: A re-formulation. *Social Problems, 21,* 145–159.

Sutherland, E. H. (1940). White-collar criminality. *American Sociological Review, 5,* 1–12.

Turner, J. H. (1991). *The structure of sociological theory* (5th ed.). Belmont, CA: Wadsworth.

Turner, J. H. (1998). *The structure of sociological theory* (6th ed.). Belmont, CA: Wadsworth.

Turner, J. H. (2003). Dialectical exchange theory: Peter M. Blau. In *The structure of sociological theory* (7th ed., pp. 294–307). Belmont, CA: Wadsworth/Thomson Learning.

Turner, J. H., Beeghley, L., & Powers, C. H. (1995a). The origin and context of Auguste Comte's thought. In *The emergence of sociological theory* (3rd ed., pp. 13–28). Belmont, CA: Wadsworth.

Turner, J. H., Beeghley, L., & Powers, C. H. (1995b). The origin and context of Emile Durkheim's thought. In *The emergence of sociological theory* (3rd ed., pp. 284–309). Belmont, CA: Wadsworth.

Turner, J. H., Beeghley, L., & Powers, C. H. (1995c). The origin and context of Karl Marx's thought. In *The emergence of sociological theory* (3rd ed., pp. 102–128). Belmont, CA: Wadsworth.

Turner, J. H., Beeghley, L., & Powers, C. H. (1995d). The origin and context of Max Weber's thought. In *The emergence of sociological theory* (3rd ed., pp. 168–189). Belmont, CA: Wadsworth.

Turner, J. H., Beeghley, L., & Powers, C. H. (1995e). The sociology of Auguste Comte. In *The emergence of sociological theory* (3rd ed., pp. 29–46). Belmont, CA: Wadsworth.

Turner, J. H., Beeghley, L., & Powers, C. H. (1995f). The sociology of Emile Durkheim. In *The emergence of sociological theory* (3rd ed., pp. 310–350). Belmont, CA: Wadsworth.

Turner, J. H., Beeghley, L., & Powers, C. H. (1995g). The sociology of Karl Marx. In *The emergence of sociological theory* (3rd ed., pp. 129–167). Belmont, CA: Wadsworth.

Turner, J. H., Beeghley, L., & Powers, C. H. (1995h). The sociology of Max Weber. In *The emergence of sociological theory* (3rd ed., pp. 190–232). Belmont, CA: Wadsworth.

Weber, M. ([1918]1946). Science as a vocation. In H. H. Gerth & C. W. Mills (Eds.), *From Max Weber: Essays in sociology* (pp. 129–156). New York, NY: Oxford University Press.

Weber, M. (1949). "Objectivity" in social science and social policy. In *The methodology of the social sciences* (pp. 49–112). New York, NY: Free Press.

Weber, M. ([1914]1968). The distribution of power within the political community: Class, status, party. In *Economy and society: An outline of interpretive sociology* (pp. 926–940). New York, NY: Bedminster.

CHAPTER 2

Notes

1. Ryan (1981) discussed the need for people to have access to resources such as medical care, quality education, and housing, resulting in income inequality not having such a dire effect on people with low incomes.

2. For a succinct overview of libertarian, conservative, and liberal ("social democratic") philosophies, see Fine and Shulman's (2003, pp. 6–13) *Talking Sociology*.

3. See, for example, the newspaper article by King (2005). This article discusses the continuing debate about whether or not creationism, or a more recent version of creationism called *intelligent design,* should be taught in a science classroom or in any classroom in a public school.

4. This principle can also be applied to other countries that have congresses and parliaments.

5. Broder (2002) discussed how decreasing tax cuts at the federal level was resulting in less aid for state governments that in turn needed to decrease state funding such as Medicaid for the poor and cut aid to local governments. He noted that

the federal tax cuts, besides decreasing federal surpluses and increasing federal deficits, meant that "state and local governments are raising taxes and slashing vital services in order to balance their budgets" (p. A11). Hence, the shortsightedness of decreasing taxes has numerous negative effects on state and local governments and on families, especially lower-income ones.

6. As Schumpeter (1976) noted, "The first and foremost aim of each political party is to prevail over the others in order to get into power or to stay in it" (p. 279).

7. For a discussion of American values, see Williams's (1970) *American Society*.

8. Eitzen and Sage (1997) noted that the University of Tennessee of the Southeastern Conference broke the racial barrier when it signed an African American football player for the 1966 to 1967 school year.

9. When I was an undergraduate at the University of Tennessee during the early 1960s, African Americans did not live on campus, were not in the fraternities and sororities, and were not athletes for the university. The few black students who were attending the university at the time lived in African American homes. They would take the bus across town in Knoxville, attend classes, and return to the private homes during the evening. As a result, the African American students were less likely to participate in extracurricular activities than were the White students who lived in the dorms and had much more access to extracurricular activities.

10. Max Weber, the great German sociologist, helped us to realize the potential role that values can play in social action in his book, *The Protestant Ethic and the Spirit of Capitalism* (Weber, [1905]1958).

11. See, for example, Blau's (1964) *Exchange and Power in Social Life*. A key point that exchange theory makes is that not just financial relationships are exchange relationships and that nearly all social relationships have some form of exchange to them. Turner (1991) converted Blau's ideas into interrelated propositions that can be tested empirically for their validity. For example, one of Turner's propositions from Blau is the following: "The more profit people expect from one another in emitting a particular activity, the more likely they are to emit that activity" (p. 331).

References

Berger, P. L., & Kellner, H. (1981). *Sociology reinterpreted: An essay on method and vocation*. Garden City, NY: Anchor.

Blau, P. M. (1964). *Exchange and power in social life*. New York, NY: Wiley.

Blumer, H. (1971). Social problems as collective behavior. *Social Problems, 18*, 298–305.

Broder, D. S. (2002, July 31). The states' dilemma. *Louisville Courier–Journal*, p. A11.

Durkheim, E. (1933). *The division of labor in society* (G. Simpson, Trans.). New York, NY: Free Press.

Eitzen, D. S., & Leedham, C. S. (1998). *Solutions to social problems: Lessons from other societies.* Boston, MA: Allyn & Bacon.

Eitzen, D. S., & Leedham, C. S. (2001). *Solutions to social problems: Lessons from other societies* (2nd ed.). Boston, MA: Allyn & Bacon.

Eitzen, D. S., & Sage, G. H. (1997). *Sociology of North American sport* (6th ed.). Madison, WI: Brown & Benchmark.

Fine, G. A., & Shulman, D. (2003). *Talking sociology* (5th ed.). Boston, MA: Allyn & Bacon.

Kerbo, H. R. (2006). *Social stratification and inequality: Class conflict in historical, comparative, and global perspective* (6th ed.). Boston, MA: McGraw–Hill.

King, R. (2005, August 22). Evolution debate is playing out in Hoosier schools. *Louisville Courier–Journal,* pp. B1–B2.

Kingdon, J. W. (1993). How do issues get on public policy agendas? In W. J. Wilson (Ed.), *Sociology and the public agenda* (pp. 40–50). Newbury Park, CA: Sage.

Lenski, G. E. (1984). *Power and privilege: A theory of social stratification.* Chapel Hill: University of North Carolina Press.

Marx, K., & Engels, F. ([1848]1978). *The Communist manifesto.* Chicago, IL: Charles H. Kerr.

Mills, C. W. (1956). *The power elite.* London, UK: Oxford University Press.

Peyrot, M. (1984). Cycles of social problem development: The case of drug abuse. *Sociological Quarterly, 25,* 83–95.

Piven, F. F., & Cloward, R. A. (1971). *Regulating the poor: The functions of public welfare.* New York, NY: Vintage.

Ryan, W. (1981). *Equality.* New York, NY: Vintage.

Schoenfeld, A. C., Meier, R. F., & Griffin, R. J. (1979). Constructing a social problem: The press and the environment. *Social Problems, 27,* 38–61.

Schumpeter, J. A. (1976). *Capitalism, socialism, and democracy.* New York, NY: Harper & Row.

Turner, J. H. (1991). *The structure of sociological theory* (5th ed.). Belmont, CA: Wadsworth.

Weber, M. ([1905]1958). *The Protestant ethic and the spirit of capitalism.* New York, NY: Scribner.

Weiss, C. H. (1993). The interaction of the sociological agenda and public policy. In W. J. Wilson (Ed.), *Sociology and the public agenda* (pp. 23–39). Newbury Park, CA: Sage.

Williams, R. M. Jr. (1970). *American society: A sociological interpretation* (3rd ed.). New York, NY: Knopf.

Wilson, W. J. (1993a). Can sociology play a greater role in shaping the national agenda? In W. J. Wilson (Ed.), *Sociology and the public agenda* (pp. 3–22). Newbury Park, CA: Sage.

Wilson, W. J. (1993b). *The truly disadvantaged: The inner city, the underclass, and public policy.* Chicago, IL: University of Chicago Press.

CHAPTER 3

Notes

1. For a further discussion of these three dimensions of inequality, see Weber's ([1914]1968, pp. 926–940) *Economy and Society.*

2. Marx ([1867]1967), in *Capital: A Critique of Political Economy,* noted how those who have money in a capitalistic society will also have more power.

3. For a discussion of who holds certain positions and therefore has more power in our society, see Mills's (1959a) *The Power Elite.*

4. For an excellent discussion of people of the corporate class and how they are employed as top officers in one large corporation and serve on the boards of other large corporations, see Kerbo's (2009) *Social Stratification and Inequality.*

5. For a revealing discussion of this process, see Barlett and Steele's (1992) *America: What Went Wrong?*

6. Marx and Engels ([1848]1992) put it this way: "The ruling ideas of each age have ever been the ideas of its ruling class" (p. 40). In an updated variation on this same theme, see Bookman's (2002) newspaper article.

7. For an excellent discussion of Weber's ideas on legitimacy and related consequences, see Turner, Beeghley, and Powers's (2002) *The Emergence of Sociological Theory.*

8. In one of my recent social problems classes, no one voted to increase inequality, 12.5% voted to maintain the current inequality, and 87.5% voted to decrease the inequality in our country. The breakdown of conservatives and liberals in the class was interesting. Among conservative students, 30% wanted to keep the current inequality, whereas 70% wanted to decrease it. Among liberal students, 100% wanted to decrease inequality. So, even though the liberals were more in favor of decreasing the current inequality than were conservatives, a strong majority of conservative students wanted to decrease inequality as well.

References

Barlett, D. L., & Steele, J. B. (1992). *America: What went wrong?* Kansas City, MO: Andrews & McMeel.

Berger, P. L., & Kellner, H. (1981). *Sociology reinterpreted: An essay on method and vocation.* Garden City, NY: Anchor.

Bookman, J. (2002, January 13). "Little guys"—you and I—squeezed out. *Louisville Courier-Journal,* p. D1.

Brinkerhoff, D. B., & White, L. K. (1985). *Sociology.* St. Paul, MN: West.

Eitzen, D. S., Zinn, M. B., & Smith, K. (2009). *Social problems* (11th ed.). Boston, MA: Allyn & Bacon.

Kerbo, H. R. (2000). *Social stratification and inequality: Class conflict in historical, comparative, and global perspective* (4th ed.). Boston, MA: McGraw–Hill.

Kerbo, H. R. (2009). *Social stratification and inequality: Class conflict in historical, comparative, and global perspective* (7th ed.). Boston, MA: McGraw–Hill.

Krugman, P. (2006a, March 27). Looking at income disparity. *Louisville Courier-Journal*, p. A9.

Krugman, P. (2006b, March 1). Rise of the American oligarchy. *Louisville Courier-Journal*, p. A7.

Macionis, J. J. (2010). *Sociology* (13th ed.). Boston, MA: Prentice Hall.

Macionis, J. J. (2015). *Society: The Basics* (13th ed.). Boston, MA: Pearson.

Marx, K. ([1867]1967). *Capital: A critique of political economy* (Vol. 1). New York, NY: International Publishers.

Marx, K., & Engels, F. ([1848]1992). *The Communist manifesto*. New York, NY: Bantam.

Mills, C. W. (1959a). *The power elite*. London: Oxford University Press.

Mills, C. W. (1959b). *The sociological imagination*. London: Oxford University Press.

Turner, J. H., Beeghley, L., & Powers, C. H. (2002). *The emergence of sociological theory* (5th ed.). Belmont, CA: Wadsworth.

Waggoner, J. (2014, December 24). "Stocks Deliver Holiday High." *USA Today*, p. 1B.

Weber, M. ([1914]1968). *Economy and society: An outline of interpretive sociology*. New York, NY: Bedminster.

CHAPTER 4

Notes

1. Eitzen and Zinn (2003), in their book *Social Problems*, reported that 12.1 million American children (under 18 years of age) were poor as of 1999 (p. 184) and that, although the overall poverty rate in the United States was 11.8% in 1999, the poverty rate for children was 16.9% (p. 183). Children make up 40% of all the poor people in the United States (p. 210).

2. Yetter (2003) noted that mostly poor single mothers "are being forced to quit jobs or drop out of school, and some will wind up back on the welfare rolls," according to state officials and advocates who work with the poor (p. A1). Yetter noted that 25 states "are not able to serve all families who apply" (p. A4). Khrystal Johnson of Louisville, Kentucky, said, "I can't afford with my weekly paycheck to put two kids in day care" (p. A4). Johnson estimated that her day care costs are $230 per week for her two children. Also, an unintended consequence of the lack of funding, noted Yetter, is that it will "cause parents to place children in inadequate care or leave them alone" (p. A4).

3. See TaxCreditResources.org (n.d.a). Currently, 14 states plus the District of Columbia have state programs.

4. See TaxCreditResources.org (n.d.b), which reported that in 1999, the earned income tax credit lifted 4.8 million people above the poverty line.

5. We would need to discuss various ways to do this. For example, we could look into the possibility of issuing something like a credit card that, when used to pay the cashier, would indicate the person's most recent yearly income.

6. See U.S. Department of Labor (n.d.). For a good overview of the program, see also Almanac of Policy Issues (n.d.).

7. In *The Structure of Sociological Theory,* Turner (1991) created a number of theoretical propositions from the ideas of Max Weber. The two propositions that are important for the preceding discussion are as follows: (1) "The lower the rates of mobility of social hierarchies of power, prestige, and wealth, the more intense the level of resentment among those denied opportunities and, hence, the more likely they are to withdraw legitimacy" (p. 198); and (2) "The greater the degree of withdrawal of legitimacy from political authority, the more likely is conflict between superordinates and subordinates" (p. 198).

8. For a succinct discussion on our housing crisis, see Eitzen and Zinn's (2003, pp. 157–162) *Social Problems.*

9. Eitzen and Zinn (2003, p. 159) noted that whereas as much as 40% of the housing in Germany, France, and The Netherlands is owned by the government, only 1.3% of U.S. housing is publicly owned.

References

Almanac of Policy Issues. (n.d.). *Unemployment compensation.* Retrieved from http://www.policy-almanac.org/social_welfare/archive/unemployment_compensation.shtml

Aversa, J. (2009,December 29). Are we facing a decade with fewer jobs? *Madison Courier,* pp. A1 & A8.

Cornell Law School. (n.d.). *Unemployment compensation law: An overview.* Retrieved from http://www.law.cornell.edu/topics/unemploymentcompensation.html

Eitzen, D. S., & Zinn, M. B. (2003). *Social problems* (9th ed.). Boston, MA: Allyn & Bacon.

The final bill at a glance., (2010, March 23). *The Louisville Courier-Journal,* p. A4.

Friedman, M. (1962). *Capitalism and freedom.* Chicago, IL: University of Chicago Press.

Gans, H. J. (1995). *The war against the poor: The underclass and antipoverty policy.* New York, NY: Basic Books.

In.Gov. (2009). *Indiana sales tax changed to 7 percent—Effective April 1, 2008.* Retrieved from http://www.in.gov/dor/3885.htm

Kerbo, H. (2009). *Social stratification and inequality: Class conflict in historical, comparative, and global perspective* (7th ed.). Boston, MA: McGraw–Hill.

Palen, J. J. (1997). *The urban world* (5th ed.). New York, NY: McGraw–Hill.

Pear, R. (1999, October 4). 44.3 million have no health insurance. *Louisville Courier-Journal,* p. A1.

Sanders, B. (2000, Spring). The "booming" economy. *Sanders Scoop,* p. 3. (Sanders for Congress newsletter).

TaxCreditResources.org. (n.d.a). *State ETC programs.* Retrieved from http://www .taxcreditresources.org

TaxCreditResources.org. (n.d.b). *What is the earned income credit (EIC)?* Retrieved from http://www.taxcreditresources.org

Turner, J. H. (1991). *The structure of sociological theory* (5th ed.). Belmont, CA: Wadsworth.

Unemployment hits 9-year high. (2003, July 4). *Louisville Courier–Journal,* p. A1.

University of Texas. (n.d.). *Unemployment rate, Austin–Round Rock MSA, Texas, and U.S., 1999–2003.* Retrieved from http://www.utexas.edu/depts/bbr/austindex/ snapshot/unemployment/unemprate.pdf

U.S. Department of Health and Human Services. (January, 2015). *The 2015 HHS poverty guidelines.* Retrieved from http://www.liheapch.acf.hhs.gov/profiles/ povertytables/FY2015/popstate.htm

U.S. Department of Labor. (n.d.). *History of federal minimum wage rates under the Fair Labor Standards Act, 1938–1996.* Retrieved from http://www.dol.gov/esa/ minwage/chart.htm

U.S. Department of Labor. (2010). *Unemployment insurance extended benefits.* Retrieved from http://workforcesecurity.doleta.gov/unemploy/extenben.asp

Waggoner, J. (2015, March 7). Jobs leap, markets weep. *USA Today,* p. 1B.

Waitress lauds wage increase in radio show. (2007, August 19). *Louisville Courier– Journal,* p. A4.

Wilson, W. J. (1997). *When work disappears: The world of the new urban poor.* New York, NY: Knopf.

Yetter, D. (2003, June 23). Many needy parents denied child-care help: State's long waiting list may push some on welfare. *Louisville Courier–Journal,* pp. A1, A4.

Zaldivar, R., & Espo, D. (2009, June 24). Sebelius to press lawmakers on health care. *Madison Courier,* p. A1.

CHAPTER 5

Notes

1. For three different political views on affirmative action, see Fine and Shulman (2003).

2. Kinsley (2003) stated that race will continue to be seen as a legitimate variable to be used to decide who gets into a school just as other variables, such as whether the applicant is an athlete, plays a musical instrument, is an artist, has parents who give a lot of money to the school, has parents who are alumni, or has high grades, are used. Also, Thomas (2003) noted, "There is not a single word in the U.S. Constitution about educating citizens of the United States, nor is there a word about diversity as a 'compelling interest' of the government" (p. A7). He added that

we need to place more emphasis on primary and secondary education in our country because this "would ensure that minority (and majority) kids learn their subjects and qualify for admission based on merit" (p. A7).

3. There are a number of reasons given to justify implementing and continuing affirmative action: (a) the 200 years of slavery and 100 years of blatant and severe prejudice, discrimination, and segregation; (b) the current institutional discrimination that puts minorities at a disadvantage, including the "last hired, first fired" policy and the reliance on property taxes for the funding of public schools; and (c) the results of the past 300 years of discrimination. For example, African Americans are disproportionately poor and unemployed and have little wealth compared with Whites and hence are at a disadvantage due to the lower incomes they have, the less wealth they have, the poorer quality schools their children attend, the fewer family resources available to educate their children, and the poorer and more unsafe neighborhoods in which they live. Consequently, as Farley (1995) stated in *Majority–Minority Relations*, "American society has not yet attained the ideal of equal opportunity" (p. 443).

4. For two sources that seem to be saying that economic factors, rather than racial factors, are increasingly playing an influential role in the upward mobility of minorities, see Wilson's (1978) *The Declining Significance of Race,* where he stated that "the current problems of lower-class blacks are substantially related to fundamental structural changes in the economy" (pp. 21–22). See also Conley's (1999) *Being Black, Living in the Red.* Conley found that wealth, rather than skin color, had greater predictability of outcomes for minorities (p. 134) and that therefore there needs to be a corresponding "shift to a class-based affirmative action policy— that is, implementing educational, hiring, and contracting preferences that are based on *class* and not skin color" (p. 152, emphasis added).

5. Wilson (1987) stated that policies such as affirmative action are seen by many Americans as favoring minorities and discriminating against nonminorities, with the result that "the more the public programs are perceived by members of the wider society as benefiting only certain groups, the less support those programs receive" (p. 118). Similar to Wilson's argument, Fishkin (1983) asserted that social policy needs to be based on the principle of equality of life chances where those who are truly disadvantaged, regardless of their race/ethnicity, would be helped to be upwardly mobile.

References

Conley, D. (1999). *Being black, living in the red: Race, wealth, and social policy in America.* Berkeley: University of California Press.

Farley, J. E. (1995). *Majority–minority relations* (3rd ed.). Englewood Cliffs, NJ: Prentice Hall.

Fine, G. A., & Shulman, D. (2003). Race and ethnicity: Should minorities be given preferential treatment in admission to higher education and hiring? In *Talking sociology* (5th ed., pp. 131–151). Boston, MA: Allyn & Bacon.

Fishkin, J. S. (1983). *Justice, equal opportunity, and the family.* New Haven, CT: Yale University Press.

Gans, H. J. (1995). Joblessness and antipoverty policy in the twenty-first century. In *The war against the poor: The underclass and antipoverty policy* (pp. 133–147). New York, NY: Basic Books.

Greenhouse, L. (2003, June 24). Affirmative action upheld, with limits. *Louisville Courier–Journal,* pp. A1, A4.

Kinsley, M. (2003, June 26). What diversity? Think fuzzy. *Louisville Courier–Journal,* p. A7.

Macionis, J. J. (2015). Society: The basics (13th ed.). Boston, MA: Pearson.

Merton, R. K. (1967). Manifest and latent functions. In *On theoretical sociology: Five essays, old and new* (pp. 73–138). New York, NY: Free Press.

Page, C. (2008, May 11). A loving couple's legacy. *Louisville Courier–Journal,* p. H1.

Thomas, C. (2003, June 26). Diversity: Not a compelling interest. *Louisville Courier–Journal,* p. A7.

Washington, J. M. (1986). I have a dream. *A testament of hope: The essential writings and speeches of Martin Luther King, Jr.* (pp. 217–220). New York, NY: Harper-Collins.

Wilson, W. J. (1978). *The declining significance of race: Blacks and changing American institutions.* Chicago, IL: University of Chicago Press.

Wilson, W. J. (1987). *The truly disadvantaged: The inner city, the underclass, and public policy.* Chicago, IL: University of Chicago Press.

CHAPTER 6

Notes

1. See "State Welfare Cutbacks" (2002) and, in Kentucky, Yetter (2003). The latter article noted that 25 states "are not able to serve all families who apply" (p. A4). Several single mothers who were interviewed felt that, without child care subsidies and with their low wages, "they will be forced to quit jobs" (p. A4). With low wages and no child care subsidies, they regret that they must return to welfare. To the degree that this is a pattern throughout our country, our society could be better served by providing more subsidies for child care so that these mothers can continue in their jobs and have the chance for some kind of upward mobility.

2. See Blumberg (1984) and Turner (2003), where Turner reformulates Blumberg's theoretical ideas into a number of interrelated theoretical propositions (p. 184).

3. See Clawson and Gerstel (2004, pp. 94–95). Also, in this same edition, see two other articles that discuss paid maternity leaves: Gornick and Meyers (2004, pp. 100–102) and Christopher (2004, p. 109).

4. Christopher (2004) went on to note, "Macroeconomic factors were far more important influences on the unemployment rate" (p. 111).

References

Armas, G. C. (2004, June 4). In most jobs, it pays to be a man, report says. *Louisville Courier–Journal*, p. A1.

Blumberg, R. L. (1984). A general theory of gender stratification. *Sociological Theory*, 2, 23–101.

Cheatham, D. (2009, May 19). Speech to Hanover College sociology of sport class. Hanover, Indiana.

Christopher, K. (2004). Family-friendly Europe. In D. S. Eitzen & C. S. Leedham (Eds.), *Solutions to social problems* (3rd ed., pp. 107–111). Boston, MA: Allyn & Bacon.

Clawson, D., & Gerstel, N. (2004). Caring for our young: Child care in Europe and the United States. In D. S. Eitzen & C. S. Leedham (Eds.), *Solutions to social problems* (3rd ed., pp. 90–97). Boston, MA: Allyn & Bacon.

Congress by the numbers. (2015, January 18). *USA Today*, p. 5B.

Crone, J. A. (1998). Poverty. In C. L. Banston III (Ed.), *Encyclopedia of family life* (pp. 1060–1065). Pasadena, CA: Salem Press.

Dionne, E. J. (2015, January 22). Obama pushes past GOP roadblocks. *Indianapolis Star*, p. A-17.

Eitzen, D. S., & Sage, G. H. (2009). *Sociology of North American sport* (8th ed.). Boston, MA: McGraw–Hill.

Eitzen, D. S., & Zinn, M. B. (2003). *Social problems* (9th ed.). Boston, MA: Allyn & Bacon.

Evans, S. M. (1989). *Born for liberty: A history of women in America*. New York, NY: Free Press.

Farley, J. E. (1995). *Majority–minority relations* (3rd ed.). Englewood Cliffs, NJ: Prentice Hall.

Gornick, J. C., & Meyers, M. K. (2004). Support for working families: What the United States can learn from Europe. In D. S. Eitzen & C. S. Leedham (Eds.), *Solutions to social problems* (3rd ed., pp. 98–106). Boston, MA: Allyn & Bacon.

Groppe, M., & King, L. (2015, January 21). Mostly good news for Indiana. *Indianapolis Star*, pp. A1 & A4.

History, Art & Archives, U.S. House of Representatives, Office of the Historian, Women in Congress, 1917–2006. (2007). *A changing of the guard: Traditionalists, feminists, and the new face of women in Congress, 1955–1976*. Washington, DC: U.S. Government Printing Office. Retrieved from http://history.house.gov/Exhibitions-and-Publications/WIC/Historical-Essays/Changing-Guard/Introduction

Kerbo, H. R. (2009). *Social stratification and inequality: Class conflict in historical, comparative, and global perspective* (7th ed.). Boston, MA: McGraw–Hill.

Korte, G. (2015, January 16). Obama pushes paid sick leave expansion. *USA Today*, p. 3B.

Macionis, J.J. (2015). Society: The Basics (13th ed.). Boston, MA: Pearson.

Marcus, R. (2015, January 22). Adopt one of Obama's two proposals. *Louisville Courier-Journal*, p. A15.

McCombs, B. (2013, October 6). Mormon leader: Need women at home. *Louisville Courier-Journal*, p. A4.

Mishel, L., Bernstein, J., & Shierholz, H. (2009). *The state of working America: 2008/2009*. Ithaca, NY: ILR Press.

O'Donnell, J., & Ungar, L. (2015, February 19). Obamacare sign-ups surge. *USA Today*, p. 1B.

Robinson, E. (2009, July 14). Neutrality that never was. *Louisville Courier–Journal*, p. A5.

Rosser, P. (2005, Fall). Too many women in college? *Ms.*, pp. 42–45.

Rudavsky, Shari. (2015, January 15). Deadline nears to enroll for health insurance. *Indianapolis Star*, p. A-9.

State welfare cutbacks will slash child care, job training programs. (2002, September 11). *Madison Courier*, p. A2.

Turner, J. H. (2003). Feminist conflict theory. In *The structure of sociological theory* (7th ed., pp. 182–194). Belmont, CA: Wadsworth/Thomson Learning.

Yetter, D. (2003, June 23). Many needy parents denied child-care help. *Louisville Courier–Journal*, pp. A1, A4.

CHAPTER 7

Notes

1. In *Savage Inequalities*, Kozol (1991) observed how there was no staff to teach machine shop even though the school had a machine shop.

2. Before I went for my PhD in sociology so that I would be able to teach at the college level, I taught for 3 years in a public high school. Even though I had bachelor's and master's degrees in world history as a major and sociology and political science as minors, I never taught a world history course, but I did teach an economics course even though I had taken only one college economics class. So, the subject area in which I had an interest and depth of knowledge of the subject matter, I never taught. But a subject area in which I had little interest and little knowledge of the subject matter, I was assigned to teach.

3. The National Education Association (NEA, n.d.a) asserted, "It is unacceptable for teachers to be assigned out-of-field. Such assignments are a disservice to students and teachers alike."

4. The NEA (n.d.a) asserted, "Teacher compensation is a significant deterrent to recruitment. Teachers are still paid less than professions that require comparable education and skills. Teachers still are not valued and respected to the extent of their actual contributions to society." Moreover, not only is recruiting teachers a challenge due to their low pay, but keeping them is also a problem. The NEA reported that "20 percent of all new hires leave the classroom within three years." In urban districts, "close to 50 percent of newcomers flee the profession during their first five years of teaching." Besides low compensation, those who leave say "they feel overwhelmed by

the expectations and scope of the job. Many say they feel isolated and unsupported in their classrooms or that expectations are unclear."

5. Kozol (1991) noted how in schools in East St. Louis, Illinois, 280 teachers were laid off, along with 166 cooks, 25 teacher aides, and 18 painters, electricians, engineers, and plumbers (p. 24). Loss of 280 teachers caused the size of the East St. Louis classes to get larger, which is the opposite of what needs to happen in a low-income, poverty-ridden city. He noted that the teachers' paychecks were arriving 2 weeks late and stated, "The city warns its teachers to expect a cut of half their pay until the fiscal crisis has been eased" (p. 24). Also, Fruchter (1998) noted, "We have sufficient evidence that reducing class size and providing intensive professional development, particularly in the early grades, significantly increases student achievement" (p. 15).

6. The American Federation of Teachers (AFT, n.d.a) reported, "The Tennessee STAR [Student Teacher Achievement Ratio] study followed a group of students from kindergarten through third grade, randomly assigning these students to one of three types of classes: small (13–17 students); regular (22–25 students); and regular with an aide. With four years of data, researchers found that students in small classes significantly outperformed the other students in both math and reading, every year, at all grade levels, across all geographic areas."

7. The National Education Association (n.d.b) reported research on a longitudinal study done in Tennessee titled Student Teacher Achievement Ratio (STAR).

8. See NEA (n.d.b). The NEA also quoted the U.S. Department of Education: "A growing body of research demonstrates that students attending small classes in the early grades make more rapid educational progress than students in larger classes, and that these achievement gains persist well after students move on to larger classes in later grades."

9. The AFT (n.d.a) noted that with respect to the state of Tennessee's STAR research on the relationship between class size (the independent variable) and reading and math scores (the dependent variables), "lower class size makes a big difference for children, particularly poor children." The AFT stated that lowering class size in combination with "high academic standards and a challenging curriculum, safe and orderly classrooms, and qualified teachers [is] also necessary."

10. The NEA (n.d.c) stated, "Every child deserves the opportunity to learn in a classroom that is modern and equipped with the latest in educational technology. Too many students—one in three, according to the U.S. General Accounting Office—attend classes in schools that fail to meet these criteria." The NEA further noted that a study by the U.S. General Accounting Office some years ago estimated that it would take $112 billion to restore our nation's schools to "good overall condition"; given the intervening years and given the increasing enrollments and greater costs in new school construction, the NEA estimates that the cost in 2003 would be approximately $200 billion. Besides the disrepair and the overcrowding, the NEA noted that "forty-six percent of the public schools in America lack the electrical and communication wiring to support today's computer systems." As a part of the American Recovery and Reinvestment Act passed by Congress to

stimulate the economy, the U.S. Department of Education was given $100 billion in order "to avert teacher layoffs" (U.S. Department of Education, 2009). This attempt to stimulate the economy may turn out to be of great benefit for the nation's schools.

11. Kozol (1991) stated that when he traveled throughout the country during the years of 1988 and 1989 and visited many public schools, "Looking around some of these inner-city schools, where filth and disrepair were worse than anything I'd seen in 1964, I often wondered why we would agree to let our children go to school in places where no politician, school board president, or business CEO [chief executive officer] would dream of working" (p. 5). The football field had a couple of metal pipes but no crossbar for goalposts, and the school did not have a washing machine to wash the football uniforms, which were 9 years old (p. 25). Kozol noted that there was no heat in the weight room and no staff to teach machine shop even though the school had a machine shop and that the science labs "are 30 to 50 years outdated." The physics lab had no equipment, and the typewriters did not work (p. 30).

12. Kozol (1991) noted that the teachers in East St. Louis "are running out of chalk and paper" (p. 24).

13. Kozol (1991) discussed the lack of safety in the schools: "The doors [of the schools] were guarded. Police sometimes patrolled the halls. The windows of the schools were often covered with steel grates. Taxi drivers flatly refused to take me to some of these schools" (p. 5).

14. Hooper (2005) reported that the Indianapolis public schools are creating smaller high schools to have higher quality education and to keep more students in school. She reported that one third of the students drop out and that one third graduate without skills to go to college or to work (p. B5). Her article went on to report that the billionaire Bill Gates "believes so strongly that smaller is better that the foundation he and his wife support is sinking billions into helping districts make the change" (p. B5).

15. The NEA (n.d.d) took the stance that one way to make schools safer is to "provide resources for smaller classes and smaller schools." Also, Fruchter (1998) stated that we have "a growing mass of evidence that reducing scale by creating smaller schools raises student achievement, reduces dropping out, and increases graduation rates at the high school level" (p. 15).

16. Turner (2003, pp. 134–136) discussed Max Weber's proposition that as there are lower rates of mobility among subordinates of a social system, these subordinates will be more likely to withdraw their belief in the legitimacy of the current political authority and be more likely to pursue conflict with superordinates.

17. See Friedman (1982) for an early statement of the voucher system, where education would be taken out of the hands of government more and more and where individual citizens would choose where and what kind of education they wanted their children to have. In other words, Friedman wanted education to be more in the realm of the marketplace than under the authority of the government.

18. The AFT (n.d.c) noted, "Private and religious schools currently have almost complete autonomy with regard to who they teach." The public would want any private and religious schools to be accountable given that these schools would be using public money. Yet in research cited in this article, the AFT noted that these private and religious schools "would not be willing to participate in a voucher plan that requires them to meet the kind of accountability standards that the public desires." This report found that in the school districts studied, even if no conditions were made on these schools, the private and religious schools could accommodate at most only 3.5% of the public school enrollment. This would mean that 96.5% of the students would be left behind, still attending poor-quality public schools. Hence, we would be far from solving our public education problem.

19. A newspaper editorial ("After the Voucher Ruling," 2002) noted that in the situation in Cleveland, Ohio, "despite legislative intent, suburban public schools and well-off private ones are not participating" (p. A8). The editorial went on to assert that Kentucky and Indiana are finding more promising ways "than spending a lot of money to send relatively few students to religious schools that are publicly unaccountable and economically marginal" (p. A8). It made a final point that is worth considering: "Further, there's a real threat of creating a vicious circle. Public schools could become even more overburdened and undersupported as they are left with even higher proportions of the special education or behaviorally troubled youngsters private schools won't accept or keep" (p. A8).

20. Gutmann (2000) stated, "If we [the citizens of this country] were committed to giving poor parents what most parents want for their children, we would not follow the voucher route; we would do whatever it takes to improve public schools" (p. 20).

21. Gutmann (2000) asserted, "A successful voucher movement in this country would therefore provide an enormous subsidy to affluent parents" (p. 20).

22. The AFT (n.d. b) reported on a national representative sample of more than 1,000 adults who were asked the question of whether we should allow students and parents to choose a private school to attend at public expense; the survey showed that 44% of the respondents favored this, and 50% were against it. Moreover, when asked how the private schools should be accountable with this public tax money, 92% of the respondents said there should be no discrimination based on race, 88% said the private schools should meet state curriculum standards (as of that publication, "No state requires private schools to meet the same state curriculum standards as public schools"), 86% said only certified teachers should be employed (71% of all private school teachers are licensed versus 97.4% of all public school teachers who are licensed), and 83% said the private schools should not discriminate on the basis of religious beliefs.

23. See NEA (n.d.e). Also, the AFT (n.d.b) noted that California's "proposal to give $4,000 vouchers for students to attend private or religious schools will be a $3 billion windfall to affluent parents whose children already attend private schools." Luis Huerta, coauthor of the report used by the AFT, stated, "It's essentially tax relief for the well off."

References

After the voucher ruling. (2002, June 29). *Louisville Courier–Journal,* p. A8.

American Federation of Teachers. (n.d.a). *Small class size: Education reform that works.* Retrieved from http://www.aft.org

American Federation of Teachers. (n.d.b). *Voucher home page reports.* Retrieved from http://www.aft.org

American Federation of Teachers. (n.d.c). *Vouchers and the accountability dilemma.* Retrieved from http://www.aft.org

Carroll, R. (2003, August 20). Most oppose vouchers, want teachers paid more. *Madison Courier,* p. A9.

Friedman, M. (1982). The role of government in education. In *Capitalism and freedom* (pp. 85–107). Chicago, IL: University of Chicago Press.

Fruchter, N. (1998, Fall/Winter). American public education: Crisis and possibility. *New Labor Forum,* pp. 9–16.

Gutmann, A. (2000, Summer). What does "school choice" mean? *Dissent,* pp. 19–24.

Hooper, K. (2005, August 21). Less is more for students in Indy: Overhaul creates smaller schools. *Louisville Courier–Journal,* pp. B1, B5.

Kerbo, H. R. (2012). *Social stratification and inequality: Class conflict in historical, comparative, and global perspective* (8th ed.). Boston. MA: McGraw–Hill.

Kozol, J. (1991). *Savage inequalities: Children in America's schools.* New York, NY: Crown.

Merton, R. K. (1968). Social structure and anomie. In *Social Theory and Social Structure* (enlarged ed., pp. 185–214). New York, NY: Free Press.

Mills, C. W. (1959). *The sociological imagination.* London, UK: Oxford University Press.

National Education Association. (n.d.a). *Attracting and keeping quality teachers.* Retrieved from http://www.nea.org

National Education Association. (n.d.b). *Class size.* Retrieved from http://www.nea.org

National Education Association. (n.d.c). *School modernization.* Retrieved from http://www.nea.org

National Education Association. (n.d.d). *School safety.* Retrieved from http://www.nea.org

National Education Association. (n.d.e). *Vouchers.* Retrieved from http://www.nea.org

Rodriguez, N. C. (2003, February 5). School systems consider job, program cuts. *Louisville Courier–Journal,* p. A1.

Turner, J. H. (2003). *The structure of sociological theory* (7th ed.). Belmont, CA: Wadsworth/Thomson Learning.

U.S. Department of Education. (2009, February 19). *U.S. education secretary announces state-by-state dollars in New York.* Retrieved from http://www.ed.gov/news/pressreleases/2009/02/02192009.html

CHAPTER 8

Notes

1. For a more extended discussion of slavery and its consequences, see Franklin and Moss's (1994) *From Slavery to Freedom*.

2. Hraba (1994) discussed various Indian nations and how each of them had its own distinct way of life, including different customs, religions, dress, and ways of economic survival (pp. 202–213).

3. See Hraba (1994, pp. 219–231). For a good discussion of the current situation of Native Americans, see Aguirre and Turner's (2001, pp. 104–133) *American Ethnicity*.

4. See Merton's (1968, pp. 185–214) article in *Social Theory and Social Structure*. See also Cloward and Ohlin's (1960) *Delinquency and Opportunity*.

5. Eitzen and Leedham (2004) asserted that one of the major causes of crimes, especially violent crimes such as robbery, assault, murder, and rape, is the greater proportion of Americans living in poverty compared with rates of poverty and crime in other industrialized countries. They also suggested that a second cause of more violent crime can be seen when a country has a weaker safety net for the poor, such as the United States does compared with other industrialized countries (p. 190).

6. Eitzen and Leedham (2004) asserted that one of the four factors that cause crime, especially violent crime, is a large gap between the rich and the poor. They noted, "The United States has the greatest inequality gap among industrialized nations" (p. 190).

References

Aguirre, A. Jr., & Turner, J. H. (2001). *American ethnicity: The dynamics and consequences of discrimination* (3rd ed.). Boston, MA: McGraw-Hill.

Booth, M. (2007). Deaths reflect gun use in U.S. In D. S. Eitzen (Ed.), *Solutions to social problems: Lessons from other societies* (4th ed., pp. 205–207). Boston, MA: Allyn & Bacon.

Brooks, D. (2015). *The road to character*. New York, NY: Random House.

Cloward, R. A., & Ohlin, L. E. (1960). *Delinquency and opportunity: A theory of delinquent gangs*. New York, NY: Free Press.

Davidson, P. (2014, December 29). Hourly pay on the rise in 21 states. *USA Today*, p. 5B.

Durkheim, E. ([1895]1966). What is a social fact? In *The rules of sociological method* (pp. 1–13). New York, NY: Free Press.

Eitzen, D. S. (2007). *Solutions to social problems: Lessons from other societies* (4th ed.). Boston, MA: Pearson/Allyn & Bacon.

Eitzen, D. S., & Leedham, C. S. (2004). Crime and crime control. In *Solutions to social problems: Lessons from other societies* (3rd ed., pp. 190–208). Boston, MA: Allyn & Bacon.

Eitzen, D. S., Zinn, M. B., & Smith, K. E. (2009). *Social problems* (11th ed.). Boston, MA: Pearson/Allyn & Bacon.

Franklin, J. H., & Moss, A. A., Jr. (1994). *From slavery to freedom: A history of African Americans* (7th ed.). New York, NY: McGraw–Hill.

Hraba, J. (1994). *American ethnicity* (2nd ed.). Itasca, IL: F. E. Peacock.

Kerbo, H. (2012). *Social stratification and inequality: Class conflict in historical, comparative, and global perspective* (8th ed.). New York, NY: McGraw-Hill.

Marx, K. ([1844]1964). Estranged labor. In *The economic and philosophic manuscripts of 1844* (pp. 106–119). New York, NY: International Publishers.

Marx, K. ([1845]1967). *Capital*. New York, NY: International Publishers.

Marx, K., & Engels, F. ([1848]1992). *The Communist manifesto*. New York, NY: Bantam.

Merton, R. K. (1968). Social structure and anomie. In *Social theory and social structure* (enlarged ed., pp. 185–214). New York, NY: Free Press.

O'Donnell, J. (2015, February 5). Health care sign-ups estimated at nearly 10M as deadline looms. *USA Today*, p. 3B.

O'Donnell, J., & Ungar, L. (2015, February 12). Health enrollment passes projection. *USA Today*, p. 3B.

O'Donnell, J., & Ungar, L. (2015, February 19). Obamacare sign-ups surge. *USA Today*, p. 1B.

Paternoster, R. (1989). Absolute and restrictive deterrence in a panel of youth: Explaining the onset, persistence/desistance, and frequency of delinquent offending. *Social Problems, 36,* 289–309.

Population Reference Bureau. (2014). *2014 world population data sheet*. Washington, DC: Author.

Ritzer, G. (2005). *Enchanting a disenchanted world: Revolutionizing the means of consumption* (2nd ed.). Thousand Oaks, CA: Pine Forge.

Rudavsky, S. (2015, January 15). Deadline nears to enroll for health insurance. *Indianapolis Star*, p. A-9.

Shell, A. (2015, January 2). Stocks score hat trick of 10% gains. *USA Today*, p. 4B.

University of Texas. (n.d.). *Unemployment rate, Austin–Round Rock MSA, Texas, and U.S., 1999–2003*. Retrieved from http://www.utexas.edu/depts/bbr/austindex/snapshot/unemployment/unemprate.pdf

U.S. Unemployment Rate. (2009, June). http://www.google.com/publicdata ?ds=usun employment&met=unemployment_rate&tdim=true&q=U.S.&Unemployment &Rate

Waggoner, J. (2015, March 7). Jobs leap, markets weep. *USA Today*, p. 1B.

Zaldivar, R., & Espo, D. (2009, June 24). Sebelius to press lawmakers on health care. *Madison Courier*, p. A1.

CHAPTER 9

Notes

1. Nadelmann (1988) states, "All of the health costs of marijuana, cocaine, and heroin combined amount to only a small fraction of those caused by tobacco and alcohol" (p. 24). More recent data reported by the Centers for Disease Control (2006) continue to affirm Nadelmann's assertion.

2. Brownstein (1992) noted, "Efforts to reduce the supply of imported drugs through interdiction have resulted in an expansion of the domestic supply of marijuana, more violence, and possibly even assistance to major drug dealers through elimination of weaker competitors" (p. 220).

3. Nadelmann (1988) noted, "Many illicit drug users commit crimes such as robbery and burglary, as well as drug dealing, prostitution, and numbers running, to earn enough money to purchase the relatively high-priced illicit drugs. . . . If the drugs to which they are addicted were significantly cheaper—which would be the case if they were legalized—the number of crimes committed by drug addicts to pay for their habits would, in all likelihood, decline dramatically. Even if a legal drug policy included the imposition of relatively high consumption taxes in order to discourage consumption, drug prices would probably still be lower than they are today" (p. 17).

4. Nadelmann stated, "Illegal markets tend to breed violence. . . . During Prohibition, violent struggles between bootlegging gangs and hijackings of booze-laden trucks and sea vessels were frequent and notorious occurrences. . . . Most law enforcement officials agree that the dramatic increases in urban murder rates during the past few years [this article was published in 1988] can be explained almost entirely by the rise in drug dealer killings" (p. 18).

5. Nadelmann (1988) noted, "Repeal of Prohibition came to be seen not as a capitulation of Al Capone and his ilk, but as a means of both putting the bootleggers out of business and eliminating most of the costs associated with the Prohibition laws" (p. 13).

6. Szasz (1972) argued, "Like most rights, the right of self-medication should apply only to adults" (p. 77).

7. Nadelmann (1988) noted, "If the marijuana, cocaine, and heroin markets were legal, state and federal governments would collect billions of dollars annually in tax revenues" (p. 16).

8. Becker (2001) also suggested this approach because "legalizing drugs is a venture into the unknown" (p. 32).

9. Brown (1975) noted that the National Commission on Marijuana and Drug Abuse, created by Congress in 1970, recommended that the possession of marijuana "for personal use no longer be a federal or state offense" (p. 114).

10. Eitzen, Zinn, and Smith (2009) cited that it costs $80,000 to build each new cell and costs approximately $25,000 per year to house a prisoner (p. 404).

11. Nadelmann (1988) agreed. He stated, "Legalization is repeatedly and vociferously dismissed, without any attempt to evaluate it openly and objectively.

The past twenty years have demonstrated that a drug policy shaped by exaggerated rhetoric designed to arouse fear has only led to our current disaster. Unless we are willing to honestly evaluate our options, including various legalization strategies, we will run a still greater risk: We may never find the best solution for our drug problems" (p. 31).

12. See Cart (1999). New Mexico Governor Gary Johnson advocated legalizing all drugs and suggested that this issue needs to be discussed, but he heard a lot of negative criticism just for bringing up the issue.

References

Becker, G. (2001, September 17). It's time to give up the war on drugs. *Business Week,* p. 32.

Brown, B. S. (1975). Drugs and public health: Issues and answers. *Annals of the American Academy of Political and Social Sciences, 417,* 110–119.

Brownstein, H. H. (1992). Making peace in the war on drugs. *Humanity and Society, 16,* 217–235.

Cart, J. (1999, November 12). Governor's support for drugs sparks New Mexico firestorm. *Louisville Courier–Journal,* p. A4.

Carson, E. (2014). Prisoners in 2013. Bureau of Justice Statistics, Office of Justice Program, U.S. Department of Justice, http://www.bjs.gov/content/pub/pdf/p13.pdf

Eitzen, D. S., & Zinn, M. B. (2009). *Social problems* (11th ed.). Boston, MA: Allyn & Bacon.

Eitzen, D. S., Zinn, M. B., & Smith, K. E. (2009). *Social problems.* (11th ed.). Boston, MA: Pearson/Allyn & Bacon.

Eitzen, D. S., Zinn, M. B., & Smith, K. E. (2011). *Social problems.* (12th ed.). Boston, MA: Pearson/Allyn & Bacon.

Ferner, M. (2015, January 26). Legalizing Marijuana Is The Fastest Growing Industry In The U.S.: Report. *Huffingtonpost.com.* Retrieved from http://www.huffingtonpost.com/2015/01/26/marijuana-industry-fastest-growing_n_6540166.html

Fine, G. A., & Shulman, D. (2003). *Talking sociology* (5th ed.). Boston, MA: Allyn & Bacon.

Marcus, R. (2014, June 26). Beware consequences of legalizing marijuana. *Indianapolis Star,* p. A-23.

Myers, L. (2001). Cultural divide over crime and punishment. In D. S. Eitzen & C. S. Leedham (Eds.), *Solutions to social problems: Lessons from other societies* (2nd ed., pp. 233–239). Boston, MA: Allyn & Bacon.

Nadelmann, E. A. (1988, Summer). The case for legalization. *Public Interest,* pp. 3–31.

Neubeck, K. J., Neubeck, M. A., & Glasberg, D. S. (2007). *Social problems: A critical approach* (5th ed.). Boston, MA: McGraw-Hill.

Szasz, T. S. (1972, April). The ethics of addiction. *Harper's,* pp. 74–79.

Substance Abuse and Mental Health Services Administration. (2014). *Results from the 2013 National Survey on Drug Use and Health: Summary of National Findings.*

NSDUH Series H-48.HHS Publication No. (SMA) 14-4863. Rockville, MD: Substance Abuse and Mental Health Services Administration. Retrieved from http://www.samhsa.gov/data/sites/default/files/NSDUHresultsPDF-WHTML2013/Web/NSDUHresults2013.pdf

U.S. Department of Health and Human Services. (2015). *The health consequences of smoking—50 years of progress: A report of the surgeon general.* Atlanta: U.S. Department of Health and Human Services, Centers for Disease Control and Prevention, National Center for Chronic Disease Prevention and Health Promotion, Office on Smoking and Health. Retrieved from http://www.cdc.gov/tobacco/data_statistics/sgr/50th-anniversary/index.htm

Zeese, K. (2006). The futility of drug prohibition. *Alternet* (December 13). http://www.alternet.org/story/45010

CHAPTER 10

Notes

1. This was reported on the *NewsHour with Jim Lehrer,* January 9, 2006. One interviewee reported that 46 million Americans are currently uninsured. It was also reported that 69% of American corporations offered health coverage in 2000, whereas only 60% of American corporations offer coverage today (2006). Because health insurance costs so much, and because the cost is going up at 8% or more each year (as reported on the *NewsHour*), corporations are finding it harder and harder to offer coverage. To cut their costs so as to remain competitive or become more competitive in their respective markets, more and more corporations are reducing or eliminating health insurance coverage for their employees. This trend will put more pressure on the current president and future presidents, as well as the current Congress and future Congresses, to do something in the area of health care for Americans. Zaldivar and Espo (2009, June 24, p. A1) report that 50 million Americans are without health care.

2. Unger (2006) noted, "Many people cannot afford to see a doctor and live with the threat of financial ruin if they get sick" (p. A1).

3. See Carroll (2003, p. A1). By the way, the new prescription drug plan took effect January 1, 2006, not without some problems. Pear (2006b) noted that people who had signed up were not on the government's list of subscribers, that insurers did not have a way of identifying poorer people who were entitled to extra help, and that pharmacists were on the phone for hours trying to reach insurers to work out the various problems. The new program, Pear noted, appeared to be "too complicated for many people to understand" (p. A12). He stated that this new prescription drug plan "is the most significant expansion of Medicare since creation of the program in 1965" (p. A12). Also, Howington (2006) reported that in 70% of the cases in Kentucky, there were problems in getting prescriptions (p. A1). Retired people were not on the new lists even though they had signed up to be on the lists, and poor

people who are on Medicaid were supposed to get their prescription drugs through Medicare, but "Medicare plans wouldn't pay" (p. A1). A major problem, the article noted, was that there was not enough time to sign up 42 million Americans between the sign-up time of November 15, 2005, and the time the new prescription drug plan kicked in on January 1, 2006.

4. Jewell (2003) reported that Republican congresspersons such as Dan Burton of Indiana and Jo Ann Emerson of Missouri desired the importation of prescription drugs as a way to decrease costs of prescription drugs for the elderly. This article reported that the Eli Lilly drug company, with headquarters in Indianapolis, Indiana, got 100 of its employees to go to a forum promoting the importation of drugs to speak against this importation. Also, Frommer (2003) reported that the drug industry spent $29 million in lobbying—"more than any other industry" (Frommer, 2003, p. A10). Besides the lobby that spent $8.5 million to work against allowing Americans to buy prescription drugs from Canada, individual drug companies also spent their own money to stop the importation of prescription drugs at lower prices; for example, Eli Lilly spent $2.9 million, Bristol–Myers Squibb spent $2.6 million, Johnson & Johnson spent $2.2 million, and Pfizer spent $1.8 million. Ira Loss, a senior health care analyst for the Washington Analysis Corporation, stated, "They [the drug companies] make a lot of money, and they are trying to protect their interests" (Frommer, 2003, p. A10). Frommer reported that the drug industry "enjoyed about $150 billion in U.S. sales last year" (2003, p. A10).

5. Graig (1999) noted, "Many U.S. companies complained that high health care costs put them at a competitive disadvantage with regard to foreign competitors in countries with nationalized health care systems" (p. 18). Graig (1999) reported further that although few employers viewed health care costs as a problem in 1980, two thirds of the executives in a 1990 survey viewed "health benefits costs to be the leading issue companies faced at that time" (p. 19).

6. This was reported on the *NewsHour with Jim Lehrer,* January 12, 2006.

7. Kerbo (2006) noted that good health is unequally distributed in that people with lower incomes will often face the following conditions: (a) poor nutrition, (b) less sanitary living conditions, (c) less knowledge about how to have better health, and (d) more unhealthy work environments, such as working with dangerous machines and chemicals (p. 38).

8. Also, Globerman (1990) noted that there are physicians who are "committed to the well-being of the collective, who support government-run universal health insurance" (p. 12), but that there are also physicians who "oppose government intervention and support free-enterprise medicine" (p. 12). For the physicians who want more free enterprise medicine, the reasons why they want this are "professional ideology, free enterprise ideology, and economic self-interest" (p. 13). So, even though Canada has a universal health care system, there are doctors in Canada who want to abolish this system. A number of these doctors want to bill the patients over and above what the government will reimburse them for services rendered, for example, approximately 12% of doctors "extra-bill" patients (p. 15).

9. Pear and Bogdanich (2003) reported, "Drug companies say they support covering prescription drugs under Medicare. But in the last few years, they have invested several hundred million dollars in campaign contributions, lobbying, and advertising to head off price controls" (p. A7).

10. In a classic work in sociology, *The Social Construction of Reality,* Berger and Luckmann (1966) argued that we, as humans, create our own social reality of norms, values, beliefs, and institutions. These norms, values, beliefs, and institutions may be different in different cultures and at different times in history, but they are created by humans over time. Sometimes people forget this and believe that these things have always been and will always be. Berger and Luckmann reminded us how much we socially construct how we live.

11. Daniels and colleagues (1996) presented data showing that "the lowest fifth of the nation has no money left over for medical bills, health insurance premiums, movie going, or any other expenses" (p. 50). So, the lowest 20% of Americans do not make enough money to have health insurance. Moreover, Daniels and colleagues pointed out that the next 20% of Americans do not have much left over after paying their expenses. So, in reality, approximately 40% of Americans either cannot afford health care coverage or have a difficult time in making enough money to pay for health insurance.

12. Graig (1999) discussed the first national health care plan begun under the German leader Otto von Bismarck in 1871. Graig noted that in Bismarck's health care system "all members of society should have access to health care regardless of ability to pay, and . . . the costs of health care would be spread across the population" (p. 47). Bismarck was responding to the rise of socialism and wanted to retain the loyalty of the workers by implementing such a health care plan. People paid into this plan via their employers and paid into the plan more or less depending on their incomes (p. 47).

13. Daniels and colleagues (1996) asserted that "any health reform must retain a strong emphasis on public health and prevention" (p. 54).

14. Others have come up with similar criteria. For example, Daniels and colleagues (1996) discussed 10 criteria, some of them similar to my criteria. For example, they stated that a new health care system needs to be accessible to all (my Criterion 2), that it needs to be comprehensive in benefits and be uniform in benefits (similar to my Criteria 3 and 4 where all Americans will receive good-quality care and receive it in a timely way), and that it needs to be accountable to the public (similar to my Criteria 8, 9, and 10 where health professionals, drug companies, hospitals, and insurance companies are paid reasonably or are compensated reasonably) (pp. 32–34).

15. See Health Canada (n.d.a), where the Canadians solve the problem of a waiting period by having the province the person is moving from continue to pick up the person's health care coverage for a 3-month waiting period when the person moves to another province and applies for health care coverage.

16. Yetter (2005) noted, "Children are doing without dental care because their parents don't have a car or other means to take them out of the county to a dentist" (p. A2).

17. We are already beginning to see preliminary attempts at providing more nutritious food at public schools. See, for example, Schneider's (2006) newspaper article.

18. This was reported on the *NewsHour with Jim Lehrer,* January 12, 2006.

19. See "Medicare Q & A" (2003, p. A7). Medicare is a federal program, whereas Medicaid is a joint federal and state program where the "programs vary from state to state." Also, Sherman (2003) noted that whereas the federal government pays for all of the Medicare bill, the "states pay about a third of the cost of Medicaid" (p. A5). From the state governors' perspectives, because most of them are facing large deficits in their state budgets, they are hoping that the federal government can take over the cost of prescription drugs given that this would help to cut the states' Medicaid costs, potentially by $7 billion.

20. For a succinct discussion of the libertarian view, see Fine and Shulman's (2003, pp. 6–9) *Talking Sociology.*

21. See Archer (1998, p. 77), who suggested changes that could be made in the current system even if we do not go to a national health care system that would greatly improve managed health care: "(1) Pay managed care plans in a manner that creates a financial incentive to recruit patients in poor health and provide them with quality care, and (2) mandate that plans disclose information that can permit evaluation of plan treatment practices" (p. 78). Under this situation, the government would need to pay HMOs enough to give them an incentive to include seriously ill people in their plans. Also, the government would need to stipulate that all HMOs disclose what services they provide so that people can decide which HMO they want to join. Currently, people do not have this information with which to decide what is in their best interest. Also, Newhouse (1996) noted that one of the potential problems managed care raises is that "above average spenders, for example those with chronic illness, may be shunned by every plan" (p. 1719).

22. See Graig (1999). German public opinion "was enraged by the wide disparity in income levels between physicians and other workers" (p. 62). Doctors during the 1970s made five to six times more than the average worker.

23. Marmor (1996) outlined how there were four times in American history when there were attempts "to enact national health insurance" (p. 672). He went on to state, "Now, as then, entrenched interests tried to block national health insurance by skillfully manipulating our deepest fears to protect what they regarded as their interests" (p. 672).

24. See Pear (1999, p. A1). The 46 million figure was reported on the *NewsHour with Jim Lehrer,* January 9, 2006. Also, see Zaldivar and Espo (2009, June 24, p. A1).

25. See Wheeler (2003, p. A4), Dalrymple (2003, p. A10), and Yetter (2003a, pp. A1, A6; 2003b, pp. A1, A6). See also Stolberg (2006, p. A1). By narrow margins in both the Senate and the House, a bill to cut spending on Medicare, Medicaid, and student loans passed. As a consequence, more elderly and poor will have problems receiving health care.

References

Adams, H. J. (2009, September 1). Hill hears plenty on health care. *Louisville Courier–Journal*, pp. A1 & A2.

Alonso-Zaldivar, R. (2009a, November 9). Health bill faces hurdles in Senate. *Louisville Courier–Journal*, pp. A1 & A4.

Alonso-Zaldivar, R. (2009b, October 15). Health bill gets new GOP lift. *Louisville Courier–Journal*, p. A3.

Alonso-Zaldivar, R. (2009c, September 7). Obama still eyes public health plan. *Louisville Courier–Journal*, pp. A1 & A4.

Archer, D. (1998, Summer). From a Medicare rights advocate: Problems and solutions in Medicare managed care. *Generations*, 22(2), 77–78.

Babington, C. (2009, September 2). Obama may get more specific about health care. *Madison Courier*, p. A8.

Babington, C., & Loven, J. (2009, September 4). Obama seems open on health—to liberals' dismay. *Madison Courier*, pp. A1 & A8.

Beauchamp, D. E. (1996). *Health care reform and the battle for the body politic*. Philadelphia, PA: Temple University Press.

Berger, P. L., & Luckmann, T. (1966). *The social construction of reality: A treatise in the sociology of knowledge*. New York, NY: Anchor.

Brill, S. (2015). *America's bitter pill: Money, politics, backroom deals, and the fight to fix our broken healthcare system*. New York, NY: Random House.

Budrys, G. (2003). *Unequal health: How inequality contributes to health or illness*. Lanham, MD: Rowman & Littlefield.

Carroll, J. R. (2003, September 14). Canada's lure: Low-cost prescription drugs. *Louisville Courier–Journal*, pp. A1, A7.

"Current U.S. inflation rates: 2005-2015." (2015). U.S. Inflation Calculator. Retrieved from http://www.usinflationcalculator.com/inflation/current-inflation-rates

Dalrymple, M. (2003, September 22). States trim Medicaid to balance budgets. *Madison Courier*, p. A10.

Daniels, N., Light, D. W., & Caplan, R. L. (1996). *Benchmarks of fairness for health care reform*. New York, NY: Oxford University Press.

Durbin, D. A. (2005, November 22). UAW calls GM moves devastating. *Madison Courier*, pp. A1, A10.

Elliott, P. (2009, June 12). Obama challenges critics on health care. *Louisville Courier–Journal*, p. A3.

Espo, D. (2009, November 8). Health bill: A historic moment. *Louisville Courier–Journal*, pp. A1 & A18.

Feldman, R. (2006, February 21). Ailing health system needs more than a few Band-Aids. *Indianapolis Star*, p. A6.

The final bill at a glance., (2010, March 23). *The Louisville Courier-Journal*, p. A4.

Fine, G. A., & Shulman, D. (2003). *Talking sociology* (5th ed.). Boston, MA: Allyn & Bacon.

Fritze, J. (2009, September 15). Average family health insurance policy: $13,375, up 5%. *USA Today*. Retrieved from http://www.usatoday.com/money/industries/health/2009-09-15-insurance-costs_N.htm

Frommer, F. J. (2003, October 13). Drug lobby spends heavily against drug importation bill. *Madison Courier*, p. A10.

Gerth, J., & Rose, S. (2009, September 3). Crowd challenges health bill. *Louisville Courier–Journal*, pp. A1 & A4.

Globerman, J. (1990). Free enterprise, professional ideology, and self-interest: An analysis of resistance by Canadian physicians to universal health insurance. *Journal of Health and Social Behavior, 31,* 11–27.

Graig, L. A. (1999). *Health of nations* (3rd ed.). Washington, DC: Congressional Quarterly Press.

Groppe, M. (2009, September 7). Health care debate stalls. *Louisville Courier–Journal,* pp. B1 & B4.

Health Canada. (n.d.a). *Canada Health Act: Overview.* Retrieved from http://www.hc-sc.gc.ca/hcs-sss/medi-assur/overview-apercu/index_e.html

Health Canada. (n.d.b). *Health care system.* Retrieved from http://www.hc-sc.gc.ca/hcs-sss/index_e.html

Hiatt, F. (2009, July 24). Obama: How we'll close the fiscal gaps. *Louisville Courier–Journal,* p. A11.

Highlights of the plans. (2009, September 20). *Louisville Courier–Journal,* p. A10.

Howington, P. (2006, February 1). Health savings accounts: HSAs more popular, draw criticism. *Louisville Courier–Journal,* pp. A1, A7.

Jewell, M. (2003, September 17). Lilly loudly fights drug importation plan. *The Madison Courier,* p. A2.

Kerbo, H. R. (2006). *Social stratification and inequality: Class conflict in historical, comparative, and global perspective* (6th ed.). Boston, MA: McGraw–Hill.

Kerbo, H. R. (2009). *Social stratification and inequality: Class conflict in historical, comparative, and global perspective* (7th ed.). Boston, MA: McGraw–Hill.

Kerbo, H. R. (2012). *Social stratification and inequality: Class conflict in historical, comparative, and global perspective* (8th ed.). Boston, MA: McGraw–Hill.

Lester, W. (2003, October 20). Poll finds support for changing health system, prescription laws. *Louisville Courier–Journal,* p. A5.

Macionis, J. J. (2008). *Sociology* (12th ed.). Upper Saddle River, NJ: Pearson/Prentice Hall.

Marcus, R. (2009, July 29). A route to reform? *Louisville Courier–Journal,* p. A9.

Marmor, T. R. (1996). The politics of universal health insurance: Lessons from the past? *Journal of Interdisciplinary History, 26,* 671–679.

Marx, K., & Engels, F. ([1848]1992). *The Communist manifesto.* New York, NY: Bantam.

Maynard, M. (2006, January 24). Ford eliminating up to 30,000 jobs and 14 factories. *New York Times,* pp. A1, C6.

Medicare Q & A. (2003, June 29). *Louisville Courier–Journal,* p. A7.

Milbank, D. (2009, September 11). The Republican response arriving a little early. *Louisville Courier–Journal*, p. A9.

Newhouse, J. P. (1996). Health reform in the United States. *Economic Journal*, pp. 1713–1724.

Obama's chance to recast debate. (2009, September 6). *Louisville Courier–Journal*, p. H2.

O'Donnell, J., & Ungar, L. (2015, February 2). Feds grant another ACA extension. *USA Today*, p. 1B.

O'Donnell, J., & Ungar, L. (2015, February 19). Obamacare sign-ups surge. *USA Today*, p. 1B.

Pear, R. (1999, October 4). 44.3 million have no health insurance. *Louisville Courier-Journal*, p . A1.

Pear, R. (2006b, January 16). President tells insurers to aid new drug plan. *The New York Times*, pp. A1, A12.

Pear, R., & Bogdanich, W. (2003, September 5). Problems with Medicare drug bill. *Louisville Courier–Journal*, p. A7.

Premiums and worker contributions among workers covered by employer sponsored coverage, 1999–2014. (2015). *Kaiser Family Foundation*. Retrieved from http://kff.org/health-costs/report/2014-employer-health-benefits-survey

Reid, T. R. (2009). *The healing of America: A global quest for better, cheaper, and fairer health care.* New York, NY: Penguin Press.

Rudavsky, Shari. (2015, January 15). Deadline nears to enroll for health insurance. *Indianapolis Star*, p. A-9.

Schneider, M. B. (2006, February 21). Healthy choices at school. *Indianapolis Star*, pp. A1, A4.

Sherman, M. (2003, August 5). Governors urge federal deal to ease drug costs for states. *Louisville Courier–Journal*, p. A5.

Stolberg, S. G. (2006, February 3). House approves budget cutbacks of $39.5 billion. *New York Times*, p. A1.

Unger, L. (2006, January 30). Support swells for universal health care. *Louisville Courier–Journal*, pp. A1, A10.

Walker, F. A. (1969). Compulsory health insurance: "The next great step in social legislation." *Journal of American History, 56,* 290–304.

Weber, M. ([1914]1968). The distribution of power within the political community: Class, status, party. In *Economy and society: An outline of interpretive sociology* (pp. 926–940). New York, NY: Bedminster.

Weigel, J. G. (2006, January 30). Medicare's new prescription drug plan: VA plan already set up. *Louisville Courier–Journal*, p. A9.

Werner, E. (2009a, October 18). Dems at odds on health care. *Louisville Courier–Journal*, p. A3.

Werner, E. (2009b, July 29). Health care not budging in House. *Louisville Courier–Journal*, p. A3.

Wheeler, L. (2003, September 23). States tightening spending on Medicaid even further. *Louisville Courier–Journal*, p. A4.

Yetter, D. (2003a, August 31). Burden of care overwhelms unprepared families. *Louisville Courier–Journal,* pp. A1, A6.

Yetter, D. (2003b, September 18). Panel urges halt to Medicaid cuts. *Louisville Courier–Journal,* pp. A1, A6.

Yetter, D. (2005, December 29). Poor youths lack dental care. *Louisville Courier–Journal,* pp. A1–A2.

Zaldivar, R. (2009a, October 14). Health care legislation back behind closed doors. *Louisville Courier–Journal,* pp. A1 & A10.

Zaldivar, R. (2009b, July 24). Senate delays vote on health-care plan. *Louisville Courier–Journal,* pp. A1 & A5.

Zaldivar, R., & Espo, D. (2009, June 24). Sebelius to press lawmakers on health care. *Madison Courier,* p. A1.

CHAPTER 11

Notes

1. Kerbo (2006) noted, for example, that the "gap between the average worker's pay and that of top corporate executives has shown a staggering increase from 40 to 1 in 1990 to 419 to 1 in 1998" (p. 23). Also, in the fifth edition of Kerbo's (2003) book, see Tables 2–4 and 2–5, where worker pay ranks 9th among the 13 industrialized nations, whereas chief executive officer salaries are the highest among these industrialized nations (p. 31).

2. Groppe (n.d.) stated that Indiana is one of seven states "that tax the incomes of three- or four-person families earning less than three-quarters of the poverty line."

3. Kerbo (2006) noted that of 12 industrialized countries, the United States does the least to decrease poverty within its borders (p. 251).

4. See LeVay's (1991) journal article. Also, for one of the first extensive studies on the sexual behavior of humans, see Kinsey, Pomeroy, and Martin's (1948) *Sexual Behavior in the Human Male* and Kinsey, Pomeroy, Martin, and Gebhard's (1953) *Sexual Behavior in the Human Female.* For a more recent study on the biology of homosexuality, see Hamer and Copeland's (1994) *The Science of Desire.* In the study on the sexual behavior of the human male, Kinsey and colleagues (1948) made the following pertinent point: "Males do not represent two discrete populations, heterosexual and homosexual. The world is not to be divided into sheep and goats. Not all things are black nor all things white. It is a fundamental of taxonomy that nature rarely deals with discrete categories. Only the human mind invents categories and tries to force facts into separated pigeon-holes. The living world is a continuum in each and every one of its aspects. The sooner we learn this concerning human sexual behavior, the sooner we shall reach a sound understanding of the realities of sex" (p. 639).

5. See the two studies by Kinsey and colleagues (1948, 1953), where in actuality, individual Americans are various degrees of being heterosexual and homosexual.

6. For more recent research on sexuality and how complex it can be (for example, people can be attracted to the same sex, people can engage in sexual behavior with the same sex, people can identify with a certain sexual orientation or some combination of these dimensions), see Michael, Gagnon, Laumann, and Kolata's (1994) *Sex in America*.

7. See Merton (1968, pp. 185–214) and Cloward and Ohlin (1960). Both works made connections among the social structure, the opportunities available, and the crime that can result.

8. One of the theoretical propositions that Turner (2003) constructed from the works of Max Weber in constructing a theory of conflict deals with the notion that as there are lower rates of social mobility, "subordinates are more likely to withdraw legitimacy from political authority" (p. 135). As people find less legitimacy in the existing social structure, they are more likely to look for other means to survive and get ahead in that social structure.

References

Cloward, R. A., & Ohlin, L. E. (1960). *Delinquency and opportunity: A theory of delinquent gangs*. New York, NY: Free Press.

Cooley, C. H. (1964). *Human nature and the social order*. New York, NY: Schocken.

Davidson, P. (2014, December 29). Hourly pay on the rise in 21 states. *USA Today*, p. 5B.

Ferner, M. (2015, January 26). Legalizing marijuana is the fastest growing industry in the U.S.: Report. *Huffington Post*. Retrieved from Huffingtonpost.com, http://www.huffingtonpost.com/2015/01/26/marijuana-industry-fastest-growing_n_6540166.html

Groppe, M. (n.d.). Many poor Hoosiers struggling, groups say. *Indystar.com*. Retrieved from http://www.indystar.com/apps/pbcs.dll/article?aid=/20060224/news02/602240431

Hamer, D., & Copeland, P. (1994). *The science of desire: The search for the gay gene and the biology of behavior*. New York, NY: Simon & Schuster.

Kerbo, H. R. (2003). *Social stratification and inequality: Class conflict in historical, comparative, and global perspective* (5th ed.). Boston, MA: McGraw–Hill.

Kerbo, H. R. (2006). *Social stratification and inequality: Class conflict in historical, comparative, and global perspective* (6th ed.). Boston, MA: McGraw–Hill.

Kerbo, H. R. (2012). *Social stratification and inequality: Class conflict in historical, comparative, and global perspective* (8th ed.). Boston, MA: McGraw–Hill.

Kinsey, A. C., Pomeroy, W. B., & Martin, C. E. (1948). *Sexual behavior in the human male*. Philadelphia, PA: W. B. Saunders.

Kinsey, A. C., Pomeroy, W. B., Martin, C. E., & Gebhard, P. H. (1953). *Sexual behavior in the human female*. Philadelphia, PA: W. B. Saunders.

Kozol, J. (1991). *Savage inequalities: Children in America's schools*. New York, NY: Crown.

Laumann, E. O., Gagnon, J. H., Michael, R. T., & Michaels, S. (1994). *The social organization of sexuality: Sexual practices in the United States.* Chicago, IL: University of Chicago Press.

LeVay, S. (1991). A difference in hypothalamic structure between heterosexual and homosexual men. *Science, 253,* 1034–1037.

Liebow, E. (1967). *Tally's corner: A study of Negro streetcorner men.* Boston, MA: Little, Brown.

Macionis, J. J. (2008). *Sociology* (12th ed.). Upper Saddle River, NJ: Pearson/Prentice Hall.

Merton, R. K. (1968). Social structure and anomie. In *Social theory and social structure* (enlarged ed., pp. 185–214). New York, NY: Free Press.

Michael, R. T., Gagnon, J. H., Laumann, E. O., & Kolata, G. (1994). *Sex in America: A definitive survey.* Boston, MA: Little, Brown.

O'Donnell, J., & Ungar, L. (2015, February 19). Obamacare sign-ups surge. *USA Today,* p. 1B.

Quigley, F. (2014, December 18). It's time to close CEO-to-worker pay gap. *Indianapolis Star,* A-17.

Roberts, C., & Roberts, S. (2015, April 3). Pence backtrack of RFRA didn't go far enough. *Madison Courier,* p. A4.

Robinson, E. (2015, January 19). King still resonates on economic issues. *Indianapolis Star,* A-9.

Roughgarden, J. (2004). *Evolution's rainbow: Diversity, gender, and sexuality in nature and people.* Ewing, NJ: University of California Press.

Rudavsky, Shari. (2015, January 15). Deadline nears to enroll for health insurance. *Indianapolis Star,* p. A-9.

Stone, L. (1985). Sex in the West: The strange history of human sexuality. *New Republic,* pp. 25–37.

Turner, J. H. (2003). Early conflict theory. In *The structure of sociological theory* (7th ed., pp. 131–161). Belmont, CA: Wadsworth/Thomson Learning.

Waggoner, J. (2015, March 7). Jobs leap, markets weep. *USA Today,* p. 1B.

Wang, S. (2015, June 27). Landmark U.S. Supreme Court Decision: Just Marriage. *Indianapolis Star,* pp. A1 and A4.

Wolf, R. (2014, October 5). Gay marriage all but inevitable. *USA Today,* p. 1B.

Wolf. R. (2015, February 28). Gay marriage hits high court. *USA Today,* p. 3B.

CHAPTER 12

Notes

1. For interesting data to study on this matter and for a comparative look among and between countries and over time, see the *1990 World Population Data Sheet* (Population Reference Bureau, 1990), which reported that the world's doubling time in 1990 was every 39 years. The *1997 World Population Data Sheet* (Population Reference Bureau, 1997) reported that the doubling time was 47 years. The *2003*

World Population Data Sheet (Population Reference Bureau, 2003) showed a 1.3% increase in population per year, meaning that the world's population is doubling every 54 years. The *2009 World Population Data Sheet* (Population Reference Bureau, 2009) showed a 1.2% increase in population per year, meaning that the world's population is doubling every 58 years. Also, the *2014 World Population Data Sheet* (Population Reference Bureau, 2014) still showed a 1.2% increase in population per year, meaning that the world's population is still doubling every 58 years.

2. As we have learned since the onset of the war with Iraq, when Saddam Hussein was in power, he favored the Sunni ethnic group in Iraq while discriminating against the Shiites and Kurds with respect to the distribution of resources in that country. The unequal distribution of resources has been a key reason for the conflict in Northern Ireland between the Catholics and the Protestants. The same was true after the breakup of Yugoslavia, where the Serbian ethnic group came to have more power and more resources than did other ethnic groups (Gelles & Levine, 1999, pp. 313–315). During the past few years, we have seen people from the Darfur region of Sudan being beaten, killed, and run out of their homes and have seen their homes and entire villages being set afire by rebel forces and, at times, with the help of the Sudanese government. Brinkley and Polgreen (2006) reported, "More than 200,000 people have died and two million more have been driven from their homes since the conflict began in February, 2003" (p. A3).

3. For example, in western, central, and eastern Africa, families are having approximately five to six children per family, yet the average income of these families is less than $1,700 per year, and some countries have an average income of less than $800 per year. See Population Reference Bureau (2009).

4. Forrester (1975) noted that a lot of countries and families would highly resist international controls on them in terms of family planning. Hence, providing access, education, and transportation would help not only to decrease the birth rate but also to give people freedom.

5. For the George W. Bush administration of 2000 to 2008, see Associated Press (2002, p. A4). For the George H. W. Bush administration of the late 1980s and early 1990s, see Gore (2000, pp. 315–316). For the Obama decision, see Daniel Nasaw (2009).

6. Livernash and Rodenburg (1998) discussed the problems between developed and developing countries and possible solutions to world problems, where the developing nations have emphasized the need to forgive debt, but the developed countries have emphasized family planning policies to decrease the population (pp. 9–10).

References

Associated Press. (2002, July 23). U.S. will withhold $34 million from U.N. birth-control program. *Louisville Courier–Journal*, p. A4.

Brinkley, J., & Polgreen, L. (2006, May 2). U.S. diplomat heads to Nigeria to try to unsnarl Darfur talks. *New York Times*, p. A3.

Eitzen, D. S., Zinn, M. B., & Smith, K. E. (2009). *Social problems.* (11th ed.). Boston, MA: Pearson/Allyn & Bacon.

Eitzen, D. S., Zinn, M. B., & Smith, K. E. (2011). *Social problems*. (12th ed.). Boston, MA: Pearson/Allyn & Bacon.

Epstein, J. H. (1998, October). Declining growth in population raises hopes. *Futurist*, p. 8.

Forrester, J. W. (1975, October). The road to world harmony. *Futurist*, pp. 231–234.

Gelles, R. J., & Levine, A. (1999). *Sociology: An introduction* (6th ed.). Boston, MA: McGraw–Hill.

Gore, A. (2000). *Earth in the balance: Ecology and the human spirit*. Boston, MA: Houghton Mifflin.

Kerbo, H. R. (2006). *World poverty: Global inequality and the modern world system*. Boston, MA: McGraw–Hill.

Kerbo, H. R. (2012). *World poverty: Global inequality and the modern world system*. Boston, MA: McGraw–Hill.

Livernash, R., & Rodenburg, E. (1998, March). Population change, resources, and the environment. *Population Bulletin*, pp. 2–40.

McKee, M., & Robertson, I. (1975). *Social Problems*. New York, NY: Random House.

Nasaw, D. (January 23, 2009). Obama reverses "global gag rule" on family planning organizations. Retrieved from http://www.guardian.co.uk/world/2009/jan/23/barack-obama-foreign-abortion-aid

Population Reference Bureau. (1990). *1990 world population data sheet*. Washington, DC: Author.

Population Reference Bureau. (1997). *1997 world population data sheet*. Washington, DC: Author.

Population Reference Bureau. (2003). *2003 world population data sheet*. Washington, DC: Author.

Population Reference Bureau. (2009). *2009 world population data sheet*. Washington, DC: Author. Retrieved from http://www.prb.org/Publications/Datasheets/2009/2009wpds.aspx

Population Reference Bureau. (2014). *2014 world population data sheet*. Washington, DC: Author.

Rosenfield, A. G. (2000). After Cairo: Women's reproductive and sexual health, rights, and empowerment. *American Journal of Public Health, 90*, 1838–1840.

Stoltenberg, T. (1989). Devising world policy options for sustainable growth. *Development, 1*, 19–25.

CHAPTER 13

Notes

1. See Gore (2000, p. 30). For the human authorship of much of our current environmental problems, see also Lori Hunter's (2001) *The Environmental Implications of Population Dynamics*.

2. For an excellent article on the pollution and waste problems of Mexico City, Mexico, see Harris and Puente (1990).

3. Gore (2000) stated that during the 20th century, "the average global surface temperature climbed one degree Fahrenheit and sea levels rose four to ten inches" (p. xiv). He also noted that data collected indicate that "the north polar cap has thinned 2 percent in just the last decade" (p. 23).

4. Romm (1991) reported that a National Academy of Sciences study, "which predicted a 1–5 degree rise, refused to rule out the possibility of a runaway greenhouse effect, with 'altered weather patterns' and 'a sea level several meters higher than it is today.'" (p. 35).

5. Romm (1991) stated that in our post–cold war world, "it is clear that America's current practice of focusing on short-term military threats will be singularly inadequate for dealing with broader, longer-term threats to the environment and the protection of vital resources" (p. 31).

6. Boeker and Van Grondelle (2000) discussed what will probably happen with the Kyoto Protocol and how, instead of counting national emissions by each country, the emissions should be connected to where the profit is; otherwise, developed countries could put more of their companies in developing countries, and the emissions would be counted as being produced by those countries rather than by the developed countries (p. 84).

7. Murshed (1993) asserted that the process of international agreement making will be crucial if we are to address and solve our environmental problems (p. 41).

8. The final chapter of Gore's (2000) book, titled "A Global Marshall Plan" (pp. 295–360), has an extensive set of suggestions on how we can solve the environmental problem. Anyone who seriously wishes to solve the environmental problem needs to read and consider what Gore has proposed.

9. Blumenthal (n.d.) reported, "The U.S. Army Corps of Engineers proposed to study how New Orleans could be protected from a catastrophic hurricane, but the Bush administration ordered that the research not be undertaken." Blumenthal went on to say, "By 2003 the federal funding for the flood control project essentially dried up as it was drained into the Iraq war." He also noted that in 2004, "the Bush administration cut funding requested by the New Orleans district of U.S. Army Corps of Engineers for holding back the waters of Lake Pontchartrain by more than 80 percent." So, the chaos for not planning ahead was overwhelming in this instance. Hence, there is a critical need for planning and research and for setting aside funding to address potential catastrophes.

10. See Gore (2000, p. xvii). Gore took this position in opposition to what then Texas Governor George W. Bush would eventually do as U.S. president.

11. See Carroll (2002a, p. A10). Thelma Wiggins, spokeswoman for the Nuclear Energy Institute, was quoted as follows: "The nuclear industry has an impeccable safety record," she said. "We have been transporting fuel for more than 35 years. There's been more than 3,000 shipments covering 1.7 million miles with no injuries, no fatalities, and no injury to the environment."

12. For an excellent discussion on vested interests and the influence of economic interests over environmental interests, see Van der Straaten and Ugelow (1993).

References

Associated Press. (2002, July 24). Bush signs bill for Yucca Mountain dump. *Louisville Courier–Journal*, p. A10.

Blumenthal, S. (n.d.). No one can say they didn't see it coming. *Spiegel Online*. [Online English site.]

Boeker, E., & Van Grondelle, R. (2000). The environment as a human right. *International Journal of Human Rights, 4*, 74–93.

Borenstein, S. (2015, January 17). Sizzle: NOAA, NASA say 2014 warmest year on record. *Madison Courier*, pp. A1 & A6.

Brown, L. (2009). *Plan B 4.0: Mobilizing to save civilization.* New York, NY: W. W. Norton.

Bruggers, J. (2014, June 3). EPA touts flexibility. *Louisville Courier-Journal*, pp. A1 & A12.

Carroll, J. R. (2002a, July 7). Large amount of nuclear waste could pass through area, analysis shows. *Louisville Courier–Journal*, pp. A1, A10.

Carroll, J. R. (2002b, July 10). Senate backs nuclear-waste storage site. *Louisville Courier–Journal*, pp. A1, A5.

Darst, T. (2014, October 8). Look to sun for electricity. *Louisville Courier-Journal*, p. A13.

Durbin, D. A. (2005, November 22). UAW calls GM moves devastating. *Madison Courier*, pp. A1, A10.

Ehrlich, P. R., Daily, G. C., Daily, S. C., Myers, N., & Salzman, J. (1997, December). No middle way on the environment. *Atlantic Monthly*, pp. 98–104.

Eitzen, D. S., & Leedham, C. S. (2001). *Solutions to social problems: Lessons from other societies* (2nd ed.). Boston, MA: Allyn & Bacon.

Eitzen, D. S., & Zinn, M. B. (2000). *Social problems* (8th ed.). Boston, MA: Allyn & Bacon.

Friedman, T. (2006, January 28). What Bush's speech should say. *Louisville Courier–Journal*, p. A9.

Good for us, good for GM? (August 26, 2009). *Louisville Courier–Journal*, p. A9.

Gore, A. (2000). *Earth in the balance: Ecology and the human spirit.* Boston, MA: Houghton Mifflin.

Groppe, M. (2014, June 2). State power plants set for limits. *Indianapolis Star*, A1 and A9.

Harris, N., & Puente, S. (1990). Environmental issues in the cities of the developing world: The case of Mexico City. *Journal of International Development, 2*, 500–532.

Holy, N. (2014, December 10). Indiana needs to look to Germany's solar example. *Indianapolis Star*, p. A11.

Hunter, L. (2001). *The environmental implications of population dynamics.* Santa Monica, CA: RAND.

Intergovernmental Panel on Climate Change. (2001). *Climate change 2001: Impacts, adaptation, and vulnerability.* New York, NY: United Nations Environmental Program and World Meteorological Organization.

Jan, G. (1995). Environmental protection in China. In O. P. Dwivedi & D. K. Vajpeyi (Eds.), *Environmental policies in the Third World: A comparative analysis* (pp. 71–84). Westport, CT: Greenwood.

Kahn, H., & Brown, W. (1975, December). A world turning point: And a better prospect for the future. *Futurist,* pp. 284–287, 329–334.

Koch, W. (2014, June 3). Carbon emission cuts could shift energy mix. *Indianapolis Star,* pp. 4B & 5B.

Koch, W., & Kelly, J. (2014, June 9). Retiring coal plants won't do much to clear air. *USA Today,* p. 1B.

Marchetti, C. (1986). Environmental problems and technological opportunities. *Technological Forecasting and Social Change, 30,* 1–4.

Maynard, M. (2006, January 24). Ford eliminating up to 30,000 jobs and 14 factories. *New York Times,* pp. A1, C6.

Moberg, D. (1993, June 14). Late to the station. *In these times,* pp. 14–17. Chicago, IL: Chicago Institute of Public Affairs.

Moore, C. (1995, January/February). The green revolution in the making. *Sierra,* pp. 50–52, 126–130.

Murshed, S. M. (1993). The North–South economic interaction and the environment. *Asia–Pacific Journal of Rural Development, 3,* 41–53.

Out of denial. (2002, June 5). *Louisville Courier–Journal,* p. A6.

Pimentel, D., Tort, M., D'Anna, L., Krawic, A., Berger, J., Rossman, J., Mugo, F., Doon, N., Shriberg, M., Howard, E., Lee, S., & Talbot, J. (1998). Ecology of increasing disease: Population growth and environmental degradation. *BioScience, 48,* 817–827.

Population Reference Bureau. (1990). 1990 *World population data sheet.* Washington, DC: Population

Population Reference Bureau. (2014). 2014 *World population data sheet.* Washington, DC: Population Reference Bureau.

Renner, M. (2000). Vehicle production increases. In L. R. Brown, M. Renner, & B. Halweil (Eds.), *Vital signs 2000* (pp. 86–87). New York, NY: Norton.

Ritzer, G. (2005). *Enchanting a disenchanted world: Revolutionizing the means of consumption* (2nd ed.). Thousand Oaks, CA: Pine Forge.

Romm, J. (1991, July/August). Needed—A no-regrets energy policy. *Bulletin of the Atomic Scientists,* pp. 31–36.

Sanburn, J. (2015, March 9). A burst of energy. *Time,* pp. 34–36, 38.

Star Editorial Board Opinion. (2014, June 8). Too reliant on coal. *Indianapolis Star,* p. A17.

Star Editorial Board Opinion. (2014, June 3). Press for compromise on new coal plant rules. *Indianapolis Star,* p. A11.

Tuohy, J. (2015, January 11). Car-sharing worth a look. *Indianapolis Star*, p. A-22.

Van der Straaten, J., & Ugelow, J. (1993, Winter). Environmental policy in the Netherlands: Change and effectiveness. *Dutch Crossing*, pp. 130–158.

Verrengia, J. B. (2002, July 22). Pollution blamed in killer drought. *Louisville Courier–Journal*, p. A2.

CHAPTER 14

Notes

1. It would seem that to have extended peace and unity in our society would require taking back much freedom and many rights and allowing only a set of common values. Because most of us do not want such a restrictive society, we accept the fact that built into our current society is—whether we like it or not—the potential for continual disagreement, dissatisfaction, opposition, and conflict. However, on further reflection, most of us would not want it any other way.

2. New technologies (for example, computers), new ideologies (for example, attempting to build a sustainable society and world [Brown, 1987]), and recent social movements (for example, for African Americans, Native Americans, Hispanic Americans, women, gays, and the elderly) all have been major independent variables promoting social change in our society by producing new kinds of jobs, moving toward closer to equal opportunity for many groups of people, and creating new ways of how we can look at our world.

3. Karl Marx pointed this out in a number of his works. For example, see *Communist Manifesto* (Marx, [1848]1947), *The Economic and Philosophic Manuscripts of 1844* (Marx, [1844]1964), and *Capital* (Marx, [1867]1967). For a more recent work on the creation of social structures by humans, see Berger and Luckmann's (1966) *The Social Construction of Reality*.

References

Berger, P. L. (1963). *Invitation to sociology: A humanistic perspective*. Garden City, NY: Anchor.

Berger, P. L., & Luckmann, T. (1966). *The social construction of reality*. Garden City, NY: Doubleday.

Blumer, H. (1971). Social problems as collective behavior. *Social Problems, 18*, 298–305.

Brill, S. (2015). *America's bitter pill: Money, politics, backroom deals, and the fight to fix our broken healthcare system*. New York, NY: Random House.

Brown, L. R. (1987). *Building a sustainable society*. New York, NY: Norton.

Durkheim, E. ([1895]1966). What is a social fact? In *The rules of sociological method* (pp. 1–13). New York, NY: Free Press.

Ferrari, A. (1975). Social problems, collective behavior, and social policy: Propositions from the war on poverty. *Sociology and Social Research, 59,* 150–162.

Heilbroner, R. L. (1991). Three socio-economic capabilities for response. In *An inquiry into the human prospect* (pp. 77–121). New York, NY: Norton.

Kerbo, H. (2009). *Social stratification and inequality: Class Conflict in historical, comparative, and global perspective* (7th ed.). Boston, MA: McGraw-Hill.

Martin, D. (August 22, 2009). Indiana jobless rate holding steady at 10.6%. *Louisville Courier–Journal,* pp. A1 & A10.

Marx, K. ([1848]1947). *Communist manifesto.* Chicago, IL: Charles H. Kerr.

Marx, K. ([1844]1964). *The economic and philosophic manuscripts of 1844.* New York, NY: International Publishers.

Marx, K. ([1867]1967). *Capital.* New York, NY: International Publishers.

Merton, R. K. (1967). Manifest and latent functions. In *On theoretical sociology: Five essays, old and new* (pp. 73–138). New York, NY: Free Press.

Mills, C. W. ([1959]2000). *The sociological imagination.* Oxford, UK: Oxford University Press.

Index